"The ministry of women in the Church continues to be a vital issue. This new collection presents us with an ample dossier of carefully researched essays on the history of women deacons and the possibility of restoring this valuable ministry today. We owe Phyllis Zagano a debt of gratitude for collecting these pieces, many of them appearing for the first time in English. This book deserves serious attention by historians, theologians, and Church leaders alike."

—John Baldovin, SJ
Boston College School of Theology & Ministry

"This helpful collection of academic essays, many of them newly translated into English, shows that the idea of reconstituting the diaconate for women has been around for a very long time. Phyllis Zagano is second to none in the pursuit of this question, and her introduction summarizes beautifully what everyone should know who is interested in the issue."

—Carolyn Osiek, RSCJ
Charles Fischer Professor of New Testament Emerita
Brite Divinity School

"Since the reestablishment of the permanent diaconate at the Second Vatican Council, some 42,000 men have been ordained throughout the world to serve as deacons. At the same time, there has been a parallel conversation about the possibility of women as ordained deacons. Dr. Zagano and her collaborators have collected important articles on the history and theology of the diaconate for women, some translated into English for the first time. This volume is an indispensable resource for the continuing discussion."

—Emil A. Wcela
Auxiliary Bishop Emeritus
Diocese of Rockville Centre, New York
Past President, Catholic Biblical Association

Women Deacons?
Essays with Answers

Edited by
Phyllis Zagano

A Michael Glazier Book

LITURGICAL PRESS
Collegeville, Minnesota

www.litpress.org

A Michael Glazier Book published by Liturgical Press

Cover design by Ann Blattner. Cover image: Thinkstock Images by Getty.

1	2	3	4	5	6	7	8	9

Library of Congress Cataloging-in-Publication Data

Names: Zagano, Phyllis, editor.
Title: Women deacons? : essays with answers / edited by Phyllis Zagano.
Description: Collegeville, Minnesota : Liturgical Press, 2016. | "A Michael
    Glazier book." | Includes bibliographical references.
Identifiers: LCCN 2015035245 | ISBN 9780814683125 | ISBN 9780814683378
    (ebook)
Subjects: LCSH: Deaconesses—Catholic Church.
Classification: LCC BX1912.2 .W64 2016 | DDC 262/.142082--dc23
LC record available at http://lccn.loc.gov/2015035245

Contents

Contributors

Yves Congar, OP (1904–1995), an ecclesiologist and early advocate of ecumenism, was a major influence at the Second Vatican Council and was a member of the International Theological Commission of the Congregation for the Doctrine of the Faith from its inception in 1969 until 1986.

Philippe Delhaye (1912–1990) was professor at Louvain and member of the Belgian Royal Academy of Sciences and Letters, and he was a member of the International Theological Commission of the Congregation for the Doctrine of the Faith from its inception in 1969 and its secretary general from 1972 until 1990.

Peter Hünermann was professor of dogmatics at Münster from 1971 to 1982, and then at Tübingen until his retirement in 1997. He is past president of the Catholic Academic Exchange Service (KAAD) and founding president of the European Society for Catholic Theology.

Valerie A. Karras holds the PhD in church history from The Catholic University of America, Washington, and the ThD in patristic theology from the Aristotle University of Thessaloniki and has taught at St. Louis University and the Perkins School of Theology at Southern Methodist University.

Corrado Marucci, SJ, is professor of biblical exegesis at the Pontifical Oriental Institute, Rome, and director of *Orientalia christiana periodica*. He is a member of the Studiorum Novi Testamenti Societas and of the Associazione Biblica Italiana.

Pietro Sorci, OFM, is professor of liturgy at the Theological Faculty of Sicily "San Giovanni Evangelista" and a member of the Pontifical Academy of Theology. He is a former president of the liturgical commission of the Archdiocese of Palermo, Italy.

Jennifer H. Stiefel is a deacon of the Episcopal Church. Now retired, she is a former director of the Bishop's School of Theology and member of the Board of Examining Chaplains, Denver, Colorado. Her doctorate is from Union Theological Seminary, New York.

Cipriano Vagaggini, OSB Cam (1909–1999), was a significant figure during the Second Vatican Council, especially in the creation of the document on the liturgy, *Sacrosanctum Concilium*, and was a member of the International Theological Commission of the Congregation for the Doctrine of the Faith, from its inception in 1969 to 1986.

Phyllis Zagano is senior research associate-in-residence and adjunct professor of religion at Hofstra University, Hempstead, New York. She is a member of the Catholic Theological Society of America, the College Theology Society, and the American Academy of Religion, for which was founding co-chair of the Catholic Studies Group.

Ugo Zanetti is a Byzantine rite priest and monk of Chevetogne Benedictine Monastery, ordained as a Jesuit in 1978. A member of the Bollandists, he retired from Institut Orientaliste of the Université Catholique de Louvain in 2001.

Acknowledgments

Philippe Delhaye, "Rétrospective et prospective des ministères féminins dans L'Eglise," *Revué théologique de Louvain* 3 (1972), 55-75. Reprinted with permission of *Revué théologique de Louvain*.

Peter Hünermann, "Conclusions Regarding the Female Diaconate," *Theological Studies* 36 (1975): 325–33. Valerie A. Karras, "The Liturgical Function of Consecrated Women in the Byzantine Church," *Theological Studies* 66 (2005): 96–116. Phyllis Zagano, "Remembering Tradition: Women's Monastic Rituals and the Diaconate" *Theological Studies* 72 (2011): 787–811. Reprinted with permission of *Theological Studies*.

Corrado Marucci, "Il 'diaconato' di Febe (*Rom.* 16,1-2) secondo l'esegesi moderna," in *Diakonia, Diaconiae, Diaconato. Semantica e Storia nei padri della Chiesa* (Roma: Istitutum Patristicum Augustinianum, 2010), 685–95. Reprinted with permission of Istituto Patristicum Augustinianum.

Corrado Marucci, "Storia e valore del diaconato femminile nella Chiesa antica," *Rassegna di Teologia* 38 (1997), 771-795. Reprinted with permission of *Rassegna di teologia*.

Pietro Sorci, "Diaconato e altri ministeri liturgici della donna," in *La Donna nel pensiero cristiano antico*, ed. Umberto Mattioli, 331–64. (Genova: Marietti Editore, 1992). Reprinted with permission of Pietro Sorci.

Jennifer H. Stiefel, "Women Deacons in 1 Timothy: A Linguistic and Literary Look at 'Women Likewise . . .' (1 Tim 3.11)," *New Testament Studies* 41 (1995): 442–57. Reprinted with permission of Cambridge University Press.

Cipriano Vagaggini, "La diaconessa nella tradizione bizantina," *Il Regno* 32 (1987): 672–73. Reprinted with permission of *Il Regno*.

Cipriano Vagaggini, "L'ordinazione delle diaconesse nella tradizione greca e bizantina," *Orientalia Christiana Periodica* 40 (1974): 146–89. Reprinted with permission of Edizioni Orientalia Christiana.

Ugo Zanetti, "Y eut-il des diaconesses en Égypte?,"*Vetera Christianorum* 27 (1990): 369–73. Reprinted with permission of Edipuglia, SRL.

At the time of publication, the following permission was pending:
Yves Congar, "Variétés des ministères et renouveau diaconal," *Diacres aujourd'hui* 7 (1969): 2–3.

Introduction

While the restoration of women to the ordained diaconate in the Catholic Churches has become a major topic of discussion in many quarters, significant and serious prior work on the question has receded into the unexamined past for much of the English-speaking world. Two critical reasons stand out: first, significant work in French and Italian remained untranslated until now; second, some of the works in French and Italian translated here were dismissed in a footnote regarding the question of whether women deacons received the "imposition of hands" as in other major ordinations to a study document on the diaconate published by the International Theological Committee (ITC) in 2002.

Each essay in this collection fairly discusses the major historical questions regarding women in the diaconate: Were they ordained to the major order of deacon? What were their tasks and functions? Can they belong to the renewed order of deacon today?

The ITC did not fully answer these questions. Regarding women in the diaconate, it concluded (1) the "deaconesses" of history were not equivalent to the deacons; (2) the unity of the sacrament of Order is clear, and the presbyterate and episcopate are distinct from the ministry of the diaconate; (3) it pertains to the Church's ministry of discernment to pronounce authoritatively the question of women in the diaconate. Since the ITC study document's publication, canons 1008 and 1009 of the Code of Canon Law have been revised to more clearly distinguish the presbyterate and the diaconate, as in the previously published Catechism of the Catholic Church.

The 2002 ITC study document, first published in French as "Le Diaconate: Evolution et Perspectives," languished for many years on the Vatican website only in French and Italian. Later, an English translation prepared by the Catholic Truth Society in London appeared on the website. Still later, other translations to German, Hungarian, Polish, Portuguese, Russian, and Spanish gradually appeared. Some discussion has begun in these language groups, principally guided by the 2002 ITC study document.

Some have noted problems with the current English translation. The study document's English title, "From the Diakonia of Christ to the Diakonia of the Apostles," translates the title of its first chapter, not the title of the entire document. The ensuing English translation skews the document even further from the history of women ordained as deacons in the Churches East and West over the centuries. The serious reader is well advised to read the French original.

Although the 2002 study document is the most recent commentary on women deacons issued from Vatican sources, it has no legislative weight. It is neither a Decree, nor an Instruction, nor a Declaration, nor a Circular Letter, nor a Directory. It is not a Notification, a Norm, nor an Ordinance, nor an Indult, nor a Rescript. In short, it is simply a study document, and one with a rather checkered history.

The diaconate was a topic of great discussion during the Second Vatican Council. In addition to the determinations and recommendations by the assembled bishops to restore the diaconate as a permanent order in the Church, some bishops asked (publicly or privately) about restoring women to the ordained diaconate. Their discussions did not carry forth to the documents regarding the diaconate, which specified male candidates and allowed for married men to be ordained. Since that time, the diaconate has grown to include approximately 42,000 men, and no women. The essays in this volume continue the conversation begun at Vatican II about restoring women to the ordained diaconate.

Following the close of Vatican II, the very fact and function of the diaconate continued as a topic of concern. Yves Congar added some commentary on the diaconate as a permanent office in a short book review titled "Variétés des ministères et renouveau diaconal" in the small publication, *Diacres aujourd'hui*. In 1972, another scholar, ITC secretary Philippe Delhaye, presented a strong essay in *Revué théologique de Louvain* supporting the proposition that women could be ordained as deacons. While Delhaye argues (in support of Roger Gryson, whose work he responds to) that women are capable of receiving Holy Orders, he does not think the Church has the right to modify its beliefs on priesthood. According to both Congar and Delhaye, there appeared to be no objective barrier to restoring women to the ordained diaconate.

Soon, Pope Paul VI asked about women in the diaconate. Could women be ordained as deacons? The answer came from the respected scholar of Eastern liturgy and ITC member, Cipriano Vagaggini, OSB Cam (1909–1999): "Yes." However, neither Vagaggini's nor Delhaye's scholarly essays joined other study documents then coming from the

ITC, which at the time included the world's most prestigious theologians. Delhaye's work had already been published in Belgium, at Louvain. Two years later, Vagaggini's essay appeared in Rome, in *Orientalia christiana periodica*, a publication of the Pontifical Biblical Institute of Gregorian University then under the editorial direction of Robert F. Taft, SJ.

Vagaggini's essay, "L'ordinazione delle diaconesse nella tradizione greca e bizantina," gives perhaps the strongest detailed evidence for the relatively common practice of ordaining women as deacons in the Eastern Churches. Vagaggini concludes that women can again be given diaconal ordination equal to the ordinations of male deacons and that restrictions against women performing certain functions of male deacons (distributing Communion, etc.) no longer exist.

Delhaye's, Vagaggini's, and the findings of others gained notoriety in scholarly circles, and in the years following two liturgy scholars, Roger Gryson (1938–) and Aimé Georges Martimort (1911–2000), wrote competing works on women as deacons.[1] Using identical sources, Gryson's *The Ministry of Women in the Early Church* and Martimort's *Deaconesses: An Historical Study* came to opposing conclusions. Martimort, particularly, profoundly disagrees with Vagaggini and calls Vagaggini's *Orientalia* article a "seductive presentation of a case" (for ordaining women as deacons).[2] Even so, Martimort does not completely close the case on women deacons.

During the 1970s and 1980s, discussion and debate about women as deacons continued, often eclipsed by discussion about women as priests. However, in 1987 Vagaggini was asked to make an intervention before the Synod of Bishops on the Laity, which gathered 231 bishops and sixty lay auditors. Of the four topics under consideration by the synod, the fourth, "women in the church," found Milwaukee Archbishop Rembert Weakland asking that women be included in all non-sacerdotal ministries and Vagaggini presenting a précis of his longer argument: "La diaconessa nella tradizione bizantina," later published in the Italian journal, *Il Regno*.

The question of restoring women to the diaconate, however, remained (and remains) conjoined to the question of women as priests, in part due

---

[1] Roger Gryson, *The Ministry of Women in the Early Church*, trans. Jean Laporte and Mary Louise Hall (Collegeville, MN: Liturgical Press, 1976); original: *Le ministère des femmes dans l'Eglise ancienne. Recherches et synthesis, Section d'histoire* 4 (Gembloux: J. Duculot, 1972); Aimé Georges Martimort, *Deaconesses: An Historical Study*, trans. K. D. Whitehead (San Francisco: Ignatius Press, 1986); original: *Les Diaconesses: Essai Historique* (Rome: Edicioni Liturgiche, 1982).

[2] Martimort, *Deaconesses*, 75.

to the general decline of the diaconate in the West as it became simply a step on the way to priesthood. However, many Eastern Churches retained the tradition of women deacons.

The 2002 ITC document reflects the argument that to be ordained deacon one must be eligible to be ordained priest, noting one small commentary that the deacon must be suitable for "higher orders." (The ITC seems to take this as meaning priesthood, although the episcopacy is more certainly meant.) However, the diaconate of women had never been seen as a step on the way to priesthood, even as it was absorbed into many abbeys and monasteries and later conjoined with the office of abbess or prioress.

In the early 1990s, scholarship on women deacons increased: In 1990 Ugo Zanetti, OSB, looked at the possibility of women deacons in Egypt and answered in the affirmative with a linguistic study, "Y eut-il des diaconesses en Égypte?," published in *Vetera christianorum*. In 1992, Franciscan Pietro Sorci joined the discussion with his essay, on the diaconal ministries of women, "Diaconato ed altri ministeri liturgici della donna" in a book-length collection titled *La Donna nel pensiero cristiano antico*. Considerations also appeared in English: Anglican deacon J. H. Stiefel presented a significant study on the mention of deacons in Scripture: "Women Deacons in 1 Timothy: A Linguistic and Literary Look at 'Women Likewise . . .' (1 Tim 3.11)," in *New Testament Studies*, which definitively argues that the women so mentioned were most assuredly deacons.

In the early 1990s, the history of women in the diaconate remained a point of discussion. Who were they? What did they do? Were they ordained? Depending on the writer's expertise, one or another of these points found emphasis. Most scholars—including it seems the members of the ITC—had no problem with ordaining women as deacons. In fact, from 1992 to 1997, a subcommittee of the ITC prepared a short French-language study document opining just that. The paper, perhaps seventeen or eighteen pages in length, was printed and numbered. The president of the ITC and prefect of the Congregation for the Doctrine of the Faith, Cardinal Joseph Ratzinger, refused to sign it. The question of women in the diaconate was sent back to a newly configured committee, which retained only Henrique de Noronha Galvão, a former graduate student of Ratzinger, as its newly appointed chair.

Concurrent with the non-publication of the first findings of the ITC in 1997, Corrado Marucci, SJ, reviewed the history of women in the diaconate in a detailed work, "Storia e valore del diaconato femminile nella Chiesa antica," which appeared in Italian in *Rassegna di Teologia*. Like Vagaggini, Marucci reviews the history of women ordained as deacons, in this article emphasizing their tasks and functions and arguing in even more detail than Vagaggini on behalf of the historicity of their ordinations.

Meanwhile, the ITC, now reconfigured somewhat with new membership, and a smaller subcommittee newly appointed to rewrite or create anew a study document that addressed women in the diaconate, worked from 1997 to 2002 to complete a document that Cardinal Ratzinger would approve. Among the committee members was Gerhard L. Müller. Several sections of Müller's 2000 book, *Priestertum und Diakonat*, appear (without citation) in the 2002 document.[3] Müller was named bishop of Regensburg shortly after the 2002 document's publication, then followed Cardinal William Levada as prefect of the Congregation for the Doctrine of the Faith (and therefore president of the ITC) in 2012.

Despite the fact that the 2002 ITC study document is the most recent comment from Rome regarding women in the diaconate—*Inter insignores* (1976) and *Ordinatio sacerdotalis* (1994) pointedly leave the diaconate aside—there is the common misperception by many in the church that women are barred from the diaconate by more than a merely ecclesiastical law. As the discussion has continued, we find calls within the Orthodox Churches to more widely restore the practice of ordaining women as deacons, even as scholars search through history to determine how the earliest women deacons functioned liturgically. In 2005, Greek Orthodox scholar Valerie A. Karras published "The Liturgical Function of Consecrated Women in the Byzantine Church" in the journal *Theological Studies*.

Other relatively recent scholarship underscores the fact that the female diaconate in the West was relegated to monasteries, where it remains to this day in some churches of Orthodoxy. My own 2011 article, "Remembering Tradition: Women's Monastic Rituals and the Diaconate," also in *Theological Studies*, reviews the conflation of ceremonies within monasteries, while demonstrating that remnants of diaconal ordination remain within Carthusian women's traditions practiced to this day.

---

[3] See Gerhard L. Müller, *Priesthood and Diaconate* (San Francisco: Ignatius Press, 2002) trans. by Michael J. Miller of *Priestertum und Diakonat. Der Empfänger des Weihesakramentes in schöpfungstheologischer und christologischer Perspecti* (Freiburg: Johannes Verlag, 2000).

Finally, in a 2010 edited work, *Diakonia, Diaconiae, Diaconato. Semantica e Storia nei padri della Chiesa,* Corrado Marucci, SJ, discusses the only scriptural reference to a deacon by name: Phoebe. Within his article, "Il 'diaconato' di Febe (*Rom*.16,1-2) secondo l'esegesi moderna," we find even more evidence of the long history of women as deacons.

The final essay in this collection is actually one of the earliest. Written by German priest Peter Hünermann in 1975, "Conclusions Regarding the Female Diaconate" presented a summary of the arguments for women as deacons in *Theological Studies*. Its conclusions, now more than forty years old, represent the discussions in the many German works not otherwise found here except within the bibliography of sources. It is interesting that at this point in time, there are no scholars writing against the inclusion of women in the renewed diaconate. Some German-language work now in translation, such as the previously mentioned book by Müller, and work by the German Mariologist Manfred Haucke, and Martimort's French-language book of the 1980s still influences the one or two persons who write against women deacons. What unfortunately passes for informed discussion on the matter is too often relegated to Internet-level hearsay. This collection is aimed at presenting the entire story, the majority of which the ITC may have accepted between 1992 and 1997 but which it eventually eviscerated in 2002.

I am deeply appreciative of the many individuals and organizations that have supported this year-long project of reviewing the literature and translating from Italian and French some very important essays that the ITC seems to have discounted.

The majority of the initial translation work was done by Dr. Carmela Leonforte-Plimack, my able assistant at Hofstra University, whose attention to linguistic detail is unmatched. I give deep thanks as well to the many who helped with, and in some cases did first drafts of, some translations: Gabrielle Corbally, RSHM, and Drs. Peter J. Houle, Valerie Karras, Amanda Quantz, and Robert F. Taft, SJ. I am especially grateful to Corrado Marucci, SJ, and Ugo Zanetti, OSB, each of whom reviewed the initial translations of their works. Needless to say, the errors that may remain are mine alone.

I am grateful as well to those at Hofstra University who made this project easier, even possible, by their expert assistance: Dr. Steven D. Smith, Comparative Literature and Languages, Dr. David Woolwine, reference librarian, and the Hofstra Interlibrary Loan Staff; Monica Yatsyla, manager of Instructional Design Services, and the staff and student workers of Faculty Computing Services; Department of Religion student assistant Sarah Estebahn and the department's senior assistant Joanne Herlihy.

Finally, I thank Hans Christoffersen, publisher of the academic and trade markets, and all at Liturgical Press who had a hand at bringing this work forward, especially Ann Blattner, Lauren L. Murphy, and Colleen Stiller.

These join the many others who learned about the project as it was underway and offered support and advice. I am especially indebted to The Wiegand Family Charitable Fund and to other private donors for the financial support that allowed creation of this work and brings it forward, and particularly to Jeff and Kathy Wiegand for their enthusiastic belief in the future of women deacons in the Catholic Churches.

May the conversation continue.

Phyllis Zagano
July 22, 2015
Feast of St. Mary Magdalene

1

The "Diaconate" of Phoebe (Rom 16:1-2) According to Modern Exegesis

Corrado Marucci

The Modern Exegesis

Without doubt, for all modern exegetes the greatest problem posed by the sixteenth chapter of the letter to the Romans is deciding whether this chapter, which consists almost exclusively of greetings to figures unknown to us (except for the couple Priscilla and Aquila), was originally linked to the previous fifteen [chapters] as we read them today, or rather it was first sent to Ephesus, either with or without prior letters, and then, for some unclear reason, added to the letter to the Romans. A second interest that animates commentators regards the varied world of Paul's collaborators, which in Romans 16 emerges in its entire complexity (no fewer than twenty-six friends of the apostle are named, eight among them send greetings together with Paul, and fourteen/fifteen of them are women).[1] In this short paper I am only interested in a more limited topic, that is, the issue found in the first line of the chapter, which in the twenty-seventh edition of the Nestle-Aland (1993) reads: συνίστημι δὲ ὑμῖν Φοίβην τὴν ἀδελφὴν ἡμῶν, οὖσαν [καὶ] διάκονον τῆς ἐκκλησίας τῆς ἐν Κεγχρεαῖς. The text is practically certain; the sole doubt concerns the presence or absence of the conjunction καί after οὖσαν: this presence is attested to only by some witnesses of the neutral text (P46 [Chester Be-

"Il 'diaconato' di Febe (*Rom.* 16,1-2) secondo l'esegesi moderna," in *Diakonia, Diaconiae, Diaconato. Semantica e Storia nei padri della Chiesa* (Roma: Institutum Patristicum Augustinianum 2010), 685–95.

[1] The uncertainty of the number is due to the person indicated in v. 7, in the accusative case, in the capital codices with the letters IOYNIAN, which, according to the implied accent and added later, may refer either to a nominative Ἰουνιᾶς (masculine hypocorism of Iunianus) or to Ἰουνία (feminine Iunia).

1

atty II, c. 200²], N2, B, C*, *bo*), while it is lacking in the majority of manuscripts. NA27 puts it in square brackets, which means that according to the committee of five curators its presence is not thoroughly certain. Given that this preposition is lacking in the greater number of both small and capital letter manuscripts, its presence seems difficult to maintain, notwithstanding the great value of the Chester Beatty papyrus. As to the so-called internal criteria, the presence of the conjunction seems unnecessary (the result would be "Phoebe our sister, who is *also* deaconess in the church of Cenchraea"). Neither of the two editions of the *Textual Commentary on the Greek New Testament* by Bruce Metzger discusses the variant, and the majority of commentators and translations omit it.[3]

When considering the content of the chapter, there is nearly unanimous agreement in identifying Phoebe, whom Paul here recommends, with the person entrusted to carry the actual letter to the Romans; this indicates that Paul regards her as highly trustworthy. Given the pagan origin of the name Φοίβη, well known in Greek mythography,[4] it should here be the case of a pagan convert to Christianity, according to some a *liberta* [freed slave], a fact that the Apostle expresses by using the familiar term of "sister" (implying in the faith). In this regard, however, Father Huby is correct in indicating that Judaic epigraphy in imperial Rome does not allow complete certainty of this, due to the fact that there were

---

[2] According to K. and B. Aland, *Der Text des Neuen Testaments* (Stuttgart, 1989, 103.109) exponent of the *freier Text*.

[3] Among the not few exceptions we recall those by Father Lagrange in his commentary at p. 362, by H. Schlier, and by Dunn.

[4] This name means "the resplendent." Phoebe is above all one of the Titan goddesses, daughters of Uranus and Gaia, who begets two daughters Leto and Asteria from her marriage to Coeus; Leto then begets Apollo and Artemis. To Phoebe is sometimes attributed the establishment of the Delphic oracle, which she then gave to her grandson Apollo. Another Phoebe is one of the Leucippides, who is married to Castor or Pollux. Finally one of the five Heliades, daughters of the Sun (Elios), is named Phoebe. Even Eusebius of Caesarea, in his *Praep. Ev.*, twice recalls the Phoebe of Greek mythology (IV,23,7 and VI,1,2), as do various ecclesiastical writers after him. The historical figures carrying the name are rare: Suetonius, in his *Aug.* 65, 1, recalls Phoebe, a freed slave of Augustus's daughter Julia, who commits suicide after discovering Julia's adultery; the Supplement X of PRE (1965) records the existence of a Phoebe Vocontia, *emboliaria*, of whom CIL VI 10 127 (= Dess. 5262) commemorates the premature death at only twelve years of age. Further information in Gibson, *cit.*

Jewish women called Aphrodisia or Dionysia.[5] According to the greater number of exegetes, the fact that the second title of Phoebe (διάκονος) is introduced by the present participle οὖσαν means that she is still such at the moment of sending [the letter], perhaps even that the mission to Rome is part of her functions. The sphere of such functions is the community, the ἐκκλησία, of Cenchraea, which is the easternmost of the three ports in Corinth, around seven kilometers southeast of Corinth, on the Sinus Saronicus (Saronic Gulf), a lively center of commerce toward the east, developed by the Roman administration.[6]

Now, speaking of Phoebe, it is fairly surprising that in v. 2 the Apostle gives her the title of προστάτις, not only of many faithful, but of Paul himself. This term too, which is the feminine of προστάτης[7] (used eight times in the Septuagint,[8] but not elsewhere in the New Testament), is not thoroughly univocal, although a juridical connotation limited to the meaning of assistant in trial issues is not to be excluded, but most probably it implies a role of patron or lawyer, like the Latin *patrona*.[9] On the other hand, the context excludes the meaning of "female president" or "overseer." Obviously, one should wonder whether this function of Phoebe as προστάτις has to do with that of διάκονος presented in the first line.

However, in Romans 16:1-2, the term that has attracted the most attention is without a doubt διάκονος, which is attributed to Phoebe. It is a noun and an adjective with one ending, common in classical Greek from

---

[5] Cf. J. Huby, Épître *aux Romains* (Paris, 1940), 496.

[6] The doubts and the alternative hypothesis of W. Michaelis (cf. "*Kenkreá*," in ZNW, 25, 1926, 144–54) have not encountered any approval among scholars: the German exegete, on the basis of the fact that there exist at least five other Κεγκρεαί thinks that the one implied in Rom 16:1 could be a town in Troad (Troas).

[7] The feminine is largely used in secular Greek: cf. Sophocles, *Oedipus Col.* 458 (according to the Jebb edition 1884–1896); Appian, *BellCiv.* 1, 1; Cornutus, *Theologiae Graec. Comp.* (Lang, 37, ll. 20s.); Lucian, *bis accusatus* 29i, *Charid.* 10; Cassius Dio 42, 39; *Papyri Graecae Magicae Osl.*I, 338 etc. The masculine had a true technical meaning in both pagan (cf. OGIS 209; SIG 1109,13; CIG I, 126) and Jewish religious contexts (cf. Schürer[4] III, 89). Further details in G. Heinrici, in *Zeitschrift für wissenschaftliche Theologie* 19 (1876): 516ff.

[8] Cf. 1 Chr 27:31; 29:6; 2 Chr 8:10; 24:11 (twice); 1 Ezra 2:12; Sir 45, 24BSA, and 2 Mac. 3:4. The term translates flexions of פקד and of שׂר.

[9] According to Mommsen (*Römisches Strafrecht*, Leipzig, 1899, 378 n.1) during the [Roman] principality, *patronus* (*causae*) is synonym for *advocatus*, even if less used (cf. Tacitus, *dial.* 1; Pliny, *ep.*3:4 etc.).

the time of the tragedians onward, corresponding to the Latin *minister*, that is, *servant* (as opposed to δοῦλος, Latin *servus*, that is, slave). To the same semantic group also belongs ὑπηρέτης, used twenty times in the New Testament meaning "servant, collaborator," also in a spiritual and apostolic context. The etymology of διάκονος is uncertain; the case against a derivation from διά + κόνις (one who raises the dust for being in a hurry, analogically with ἐγ-κονέω = hasten) is supported by the fact that the α in διάκονος is long while the α in διά is short.[10] Therefore, the term probably originated from the obsolete forms διάκω/διήκω. In the Septuagint the term is present only six or seven times (Esth 1:10; 2:2; 6:1;[11] 6:3-5; 4 Macc. 9:17; Prov 10:4); whenever an original Hebrew term is present it reads *na'ar* or *šāraṭ*. In the Hellenistic epigraphies διάκονος is used in the sense of "server in a temple."[12] In the New Testament the root διακον- is found in three flexions: the verb διακονέω (thirty-six/thirty-seven times), the noun διακονία (thirty-three/thirty-four times[13]), and the noun διάκονος (twenty-nine times). The feminine ἡ διάκονος is not frequent, but it is well documented even outside the New Testament;[14] in addition, canon 15 of the Council of Chalcedon (451) required that διάκονον μὴ χειροτονεῖσθαι γυναῖκα πρὸ ἐτῶν τεσσαράκοντα (the official Latin text has *diaconissa!*). In

[10] Chantraine, in his *Dictionnaire* étymologique *de la langue grecque* admits this etymology among the possible ones, as Frisk had cautiously done, and he explains the change of quantity in the α of διάκονος with the fact that the term was very old.

[11] According to the text of the Sistine edition of 1587; all the other manuscripts have διδάσκαλος.

[12] Cf. Buckler-Robinson, in *American Journal of Archeology* 20 (1914): 45.

[13] The uncertainty of this reoccurrence as well as of that of the previous term derives from the presence of some variations valued differently in NA[26] than in the previous editions.

[14] Cf. Aristophanes, *Eccles*.1116 (fourth/fifth c. BC); Demosthenes 762 (=XXIV, 197); 1155 (=XLVII, 52) (?) of the fourth century; Heraclitus the Stoic, *Allegoriae* (or *Quaestiones Homericae*) 28, 5 (Bonn, 1919, 43, l.15) of the first century BC or AD; Epictetus II, XXIII, 8; III, VII, 28; (AD first c.); Flavius Josephus, *Ant.* 1, 298; *Vita Aesopi* G 7 P. (of a woman at the service of the goddess Isis); *CIG* 3037,5(?).14; (Metropolis in Lidia); Marco Diacono, *Vita Porphyrii* 102 (a.p. 81,6 of the Bibliotheca Scriptorum Graecorum et Romanorum Teubneriana of 1895) of the beginning of the fifth century (?); *Mitteilungen des Dt. Arch. Instituts, Athenische Abt.* 14 (1889), 210; H. Usener, Hg., *Legenden der helgen Pelagia*, Bonn, 1879, 11, l. 18, perhaps fifth century (the old translation into Italian by various authors, *Pélagie la péninente*, Paris, 1984, II, 236f; here, however, the critical text suggested by the authors has διακόνισσα: cf. I, 88, l. 249).

ecclesiastical Greek this would be soon replaced by διακόνισσα.[15] In Philo of Alexandria's works the root διακον- is present thirteen times, five as a noun.[16] Flavius Josephus, a contemporary of the evangelist Luke, uses διάκονος fourteen times in the slightly different meaning of server, cup-bearer, assistant, medium, and mediator,[17] and he uses διακονία in the sense of religious service only a few times (*Ant.* 5, 34).

In the twenty-nine occurrences within the New Testament the root often has an impractical meaning, rather it has a discerning, spiritual, or even mystical sense: in Colossians 1:25 Paul defines himself as διάκονος of the Church, of the Body of Christ, *according to the* οἰκονομία τοῦ θεοῦ *granted to me to realize his word among you*; in Romans 15:8 even Christ has become διάκονος περιτομῆς!

Given that at least during the entire first millennium there existed, mostly in the East and more rarely in the West, the female diaconate analogous to the male diaconate,[18] the question that essentially all modern exegetes pose regards the relation of this with the feminine term διάκονος in Romans 16:1. Indeed, from the logical point of view there are three possibilities: (1) it [διάκονος] has a noble meaning, but not ministerial in a technical sense; it means more or less "who is at the service"; (2) the noun mirrors an ecclesial situation where a ministerial significance of the diaconate, and, furthermore, precisely of a diaconate of women, is outlined; (3) finally, Romans 16:1 is the first evidence of a true and proper female diaconate, parallel to the male diaconate (testified to in Phil 1:1; 1 Tim 3:8-12; 4:6; Titus 1:9), even though in a basic form, as for the other ministries that emerge in the New Testament (bishops, presbyters, deacons, true widows, teachers, etc.). Any conclusion must take into account the fact that some exegetes date the epistle to the Romans to the spring of 55 or 56 (Kümmel, Friedrich, Bornkamm), others to the beginning of 57 or 58 (Schlier, Bruce), others yet to 58 (Wikenhauser-Schmid, Michel, Kalsbach): in any case around twenty-five years after the death of Jesus, that is, in an era when the ecclesial fabric was at its beginning.

---

[15] Cf. IG 3, 3527; First Council of Nicaea, *can.* 19 (twice); *Const. ap.* 3:7; *CI* 1, 2, 13 etc.

[16] It is *de post. Caini* 165; *gig.* 12; *Ios.* 241; *de vita Mois.* I, 199 and *de vita cont.* 75.

[17] Cf. *Bellum* 3, 354.388.626, *Ant.* 1, 298; 6, 52; 7, 201. 224; 8, 354; 9, 54. 55; 11,188. 228.255; 12, 187.

[18] See evidence in Marucci, *op. cit.*

Analysis of the thirty or so most important commentaries on the epistle to the Romans of the last one hundred years,[19] of the liturgical translations into the major European languages, of the dictionaries of biblical theology, and of the scanty literature on the subject has led me to establish the actual presence of all the three above-mentioned possibilities. The first meaning, though, is definitely in the minority, more hinted at than anything else;[20] for the other two it is obvious that the boundary is uncertain and variable. Those in favor of an at least vaguely ministerial meaning [of the term] consider its activities as care of the sick, aid to the poor, and assistance to the bishop during the baptism of women.[21]

It seems to me that among the conclusions we can draw from this analysis, the first is that, at least this time, no denominational influences are detected regarding the choices made. The Catholic Jerusalem Bible, for example, in the famous first edition of 1995 (attributed to the Jesuit father S. Lyonnet) had *deaconesses*, a translation also present in the 1998 edition, while the 1984 *revidierte Fassung der Lutherbibel* has "(Phoebe), die im Dienst der Gemeinde von Kenkree ist"; the current *Einheitsübersetzung* for the Psalms and the New Testament, which is also the official text for the German evangelical churches, does likewise ("Dienerin der Gemeinde . . ."). Uncertain is the *Orthodox Study Bible* of the St. Athanasius Academy (2008), which translates "who is a servant of the Church in Cencree"

---

[19] I am referring here to F. Godet (1890), Th. Zahn (1910), M.-J. Lagrange (1922[3]), R. Cornely (1927[2]), J. Huby (1940), O. Kuss (1940), C. H. Dodd (1947[repr]), Pirot/Clamer (1948), A. Nygren (19593), A. Schlatter (1959[3]; English: 1995), H. W. Schmidt (1962), J. Murray (1965), O. Michel (1966), P. Althaus (1971), E. Käsemann (1974[2]), H. Schlier (1979[2]), G. Barbaglio (1980), C. E. B. Cranfield (1980–1981), U. Wilckens (1982), A. Maillot (1984), D. Zeller (1985), J. D. G. Dunn (1988), W. Schmithals (1988), C. K. Barrett (1991[2]), J. A. Fitzmyer (1993), B. Byrne (1996), H. Krimmer (1996), D. J. Moo (1996).

[20] The strongest objections against a ministerial interpretation of the "diaconate" of Phoebe are in Michaelis *op. cit.*, 146; Delling, *Gottesdienst*, 141, and Kalsbach in the article of *RAC* III, 917 cited in the bibliography.

[21] As far as the biblical or philological lexicons are concerned: according to Thayer διάκονος of Romans 16:1 is to be translated as *deaconess*, meaning "a woman to whom the care of either poor or sick women was entrusted"; Beyer, in his entry in *ThWNT* regarding the root διακον-, does not take a stand on the significance of διάκονος in the case of Phoebe; strangely the known philologist M. Zerwick in his *Analysis philological N.T.* (as Rienecker) does not explain the term διάκονος in Romans 16:1; on the contrary, Grosvenor's English edition translates it as "deaconess."

but which in a footnote, however, explains that she was *deaconess*; the *New Revised Standard Version* (Oxford, 1989), which is published by the Church of England, in the text has *a deacon*, and in a footnote adds "or *minister*." What concerns the various official translations by CEI [Italian Episcopal Conference] is a mystery: the word used in the 1971 edition was "deaconess of the Church of C."; even the text of the new liturgical version of the New Testament published in 1997 had "deaconess" (379) and yet the final text of the whole Bible, which is now official for the liturgy, has "Phoebe, who is at the service of the Church of C."[22] In the footnotes, however, the text mitigates this, explaining that she was "responsible" for that Church (624). For a Catholic it might be interesting to note that the Vulgate, which translates Philippians 1:1 with *diaconibus*, 1 Timothy 3:8 with *diaconos*, and 1 Timothy 3:12 with *diacones*,[23] for Romans 16:1 has *quae est in ministerio ecclesiae*, as for all the other occurrences of διάκονος, thus implying that for the translator (Jerome) the term in Romans 16:1 has a generic, not a ministerial, meaning; in the other occurrences of Romans (13:4 [twice], which refers to civilian authority, and 15:8, which refers to Christ) such revered translation has *minister*. The *Nova Vulgata* is only slightly different: *quae est* ministra *ecclesiae, quae est in Cencris*. As to the Castilian, the *Sagrada Biblia* of BAC, edited by Nácar Fuster and Colunga (1964), translated "Os recomiendo a nuestra hermana Febe, *diaconissa* de la iglesia de C."; also Alonso Schökel and Mateos choose *diaconissa* in the 1975 *Nueva Biblia Española* of 1975.

Second, we must note that during the twentieth century there has been no evolution of or dialectic with regard to the three alternatives, perhaps because of the relatively limited importance of the issue.

Finally, for many commentators the text would demonstrate implicitly that Roman Christians knew what a deacon was, given that Paul does not feel the need to render the meaning explicit.

---

[22] Cf. *La Sacra Bibbia* (Rome, 2008), 2144. The 1961 Salani Bible, edited by the Pontifical Biblical Institute (Giovanni Re S.I. was responsible for Romans), and in 1966 the Marietti Bible (translated by Algisi) did the same.

[23] As we can see, since it is a Grecism, the translator fluctuates between the second and the third declension; later the terms *diaconus* and *diaconissa* will prevail. For all three occurrences there exist manuscripts with variations with regard to the terms given in the text (*diaconis* for Phil 1:1; *diacones* for 1 Tim 3:8; and *diaconi* for 1 Tim 3:12).

The Ecclesial Tradition

Before drawing any conclusion regarding the diaconate of Phoebe it is certainly useful to overview briefly the works of the major ecclesiastical writers.

Origen's (c. 185–254) commentary on the epistle to the Romans has come to us complete, but certainly summarized, in the Latin version by Rufinus of Aquileia, finished by AD 406; although Rufinus's declared intention is to spread Origen's thought throughout the West, one wonders how much in the Latin text belongs to Origen and how much to Rufinus. Many Greek fragments have also been gathered from various sources, but this is no help because none treats chapter 16. The Latin text contains great praise of Phoebe's virtues and often affirms that she and other women in the Church are *ministrae* or *in ministerio ecclesiae*.[24] Despite attempts to the contrary, it appears that in essence Origen gives no new information about the Pauline text.

In a commentary—probably spurious—by Jerome we find for the first time words that will reoccur often in the writings of Western exegetes: *(in ministerio Ecclesiae) sicut etiam nunc in Orientalibus diaconissae in suo sexu ministrare videntur in baptismo, sive in ministerio verbi, quia privatim docuisse feminas invenimus, sicut Priscillam [. . .].*[25]

Ambrosiaster, writing between 366 and 384, contemporary of the translation prior to the Vulgate, translates the debated Greek term in Romans 16:1 with *ministra*, but in his brief commentary he repeats the term without explaining in detail what it means.[26]

John Chrysostom (344?–407) briefly recalls Phoebe in six places within his numerous works. First of all, obviously, in the XXX homily on the letter to the Romans:[27] he repeatedly underlines the exceptional praise the Apostle sings of her, but Chrysostom does not specify the meaning of the term διάκονος.

We find even less in the XIII homily, which comments on the third chapter of the letter to the Philippians,[28] in the *de profectu evangelii*,[29] in the *homilia, dicta postquam reliquiae martyrum*,[30] in the *homilia de studio*

---

[24] Cf. T. Heither, Hg., *Origenes. Römerbriefkommentar* [Fontes Christ. 2], I, 242–45.
[25] PL 30, 714.
[26] Cf. CSE 81, 476f.
[27] Cf. PG 60, 663f.
[28] Cf. PG 62, 280.
[29] Cf. PG 51, 315.
[30] Cf. PG 63, 471.

praesentium,[31] and finally in the *de laudibus Pauli* 3:7.[32] Perhaps it is a little amazing that this bishop, by whom no fewer than seventeen letters to the deaconess Olympia have survived,[33] does not even say one word about the "diaconate" of Phoebe.

The writings of *Pelagius*, the Breton ascetic active first in Rome, then in Carthage and in the East between 384 and c. 430, have been handed down under a false name, but today they are unanimously recognized. These works include a commentary on the letter to the Romans. When speaking about Phoebe, Pelagius identifies her as the messenger carrying the letter and explains her ministry with the same words of Pseudo-Jerome: *sicut etiam nunc in Orientalibus diaconissae in suo sexu ministrae videntur in baptismo, sive in ministerio verbi, quia privatim docuisse feminas invenimus, sicut Priscillam.*[34]

Cyril of Alexandria (d. 444) in his commentary on the letter to the Romans does not comment on chapter 16. In his *Adv. libros athei Iuliani* II, 25 he recalls the Phoebe of Greek mythology.[35]

Theodoret of Cyrus (393?–c. 446), who knew several deaconesses, mentions Phoebe three times. In his *praefatio in epist. S. Pauli* he simply cites Romans 16:1; when explaining the line he affirms that although Cenchrae was a small city, the community was so large as to need a woman deacon; it appears to Theodoret that the help Paul mentions concerns Phoebe's hospitality toward him [the Apostle]. Commenting on 1 Timothy 5:10 Theodoret also recalls Phoebe in passing.[36]

In the commentary attributed to *Primasius* (which is in reality the Orthodox elaboration of Pelagius's commentary by the school of Cassiodorus) Romans 16:1 is explained: *quomodo diacones sunt, sive in ministerio verbi: nam et feminae tunc in suo sexu docebant . . .*[37]

John of Damascus (c. 650–754) also wrote a commentary on the letters of Saint Paul, which Altaner describes as a compilation of excerpts from the works of John Chrysostom, Cyril of Alexandria, and Theodoret. As

---

[31] Cf. Ibid., 489f. (here Chrysostom repeatedly wonders how it was possible that Phoebe was προστάτις of Paul himself).

[32] Cf. SCh 300, 174.

[33] Cf. SCh 13.

[34] Cf. PL 30, 714f.

[35] Cf. SCh 322, 256.

[36] Respectively, PG 82,41. 217. 820.

[37] PL 68, 504f.

for chapter 16 of Romans the Damascene relates the entire Pauline text but only comments briefly on a few lines, although not on the first two.[38]

Sedulius Scotus, active in Liege from 848 to 858, does as do many previous and later Latin exegetes: in his brief commentary on Romans 16:1 he repeats the opinion quoted above from Pseudo-Jerome and Pelagius, that is *(in ministerio Ecclesiae) sicut etiam in Orientalibus locis diaconissae mulieres in suo sexu ministrae videntur in baptismo sive in ministerio verbi, quia privatim docuisse feminas invenimus (sicut Priscilla) [. . .].*[39]

Both the *Pseudo-Ecumenius* (eighth century?) and *Theophylact* [of Ochrid] (eleventh century) in their writings on the letter to the Romans report the Pauline text, but they do not give any explanation of the term διάκονος.[40]

Attone, bishop of Vercelli from 924 to 964, in his Epistle VIII proves to be one of the few to explain relatively extensively, to a presbyter named Ambrose, what one must think of such terms as *presbytera, diacona, ministra,* and *abbatissa* which, other than in Romans 16:1 in the case of Phoebe, occur in several canons of synods and councils. In his opinion, for the needs of the churches of the first centuries *non solum viri, sed etiam feminae praeerant Ecclesiis,* something that the council of Laodicea would later prohibit (canon 11). Among the reasons for justifying a female ministry he explicitly recalls their greater ease in approaching pagan women and the decency required for the baptism of adult women. All this, says Attone, *nunc jam minime expedit,* given the custom of infant baptism of his time. According to Attone it was not advisable for abbesses to be called *diaconae,* as appears was the practice in the past, given that the two terms (*abbatissa* and *diacona*) are contradictory.[41]

Among the Latin writers, *Peter Abelard* (1079–1142), is one of the most comprehensive when considering Romans 16:1: he reports the words of the commentary attributed to Jerome (mentioned above), then the words of Epiphanius, who opposed the ordination of women, then the words of Cassiodorus and of Claudius, bishop of Turin. From the various quotations, which he partially repeats in epistle VII and in the *sermo* XXXI, positive judgments emerge about the ministry of women in the Church, as well as one negative evaluation. We get the impression that Abelard tends to favor the positive judgments.[42]

---

[38] Cf. PG 95, 565ff.
[39] PL 103, 123 (there is a simple mention of Phoebe also in col. 127a).
[40] Cf. PG 134, 113ff.
[41] Cf. PL 118, 628 and, resp., 124, 550.
[42] Cf. PL 178, 239 ff. 572. 586. 788. 971ff.

Peter Lombard (c. 1095–1160), who in his time was a famous interpreter of the Pauline letters, limits himself, though, to twice recalling Romans 16:1 without explaining what comprised Phoebe's diaconate.[43]

Thomas Aquinas (1225–1274), in an article of the *Summa Theologica* titled *Utrum religiosis liceat saecularia negotia tractare* (STh 2a.2ae.187.2), mentions the case of Phoebe as *Sed contra*, to demonstrate the fact that religious can deal with *secularia negotia* when charity requires. Commenting on Romans 16:1-2, he then recalls Phoebe three times; the only interesting observation is that the apostle must recommend her because, even though she has dedicated herself to God, she has no authority without that recommendation (*Super Rom.* 16:1).

Among the post-Tridentine authors, one must emphasize that W. Estius (1542–1613), the distinguished Dutch theologian called *doctor fundatissimus* by Benedict XIV, when commenting on Romans 16:1-2 and, as far as I know, for the first time on Phoebe's "diaconate," formulates the thesis that would later prevail in Catholic manuals thusly: *non quod in ecclesia sacro diaconatus officio functae fuerint aliquando mulieres, quibus nec loqui in ecclesiis permissum est, 1 Cor. 14 [. . .] sed quia* [scl. Phoebe] *solita esset suscipere et fovere ministros verbi Dei etc. [. . .] Erant enim olim quae appellabantur diaconissae, non altari servientes, sed aliis quibusdam ecclesiae ministeriis addictae.*[44]

An interesting confirmation of the fact that the ancient [writers] also saw the beginning of the female diaconate in Romans 16:1 is the inscription found in Jerusalem on the Mount of Olives, according to some dating back to the sixth century, which speaks of a deaconess named Sophia, ἡ δευτέρα Φοίβη.[45]

Ancient martyrologies, including the Roman martyrology up to the present time, have Phoebe among the saints of September 3.

Conclusions

At the end of this brief overview of the history of the interpretation of Romans 16:1, allow me some personal considerations, which may also serve as an attempt to synthesize:

---

[43] Cf. PL 191, 1299, 1527.
[44] *In Beati Pauli Epistolas Commentaria . . . auctore G. Estio*, Parisiis et denuo Neapoli 1741, T.I, 364.
[45] Text in *RB* 1 (1904): 260–62.

1) Among the three alternatives I have presented, there is no uniform or prevailing position among exegetes.

2) On the contrary, in my opinion, the fact that Romans 16:1 qualifies Phoebe through an aside that neither uses a finite verb form of διακονέω nor a participle such as διακονοῦσα, but rather says "who is διάκονος of the church of Cenchreae" make us tend decisively toward an interpretation [of διάκονος] where the noun signifies above all a title, a stable function, a ministry not purely civic rather ecclesiastical, although we cannot further specify whether it was a perpetual function, let alone whether it was "sacramental."

3) The fact that the text was written around twenty-five years after the beginning of the Christian tradition does not appear to me as relevant as some contemporary [exegetes] claim; I am not aware of any scholar who, up to now, has convincingly identified, so to speak, gradient growth in ecclesiastical structures; in the attempt to move the birth of the various ministries to very late dates the wish (of Protestant origin) takes precedence over scriptural and historical evidences.

4) The fact that a woman performs such "ministry" cannot appear *a priori* impossible for those who bear in mind the general climate of equality of the sexes that emerges in the New Testament.

5) The second title attributed to Phoebe, προστάτις of many in the community, should not be linked directly to the title of deaconess; the same is true for her task (hypothetical but probable) of carrying Paul's letter itself to the [Christian] community in Rome.

6) It does not seem to me there is any certain link of Phoebe's "diaconate" with the institution of the "true widows" (τὰς ὄντως χήρας cf. 1 Tim 5:3ff.) or with the women mentioned in 1 Timothy 3:11 in the passage dealing with deacons.

7) The survey of Greek and Latin ecclesiastical writers leads one to say that almost no one of them delves into the definition of the "ministry" of the Phoebe of Romans 16:1, except with a few words; for some Latin writers of the late Middle Ages (beginning with Attone) Phoebe recalls the idea that there were deaconesses in the ancient Church, especially in the East, an institution that later became increasingly rare, if not truly extinct.

Translated by Carmela Leonforte-Plimack with Phyllis Zagano

2

Women Deacons in 1 Timothy:
A Linguistic and Literary Look at "Women Likewise . . ." (1 Tim 3:11)

Jennifer H. Stiefel

A. Introduction

1 Timothy 3:11 has long been recognized as an anomalous element in the discussion of deacons in 3:8-13,[1] to which topic the author of the Pastorals has turned his attention as the second of the two offices described in the first half of chapter 3. Interpreters have struggled to identify the women addressed in this verse. Answers have scarcely been lacking, responses notable for their variety and for the unspoken assumptions delimiting the possibilities entertained. This paper, by scrutinizing the syntax of 3:11 and the structure of the passage on διάκονοι, "deacons," discerns new evidence for the identification of these women as partners in ministry with the explicitly named men of the passage.

B. The Genre of the Passage

It is clear that in the larger passage, 1 Timothy 3:1-13, the author is arguing neither for the establishment of a particular set of offices, in contrast to the discussion in Titus, nor for their preservation, in contrast to the focus of Ignatius's letters. Nor are the functions of bishop and deacons described, but rather, while assuming the existence of the

"Women Deacons in 1 Timothy: A Linguistic and Literary Look at 'Women Likewise . . .' (1 Tim 3.11)," *New Testament Studies* 41 (1995): 442–57.

[1] A text and translation of this passage are provided in chart 1 on p. 20; a text and translation of 3:11 are found in section C. The Greek text is taken from the UBSGNT [United Bible Society's Greek New Testament], 3rd ed., corrected; the English translation from the NRSV with some emendation on my part to make the grammatical structure evident.

offices, the author provides a character outline for those who hold these positions.[2] Models for such lists of qualifications exist in both Hellenistic and Jewish sources (e.g., 1QS, the community rule of Qumran).[3] While there is disagreement on which may have influenced the other,[4] the model that gives most direct insight into the particular, even peculiar, character of the material here is the Hellenistic one.[5] A noticeable feature of the lists in 1 Timothy 3 of the qualities desirable for bishop and deacons is how unspecific they are. Although the qualities can be related to what is known from later sources about the duties of these offices, they in themselves describe a generally virtuous person, not even one of a distinctively Christian stamp. This generic flavor (suitable for everyday use) is, however, typical of Hellenistic characterizations both in literature and in life.[6] The descriptions of protagonists, whether ideal or real, are influenced by the terms of moral philosophy and, particularly in biographies, are not drawn from the actual activities of these figures but from a fixed schema. Likewise, in honorary inscriptions the virtues listed are to inspire emulation by posterity rather than to provide an accurate account of the honorand. Thus descriptions of the qualities needed in certain professions are highly general in nature. In his commentary on the Pastoral Epistles, Hans Conzelmann gives two examples: Onosander's characterization of the ideal general in Περὶ αἱρέσεως στρατηγοῦ (*De imperatoris officio* 1), and Lucian's description of the perfect dancer in Περὶ ὀρχήσεως §81 (*Saltatio* or *Pantomimus* 81), and refers to others.[7] Although Onosander goes on to say how these broad qualities are applicable to the particular role of the general, the functions, as with 1 Timothy 3:8-13, cannot be deduced from the list of virtues. There is indeed great similarity in the content of the Hellenistic and the Christian lists.[8]

Likewise in Lucian's list there is a blend of specialized and general characteristics; the dancer is to embody the highest qualities so as to effect new self-knowledge in the spectator. The very generality of such character sketches thus renders it difficult to extract any specific information from them.

---

[2] H. Conzelmann, *The Pastoral Epistles* (Philadelphia: Fortress Press, 1972), 50.

[3] J. L. Houlden, *The Pastoral Epistles* (Harmondsworth: Penguin, 1976), 77.

[4] Conzelmann, *Pastoral Epistles*, 51.

[5] H. Koester, *History and Literature of Early Christianity* (Berlin: De Gruyter, 1980) 2:302.

[6] Conzelmann, *Pastoral Epistles*, 50–51.

[7] Ibid., 158–60, cf. 51.

[8] Koester, *History*, 2:302.

C. The Content of 3:11

Let us recapitulate what has been noted about the particular vocabulary of this verse, in comparison with what is said of those directly identified in 3:8 as deacons, and elsewhere of other functionaries or groups in the church.

3:11 γυναῖκας ὡσαύτως σεμνάς, μὴ διαβόλους, νηφαλίους, πιστὰς ἐν πᾶσιν.
Women likewise [must be] serious, not slanderers, but temperate, faithful in all things.

First, these women are to be σεμνάς, "serious," the same adjective used in 3:8 for deacons. In its most general sense this adjective means "worthy of honor"; it was applied first to deities and then to estimable humans. It is a favorite encomium in the classical vocabulary; its Latin parallel is *gravitas*. Günther Bornkamm suggests "serious and worthy,"[9] while A. T. Hanson opts for "highly respectable" to give the appropriate flavor.[10] The same virtue is enjoined also upon the older men, the πρεσβύτας, of Titus 2:2.

Second, the women are not to be διαβόλους, "slanderers." In Titus 2:3 the same admonition is to be given older women, πρεσβύτιδας. In 2 Timothy 3:2-3 it is said that, "in the last days . . . people [οἱ ἄνθρωποι] will be . . . slanderers." A similar requirement is made of the διάκονοι, that they not be διλόγους, "double-tongued," a term not found in Greek literature but probably modelled on the Latin term *bilinguis*. The requirement has been also interpreted as "not saying one thing and thinking another" (Chrysostom) or as "not saying one thing to one person and another to another" (Theodoret).[11] Polycarp characterizes deacons as both μὴ διάβολοι and μὴ δίλογοι (P01. Phil 5.2).

Next, the term νηφαλίους, "temperate," implies moderation, especially regarding wine. The same quality is required of elders (Titus 2:2); the bishop is likewise to be μὴ πάροινον (no drunkard, 1 Tim 3:3) and the διάκονοι are to be μὴ οἴνῳ πολλῷ προσέχοντας (not indulging in much wine, 1 Tim 3:8), a practical concern, however it be worded.[12]

Finally, these women are to be πιστὰς ἐν πᾶσιν, "faithful in all things." While this can be taken to indicate faithfulness in a secular sense, that is,

---

[9] G. Bornkamm, "σεμνός, σεμνότης," *TDNT* 7 (1971): 195.
[10] A. T. Hanson, *The Pastoral Epistles* (Grand Rapids: Eerdmans, 1982), 42–43.
[11] C. Spicq, *Les Épîtres Pastorales* (Paris: Gabalda, 1969), 1:457; J. N. D. Kelly, *The Pastoral Epistles* (London: Black, 1963), 81.
[12] H Seesemann, "οἶνος," *TDNT* 5 (1967): 165.

reliability,[13] it is more probably to be understood as similar in meaning to the requirement of deacons in 3:9, that of "holding fast to the mystery of the faith with a clear conscience," that is, as indicating a basic Christian commitment.

The qualities required for these women are not in any way gender-specific; the Pastorals and other early Christian writings have attached them to both women and men. The vocabulary of this list thus does not serve to distinguish this group from those specified as deacons in the verses preceding. Both they and the διάκονοι are distinguished from the bishop of 3:1-7 primarily by the omission of some particular attributes (hospitability, teaching aptitude, good repute with outsiders, time since conversion) specified for an ἐπίσκοπος. The qualities esteemed for these women in no way differentiate them from the διάκονοι described in 3:8-10. As noted above, however, lack of specificity is characteristic of the genre of this passage. On the basis only of desirable qualities it would be difficult to distinguish any of the individuals described, whether ἐπίσκοπος, διάκονοι, older women, older men, or the women of 3:11. Thus, while these characteristics do not differentiate the women from the διάκονοι, they are not sufficient, taken alone, to provide a solid ground to argue for the identification of these women as διάκονοι.

D. Syntactic Features of the Text

Several syntactic features of the verse have also stimulated comments and conclusions, both quite various. Contradictory readings are understandable because the syntactical signals sent by the text itself within its context are in fact ambiguous, orienting attention in different directions. Thus the temptation is to take one signal or another as conclusive and to dismiss the rest. An examination of the signal features of the text that have already attracted notice will show the dilemma.

1. "Women"

The first of these signals is that the plural noun γυναῖκας is anarthrous, that is, it lacks the definite article, as does the initial διακόνους in 3:8. There is no qualification of the noun to indicate any specific relationship to the διάκονοι of the preceding topic. The omission of the article can be and has been read in two quite different ways.

---

[13] R. Bultmann, "πιστεύω κτλ.," *TDNT* 6 (1968): 204, n. 231.

First, it may indicate that the anarthrous noun, since it denotes persons, is being used to stand for the whole class,[14] thus here that these γυναῖκες stand for the whole class (grammatically speaking) of women in the congregation. This reading of the anarthrous noun supports an identification of these women as a group distinct from the διάκονοι, indeed as comprising, in contrast to the subset of men who are διάκονοι, the whole female population of the church.

On the other hand, terms of relationship such as πατήρ, "father," ἀνήρ, "husband," and γυνή, "wife," may be used without the article when spoken of in general (but need the article if specific individuals are meant).[15] This appears to be the usage meant by BDF's mention of the omission of the article in "closely related pairs of substantives."[16] Presumably it is this usage that is developed further in BDF §257.3 as the one occurring with πατήρ, γυνή, and the like "when anaphoral[17] is ignored." Here are cited Hebrews 12:7: υἱός . . . πατήρ, "son . . . father," in the clause "for what child is there whom a parent does not discipline?" and 1 Timothy 2:12: γυναικὶ . . . ἀνδρός, taken by BDF as "wife . . . husband," that is, "no wife . . . to have authority over her husband." This alternate reading of this syntactical feature supports an interpretation of the women as wives of the aforesaid deacons, if the διάκονοι are taken as also simultaneously equivalent to ἄνδρες, "husbands." Yet, since these are not wives in general but specifically wives of the aforementioned deacons, some possessive or relative pronoun or adjective would be more likely.[18]

---

[14] H. W. Smyth, *Greek Grammar* (Cambridge: Harvard University, 1984) §1129, p. 289; this is presumably the usage underlying the anarthrous διακόνους in 3:8.
[15] Ibid. §1140, p. 290.
[16] *BDF* (Chicago: University of Chicago, 1961) §252, p. 132; G. B. Winer, *Grammatik des neutesiamentlichen Sprachidioms*, 8th ed., ed. P. Schmiedel (Gottingen: Vandenhoeck and Ruprecht, 1894), 1:168, §19.7.
[17] That is, reference back to what is known or assumed to be known, which usually requires the article.
[18] E.g., the second member of the pair ἀνήρ/γυνή appears (1) with the article alone: Eph 5:23, 25; Col 3:18-19; Matt 18:25, 19.10; (2) with αὐτός, "of oneself," as in Eph 5:31; 1 Cor 7:39; Matt 22:24-25 (with τίς, "some man"); Matt 19:3; Mark 10:7 (with ἄνθρωπος, "man") and Matt 19:5; Mark 10:11 and parr. (with ὃς ἄν, "whoever"); (3) with ἴδιος, "one's own": Eph 5:22; 1 Pet 3:1; 1 Cor 7:2. The nouns do appear anarthrously in several references to marriage or household relations: 1 Cor 7:1, 10-13; Mark 10:2; Mark 12:19, 23; Luke 20:28, 33 (with ἀδελφός, "brother"); Luke 18:29 (with οὐδείς, "no one") where the context makes the relationship clear. 1 Cor 7:1-16 shows the variety of usages permissible or acceptable, as it has

A third, less obvious, reading of γυναῖκας is based on the use of anarthrous γυνή to specify the female counterpart or equivalent of a male exercising a given occupation or status.[19] In this usage γυνή occurs in apposition to a more specific noun:[20] e.g., γυνὴ δέσποινα, "mistress [of the household]" (*Od.* 7.347), γυνὴ ἀλετρίς, "female slave who grinds corn" (*Od.* 20.105), δμῳαὶ γυναῖκες, "female slaves taken in war" (*Il.* 9.477), γυνὴ χερνῆτις, "woman that spins for daily hire" (*Il.* 12.433). It is possible that the author intended γυναῖκας to function in such a way here, with the appropriate occupational term implied but unexpressed, that is, intending something like "Women [ones] likewise . . ." While Paul uses διάκονος (without an article) for Phoebe of Cenchreae (Rom 16:1), specifically feminine gender terms for "women deacons/deaconesses" are not attested until the fourth century; ἡ διάκονος appears for the first time in the third-century *Didascalia Apostolorum*, and διακόνισσα in canon 19 of the Council of Nicaea.[21] Clement of Alexandria in fact uses the form γυναῖκες διάκονοι (*Strom* 3.6.53), most likely in reference to this passage.[22] This third reading supports an understanding of the women as counterparts, co-workers, with the διάκονοι.

Thus this anarthrous noun can be understood in a variety of ways, giving a variety of readings for the place and relationship

---

examples of all the above possibilities. Acts 21:5 "all [of them] . . . with wives and children" could as well be translated generically "with women and children," that is, without presuming the marital status of the γυναῖκες.

[19] I owe this suggestion to Prof. A. Enermalm-Ogawa.

[20] E. Schwyzer, *Griechische Grammatik* (Munich: C. H. Beck, 1950), 2:614; cf. *LSJ*, 9th ed. (Oxford: Clarendon, 1940), s.v. γυνή.

[21] G. Stahlin, "χήρα," *TDNT* 9 (1974): 464, n. 231; M. Hauke, "Deaconesses in the Ancient Church: A Historical Sketch," in *The Church and Women: A Compendium*, ed. H. Moll (San Francisco: Ignatius Press, 1988), 126–27.

[22] "Ἴσμεν γὰρ καὶ ὅσα περὶ διακόνων γυναικῶν ἐν τῇ ἑτέρᾳ πρὸς Τιμόθεον ἐπιστολῇ ὁ γενναῖος διατάσσεται Παῦλος" (Clemens Alexandrinus, *Stromata Buch 1-VI*, ed. O. Stiihlin, GCS 2, 3rd ed. [Berlin: Akademie, 1960], 220); "We also know the directions about women deacons which are given by the noble Paul in his second letter to Timothy" (*Alexandrian Christianity*, ed. J. E. L. Oulton and H. Chadwick, LCC 2 [Philadelphia: Westminster, 1954], 65). Both editor and translators (cf. also Clement of Alexandria, *Stromateis*, trans. J. Ferguson, FC [Washington, DC: Catholic University, 1991], 289) agree in correcting Clement's reference to 1 Timothy, and also in assigning it to 1 Tim 5:9-14, the passage on widows. A reference to 1 Tim 3:11 is far more probable.

of these women with the διάκονοι and within the congregation. Further consideration of these possible identifications will follow the conclusion of the syntactic discussion.

2. ". . . (accusative noun) likewise [must be]"

A second syntactic signal is given by the framing of γυναῖκας by the verb understood to govern it and the adverb that accompanies it. 1 Timothy 3:11 repeats the syntax of 3:8, that is, the accusative plural noun is taken as governed by an understood δεῖ εἶναι "must be," found in 3:2, and the noun is accompanied by the adverb ὡσαύτως "likewise."[23] In 3:8 this clearly indicates the beginning of a further topic, that of διάκονοι, correlated to the preceding discussion of qualifications for an ἐπίσκοπος. Similarly 3:11 appears to mark the beginning of another ecclesial topic, the discussion of a third group co-ordinate to the previous two. This syntactic sign thus points to a distinction of these "women" from the preceding διάκονοι.

3. The Syntactic Structure of the Passage

Commentators have also from time to time pointed out that there is in 3:12 a return to the previous topic of discussion, that is, to the διάκονοι, now clearly identified as male by the specification of their marital status. This sequence of subjects—διάκονοι (3:8-10), γυναῖκες (3:11), διάκονοι (3:12-13)—thus functions to include the women within the topic of deacons.

What has not been remarked is the syntactic inclusion of 3:11 itself within the larger syntactic structure of the section 3:8-13. An examination of the overall structure of the passage 3:8-13 (see chart 1 below) adds another perspective to the question of the relation of verse 11 to the rest of the passage:

---

[23] Δεῖ with a string of adjectives in the accusative is also used in Lucian's description; Onosander's discussion uses a similar construction: φημὶ τοίνυν αἱρεῖσθαι "I believe, then, that we must choose," followed likewise by adjectives in the accusative; Conzelmann, Pastoral Epistles, 158, 160.

Chart 1
1 Timothy 3:8-13

A 3:8	Διακόνους ὡσαύτως σεμνούς, μὴ διλόγους, μὴ οἴνῳ πολλῷ προσέχοντας, μὴ αἰσχροκερδεῖς,
	Deacons likewise [must be] serious, not double-tongued, not indulging in much wine, not greedy for money;
3:9	ἔχοντας τὸ μυστήριον τῆς πίστεως ἐν καθαρᾷ συνειδήσει.
	holding fast to the mystery of the faith with a clear conscience.
B 3:10	καὶ οὗτοι δὲ δοκιμαζέσθωσαν πρῶτον, εἶτα διακονείτωσαν ἀνέγκλητοι ὄντες.
	And let them first be tested; then, being beyond reproach, let [them] serve as deacons.
A' 3:11	γυναῖκας ὡσαύτως σεμνάς, μὴ διαβόλους, νηφαλίους, πιστὰς ἐν πᾶσιν.
	Women likewise [must be] serious, not slanderers, but temperate, faithful in all things.
B' 3:12	διάκονοι ἔστωσαν μιᾶς γυναικὸς ἄνδρες, τέκνων καλῶς προϊστάμενοι καὶ τῶν ἰδίων οἴκων.
	Let deacons be married only once, managing their children and their households well;
C 3:13	οἱ γὰρ καλῶς διακονήσαντες βαθμὸν ἑαυτοῖς καλὸν περιποιοῦνται καὶ πολλὴν παρρησίαν ἐν πίστει τῇ ἐν Χριστῷ Ἰησοῦ.
	for **those who serve** well **as deacons** gain a good standing for themselves and great boldness in the faith that is in Christ Jesus.

3:8-9 As mentioned above, in the Greek the initial accusative plural noun (underlined in the chart) is understood as governed by an implicit δεῖ, the sentence being parallel in syntax to 3:2, "a bishop must be . . . ," with an added adverb ὡσαύτως "likewise" (also underlined) to make the parallelism explicit. The initial noun is followed by a series of adjectives and participles also in the accusative plural.

3:10 The second sentence begins with a nominative plural subject (double underlined) and two imperatives (dotted underlined), with a nominative plural participle.

3:11 As indicated above, 3:11 repeats the syntax of 3:8, with an accusative plural noun (underlined) and the adverb ὡσαύτως "likewise" (also underlined) governed by an understood δεῖ and followed by a set of modifying adjectives.

3:12 This sentence, like 3:10, begins with the subject (double underlined) in the nominative plural, with a modifying participle. The verb is again an imperative (dotted underlined).

3:13 The passage ends with a nominative plural substantival participle and a finite verb.

Chart 2

The form of the passage thus consists of two sets of

A.	-noun + adjectives/participles in the accusative (**A** 3:8-9; **A'** 3:11)

shown by a single box,

and B.	-nominative noun/pronoun + imperatives + participle (**B** 3:10; **B'** 3:12)

shown by a shadowed box. These are then

followed by a closing sentence (**C** 3:13)

shown by a double box.

Each sentence begins with its subject, in either the nominative or the accusative. This gives a structure as follows:

A. 3:8-9	acc. pl., noun + adv. modified by adjectives and participles in the accusative;
B. 3:10	nom.pl. pronoun +imperative, participle, imperative

A' 3:11	acc. pl. noun + adv. modified by adjectives in the accusative
B' 3:12	nom. pl. noun + imperative + participle

C. 3:13	**nom. pl. substantival participle** + finite verb.

There are two irregularities to this structure. The first is in the first subset where there are two imperatives to express the bipartite and dependent nature of the action, whereas there is only one imperative in the second subset. The second irregularity involves the fact that the final "adjective" in the first subset is actually a participle governing a phrase; it is paralleled by an adjectival clause in the second subset. I suggest that in both cases the second is a condensation of the first and is formally equivalent. The passage ends with a generalizing statement forming an inclusio with 3:1.[24]

Thus the passage exhibits a balanced and coherent structure. Verse 11 is an integral part of this structure; it does not obtrude by having its own separate structure, yet it occupies a leading place in its subset. Indeed 3:11 is an abbreviated mirror of 3:8-9.[25] In section A the subject is modified by five adjectival phrases; in section A' it is modified by four. The first adjectives are identical: σεμνούς/σεμνάς. The second adjectives, of similar meaning, are both negated. The third both refer to wine consumption, in negated form for the διάκονοι and in positive form for the γυναῖκες. What is not paralleled in 3:11 is the requirement for the διάκονοι not to be greedy. Finally, I suggest that the final clauses of each (3:9 and πιστὰς ἐν πᾶσιν in 3:11) are likewise equivalent in meaning and syntax. Verses 11 and 12 together mirror verses 8-10. This parallelism reinforces the coherence of the two verses as both belonging within the total framework of the discussion of diaconate. I will suggest that this tells us something of the situation of the women of 3:11, among the διάκονοι and in the Christian community.

These three syntactic signs—(1) the anarthrous γυναῖκας (with three possible readings), (2) the implicit δεῖ and the adverb ὡσαύτως, and (3) the syntactic structure of the passage—thus give the reader a mixed message about these women. In sum, while the vocabulary of the verse does not differentiate these women from any other group, specific syntactic signs point variously to the separateness, or dependence, or co-ordination of these women in relation to others, and the structure of the passage indicates their inclusion within the larger topic. It is no wonder that commentators have proposed so many different solutions to the identity of these women. By selecting only one or two of the syntactic points above, one can support any one of the variety of identifications that have been offered, but heretofore no systematic overall consideration of the syntax has been made.

E. Possible Identifications of These "Women"

1. Generic Women

A few commentators have suggested that 3:11 simply refers to the women of the congregation as a whole, a suggestion supported by un-

---

[24] J. Roloff, *Der Erste Brief an Timotheus*, EKK 15 (Zurich: Benziger/Neukirchen-Vluyn: Neukirchener, 1988), 150.

[25] Ibid., 149–50, 165.

derstanding the anarthrous γυναῖκας to refer to the general grammatical class "women." Davies calls the verse "an intrusive statement regarding women in general,"[26] a characterization supported by the perception of a general lack of organization to the letter[27]and by the generic nature of the qualities specified. Thus 3:11 would be an addendum to the discussion of women in 2:9-10, and this interpretation of the anarthrous γυναῖκας in 3:11 would parallel the interpretation of the anarthrous γυναῖκας with ὡσαύτως in 2:9, which is, however, preceded by τοὺς ἄνδρας in 2:8; "I desire then . . . that the men should pray . . . ; also that the women should dress themselves decently." Against this proposal stands the placement of 3:11 within the diaconal content.[28] I would add that the careful structural integrity of the passage also stands against it. The identification of the women as generic errs on the side of reading only the sign of syntactic disjunction from the context.

2. Wives of Deacons

This has been the traditional understanding.[29] Syntactically speaking, this identification is supported by the reading of anarthrous γυναῖκας as referring to the ἀνήρ/γυνή relationship (assumed to be implicit in male διάκονοι). Other arguments put forward in its favor are the inclusion of the verse in a discussion of deacons, conjoined with its lack of detail.[30] The assertion is also made that, if the author had meant deaconesses (that is, a separate order of women ministers) he would have said so, using some term like those of later years.[31] In Houlden's words, "The reference is more probably to [the deacons'] wives. . . . [T]he writer seems to see widows as the women's group in the official structure of the commu-nity." Responses to this identification note the absolute use of γυναῖκας,

[26] J. G. Davies, "Deacons, Deaconesses, and the Minor Orders in the Patristic Period," JEH 14 (1963): 2.

[27] C. Spicq, Les Épîtres Pastorales, 456, cf. 549, 575.

[28] Kelly, Pastoral Epistles, 83; R. Gryson, The Ministry of Women in the Early Church (Collegeville, MN: Liturgical Press, 1976), 8; H. Frohnhofen, "Women Deacons in the Early Church," TD 34 (1987): 150.

[29] Hanson, Pastoral Epistles, 43.

[30] R. M. Lewis, "The 'Women' of 1 Timothy 3.11," BSac 136 (1979): 167; Hanson, Pastoral Epistles, 43; G. Fee, 1 and 2 Timothy, Titus (Peabody, MA: Hendrickson, 1988), 88.

[31] Houlden, Pastoral Epistles, 80; D. Guthrie, The Pastoral Epistles (Grand Rapids: Eerdmans, 1990), 97; Hanson, Pastoral Epistles, 43.

which lacks any possessive or relative pronoun or adjective to make clear whose wives these are.[32] They also point out that no mention is made of requirements for the bishop's wife.[33] An identification of the women as the wives of the aforementioned deacons also fails to account for the sign of syntactic distinction [δεῖ] . . . ὡσαύτως. This identification errs on the side of assumed syntactic dependence. One may also ask why there should be only one ministering group of women in the church. Some interpreters note the ambiguities and declare themselves unable to decide between the options of "wives" or "some form of women minister."[34]

3. A Separate Group of Women Ministering to Women

Describing the women as a ministering group separate from the (male) deacons is the most frequently proposed alternative to identifying them as deacons' wives. This discussion, however, is fogged by lack of clarity in the terms chosen. The most frequently used term for a member of this group is "deaconess," but, as Raymond Brown points out, this "can be confused with a later church institution that did not have the ordained status of the deacon."[35] Indeed commentators often use the term "deaconess" or "woman deacon" while leaving unaddressed how they understand the exact status of this group;[36] it is a matter on which the church in East and West differed in the past, as presently do churches

---

[32] Fee, *1 Timothy*, 88; Lewis, "Women," 168; R. J. Karris, *The Pastoral Epistles* (Wilmington, DE: Glazier, 1979), 76.

[33] Kelly, *Pastoral Epistles*, 83; Spicq, *Les Épîtres Pastorales*, 1:460; C. E. Cerling, "Women Ministers in the New Testament Church?," *JETS* 19 (1976): 211.

[34] H. Beyer, "διακονέω, διακονία, διάκονος," *TDNT* 2 (1964): 93; Conzelmann, *Pastoral Epistles*, 58; D. E. Hiebert, "Behind the Word 'Deacon': A New Testament Study," *BSac* 140 (1983): 154.

[35] R. E. Brown, "*Episkopē* and *Episkopos*: The New Testament Evidence," *TS* 41 (1980): 334, n. 28; T. C. Oden, *First and Second Timothy, and Titus* (Louisville: John Knox, 1989), 149.

[36] Spicq, *Les Épîtres Pastorales*, 1:76, 456, 460–61; Beyer, "διακονέω, κτλ.," *TDNT* 2 (1964): 93; G. Lohfink, "Weibliche Diakone im Neuen Testament," *Die Frau im Urchristentum*, ed. G. Dautzenberg (Freiburg: Herder, 1983), 332–33; Fee, *1 Timothy*, 88; Hiebert, "The Word 'Deacon,'" 151; Karris, *Pastoral Epistles*, 76. Guthrie (*Pastoral Epistles*, 97) uses both "deaconess" and "woman deacon," hence apparently intending the former to designate a separate non-ordained status, and the latter a joint ordained one; cf. Kelly, *Pastoral Epistles*, 83. Schweizer opts for "perhaps . . . deaconesses" (E. Schweizer, "Ministry in the Early Church," *ABD*, ed. D. N. Freedman [New York: Doubleday, 1992], 4:839).

Orthodox, Catholic, or Protestant. Thus it is at times as difficult to determine exactly what a given commentator has in mind as it is to discern the intent of the text upon which comment is made.

Gryson describes the women as "a new category of minister, . . . feminine this time. . . . [T]hese women carried out a function in the community. . . . [T]heir service was analogous to that of deacons."[37] Naming them as "women deacons," yet as separate from the διάκονοι, is becoming a more widely accepted understanding of the verse.[38] In 1988, Gordon Fee noted that most recent commentators had come to favor "deaconesses" or "women who served the church in some capacity" as the meaning of γυναῖκες, while many of the newer translations at that date (NIV, NEB, GNB) still favored "wives."[39]

The reading of the group as being separate, yet likewise ministering is supported syntactically by [δεῖ] . . . ὡσαύτως, taken to signal the beginning of a third category of functionaries.[40] That their status is equivalent to that of the διάκονοι is indicated by their inclusion within the topic. The question is raised (usually in arguing for an identification as deacons' wives) why this separate group of ministers has no distinctive name, even if only αἱ διάκοναι; however, as noted in section D.1, specific terms appear only in the third and fourth centuries CE. The inclusion of this apparent third category within the topic of deacons also brings into question their existence as an independent group. These two points are addressed by the next identification proposed.

4. Women Deacons Ministering Jointly with Men Deacons

The possibility that these women were not a separate group but were included within the group of διάκονοι has only of late been envisaged as meriting consideration. Recent treatments have increasingly affirmed this identification,[41] although they have not always accompanied it with

---

[37] Gryson, *Ministry*, 8; L. Rand, "Ordination of Women to the Diaconate," *Communio* 8 (1981): 371.

[38] G. A. Denzer, "The Pastoral Letters," *JBC* (Englewood Cliffs, NJ: Prentice-Hall, 1968), §57.21; Kelly, *Pastoral Epistles*, 83; E. Schweizer, *Church Order in the New Testament*, SBT 32 (London: SCM, 1961), 86, n. 334.

[39] Fee, *1 Timothy*, 88, 90.

[40] Guthrie, *Pastoral Epistles*, 97; Fee, *1 Timothy*, 88; Kelly, *Pastoral Epistles*, 83; Lewis, "Women," 168; Karris, *Pastoral Epistles*, 75, Cerling, "Women Ministers," 211.

[41] Lewis, "Women," 171–75, but his suggestion that the women are unmarried assistants to the διάκονοι seems improbable, given the author's evident unease

careful attention to the specifics of the text. Even the most current translations make only very gingerly moves in this direction. The NJB and the
NRSV both have "women" in the text; the NJB notes that "this instruction
is probably intended for deaconesses, . . . rather than for the wives of
deacons," while the NRSV suggests marginally "Or *Their wives* or *Women
deacons*," with the *Oxford Annotated* adding "Women also shared in the
work of the deacons." Only the REB has boldly in the text "Women in
this office . . ." As we have seen, however, the inclusion of the women in
the topic of διάκονοι and their syntactic integration into the passage speak
strongly for their status as ministers as part of the group of διάκονοι. The
suggestion that γυναῖκας may function in apposition with an understood
διακόνους to specify female counterparts to the males gives an explanation for the anarthrous noun.

5. Summary

The various points made about the text are summarized as follows:

Chart 3

Features of Text Supporting Various Identifications of γυναῖκας

	Vocab. of 3.11	Inclusion in topic	Anarthrous Noun			[Δεἰ]. . . ὡσαύτως	Structure of 3.8-13
			Class	Related	Equiv.		
Generic women	–	x	✓			x	x
Deacons' wives	–	–	✓			x	x
Separate group of ministers	–	x	–	–	–	✓	x

about the activity of young widows (5:11-13); Brown, "*Episkopē*," 334; Rand, "Ordination," 371; Lohfink, "Weibliche Diakone," 332–33; L. R. Hennessey, "Diakonia
and *Diakonoi* in the Pre-Nicene Church," *Diakonia*, ed. T. Kalton and J. Williman
(Washington, DC: Catholic University, 1986), 73; Frohnhofen, "Women Deacons,"
150; Oden *Timothy and Titus*, 149; Roloff, *Timotheus*, 164–66; R. A. Wild, "The
Pastoral Epistles," *NJBC* (Englewood Cliffs, NJ: Prentice Hall, 1990), §56.34, p.
897; J. D. Quinn, "Epistles to Timothy and Titus," *ABD*, 6:561.

Women deacons included in group	–	✓			✓	✗	✓

✓ supports identification ✗ does not support identification – inconclusive

As stated in Section C, the unspecific nature of the vocabulary describing the γυναῖκες in 3:11 does not support any one particular interpretation of the women because similar terms are used both for the officeholders ἐπίσκοπος and διάκονοι and for groups of both older men and older women within the congregation. The identification of the women as generic female members of the congregation is supported specifically only by the interpretation of the anarthrous noun as referring to the class of women in general; however, the [δεῖ] . . . ὡσαύτως phrase, the inclusion within the topic, and the structure of the passage count against this reading. The identification of the women as the wives of the deacons also has little to support it, only the relationship implied by γυναῖκας following διακόνους, but, since these would be specific wives, not wives in general, such an identification appears unlikely. The inclusion of the women in the topic of deacons would support their identification as wives only if the same inclusion were made for the wives of bishops. The [δεῖ] . . . ὡσαύτως phrase and the structure of the passage count against this as against the previous identification. The identification of the women as members of a separate group of ministering women has on its side the strong support of the [δεῖ] . . . ὡσαύτως phrase, with its indication of a third group of ministers. Counting against it is that this supposedly separate group is enfolded, both in terms of vocabulary and of syntax, within the topic of διάκονοι.

These two elements, the content and the structure of the passage, both support the identification I propose, that of the γυναῖκες as women ministering along with men as deacons. The third usage suggested to account for the anarthrous nature of the noun likewise supports this understanding of the women's status and role.

What about the [δεῖ] . . . ὡσαύτως? How can this expression be accounted for? I would suggest that women are categorized elsewhere in the letter as a separate group. They have already been so addressed in 2:9-10, and in 2:11-15, their permitted role has been sharply distinguished from that of men. Again in 5:3-16 a specific group of women is addressed—those who have been widowed. Stringent directions are given to guide the congregation's care of "real widows," the urgent necessity for those widows who have families to receive their support from them is stressed, the requirements for those to be enrolled are listed, and the remarriage of young widows is strongly recommended.

In the topic of deacons, the gender of those addressed in 3:8-10 is not specified; διάκονοι could well be inclusive. Only with 3:11 is the gender of those addressed made clear; the women deacons, even within the order of deacons, appear separately, and then male deacons are specifically addressed in 3:12. Yet the behaviors that attract notice to women in chapters 2 and 5 may not be so apparent among the women deacons. Neither they, nor the male deacons, are teaching in the congregation; that function is reserved for the ἐπίσκοπος. Nor are they functioning as a separate group of women, as the widows have been. The situation may thus indeed provoke unease, yet not prohibition or redress.[42] Thus the convoluted verse with its multivalent signals images the ambivalent situation of the women described. It is probably their status within the diaconal order that shields the women deacons, a situation mirrored in their being wrapped about by the term and the syntactic structure of the διάκονοι. Such a sheltered situation would, however, probably not protect their status for long. Both Dennis R. MacDonald's *The Legend and the Apostle* and David Verner's *The Household of God* describe a community where social tensions, particularly over the roles of women, have provoked the writing of the Pastoral Epistles.[43] Such forces, focused by an emphasis on the image of household as the proper model of social relationship, would pressure women to centre their ministries, willingly or unwillingly, in the domestic sphere, and thus to vanish from notice.

[42] I would speculate that the author can come to no reason to ban the woman deacons, but cannot forbear addressing them, yet will not entitle them forthrightly as deacons. Thus androcentric language is layered over the generic reality of diaconal service by both women and men.

[43] Dennis R. MacDonald, *The Legend and the Apostle: The Battle for Paul in Story and Canon* (Philadelphia: Westminster, 1983), 54–77; David Verner, *The Household of God: The Social World of the Pastoral Epistles*, SBLDS 71 (Chico, CA: Scholars, 1983), 176–86; both MacDonald and Verner take 3:11 to refer to wives of the deacons, MacDonald, *Legend*, 71; Verner, *Household*, 100 n. 21; 133 n. 17.

F. Conclusion

The examination of 1 Timothy 3:11 from a linguistic and literary perspective has provided new information with which to evaluate the commonly advanced identifications of the women described in this verse. The evidence in 1 Timothy 3:11 for a diaconal ministry of women is strong, although not completely conclusive. Contradictory readings are understandable because the syntactical signals sent by the text itself are ambiguous, allowing some basis for a variety of interpretations. Close attention to the syntax of 3:11 and of the passage as a whole provides, however, further support for a diaconal ministry of women as partners with men. Yet the evidence for the role of women in diaconal ministry is, as in so many areas of interest, largely indirect. Had Paul neglected to mention either her name or her role, we should not have known of Phoebe, διάκονος of Cenchreae. Had they not been slaves and thus available for torture, Pliny would not have commented on the two women ministrae (probably διάκονοι) of the Christians he was investigating. The women of 1 Timothy 3:11, like these women, come to attention and written record serendipitously; their activity is not the primary focus of the text that records it. Nonetheless the record witnesses, however peripherally, to the ministry of women in this period. We see the subjects we are interested in only out of the corner of the eye of the text; its gaze is fixed elsewhere. Here as elsewhere it is clear that later conceptions of what is possible or appropriate have largely ruled, and still influence, the interpretation of the role of women in the early church. The challenge to every interpreter is to respond beyond one's own boundaries to the intimations of the text.

3

History and Value of the Feminine Diaconate in the Ancient Church

Corrado Marucci

In what follows, I synthesize the results of many studies on the existence of a feminine diaconate in the New Testament and in the history of the Church.[1] For the reader's sake I will translate all the magisterial texts and texts by ecclesiastic writers, and, when needed, I will add in parenthesis the relevant technical terms.

1. Evidence in the New Testament

Some traces of feminine ministries seem to be found in the New Testament. Other than Luke's emphasis on the presence of some women among Jesus' followers (Luke 8:1-3; cf. Mark 15:40ff.), the clearest and most ancient reference should be that of Romans 16:1ff. relating to Phoebe.[2] Paul, in entrusting her to the Romans, calls her "*diákonos* of the Church

"Storia e valore del diaconato femminile nella Chiesa antica," *Rassegna di Teologia* 38 (1997): 771–95.

[1] The most relevant studies are: A. Kalsbach, *Die altkirchliche Einrichtung der Diakonissen bis zu ihrem Erlöschen* (Freiburg i.Br., 1926), summarized by him in RAC 3, 917–28; E. D. Theodorou, Ἡ «χειροτονία» ἤ «χειροθεσία» τῶν διακονισσῶν ["He Cheirotonia e cheirothesia ton diakonisson"], in Θεολογία [Theologia] (Review of the Holy Synod of the Greek Church, Athens) 25 (1954): 576–601; 26 (1955): 57–76. R. Gryson, *Il ministero della donna nella Chiesa antica* (Città Nuova, Roma, 1974); C. Vagaggini, "L'ordinazione delle diaconesse nella tradizione greca e bizantina" in *OCP* 40 (1974): 145–89; A. G. Martimort, *Les diaconesses. Essai historique*, C.L.V. - Ed. Liturgiche (Roma, 1982); A.-A. Thiermeyer, "Der Diakonat der Frau- Liturgiegeschichtliche Kontexte und Folgerungen" in *ThGl* 173 (1993): 226–36. In these works readers wishing for an in-depth analysis will find bibliographic references covering all the topics discussed in this article.

[2] The Epistle to the Romans was written not after the beginning of the year 58. However, since then many objections have been raised questioning the belonging of chapter 16 to the original text.

of Cenchreae," which was the eastern port of Corinth. This term, which even in extrabiblical literature is both masculine and feminine, because of the context here must have a ministerial meaning, even though nothing is said about the content of such ministry. Later in this epistle Phoebe is qualified by Paul as *"prostátis* of many and of myself [Paul]." This term, which in itself usually means "president, patron, guardian," again because of the context here can hardly have a ministerial sense; for this reason it is usually translated as "[she] who has protected." However, the fact that Phoebe might have assisted and protected many, including Paul himself, certainly corroborates the ministerial meaning of the first term (*diákonos*). It is striking that from the hermeneutical point of view in this case, as in many similar cases in the ecclesiastic tradition, while the occurrences of such a term in the masculine gender (cf., for example, Phil 1:1; 1 Tim 3:8-12; or even Acts 6:1-6, where the term is not used), are easily approved as scriptural evidences of the biblical foundation of the male diaconate, in the case of occurrences in the feminine gender many questions arise, and there is a tendency to interpret them figuratively or metaphorically.

The second passage usually quoted with regard to feminine ministries is 1 Timothy 3:11.[3] After giving instructions for bishops (vv. 1-8), the author continues with instructions regarding deacons (vv. 8-10). Verse 11 concerns "the women" (*gynaîkas*), who must be "dignified, not gossips, simple, faithful in everything." Given the ministerial context, the intention of setting norms for Christian women in general should be certainly excluded. However, it is not clear exactly who are the women for whom the passage is intended. According to some, they might be wives of the newly appointed deacons; according to others they might be the women deacons in the community. Both in my opinion and in the opinion of many other contemporary exegetes,[4] this second hypothesis is far more probable. First, because of the use of the adverb "likewise" (*hōsaútōs*), which as in the case of bishops and male deacons introduces the norms. Then, because corresponding norms for the bishops' wives were previously lacking. Moreover, because had the author intended to refer to the

---

[3] The "Pastoral" Epistles are usually dated to the last decade of the first century and are defined as pseudoepigraphic, even though the arguments made for this are not convincing for all.

[4] The recent commentary on 1 Timothy by L. Oberlinner (1994) also mentions some difficulties concerning the translation of "deaconesses." Among the fathers, above all John Chrysostom supports the second hypothesis (cf. *In Ep. ad Titum Hom.* XI).

wives of the deacons earlier described, we would expect him to have said "*their* wives" (*autôn*). Finally, because in the following verses (12-13) he resumes speaking about deacons, and because the four virtues required by verse 11 seem like an adaptation for women of what is required by male deacons. The generic qualification of "women" would then derive from the fact that, as in Romans 16:1, the technical term *diakónissa* does not yet exist. Furthermore, the fact that no determination of a liturgical or functional type is involved is similar to the case of bishops and deacons.

There are many other feminine figures casually mentioned in the *corpus Paulinum* and in the Acts of the Apostles who might have had ministerial roles, but unfortunately we can only formulate hypotheses concerning them. Such is the case for Lydia in Acts 16:14-60, for Nympha in Colossians 4:15, of Euodia and Syntyche in Philippians 4:2ff., of a Mary who "has worked much" for the Christians (Rom 16:6), of Tryphaena and Tryphosa and of the "dear Persis" in Romans 16:12, and maybe of Prisca (Priscilla) in Romans 16:3 (who was a collaborator of Paul); who in Acts 18:2, 26 (together with her husband Aquila catechizes Apollo), etc. Let us finally remember the uncertainty about the gender of the individual (*Iounian*) mentioned in the accusative case together with Andronicus in Romans 16:7, upon whom the Apostle bestows the important status of "outstanding apostles." While up to some decades ago there was a certain agreement among exegetes on *Iounian's* maleness, now it seems in fact more probable that she was a woman (*Iunia*), most of all because a corresponding masculine name different from the feminine has not yet been found in any literary or epigraphic source.

2. Development in the Eastern Churches

In the decades following the closing of the canon, the only evidence relating to feminine ministries seems to be the well-known sentence of Pliny the Younger, governor of Bithynia, in his *Relatio de Christianis* for Emperor Trajan (c. AD 111–113): "Necessarium credidi ex duabus ancillis, quae *ministrae* dicebantur, quid esset veri et per tormenta quaerere" (*Ep. liber* 10,96,2; italics mine). We can certainly presume that here *ministra* translates a term from the Greek root *diacon-*.

In the third century, both Clement of Alexandria and Origen, when commenting on the corresponding passages in the New Testament, often mention the widows[5] and the women deacons. As far as what interests

---

[5] Let us remember, once and for all, that for many fathers of the Church and in many juridic decisions, the issue of feminine ministers is interwoven with

us is concerned, the fact that from such texts we cannot infer the concrete existence of deaconesses, highlighted by Gryson[6] for example, is irrelevant. It is important that, according to Origen, "this passage [Rom 16:1] teaches on the basis of apostolic authority that even women exercised ecclesiastical ministry (*feminas ministras in ecclesia*) [. . .] and that in the Church there are women with ecclesiastical ministry."[7]

In the *Didaskalía tôn Apostólôn* (c. AD 200–220, in northern Syria, the original Greek text is missing), besides "widows," who are only "appointed" and form something similar to a present-day religious order, (in the Latin translation) *diaconissae* are mentioned for the first time. Such establishes a symbolism between the persons of the Holy Trinity and the apostles on one side and the ecclesial ministers on the other, a concept that later will be widespread. As "the bishop is image of God, the deacon of Christ, and the presbyters of the apostles . . . *the deaconess is the image of the Holy Spirit*."[8] This latter analogy, which is a little odd, perhaps derives from the fact that both in Hebrew and in Syriac "spirit" is in the feminine gender. According to this text the deaconess is responsible for all catechesis for women, which in the Eastern and Greek context would be impossible, even scandalous, for male ministers "because of the pagans."[9] The deaconess helps the bishop during the baptism (by immersion) of women and, for reasons of decency, anoints the body of the neophyte; furthermore, she visits and assists Christian women who are ill. Both on the terminological and practical level deaconesses often appear as the female line of the *diaconia*, even though not in all things. The Latin translation in this regard speaks of "unum sentiendo, unum spirantes et *duo corpora in una anima portantes* cognoscite, quantum sit

---

that concerning the nature of the "(true) widows" (*hai óntōs chêrai*) in association with 1 Timothy 5:3-16. In general we can say that, similar to what happens for deaconesses, we get slightly different answers according to the various sources. In the majority of cases we can infer that the widows, although belonging to an *ordo*, were not ordained and did not perform any other ministry than being in charge of charity for their own group. However, in some texts, which we will later quote, the relationship with deaconesses seems more delicate and complex.

[6] R. Gryson, *Il ministero della donna nella Chiesa antica*, cit., 72.

[7] Origen, *Comm. in Ep. ad Rom.*, 1.X, n.17 (PG 14, 1278).

[8] Cf. Funk, ed., 104, 7–8.

[9] Note that this complies with the teaching in 1 Timothy 2:11ff.; the *Didascalia* prescribes "the bishop to choose they whom he likes from among entire population and to make them deacons, *virum ut curet res multas necessarias, mulierem ad ministerium feminarum*" (III 12,1).

ministerium diaconiae" (III 13,2; my italics). Up to this point [the *Discalia*] no source describes the rite of ordination of deaconesses, nor mentions their *cheirotonía* or *cheirothesía*, although there are no doubts that each of these existed even if in a very simple manner.

Then, as far as the fourth century is concerned, we have to mention the problematic canon 19 of the First Council of Nicaea (325), concerning the converts of the "Paulinist" sect.[10] The council, requiring rebaptism of laity joining the Catholic Church and in general requiring the reordination (*cheirotoneîn*) of clerics belonging to the sect who were deemed worthy, concluded: "Likewise then, as far as both deaconesses [*diakónissai*[11]] and all who are of the same status [*kanón*] are concerned, let us proceed as above. Furthermore, let us remember, with regard to deaconesses who are in this situation [*schêma*] they do not have any laying on of the hands [*cheirothesía*], and for this reason they are undoubtedly counted among the laity" (cf. COED p.15). The translation we have given is uncertain in several points; even the original Greek itself has one or more textual uncertainties. According to Gryson and Martimort this canon would prove that deaconesses (in the East), at the beginning of the fourth century, did not receive any ordination and therefore did not belong to the clergy. This opinion, which is supported by some real arguments, is not shared by all. In fact for some others it is indeed strange that the council fathers felt the need to remind their own faithful what (according to Gryson and Martimort) everybody knew. Binterim and Theodorou think it impossible that the great fathers of the fourth century noted for their deep respect for the Nicaean canons, for example, Basil, Gregory of Nyssa, and John Chrysostom (all of whom, as we shall see, ordained or were in contact with deaconesses), would act or think against these canons. The same thing stands for the fathers of the Council of Chalcedon, who, as we will state below, determined the minimum age for the ordination (*cheirotonía*) of deaconesses. The most probable among the alternative interpretations is that by this canon the council intends to refer only to the Paulinist deaconesses.[12]

[10] Followers of the heretical leader Paul of Samosata. His doctrines and the sect linked to his name were later a bit mythologized. At the time of the First Council of Nicaea, the sect was considered "anti-trinitarian."

[11] Canon 19 of the First Council of Nicaea is the first text we have where this neologism appears.

[12] For example, the Orthodox canonist J. Cotsonis in his "A Contribution to the Interpretation of the 19th Canon of the First Ecumenical Council," in *Revue*

In the *Ecclesiastic Canons of the Holy Apostles* (beginning of the fourth century, in Egypt, Greek text) Peter affirms that three widows must be "constituted,"[13] the third of whom must be, literally, "a good deaconess" (*eudiákonos*). The qualities that she must have are similar to those of deacons in 1 Timothy; her tasks consist in the *diakonía* to women who are ill. Then, the apostle Andrew asserts that "it is useful to establish a ministry [*diakonía*] for women." The meaning here is a ministry performed *by women*, not for the benefit of women. The Latin translation, usually faithful, reads: "Utile est, fratres, mulieribus diaconissam ordinare."

While the *Canons of Hippolytus* (c. 350, Arab text) only mention widows and not deaconesses, the forty-fourth among the *Canons of Saint Basil* (died 379) prescribes that the "deaconess" (*he diákonos*) guilty of fornicating with a pagan be excluded from taking communion for seven years. According to Gryson and Martimort, this punishment would imply that the deaconess does not belong to the clergy, members of which are deposed for such guilt. We can disagree with this conclusion.

The document of this period that deals more extensively with deaconesses is without doubt the *Apostolic Constitutions*. It is in reality a collection and a re-elaboration version in Greek of canonical and liturgical texts of various origin (the *Didascalia* of the Apostles, the *Didachè*, the *Apostolic Tradition*, perhaps the apostolic Canons) composed around 380 in Syria or in Constantinople by a writer who sympathized with Arianism (the same writer as Pseudo-Clement). Such explains the presence of some inner contrasts, which are not irrelevant. Here is established explicitly that women belonging to the "order" of widows are not ordained and hence do not belong to the clergy: for them the verb "institute" (*kathístasthai*) is used. According to the *Apostolic Constitutions* the deaconesses are gathered from among the virgins and the widows; for them both *he diákonos* and *diakónissa* are the terms used. The reason they exist is the same as in the *Didascalia*, that is, mainly the desire to avoid scandals in the apostolate to Christian women. However, unlike the *Didascalia*, in the *Constitutions* even the deaconess, as the deacon, can be charged by the bishop to other tasks, such as carrying messages. The *Constitutions* reiterate and develop the analogy between the deaconess and the Holy Spirit already found in the *Didascalia*. As in fact the Spirit does nothing

---

des Études Byzantines 19 (1961): 189–97. Likewise for Thiermeyer (*Der Diakonat der Frau*, cit., 231).

[13] To correctly evaluate this term let us bear in mind that, in this work, it is also used for the bishop, the presbyters, the lector, and the deacons.

alone, but glorifies Christ (cf. John 16:13-15), likewise also the deaconess must not do anything without the deacon, who is the symbol of Christ. Here it is established that she should be an intermediary between the women faithful and the male clergy, again because of decency. With reference to liturgical functions, the *Constitutions* do not dwell on their assisting during the baptism of women, something perhaps obvious by that time. The text clearly states that as deacons are responsible for the behavior of men during the liturgy, likewise deaconesses are responsible for the behavior of women. Although the deaconess is presented as the feminine branch of the diaconate, there is not, however, a perfect similarity with the liturgical functions of the deacon, because even here the text underscores that the deaconess "does not perform any of the things done by presbyters and deacons." The text also clearly affirms that she is of an inferior rank to the bishop and the deacon; her hierarchical position nonetheless is not always the same in all the parts of the document. Above all, she does not assist the bishop and the presbyters at the altar, nor does she help distribute communion; she neither baptizes, nor can she preach. Without doubt, here deaconesses belong to the clergy: like the male clergy, they take part in distributing the *eulogíai* (breads offered, but not consecrated) and above all they are ordained by the bishop as are all other clerics. In distinction to that for subdeacon and lector, her ordination (*cheirotonía*) takes place in the presence of presbyters, deacons, and the other deaconesses, by the laying on of the hands (*epíthesis tôn cheirôn*) and the prayer of the bishop. The *Constitutions* are the first document reporting as well the text of this prayer of ordination. With some understandable adaptation (citation of some feminine figures of the Old Testament) it has the same structure as that expected for other ordinations. It has been noted that the tasks assigned elsewhere to the deaconess are greater than those listed in the prayer of ordination. With reference to this Gryson affirms: "Nothing implies that in the mind of the author there is any difference between this ordination and that of male clerics."[14]

However, we have to specify that in the *Constitutions* the imposition of hands, the term "ordination" (*cheirotonía*), and related grammatical cases are also used for the subdeacon and the lector (in some sections even for other clerics). A more uncertain issue related to the text under examination is the juridical place of the deaconess within the clergy: in

---

[14] Gryson, op. cit., 124.

some cases she comes immediately after the deacon, that is, before the subdeacon and the lector; other times she comes instead after all the male members of the clergy. For these reasons Martimort, in a brief review of Gryson's book,[15] refuses to attribute a sacramental character in the modern sense of the term to the ordination of the deaconess, because then, coherently, one should extend such status to the subdeacon and the lector. Let us notice nonetheless that this difficulty may be overturned: given that such an argument is not raised for deacons, there is no reason why it should be valid for deaconesses. Moreover, Martimort, reclaiming a clarification by Botte, highlights the fact that the *Apostolic Constitutions* (like other apocryphal collections of the time) are only "a private compilation deriving from an unorthodox environment [. . .] and that their liturgical formularies do not come in any way from the real use of a church";[16] he also reminds that, unlike with higher clerics, the epiclesis does not refer to any founding text in the New Testament. The French liturgist concludes by affirming that "no argumentation can be based on the *Apostolic Constitutions*."[17] In his reply Gryson conceded that the text was developed in an unorthodox environment, but he asserts that for just this reason it is highly probable that the author was trying to be accepted by demonstrating, in areas of the ecclesial life where heterodox belief was not a factor, the highest fidelity to canonical and liturgical practice.[18] In his long text, written in 1982 and cited here in fn. 1, Martimort does not acknowledge Gryson's observation.[19]

The most important magisterial text on the topic we are looking at is certainly can. 15 of the Council of Chalcedon (451), which determines that no woman be ordained deaconess (*cheirotoneîsthai*) before forty and that a deaconess who, after ordination (*cheirotonía*) and having exercised her ministry, marries should be excommunicated (cf. COED p. 94). All this presupposes that the existence of ordained deaconesses was a sure and established fact; even in this case we have to bear in mind that in the texts of this council the root *cheiroton-* is used not only for the higher clergy but also for the minor clergy. The minimum age of forty years seems to

---

[15] A. G. Martimort, "À propos des ministères féminins dans l'Église," in *Bulletin de Littérature ecclésiastique* 74 (1973): 104–8.

[16] Ibid., 105. Likewise in *Les diaconesses*, cit., 42-44.

[17] Martimort, "À propos des ministères féminins dans l'Église," 108.

[18] Cf. R. Gryson, "L'ordination des diaconesses d'après les "Constitutions Apostoliques," in *Mélanges de Science Religieuse* 31 (1974): 41–45.

[19] Cf. Martimort, *Les diaconesses*, op. cit., 71, fn. 66.

be a compromise between the sixty years mentioned in 1 Timothy 5:9 and possible violations of this [rule]. The norm is repeated by the council named *In Trullo* (alias *Quinisextum*) of 691, in can. 14 (*cheirotoneísthō*).[20]

A particular evolution of the feminine ministries in the East is represented by the *Testament of Our Lord Jesus Christ*, written by monophysite groups in Syria in the second half of the fifth century and largely depending on the *Traditio Apostolica* of Hippolytus. The original Greek is lost; we have the Syriac, Coptic, Ethiopian, and Arab translations. In this work "widows who have precedence"[21] are mentioned, but scholars disagree regarding their juridical status. Some scholars, by underlining the fact that the *Testament* mentions the "ordination" of widows inside the sanctuary, as in the case of major clerics, assert that such a rite is to be understood as a true ordination. Martimort and Gryson rather, based on the fact that later in the text the "prayer for the institution of widows" is mentioned, hold an opposite view. Some problems might be raised due to the fact that the original Greek text is missing and that perhaps within it there may not be perfect internal coherence. Furthermore, they are treated in an entirely similar manner as are deacons, they hold many apostolic and juridical responsibilities with regard to women faithful, during the Mass (except during their menstruation) they stand in the sanctuary to the left of the bishop and therefore in front of deacons, who stand to his right. They receive Communion after the deacons but before the male lower clergy (cf. 1, 23, 13). In the *Testament* deaconesses are also mentioned: they have a subordinate position with respect to widows and their belonging to the clergy is at least doubtful. Compared with what is found in the *Apostolic Constitutions*, the relationship between deaconesses and widows is here overturned: it is widows who must supervise deaconesses. At the moment of the oblation these latter [deaconesses] are inside the sacred veil [inside the sanctuary] together with the clergy, but "after the subdeacons" and elsewhere they are listed even after lectors. At the moment of Communion they precede only the other women faithful. And nonetheless, the deaconess is responsible for bringing Communion to sick women on Easter (cf 2, 20, 7). Some scholars see this new function as very important in the evolution of feminine ministries.

[20] Even today the Orthodox Church considers this synod as the seventh ecumenical council.

[21] According to Martimort it should be the case of the *prokatheménai* mentioned by canon 11 of the Council of Laodicea.

Even civil legislation, first in the Theodosian Code and later in the Code of Justinian, acknowledges the existence of deaconesses, defining some of their rights and duties. Many times they are considered as belonging to the clergy and at least according to the Code of Justinian they are ordained by *cheirotonía*. Moreover, the Third Novella of the Code of Justinian determines the maximum number of clerics for the churches: in Saint Sophia of 425 clerics, the maximum number of deaconesses is forty. Their minimum age, which according to Theodosius was still sixty, is lowered by Justinian first to fifty (cf. Novella 6, 6) then definitely to forty (cf. Novella 123, 13). After ordination the deaconess, like the other higher clerics, is bound to perfect continence.

Among the Eastern fathers, we find it interesting to recall the polemic of Epiphanius of Salamis (d. 403) against the Cataphrygians and the Collyridians. Epiphanius strongly opposes, with the classical arguments, the practice of these heretical groups of admitting women among the bishops and the presbyters or even of offering sacrifices to Mary, whom they considered as a goddess, but he admits that deaconesses exist, although they can neither preach nor rule over men. With regard to Titus 2:3, he reminds us that widows are called *presbýtides* and not *presbytérides* or *hiérissai*.[22]

We know of John Chrysostom's (d. 407) large and devoted correspondence with various deaconesses; like many other theologians of the same period he is concerned with reconciling the restrictive affirmations in 1 Corinthians 14 and 1 Timothy 2 with the existence of a feminine ministry. According to him the solution lies in the distinction between preaching inside or outside the church. According to Chrysostom, the *laleîn* of 1 Corinthians 14:34 means "to annoy with chatter."[23] Similar notions are found in the works of Theodore of Mopsuestia (d. 428) and Theodoret of Kyros (d. 466). Also, fairly extensive epigraphic material proves the concrete existence of deaconesses in the Church of the East.[24]

---

[22] Cf. PG 42,744f.f; GCS 37,478.

[23] Cf. PG 52,549–623; 657–59; and 662–64.

[24] Among the most famous Eastern deaconess we remember: Celerina, Assia, Casiana, and another deaconess in contact with Theodoret of Kyros (cf., respectively, PG 83,1293=SC 111,18–20; SC 40,118; PG 83,1196=SC 98,62–64; PG 82,1101–4); the daughters of Terentius, in contact with Saint Basil (cf. PG 32,521ff.); the sister of Saint Gregory of Nyssa, Macrina, and her friend Lampadia (cf. PG 46,984–86); Theosebia, the wife (?) of Saint Gregory (cf. PG 37,321C–24); Euphemia, wife of Sergio archbishop of Ravenna (753); Olympia and her relatives

Finally, let us recall that the Byzantine church has a rite of ordination for the deaconess, substantially, analogous to that of the deacon. In both cases the site of the ordination (*cheirotonía*) is in what today we call the sanctuary, while for the subdeacon and the lector the sacristy (*diakonikón*) or the narthex are prescribed. The minister is the bishop, who imposes his hands, invokes upon the ordinandi [male or female] the gift of the Holy Spirit, and who places the diaconal stole (*orarion*) on them. However, historians of the liturgy have emphasized some differences between the two rites. Besides the fact that only the deaconess has her head covered by the *maphorion* (veil), she bows her head, while the deacon kneels until he touches the altar with his head; in the second prayer by the bishop, only for the woman are the "limits" of her future ministry explicitly recalled; the deaconess wears the stole not across, as does the deacon, but with both edges on the front and finally, after communicating, replaces the chalice on the altar without administering Communion to the faithful, whereas the deacon afterward does.[25]

In the East, at least throughout the Byzantine era, deaconesses continued to be ordained, although by now the almost exclusive practice of infant baptism, the change in habits, and the reaction to violations that occurred even in the East lead to a real atrophy of the feminine diaconate, which probably survived only in women's convents. Theodorou asserts that still today in Orthodox monasteries there exist some "ordained" deaconesses, and he specifies that this institution has never been abolished by any ecclesiastic decision and urges indeed for its "renewal." The provisions of the synod of Laodicea against any feminine ministry, which according to some Church historians also regards deaconesses,

---

Elisanthia, Martyria, and Palladia, ordained deaconesses of Constantinople by the archbishop Nektarios (cf. GCS N.F. 4, 361) and, respectively, by Saint John Chrysostom, with whom they were in correspondence (cf. PG 34,1244–50); Pentadia, Procla, and Sabiniana, aunt of John Chrysostom; Marthana mentioned in the *Peregrinatio Aetheriae* XXII, 2–3; Anastasia, Valeriana, and Jannia in correspondence with Severus of Antioch; according to Novella 3 of Justinian, reiterated by Balsamon and by Heraclius, for the Church of Saint Sophia forty deaconesses were expected; Nektaria (cf. GCS 50, 181, 16–18); Dionysia, mother of Saint Euthymius the Great (377–473), whose life was written by Cyril of Scythopolis (cf. TU 49/2, 10ff.); Eusebia (cf. GCS 50, 392,8–15); Manaride in Gaza; Syncletica virgin deaconess of the fifth century praised by Sedulio (cf. CSEL 10, 9); etc.

[25] This analysis is based on the *Barberini Euchologion* gr. 336 (Apostolic Vatican Library, eighth/ninth century, Southern Italy) and on the study by Theodorou.

were unclear and had a temporary and local significance because they were probably caused by a reaction to excesses of Montanism.[26]

Let us call to mind that for the Maronites the feminine diaconate is theoretically possible even today, based on the 1736 synod, approved by the pope *in forma specifica* in 1741, which grants bishops the authority to ordain deaconesses. In this regard, however, we must say that this synod (as in the case of other, ancient documents) is not univocal in its terminology and does not speak clearly about character of such ordination. While in fact in chapter 14, part 2 [of the synod documents], dealing with the sacrament of order, deaconesses are not mentioned, on the contrary can. 5 states "declaramus . . . Subjectum vero ordinatinis capax esse virilem sexum tantummodo," in chapter 2, part 3 (which seems to deal with more practical problems) the ordination or blessing of the deaconesses is explicitly mentioned, for whom precise norms are provided.[27] In this case it is probable that the explanation is found in the mixed nature of the long synodal document.

Finally, in the present ecumenical situation we must bear in mind that the *Armenian Apostolic Church* revived the feminine diaconate in the seventeenth century and today has at least one deaconess, Ms. Kristin Arat, ordained in Constantinople in 1982. The prescribed rite is completely identical to that used for the deacon, except for the words that refer to future priesthood. The Armenian Patriarch of Constantinople Schnork Kalustyan, in a letter addressed to the deaconess, declares that she belongs to the clergy and performs the same tasks as the deacon.[28]

3. The Situation in the Western Church

The feminine ministry was in general less prevalent and spread slowly in the West. The important *Traditio apostolica* by Hippolytus (c. 215), which according to Altaner is "fundamental for our knowledge of the ancient Roman liturgy," does not mention deaconesses. *Tertullian*

---

[26] See Canon 11 of this council; the date is uncertain although later than 350. Cf. ed. Joannu 1-2, 135, 619.

[27] Cf. Mansi 38, in general 128–64, specifically 130 and 163ff.; *Coll. Lacensis* Book. II, col. 272. The complete text is given and discussed as an example by F. Cappello, *Tractatus Canonico-Moralis de Sacramentis* (Torino: Marietti, 1951), vol. IV, 55ff.

[28] Cf. K. Arat, "Die Weihe der Diakonin in der armenish-apostolichen Kirche," in *Liturgie und Frauenfrage*, ed. Th. Berger and A. Gerhards (St. Ottilien, 1990), 67–76.

(d. after 220) declares himself absolutely against any liturgical or teaching ministry by women.[29]

Ambrosiaster firmly maintains that only a man is the image of God and that it would therefore "be a shame if women dared to talk in church." Therefore, in his opinion it is unthinkable to ordain women even only to the diaconate.

According to *Pelagius,* active in Rome from 384 to 410, who was then inactive after various condemnations, it is against nature and revelation that women would rule over and teach men, although it is admissible for deaconesses to "serve or preach to people of their own sex," as it happens in "the Eastern regions."[30]

The decisions of synods are even more restrictive. Even the (extraordinary) council of Saragossa (380) rules against the habit of claiming priestly functions by Priscillian women.[31] Later, a whole series of extraordinary councils in Gaul rule against any kind of ordination of women. Such is the case of the (anti-Priscillian) Council of Nîmes in 394 or 396,[32] of the first Council of Orange in 441,[33] of the Council of Épaone in 517,[34] and of the Council of Orléans of 533.[35] Almost all of these prohibit the use of existing rites for the future; as far as terminology is concerned, we must remember that the terms *benedictio* and *consecratio* used in the texts at that time are synonyms for *ordination.*[36] In the *Statuta Ecclesiae Antiqua* by Gennadius of Marseilles (died c. 500), after the reiteration of the "apostolic" prohibition of "teaching to men in the assembly . . . and of baptizing," it is nonetheless conceded that there would be widows or consecrated virgins to assist women in catechesis and during the administration of baptism (can. 41 and can. 100). All in all, it seems we must infer that notwithstanding the recurring prohibitions, especially in Gaul, the fact of women exercising certain ministries was a repeated occurrence, we must assume with the previous approval of the bishop. Such prohibitions must have applied only locally, since we know of the existence of deaconesses also in the West at least until the year 1054. In

---

[29] Cf. CCL 1,291,20–292,31; 688,7–13; 2,1218,4–1219,6.

[30] PL Suppl. 1,1178.

[31] Cf. Mansi 3,633ff.

[32] Cf. CCL 148,50 can.2.

[33] Ibid., 84, can.25.

[34] Cf. CCL 148A, 29 can.21.

[35] Cf. Ibid., 101, can.17.

[36] Cf. in this sense Gryson, *Il ministero della donna nella Chiesa antica,* cit., 197.

fact, besides *Helaria*, called *diacona* by her father, Saint Remigius of Reims, and the case of Saint Radegund, wife of Lothair I, King of the Franks, who according to Venanzio Fortunato was consecrated deaconess in 555 by Saint Medard of Noyon *manu superposita*, let us recall that the *Liber Pontificalis* records how, when Leo III returned to Rome in 799, the people of Rome welcomed him *cum . . . diaconissis et nobilissimis matronis.* Later, the extraordinary Council of Worms in 868 renewed canon 15 of the Council of Chalcedon and eventually three popes (Benedict VIII, John XIX, and Leo IX) granted to the respective bishops of Porto, Sylva Candida, and again Porto the right to ordain deaconesses.[37]

The Latin Church also has an *Ordo ad diaconam faciendam* including a *Missa ad diaconam consecrandam*; it is a twelfth-century document, probably based on traditions dating back to the Carolingian era.[38] The rite is completely analogous to that of the Byzantine Church: the minister is the bishop, who places the stole under the veil in a manner akin to the Byzantine mode. It is, however, undeniable that this rite emphasizes the aspect of a blessing of a vow of chastity and because of this we think the rite passed into the West when around the same time the presence of an effective diaconal ministry had also lost relevance in the East. For the most correct interpretation of the nature of such *consecratio* a more precise knowledge of the juridical status of the *canonicae* (*sanctimoniales*) in the Middle Ages than we have today would be necessary.

4. Closing Considerations

There is no doubt that for various centuries the undivided Church had deaconesses ordained with a rite similar to that used for deacons. I do not believe that the slight differences are such as to lead the historian to maintain a substantial difference in the two rites. The actual presence of deaconesses is recorded until approximately the twelfth or thirteenth century, above all in the Christian East (Syria) and in the Byzantine Church; in the West we can speak of a reality of lesser importance. In some Eastern Christian Churches and for the Catholic Maronite Church the ordination of deaconesses is theoretically still possible today. The issue of whether such ordination was understood as a "sacrament" or rather only as a "sacramental" or a "blessing," an issue of the greatest importance for the future, is a very delicate subject that I will deal with

---

[37] Cf. PL 139,1621; 132,1056; 143,598.
[38] There is a print edition: M. Hittorp, *De divinis officiis* (Köln, 1568), here 1–160.

in the second part [of this article] on the basis of the historical data summarized above.

5. Systematic Evaluation[39]

I. In the first part of this article I have attempted a synthesis of the historical evolution of the female diaconate. Purposefully I have avoided questioning the nature of such ordinations, that is, whether by applying the categories of present-day sacramental theology they were a true sacrament or rather only a blessing, i.e., a sacramental. This question, however, as anyone can see, is of fundamental importance, not only for a complete evaluation of such ordinations, but above all to respond adequately to the requests for an introduction or (according to others)

---

[39] On this subject, see F. Gillmann, "Weibliche Kleriker nach dem Urteil der Frühscholastik," in *Archiv für katholisches Kirchenrecht* 93 (1913): 239–253; S. Giner Sempere, "La mujer y la potestad de orden," in *Revista Española de Derecho Canónico* 9 (1954): 841–96; J. Daniélou, "Le ministère des femmes dans L'Église ancienne," in *La Maison-Dieu* 61 (1960): 70–96; J. G. Davies, "Deacons, Deaconesses and the Minor Orders in the Patristic Period," in *Journal of the Ecclesiastical History* 14 (1963): 1–15 (also in *Church, Ministry, and Organization in the Early Church Era*, Studies in Early Christianity 13, ed. E. Ferguson [New York, 1993], 237–51); J. Galot, *La donna e i ministeri nella Chiesa* (Assisi: Cittadella, 1973); J. F. Coyle, "The Fathers on Women and Women's Ordination," in *Église et Théologie* 9 (1978): 51–101 (also in *Women in Early Christianity*, Studies in Early Christianity 14, ed. D. M. Scholer [New York, 1993], 117–67); C. Zedda, "Ministerium feminarum?," in *Il diaconato permanente* (Naples, 1983), 237–45; H. Frohnhofen, "Weibliche Diakone in der frühen Kirche," in *Stimmen der Zeit* 110 (1985): 844–52; J.-M. Aubert, *Des femmes diacres. Un nouveau chemin pour l'Église* (Paris, 1987); R. Goldie, "Diaconato femminile?," ibid., 305–13; M. Hauke, "Überlegungen zum Weihediakonat der Frau," in *Theologie und Glaube* 77 (1987): 108–27; J. Ysebaert, *Die Amtsterminologie im Neuen Testament und in der alten Kirche* (Breda: Eureia, 1994); C. Böttigheimer, "Der Diakonat der Frau," in *Münchener Theologische Zeitschrift* 47 (1996): 253–66; U. E. Eisen, *Amtsträgerinnen im frühen Christentum* (Göttingen: Vandenhoeck, 1996); A. Miralles, "Le diaconesse: bilancio di dodici anni di pubblicazioni (1982-1993)," in *Ricerche teologiche* 7 (1996): 161–76; E. Cattaneo, *I ministeri nella Chiesa antica* (Milano: Paoline, 1997); *Diaconat, XXI siècle*, ed. A. Haquin and P. Weber (Brussels: Éditions Lumen Vitae, 1997); G. P. Montini, "Il diaconato femminile. *Lectura cursiva* di un recente documento dell'Associazione Canonistica Statunitense," in *Quaderni di diritto ecclesiale* 10 (1997): 172–91; K. Nientiedt, "Reaktivieren order neuschaffen?," in *Herder-Korrespondenz* 51 (1997): 248–53; B. Pottier, "La sacramentalité du diaconat," in *Nouvelle Revue Théologique* 119 (1997): 20–36.

a renewal of the female diaconate, requests made by some episcopal conferences,[40] by theologians, and by many ecclesial groups.

Those who today try to answer such a question are faced essentially with the following: although the issue in itself seems fairly precise and limited, when considering the works on the subject produced in the last decades we find ourselves entangled, so to speak, in a series of prior problems and difficulties that were either ignored or peremptorily solved in classical manuals but that in postconciliar theology appear instead much more undefined and in a phase of reformulation, if not in crisis. This situation is obviously present in almost all theological treatises, but the case of the female diaconate, functioning above all in the Eastern Churches at least until the end of the Byzantine era, seems particularly affected. What follows is a report of certain areas of systematic theology involved in this problem now being reassessed; where needed, I will express my opinion.

1. As it is always the case in theological matters, first of all it has to be established who bears the burden of evidence, whether we must prove that the ordinations in question were sacramental or whether they who deny such must prove their conviction. In my opinion there is no doubt that the burden of proof falls to they who maintain that the ordinations of deaconesses in the ancient Church had a sacramental dignity like that of deacons.

2. In studies on this subject, indeed not numerous and hardly ever extensive,[41] the first difficulty we encounter regards the formulation of

[40] Cf. in this regard, for example, the *votum* presented to the Holy See by the Synod of the dioceses of West Germany in *Synode* 1-75-50/51 and 61,4,3, and the *Report* titled "The Canonical Implications of Ordaining Women to the Permanent Diaconate" by the *Ad Hoc Committee of the Canon Law Society of America* (Washington, DC, 1975). [partially translated into Italian in *Il Regno-documenti* 9 (1996): 303–11]. The article by Montini noted above (n. 39) firmly and repeatedly criticizes this document, mainly from the canonical point of view. The well-known theologian K. Lehmann, bishop of Mainz, expresses a more cautious opinion in his conference "Diaconato permanente—Un bilancio provvisorio" (cf. *Il Regno* 42 [1997]: 44–54, especially in section 4). Likewise, let us finally remember *Plädoyer*, who was in favor of ordaining women deacons at the end of the international Congress on this issue held in Stuttgart-Hohenheim at the beginning of April 1997, to which the above noted article by Nientiedt refers (cf. n.39).

[41] In the above-mentioned fn. 39 we make reference to a vast selection of these studies; in this article we will also report opinions maintained, almost *en passant*, by various authors both in slightly different or even very different contexts.

the problem itself. In particular let us recall that, within the great variety of salvific and liturgical actions of the Church, the clear separation between the true sacraments on the one hand and sacramentals and simple blessings on the other is relatively late (since the tenth century) and mainly Western. Various scholars assert that it is impossible to apply notions of medieval scholasticism to liturgical actions described in documents dating back many centuries. In substance, I do not see this way of proceeding as correct. In fact, even if we must bear in mind the difficulty associated with the great diversity of cultural contexts, since it has been possible for the Church, above all medieval and modern, to clarify much concerning sacramental realities going back to the post-apostolic Church, sometimes indeed to clarify matters to the point of dogmatic definitions, likewise we cannot admit a radical impossibility of judging whether the ordinations of female deacons were or were not sacramental. Other theologians appropriately point out that even Eastern theology, in some cases in dialogue with Latin Church positions or in other cases in opposition to these, has expressed and still expresses beliefs, which either through another terminology or sometimes with facts are equivalent to the Western notion of sacramentality. It is certainly the case with sacred orders (*hierosýne*) whenever it is asserted that they were founded by Jesus Christ, with the belief that the invocation of the Holy Spirit grants the holy grace to ministers, and with the non-repeatability of single ordinations, and so forth.

3. A second source of difficulty, often either explicitly or implicitly formulated by feminist theology, arises from a real debate opened by the *dogmatic systematization of the male diaconate* and definitely caused and supported by the (re)introduction of the permanent diaconate. Even if we can suppose that some theories and difficulties formulated during meetings of scholars derive from the wish, legitimate indeed, to test hypotheses and to encourage responses among colleagues,[42] in my opinion it is impossible to deny that the entire matter is in need of a deeper and more substantial doctrinal elaboration. Above all we should better specify the typical ministry of the deacon for the Church of today and for the future, mining the important assertions of the Second Vatican Council and synthesizing them. It is clear that the famous formula of the Con-

---

[42] This is certainly the case of the proceedings, very inspiring indeed, of the meeting organized from September 13–15, 1994, in Louvain-la-Neuve by professors of the local theological faculty and by the francophone deacons of Belgium and published under the title of *Diaconat, XXI* siècle* (cf. above fn. 39).

stitutions of the Egyptian Church (III, 2), according to which the deacon "is ordained not to the priesthood, but rather to the ministry"[43] is not sufficient to solve all the problems. To not a few theologians, especially after the reintroduction of the diaconate as a stable grade of the sacred order, it seems necessary to further reflect on the relationship between the (permanent) diaconate and the presbyterate, on the one hand, and between the diaconate and the episcopacy, on the other, and to clarify how the ministry of the diaconate differs from the *diaconia*, not only legitimate, but certainly wished for, of the laity. Regarding the issue we are considering, it is very important to specify whether *agere in persona Christi* is valid only for priests or also for the diaconal ministry or, rather, whether it is valid for the diaconal ministry only with some corrections (for example, specifying that the deacon *agit in persona Christi ministri*).

It is not so much a question of (re)defining powers, although this aspect is by no means irrelevant,[44] but rather of clarifying the structure of the ministry of the New Covenant. On one hand, we know indeed that it [the ministry] is essentially one and not the case of three distinct sacraments. On the other hand, of the ministry's three sacramental grades, only two, presbyterate and episcopacy, constitute the "priesthood" of the New Testament. It is not true, as some have written, that this is a contradiction: however, we cannot deny that we are faced with a doctrinal element not easy to understand. In this regard let me here say that, in my opinion, from a dogmatic point of view the possible restoration of the female diaconate can only consist in granting to women an ordination substantially of the same kind as that of the ordination of (permanent) deacons. Therefore, whenever a "thoroughly new" future diaconate of women is mentioned, either a dangerous terminological equivocation is in play (that is to say a surreptitious attempt to convey different contents under the "protected" terminology of the diaconate), or we undermine the substance of the dogma.

4. We should now remember (and resolve) a final prior difficulty. The latest decisions of the magisterium assure us that the Church does not

---

[43] Cf. ed. Funk II, 103.

[44] In the current Latin legislation there is only one liturgical or ecclesial action among those for which the deacon is ordinary or extraordinary minister, which under certain circumstances, cannot be performed by a layperson (therefore by a woman): Eucharistic Benediction (cf. can. 943 CIC). But it is probable that the diocesan bishop may dispense from such prohibition.

have the power to confer the ministerial *priesthood* on women.[45] However, this position does not yet necessarily imply the impossibility for a woman to receive *diaconal* ordination, because, as we have mentioned above, in the Catholic terminology the term *sacerdotium* uniquely indicates only the presbyterate and the episcopate. The fact that the declaration *Inter insigniores*, mentioned in the most recent footnote, is to be interpreted in this sense is confirmed, for example, in the "Comment" by a trusted theologian commissioned by the Congregation published together with the declaration.[46] This state of affairs would have been irrelevant during all those centuries when, unfortunately, the diaconate was only a necessary grade on the path to the presbyterate, when it was lived for a very short time and not really exercised. But the reintroduction of the diaconate as a permanent grade of the order, with its own characteristics, although these latter must be further specified, makes the question concerning the value of the ordination of women in the undivided Church during the first millennium dogmatically acceptable and sensible and therefore an issue of its possible renewal.

II. Since I will attempt to specify my opinion on the significance of the diaconal ordinations of women during the first millennium, it is more than redundant to say by way of introduction that the only duty of an honest theologian is to analyze arguments concerning the history of dogmas and the history of liturgy, to find explanations, and to highlight problems and propose solutions. Above all in the category of sacraments a final and clarifying word can only come from the living magisterium of the Church, either with reference to the past, that is, to the content of such "tradition" (as only the Church is the authentic interpreter of its own traditions), and above all with regard to the future, that is to say a possible restoration of the female diaconate, given that the Church's highest rule can be only the spiritual good of the ecclesial body.

---

[45] Cf. *Declaration on the Admission of Women to the Priesthood* by the Congregation for the Doctrine of the Faith (October 15, 1976) and above all the apostolic letter *Ordinatio sacerdotalis* by John Paul II (May 22, 1994).

[46] The trusted theologian expresses himself in this way: (if deaconesses received a true sacramental ordination) "is a question to be readdressed in an exhaustive manner without preconceived ideas, but rather through a direct study of the texts; for this reason the Congregation for the Doctrine of the Faith has considered necessary to again postpone the question, rather than face it in the present document."

A second premise interjects itself into any investigation of this matter. Although the sacramentality of the (male) diaconate may not be formally defined, it is considered at least as a certain and common doctrine even by the most cautious theologians. For some theologians the sacramentality is implicitly defined by the Council of Trent, when the council declares that "non solum de sacerdotibus, sed et de diaconis sacrae Litterae apertam mentionem faciunt etc.," and when later it defines that "Si quis dixerit, in Ecclesia catholica non esse hierarchiam, divina ordinatione institutam, quae constat ex episcopis, presbyteris et ministris, an. s."[47] In fact, the Second Vatican Council and all subsequent magisterial documents as well as the new rite of ordination, indeed in addition to Pius XII's apostolic constitution *Sacramentum Ordinis* (30 November 1947), unequivocally imply that they consider the diaconate as a sacrament.[48] The new Code of Canon Law does likewise (cf. can. 1008 and following, differently than in the Eastern canon!) and the recent Catechism of the Catholic Church (cf. no. 1570 and following).

1. The first thing a historian of dogmas notices is that traditional theology and the manualists are firmly convinced that a woman is incapable of receiving the sacrament of ordination and hence also diaconal ordination. Therefore, it follows that the ordination of "deaconesses" (or of "widows") would not have been real sacramental ordinations but rather simple blessings. Other scholars hold that abbesses in convents, who truly had some jurisdictional and liturgical power within their monasteries, were called under the honorific title of "deaconesses," or else that in many cases such a title for women should be interpreted analogically with the practice, still followed in the East, of calling the wife or the mother of the presbyter or of the bishop *presbytera* or *episkopa*, respectively.

This *sententia communis* is so frequent that it does not need to be supported with many citations; we will limit ourselves to recall some sources in the footnote here.[49] As for the *argumenta*, Saint Thomas in his

---

[47] *DS* 1765 and 1776.

[48] As far as Vatican II cf. *Lumen Gentium* 29 ("[Diaconi . . .] gratia enim *sacramentali* roborati"); *Ad Gentes* 16 ("per gratiam *sacramentalem* diaconatus"); and *Orientalium Ecclesiarum* 17 (Ut antiqua *sacramenti Ordinis* disciplina . . . iterum vigeat, exoptat haec Sancta Synodus, ut institutum diaconatus permanentis . . . instauretur"). Italics mine. In the past, Gaetano and Durando, for example, have denied that the diaconate is a true sacrament.

[49] Among the Greek fathers, Epiphanius, *Haer.* 79,3 (=PG 42,744ff.); according to Thomas Aquinas cf. *In IV Sent.* d.25, q.2, a.1 (Busa I, 578) and *STh.* Suppl. q. 39,

commentaries to the *Sentences* (4, 25, 2, 1) and in his *Supplementum* of the *Summa Theologiae* expresses himself thusly: "Cum . . . in sexu femineo non possit significari aliqua eminentia gradus, quia mulier statum subiectonis habet; ideo non potest ordinis sacramentum suscipere." Cappello gives the following rationale: (a) the title of "ordination" is improper and analogical; (b) the rites concerning deaconess lack a true laying on of hands with the express invocation of the Holy Spirit; (c) the deaconesses in the ancient sources did not perform the same things as did the deacons but rather they were instituted for reasons of decency; (d) even so, such a rite was neither always nor everywhere valid in the Church, for example, it was never adopted in the Roman Church; (e) it is in reality a blessing that was never considered as a true ordination by the Church. Solá, more precisely, affirms that "even though there sometimes was the laying on of hands and the invocation of the Holy Spirit, nonetheless such *consecratio* was never considered the equivalent of a true sacrament," and he refers to the basic text of the *Apostolic Constitutions*, which we have mentioned above, according to which "diaconissa non benedicit, sed nec peragit quidquam eorum, quae presbyteri aut diaconi faciunt."[50] Moreover, two New Testament passages typically considered as against the notion of any feminine ministry are very often quoted in support of this view, 1 Corinthians 14:33b-35 and 1 Timothy 2:12-14; in distinction to what the majority of contemporary exegetes maintain, ancient, medieval, or modern theologians did not at all consider these passages as later interpolations or rules of a local nature. As canonical texts they took them literally and used them as any other New Testament passage. Finally, as far as all the preconciliar authors are concerned we can certainly admit the importance of a premise, hardly ever formulated, as follows: "Why ordain to an order only meant to prepare for the priesthood a person known as incapable of being admitted to it?"

---

a.1; similar things are found in Bonaventure and Scotus. Among the theologians of this century we recall Pohle in his *Lehrbuch der Dogmatik* (Paderborn, 1905), III, p. 569; J. Forget in *DThCath* IV, 694ff. (1911); H. Leclerq in *DACL IV/1* p. 727 (1920); F. Solá in *Sacrae Theologiae Summa* of BAC (Matriti 1962), vol. 4, especially the *scholion* at nos. 56–59 (pp. 619–22), etc. As far as the canonists are concerned, besides Devoti, cf. P. Gasparri, *Tractatus canonicus de Sacra Ordinatione* (Parisiis/ Lugduni, 1893), especially p. 80, no. 136; F. M. Cappello, *Tractatus Canonico-Moralis de Sacramentis*, cit., especially nos. 87ff. (pp. 52–59); etc. On this point even the Orthodox theologians generally agree: cf., for example, the text on sacraments by the Archimandrite B. Katsanevakis (Naples, 1954), especially at p. 246.

[50] *Apostolic Constitutions* 8,28,6 (ed. Funk, 531).

2. While all the above-mentioned observations are substantially *scholia*, or notes of less importance to the discourse on (male) sacred orders, in approximately the past thirty years the number of direct and exclusive studies essentially focused on all the aspects of ancient female ordinations done by specialists in various fields has increased. As always happens in these cases, relative certainty and unanimity have been reached on some points, while on others we are faced with theses and antitheses. We have already seen that, in the majority of the rites used for deaconesses, it was the case of a true and proper ordination, that deaconesses were ordained nearly only in the East at least for the whole Byzantine era, and that such rites have never been declared invalid or abandoned by any synodal or magisterial decision. As regards the issue of whether these ordinations were sacramental or not, which is the point of greater ecclesial relevance, we have to acknowledge that the majority of scholars we have analyzed maintain that there are not valid argumentations to deny sacramentality. On the occasion of the synod of the dioceses of the Federal Republic of Germany, three theologians of renowned merit, Y. Congar OP, P. Hünermann, and H. Vorgrimler, were asked to give their opinion on the subject in a written document. All three declared themselves in favor of the sacramentality of the ordinations at issue. Father O. Semmelroth, SJ, expressed some doubts on some of Hünermann's statements; in my opinion Hünermann replied proving their groundlessness. In addition, J. Galot, SJ, R. Gryson, and C. Vagaggini, OSB, in their works of the 1970s above mentioned (cf. fn. 39) express themselves in favor of a substantial equality between the male and the female diaconate in the undivided Church.[51] Among the scholars who have devoted themselves to this subject, the French liturgist A. G. Martimort holds a different position. In his very detailed study *"Les diaconesses"* (1982) Martimort appears to reach the conclusion that the Eastern ordinations of women deacons placed deaconesses halfway, so to speak, between the three major orders (deacon, presbyter, and bishop) and the broad series of minor ministers such as subdeacon, acolyte, ostiary [doorkeeper], psalmist, etc. (whom nowadays we know were not ordained).[52] Martimort concludes his research stating that more and deeper analysis of the

---

[51] Daniélou, in the above-mentioned article, dated 1960, gathers many historical sources, but he does not make a judgement on the sacramentality of the ancient female diaconate.

[52] We refer specifically to his conclusion: "la diaconesse byzantine n'est pas un diacre: c'est un tout autre ministère" (op. cit. 155).

ancient documents and of the various ordination rites is necessary; he reaffirms the great difficulty of interpreting these sources, and he warns against making the mistake in the future of performing on women a rite of which we do not exactly know the sacramental value. Among those who reject the notion of sacramentality, in addition we have to remember M. Hauke, whose premise is that notwithstanding its three grades the sacred order is only one and maintains that a possible sacramental ordination of women even though solely to the diaconate would likewise contradict the impossibility of ordaining women to the priesthood, recently definitively reiterated by John Paul II in *Ordinatio sacerdotalis*. In this context it is certainly useful to recall that the vast majority of Protestant theologians have no difficulty recognizing the absolute parity of ancient ordinations of [men and] women deacons and that within the Orthodox Church, which like the Catholic Church is thoroughly adverse to women priests, there are favorable opinions concerning the renewal of a true female diaconate.[53] In this regard the clearest affirmations are those by E. Theodorou, E. Gvosdev, and E. Behr-Siegel.

3. After three decades of studies and debates, I believe it is possible to maintain that nearly all the arguments lead to consider it highly probable that deaconesses in the ancient and medieval Church received a sacramental ordination analogous to that of deacons. I will summarize here below these arguments and address some difficulties concerning this affirmation.

a) *Biblical evidence:* The apostolic ministry appears to have been founded by the Lord in a generic way and structured in its three grades by the apostolic Church; exegetes are not in complete agreement about the historic periods and the modes of this structuring. Within this frame of reference, scriptural evidence for the female diaconate (which I have presented in the first section) is in reality only slightly weaker than that for the male diaconate, which essentially consists only in 1 Timothy 3:8ff.[54] The fact that

---

[53] All this of course has an ecumenical relevance for future choices, but does not necessarily make an argument. In fact, for the churches of the Reformation the ordained ministry is not a sacrament.

[54] Let us remember that the seven individuals elected by the Apostles to "serve" during the meals of the Greek widows in Acts of the Apostles 6:1ff. are never called deacons, and they are probably appointed to a much more relevant ministry, as it appears from what two of them (Stephen and Philip) do in the following part of the passage. However, the term *diákonos*, which in the New Testament occurs twenty-nine (certain) times besides the aforementioned passages

there is no record of the actual existence of deaconesses throughout the second century is clearly an *argumentum ex silentio*, which therefore cannot be used to prove the lack of historic continuity with the New Testament.[55]

b) *Classical arguments:* Some of the reasons put forward by the fathers and manualists to explain the exclusion of women from any sacramental ministry, and therefore even from the diaconate, are to be judged unacceptable today. Above all among these, the notion of a natural inferiority of women is explicitly denied by all of the latest magisterial documents concerning the role of women in the Church.[56] Other times it is essentially a *petitio principii* of this sort: since dogmatic and canonistic thought imply that women are incapable of receiving the sacrament of order, then in the case of deaconesses there was not a true sacramental ordination. The soundest arguments, which for now are certainly valid only regarding to the presbyterate, are presented by the uninterrupted tradition of the Church and what the Eastern theology calls the "iconic" nature of the presbyterial minister.

c) *The slight differences in the ordination rite:* Above all Martimort insists on some differences between the rite of ordination of the deacon and that of the deaconess; I have already described these in the first historical section of this article. I believe, along with the great majority of scholars, that the elements of equality between the two rites cannot be undermined by some slight differences. In distinction, the nature of rites performed on other minor ministers is not like a sacramental ordination. As far as Martimort's warnings are concerned, we have to reaffirm the relative clarity and sufficiency of the texts we have, and we should wonder if there is hope of finding other more explicit sources on the subject in the future. Finally, the historian of dogmas and the theologian cannot accept the elitist mentality of the researcher and keep postponing any choice on issues of such importance.

---

of 1 Timothy and Romans 16:1 (referring to Phoebe), has the technical meaning of ordained minister only in the initial greeting of Philippians 1:1 (where, from the grammatical point of view, it could also include deaconesses).

[55] In this regard let us recall the fact, too often forgotten in the analysis of the texts done in the first centuries, that the term *diákonos* as used by pre-Christian writers is both masculine and feminine; let us also remember the assertions by Clement of Alexandria (d. before 215) and above all by Origen, which I have mentioned above in the historic part.

[56] See, for example, nos. 24 and 30 of John Paul II, Apostolic Letter *Mulieris dignitatem* (15 August 1988).

Finally, in order to evaluate the importance of liturgical differences it can be helpful to recall that even the three rites presently used in the Latin Church for the ordination of a deacon, a presbyter, and a bishop differ considerably one from another, mainly with regard to the three formulae of ordination, of course, with no loss of sacramentality (cf. the Italian *editio typica* of the Roman Pontifical of 1992 no. 52,146 and 230). In my opinion the image of the deaconess established by the ancient *Didaskalia tôn Apostólon* and above all its description of the two branches of the diaconate as a *duo corpora in una anima portantes* (III 13:2) speaks in unequivocal language.[57]

d) *The diverse tasks:* From the point of view of "powers" and of *munera*, it is undeniable that the Eastern deaconess, notwithstanding all the varieties of customs and ecclesial situations, "was able to do much less" than the deacon. Essentially, apart from exceptions (most found in the Nestorian churches), her ministry was only to women. However, it is hardly possible to use this fact against the sacramentality of their ordinations: first, because it is formally the case of two utterly disparate aspects; next, because their exclusive purview was probably quite large; and finally, because even the tasks of the deacon in the history of the Church have not been stable at all. Even without recalling some practices that nowadays manuals qualify as violations,[58] some of the very important tasks a deacon performs today as an ordinary minister (for example, baptism, assistance at weddings, etc.) are unthinkable in antiquity and in the Middle Ages. The same holds true for presbyters. Historic sources often assert that the feminine diaconal ministry was introduced above all (but not only) for reasons of decency, that is, to allow entrance to areas reserved for women and for the actual immersion baptism of adult women, or for the spiritual care of sick women. In my opinion, these do not have much to do with the sacramentality of the corresponding ordinations.

---

[57] As we have already mentioned, we do not have the original Greek of this work. Two editors of the Syriac version, R. H. Connolly (*Didascalia Apostolorum*, The Syriac version [Oxford, 1929], 148) and A. Vööbus (cf. CSCO 408, p. 158), maintain that the subject of the sentence are not the two branches of the diaconate but rather the bishop and the deacon; such interpretation is accepted by Martimort (op. cit., 36 fn. 13). In my opinion the context at the most allows us to identify, on the one hand, the bishop as the subject of *portantes* and, on the other, the *ministerium diaconiae*.

[58] Such was, for example, the hearing of confession by deacons or even by lay monks during the first centuries of the Church.

Practicality and, to a certain extent, adaptation are fundamental criteria for the concrete structuring of the various ecclesial ministries.

e) *The name of the feminine ministry:* An argument thus far not employed in studies on this issue is the choice of the same name, which I think clearly supports the equality of the rites performed on the deacon and on the deaconess: first, in the Greek sources (following the use of St. Paul *in* Rom 16:1) it is first the two-gendered term *diákonos* and then the neologism *diakónissa*. Within a culture so accurate with regard to official names and titles it would truly be very strange that for approximately ten centuries women were given the title of deaconesses if what was really meant was catechists or doorkeepers. Let us recall, especially starting from the third century, that names adequately expressing the distinction from deacons were not lacking: for instance, subdeaconess (*hypodiakónissa*) or cathechist.

f) *The generic aspect of the term "to ordain":* It is true that, both by comparing the historic sources and within a same source itself, there is not absolute terminological consistency (for example, sometimes *cheirotonía* of deaconesses is mentioned, at other times *cheirothesía*) and also that the terms associated with the root *cheiroton-* are not always reserved to the group of three ministers whom today we consider as sacramentally ordained, but they are even sometimes applied to minor ministers. However, such is not at all an argument against the sacramentality of the female diaconate: in fact, this argument is never valid for the male diaconate and if anything it would lead us to say that for some ancient sources even the subdiaconate and the other minor ministries are part of the sacred order and therefore sacraments. In this regard we should remember that even the entire Latin tradition prior to the Motu Proprio *Ministeria quaedam* (15 August 1972) spoke of eight grades of order and that a great number of medieval and modern theologians believed that the subdiaconate—today abolished—was a sacrament, and some among them even believed that all the minor orders were sacraments.[59]

g) *The female diaconate as a "Trojan horse" for the presbyterate:* It is clear that for many men and women who support the sacramentality of ancient diaconal ordinations that such is considered a first step toward priesthood, more or less as has occurred within the Anglican church. But it is equally obvious that this observation can in no way influence

---

[59] As far as the subdiaconate is concerned, for example, Bonaventure, Albert the Great, Scotus, Bellarmine, Melchior Cano, Billuart, etc., perhaps even Thomas Aquinas.

judgment regarding what happened in the past. The renewal of the permanent diaconate in the Catholic Church assures us that this sacrament has meaning in itself, even without being a step toward priesthood; the renewal renders the debate conferring the sacrament on women not *a priori* contradictory to the stance of the apostolic letter *Ordinatio sacerdotalis*. Nonetheless the "political" value of the sacrament should be clearly seen, so as to avoid any misunderstanding regarding its significance.

Translated by Carmela Leonforte-Plimack with Phyllis Zagano

4

The Diaconate
and Other Liturgical Ministries of Women

Pietro Sorci

1. The State of the Question

The problem of an acknowledged liturgical ministry by women is as ancient as Christianity, even though each era has approached it according to its sensitivity and its cultural horizon. The New Testament presents it in the context of diverse experiences within the various cultural milieux, in the Patristic era in the context of the Gnostic and Montanist controversy, in the twelfth century coincidental with the spread of the ordination of women to the diaconate in the West, in the sixteenth century with the blossoming of liturgical studies caused by the Counter-Reformation.[1]

In this [twentieth] century, the resumption of the debate seems to be linked with the beginning of the feminist movement. In addition to Kalsbach's 1926 study on the deaconesses in the ancient Church,[2] by now a classic, we must mention E. Theodorou's 1954 study on the Eastern tradition,[3] and after the Second Vatican Council, the very well-documented study by R. Gryson on women's ministries in the ancient Church,[4] which, however, ends with the sixth century and discreetly poses the hypothesis

"Diaconato e altri ministeri liturgici della donna," in *La Donna nel pensiero cristiano antico*, ed. Umberto Mattioli (Genova: Marietti Editore, 1992), 331–64.

---

[1] I have provided the documentation for this discussion in my "Ministeri liturgici della donna nella Chiesa antica," in *Donna e ministero un dibattito ecumenico*, ed. Cettina Militello (Rome, 1991), 17–30.

[2] A. Kalsbach, *Die altchristiche Einrichtung der Diakonissen bis zu ihrem Erlöschen* (Freiburg, 1926). Kalsbach summarized his study for the *Reallexikon fur Antike und Christentum*, at the entry *Diakonisse*, III (1957): 917–18.

[3] E. Theodorou, Ἡ χειροτονία ἢ χειροθεσία τῶν διακονισσῶν, "Θεολογία," 25 (1954): 430–69; 26 (1955), 57–76.

[4] R. Gryson, *Le ministère des femmes dans l'Eglise ancienne* (Gembloux, 1972; Rome, 1974).

that the causes of the exclusion of women from the priesthood come from the Greco-Roman environment in which the revelation was planted.

After Gryson there is a very detailed article by C. Vagaggini on the ordination of deaconesses, which examines the rite of ordination, but which is limited to the Byzantine Church.[5]

In 1982, A. G. Martimort renewed the research, still limiting it to the diaconate but extending it to the Middle Ages, arriving at the conclusion that it is difficult to establish what the deaconesses of antiquity mentioned in theological and canonical literature and in liturgical sources were, and that in any case they cannot be considered true deacons.[6]

Nevertheless, during the past fifteen years, countless works have been published on the issue, mainly produced by the feminist movement. Among these, we must recall first of all two issues of the international review of theology *Concilium: Women in the Church* in 1976[7] and *Women in a Male Church* in 1980,[8] and especially the studies by E. Schüssler Fiorenza,[9]

[5] C. Vagaggini, *L'ordinazione delle diaconesse nella tradizione greca e bizantina*, in *OCP* 40 (1974): 145–89.

[6] A. G. Martimort, *Les diaconesses. Essai historique* (Rome, 1982). Martimort's conclusions, especially pp. 150–55; 246–51. To prove his thesis he chooses as a criterion the figure of the male deacon that emerges from the *Ordo Romanus* I of the seventh century to verify the presence or absence of a female diaconate, as if throughout the centuries the deacon did not undergo deep transformations, such as indeed occurred with the bishop and the presbyter; Martimort minimizes all the similarities and maximizes all the differences found in the ordination rites and in the functions of the deacon and the deaconess, taking for granted that the [ordained] ministry of a man and of a woman must be identical.

[7] With articles by E. Schüssler Fiorenza, *Il ruolo delle donne nel movimento cristiano primitivo*, *Concilium* 12, no. 1 (1976): 21–36; and by R. Radford Ruether, *Le donne e il sacerdozio in una prospettiva storica e sociale*, ibid., 54–67.

[8] In this, I. Raming, *Dalla libertà del Vangelo ad una Chiesa a struttura maschile. Origine e sviluppo della supremazia dell'uomo nella Chiesa*, *Concilium* 16, no. 4 (1980): 19–34, proposes an interesting hypothesis in the interpretation of the institution of widows in the New Testament, which nevertheless, at the present state of the research, does not seem to be supported by the sources. It would be the case of "a true and independent form of the feminine presbyterate, the origin of which is linked to the cultural situation of the eastern world," the tasks of which were the pastoral care of women in their homes and diaconal charitable service, of which women were deprived as a consequence of the sacerdotalization and Judaization of ecclesiastical ministry.

[9] E. Schüssler Fiorenza, *En mémoire d'elle. Essai de reconstruction des origines chrétiennes selon la théologie féministe* (Paris, 1986; New York 1983).

J. M. Aubert,[10] E. Behr Sigel,[11] as well as a very detailed article published on the journal *Studi Ecumenici* in 1988, in which C. Militello sums up the entire present debate [up to 1992] and suggests interesting solutions.[12]

Rather than on historical research, these studies focus on biblical and theological hermeneutics, which fall outside the framework of my study.

Here, I will omit the study of the New Testament, which would require an extensive analysis[13] impossible within the scope of this work, and which is certainly of great interest given that any ecclesial practice rightly or wrongly claims to be founded in it; rather, I will focus on research into liturgical sources. Bearing in mind Martimort's methodological approach,[14] I will compare historical documentation and canonical literature to liturgical sources, so as to arrive at an understanding as thoroughly complete as possible on how Churches have faced the problem of a feminine ministry.

2. The First and Second Centuries

Christian literature of the second century often mentions widows. However, they represent a category of persons assisted by the Church rather than a ministry, or, when the term is intended as technical, they constitute a state of chaste life devoted to prayer.[15]

---

[10] J. M. Aubert, *L'exil féminin. Antiféminisme et christianisme* (Paris, 1988).

[11] E. Beher-Sigel, *Le ministère de la femme dans l'Église* (Paris, 1987).

[12] C. Militello, "La donna nella Chiesa: problemi aperti," *Studi Ecumenici* 6, no. 1 (1988): 59–102.

[13] Concerning Jesus' relationship with women, cf. J. Leipold, *Die Frau in der antiken Welt und im Urchristentum* (Gütersloh, 1962), 81–98; for Matthew, cf. J. Blank, "*Frauen in den Jesusüberlieferungen*," in *Die Frau im Urchristentum*, ed. G. Dautzenberg, H. Merklein, K. Müller (Freiburg, 1983), 32–39; for Mark, ibid., 11–28; for Luke, the evangelist who most emphasizes the holiness, goodness, and willingness of women to serve and be converted, ibid., 39–68; for John, ibid., 68–88. All the biblical problems are addressed by M. Adinolfi, *Il femminismo della Bibbia* (Roma, 1981).

[14] Given the complexity of the problem and the differences from one Church to the other, it is necessary to proceed through particular monographs. Besides, it is not enough to ascertain the existence of deaconesses from a text; it is necessary to discover what they and their functions are, because the reality is extremely changeable, and above all one must find out whether the text in question was used in a specific Church or whether it has entered a compilation as a result of a copyist's decision or, moreover, whether the text survived its usage. A. G. Martimort, *Les diaconesses, op. cit.*, 8.

[15] Ignatius, writing to the Smyrnaeans, addresses a particular greeting "to the virgins called widows" (*Smirn.*, 13.1 in A. Quacquarelli, *I Padri apostolici* [Rome, 1978], 138).

The only texts showing women in ministry are the *Shepherd* [*of Hermas*], where the elderly woman (the Church) entrusts Hermas with delivering one of the two books of the revelations to Graptè, in order for her to read it to the orphans and the widows under her care;[16] and the text by Pliny the Younger, who in his well-known letter to Trajan speaks of two slaves called *ministrae* by the Christians.[17] Indeed, the Greek term that Pliny translates as *ministra* is likely to be διάκονος.

The situation witnessed by Tertullian in Africa is no different from that recorded by the apostolic fathers. Widows constitute a separate class, a particular "ordo" within the Church, alongside male members of the hierarchy. They [the widows] are asked advice concerning marriage,[18] penitents turn to them to ask for their intercession,[19] but they do not exercise any liturgical ministry.[20]

On the other hand, numerous reports come from outside the great Church. From the Apocrypha of the New Testament such as the Acts of Paul, in which Thecla baptizes herself, evangelizes Tryphaena, entrusted by the Apostle announces God's word in Iconium, and finally "enlightened" many in Seleucia with God's word;[21] the Acts of Philip, in which his sister Marianne, sent by Jesus himself, accompanies the Apostle and collaborates in his preaching.[22] Whatever value is to be attributed to these

[16] Hermas, *The Shepard*, 8.2-3, 249.

[17] Plinius, *Ep.* 10.96.8: *Necessarium credidi ex duabus ancillis, quae ministrae dicebantur, quid esset veri et per tormenta quaerere* (Durri, 74).

[18] From this practice Tertullian argues against remarriage: "How dare you ask to contract a marriage prohibited to they whom you ask: the bishop married only once, the presbyters subject to the same discipline, the widows, whose style of life you rejected with your behavior?" (*De monogamia*, 11.1, CCL 2:1244).

[19] *De pudicitia* 13.7, CCL 2:1304.

[20] The *De virginibus velandis*, 9.2-3, CCL 2:1219 shows that within the community there is an *ordo viduarum*: admission to it depends on the bishop, the conditions are those indicated by 1 Timothy 5:9-10: having become sixty, having been married only once, having brought up her children well. We can infer an analogous situation from the *Traditio apostolica* by Hippolytus: widows appear to be the privileged recipients of Christian charity. Among the widows some are instituted: they are not ordained with the laying on of hands, which is reserved to the clergy performing liturgical ministry, but are instituted for prayer, which is everybody's duty (*La tradition apostolique de saint Hippolyte*, 20 [Botte] 43; 10:31).

[21] *Atti di Paolo e Tecla* 34.39.43, in M. Erbetta, ed., *Gli Apocrifi del Nuovo Testamento, II: Atti e leggende* (Casale, 1966), 265, 266, 267.

[22] *Acts of Philip*, 95.109, here, pp. 474–76.

writings, they give testimony, if not to the practice, surely to the attempt to support claims present within the community where they originated.

Within Montanism, which developed in the second half of the second century, the role of women was decisive. The sources we have are almost entirely Catholic, and their purpose is not only to denigrate the inspiration of the Paraclete to whom Montanus appealed but principally to denigrate the activity of the two prophetesses Priscilla and Maximilla. Of these Eusebius says that they were filled with a false spirit and spoke in an inappropriate, nonsensical manner, improper to women.[23] In Pepuza, Phrygia, they dreamt they had seen Christ appearing as a woman. After experiencing the action of the Spirit they abandoned their husbands, thereby freeing themselves from male authority. They performed a ministry of penance for the forgiveness of sins: convinced that they spoke guided by the Spirit, they assured sinners led to conversion by their personal charism—their ability to read minds—of the forgiveness of their sins in the name of God.[24]

It does not seem that within the Montanist communities ordination of women with the laying on of hands was practiced: the prophetic charism rendered useless other rites for the official appointment to the ministry.

Women presiding over the Eucharist are explicitly documented only in 235, at the time of emperor Licinius Severianos, in a letter by Firmilian, bishop of Caesarea, to Cyprian.[25] This report is confirmed by Epiphanius, who affirms that among the Quintilians—a branch of Montanism—there are women bishops and women presbyters and other feminine ministries. Accordingly, indeed there would not be any difference between men and women, because in Jesus Christ there is neither male nor female (cf. Gal 3:28). However, for Epiphanius these women forget the words of Scripture: I permit no woman to teach or to have authority over a man (cf. 1 Tim 2:12), as well as the other texts affirming that the woman is the cause of sin.[26]

---

[23] Eusebius, *Storia eccl.*, 5.16.9, SCh 41:48.

[24] Ibid., 5.18.7-10, *loc. cit.*, 56–58.

[25] Among the letters of Cyprian, *Ep.* 75.10, CSEL 3:2, 816–18: *emersit istic subito quaedam mulier quae in extasim constituta propheten se preferret et quasi Sancto Spiritu plena sic ageret.* One of the things she was accused of was celebrating the Eucharist, as well as baptizing with the Catholic rite: *Ut invocatione non contemptibili sanctificare se panem et eucharistiam facere simularet et sacrificium Domino sine sacramento solitae praedicationis offeret, baptizaret quoque multos usitata et legitima verba interrogationis usurpans, ut nihil discrepare ab ecclesiatica regula videretur.*

[26] Epiphanius, *Pan.* 49.1-3, GCS 21:241–44. Another feminist movement Epiphanius attacks is that of the Collyridians, which was developed in Arabia

The Catholic reaction against these claims was harsh and intolerant, as testified, in addition to Epiphanius and Eusebius, by Hippolytus,[27] Origen,[28] and Ambrosiaster.[29]

If we add to this, on the one hand, the influence of late Judaism, very hostile toward women, as documented by Apocrypha of the Old Testament, such as the *Book of Jubilees*, the *Book of Enoch*, and the *Testament of the Twelve Patriarchs*, which were highly regarded within not a few Christian circles, and, on the other hand, the influence of the Greco-Roman culture, which excluded women from political life, we understand how the seed of Jesus' free and freeing practice and his teaching could not produce the fruits we would imagine given the affirmation of Galatians 3:28, and how Churches looked with suspicion at feminine ministry, even the diaconal ministry of women, which is admitted by Epiphanius[30] but which is resolutely denied by Ambrosiaster.[31]

---

by women from Thrace and Scythia. When they gathered they performed a particular rite in honor of the Virgin Mary using some bread, under the presidency of women. According to Epiphanius, this is a diabolical invention, not so much because the cult that only pertains to God is attributed to a creature, but because in the rite women claim to exercise priestly functions: "Never, in fact, since time immemorial a woman has ever exercised priestly functions of divine cult" (ibid., 79.3-4, GCS 37:477), not even the Virgin Mary. Who is holier than she? And yet Christ did not give her even the power to baptize, as he did not give this power to any of the women mentioned in the Gospels (ibid., 79.7.3-4, *loc. cit.* 482). This is a well-known argument, which starting from the *Didascalia Apostolorum* and from the *Constitutiones Apostolorum* (see below) would be repeated to justify the exclusion of women from the priesthood until today, in the Declaration of the Congregation for the Doctrine of the Faith, *Inter insigniores*, regarding the admission of women to the ministerial priesthood, of 1976, II-III, in *Enchiridion Vaticanum*, V, nn. 219–25.

[27] Hippolytus, *Refutatio haer.* 8.19.1, GCS 26:238.

[28] Origen, *Frammenti sulla Prima lettera ai Corinzi*, 74, *JThS* 10 (1909): 41–42 (ed. C. Jenkins).

[29] Ambrosiaster, *In ep. I ad Tim*, 3:11, CSEL 81/3, 267–68.

[30] Epiphanius, *Pan.* 79.3.6-4.1, *loc. cit.*, 478: "There are deaconesses in the Church, but they are not assigned priestly tasks. Like the male deacons, they do not perform any sacramental action, like the male deacons they are only servants. Their ministry is performed solely among women and its purpose is to safeguard decency, so that men who perform sacred rites do not see the body of a woman when unclothed at the moment of baptism, when her virginity must be certified and on the occasion of care of the sick."

[31] "Cataphrygians (as Montanists were known in Latin areas) actually look for occasions to fall into error. Given that Paul addresses women after speaking to

3. In Eastern Syria

3.1 The Didascalia Apostolorum

Western Syria was the melting pot of ancient civilizations, where Western and Semitic culture merged with the Greco-Roman civilization and where the Christian faith met Hellenistic culture. In this region, thanks as well to the greater autonomy women enjoyed in the first centuries[32] [of the Christian era], the institution of deaconesses knew its highest development. However, strangely enough, the first clear evidences of a place for women in liturgical ministry come from the eastern regions of Syria, known to be more tied to the Semitic and Judaic traditions. Even considering the scarcity of sources, the only explanation can be that such ministry was rooted in the New Testament and in the tradition of the apostolic Churches.

The first document informing us about a diaconal ministry entrusted to women in the region of Eastern Syria is the *Didascalia apostolorum*, compiled in Syria in the first half of the third century.[33]

The *Didascalia* repeatedly mentions widows, but, together with orphans, the poor, and immigrants, they are under the bishops' care.[34]

---

the deacons (1 Tim 3:8-11) they foolishly presume that even deaconesses must be ordained (*etiam ipsas diaconas ordinari debere*). Yet they know well that the apostles chose seven deacons. Perhaps at that time no woman was found suitable for this office, even though we read that there were holy women with the eleven apostles? . . . Paul prescribes that in church women must remain silent, Cataphrygians on the contrary even claim the authority of an ecclesiastical ministry for women (*illi e contra etiam auctoritatem in ecclesia vindicant ministerii*). Ambrosiaster, in ep. 1 *ad Tim* 3:11, *CSEL* 81/3, 268.

[32] For the status of women in the Hellenistic-Roman world, cf. P. Gramaglia, *Tertulliano, De virginibus velandis. La condizione femminile nelle prime comunità cristiane* (Torino, 1984), 7–19.

[33] The original Greek text is lost; we have a Syriac version dated to the beginning of the fourth century, edited by R. H. Connolly, *Didascalia Apostolorum: The Syriac Version Translated and Accompanied by the Verona Latin Fragments* (Oxford, 1929), and a Latin version of the end of the fourth century, edited by F. X. Funk, *Didascalia et Constitutiones Apostolorum*, 2 vols. (Paderborn, 1905). The *Didascalia* has served as source for the *Constituiones Apostolorum*. Several indications (the Semitic origin of the author, the references to the Apocrypha of the Old Testament) lead to locate the homeland of the *Didascalia* in Celesyria, near Edessa and Mesopotamia. In fact the Acts of Judas Thomas, most probably composed in Edessa, perhaps at the same time as the *Didascalia*, describe the baptism of women with a ritual very similar to that [found in the *Didascalia*].

[34] *Didascalia*, II, 4.1, Funk, 34. Like the Levites of the Old Testament these [widows] must receive the gifts of the faithful (II, 26.1-3, Funk, 102).

Among the widows some are "instituted," and as such they constitute the *ordo viduarum*: they must be at least fifty years of age, this ensuring that they would not remarry.[35] A widow must be occupied with nothing other than praying for donors and for the whole Church.[36] They must neither teach[37] nor baptize, although it seems some among them claimed to perform these actions.[38]

In addition to widows, the *Didascalia* mentions deaconesses. Developing further the typology of Ignatius, according to which the bishop is the image of Christ, while the presbyters are images of the apostles,[39] the *Didascalia* adds that the deaconess must be honored as a *figura* [type] of the Holy Spirit.[40] The functions [of the deaconess] are presented in book 3, chapter 12.[41] The position of the deaconess is presented as analogous to that of the deacon: men and women deacons are collaborators of the bishop, freely chosen by him. But the assignments of the deaconess are less extensive: the deacon must take care of the numerous things that are necessary; he must be ready to carry out all the bishop's orders, [to be] "his ear and his mouth,"[42] that is, to be the mediator between the bishop and the faithful; he aids the bishop during the eucharistic celebration and

[35] Ibid., III, 1.1, Funk, 182.

[36] Ibid., III 5.2, Funk, 188.

[37] "It is neither proper nor necessary for women to teach, above all about Christ and redemption through his passion. In fact, you women, and mainly you widows have not been established to teach, rather to pray and implore the Lord God. Indeed the Lord God, Jesus Christ, our master, has sent us Twelve to instruct the people and the nations. There were women disciples with us: Mary Magdalene, Mary daughter of James and the other Mary, but he did not send them with us to instruct the people. Had it been necessary for women to teach, our master himself would have ordered them to teach together with us" (ibid., III, 6.1-2, Funk, 190).

[38] "We do not advise a woman to baptize nor for anyone to be baptized by a woman, for this is a transgression of the commandment and a great danger for the person baptized and for she who baptizes. Had it been legitimate to be baptized by a woman, our master would have been baptized by Mary his mother, whereas instead he was baptized by John, as were the other people. Therefore, brothers and sisters do not put yourself in danger by acting against the law of the Gospel" (ibid., III, 9.1-3, Funk, 198–200).

[39] Ignatius, *Trall.*, 3.1 in A. Quacquarelli, *I padri apostolici, op.cit.*, 116.

[40] *Didascalia*, II, 26.6, Funk, 104.

[41] Ibid., III, 12.1-3, Funk, 208–10.

[42] Ibid., II, 28.6, Funk, 108–10.

makes sure order is maintained within the assembly.[43] Such might lead us to think that a deaconess's functions correspond to those of the deacon for what regards women. On the contrary, her ministry appears somewhat more restricted, consisting mainly in entering pagan households when the entry of a male deacon might give rise to slander, in visiting ill Christian women and washing them when they start to recover,[44] in anointing the body of women when these go down into the baptismal pool and in receiving them when they come up from it, because it is not proper for men to see their nudity, and in teaching them not to violate the baptismal seal with an unworthy life.[45]

The language of the author seems defensive: indeed, he insists on the usefulness of the deaconess's ministry, appealing to the example of the Lord who personally wanted the benefit of the assistance of women:

> We insist in saying that the ministry of a woman deacon is of great usefulness and extremely necessary, because even our Lord and Savior was assisted by women ministers ("women deacons"?): Mary Magdalene, Mary the mother of James and Joseph, the mother of Zebedee's sons. Therefore to you, (bishop,) the deaconess is necessary even for other tasks.[46]

3.2 The Practice of the Church in Chaldea and Persia

These Churches outside of the Roman Empire were evangelized from Edessa. They did not speak Greek. Little by little, under the influence

---

[43] Ibid., 57.6-7, Funk, 162.

[44] "A deaconess is necessary to go to the houses of pagans where there are women believers and to visit women who are sick and assist them in their needs, and to wash those who start to feel better" (ibid., III, 12.4, Funk, 210; cf. also III, 12, Funk, 208).

[45] "When women descend into the water, they must be anointed with the anointing oil by a deaconess. Where a woman, and especially a deaconess, is not available, he who baptizes anoints the woman being baptized. But where there is a woman, and especially a deaconess, it is not proper for women to be seen by men. At the moment of the imposition of the hand, you will anoint the head of they who are receiving baptism, men and women, and then—either you yourself baptize or you order the deacons or the presbyters to baptize—a woman will anoint the women. But let it be a man who blesses the water. Let the deaconess welcome the baptized woman, instruct her, and teach her how the seal of baptism must be kept intact in purity and holiness" (ibid., III, 12.2-3, Funk, 210).

[46] Ibid., III, 12.4, Funk, 210.

of political events and christological controversies, the majority of them constituted themselves as a separate Church, subject to the authority of the catholicos of Seleucia-Ctesiphon. The principal canonical source for this is the *Ordo e i canoni delle ordinazioni della santa Chiesa.*[47]

After explaining the duties of the various ministries (canons 5–11) and the rites of ordinations (canons 12–17), this work deals with deaconesses: "The deaconess is taken into the διακονικόν and the bishop prays over her. After having seated her in front of the altar and after she has bowed her head, the bishop imposes his hand on her head and prays over her a known prayer, which, however, is not at all similar to the specific prayer for the ordination of a deacon. The deaconess, in fact, must not approach the altar, but must only anoint for baptism: this is primarily her task."[48] In addition, during the eucharistic celebration the deaconess stands by the door of the church in the area reserved for women, not to allow entry to unbaptized men and women, and to exhort the daughters of the covenant (women religious) and the laywomen to behave well. According to the *Ordo*, then, the role of a deaconess is threefold: anointing women during baptism, guarding the doors of the church, and having responsibility for the education of women.

3.3 The Monophysite Churches of Syria and the Testamentum Domini

The "Testament of our Lord Jesus Christ" was composed in a monophysite milieu of Syria around the mid-fifth century, but the only versions of this work that have survived are in Syriac, Arabic, and Ethiopian.[49] It draws inspiration from the *Traditio Apostolica* of Hippolytus and expands it considerably. Its chapter 10, dealing with widows, is divided into four long chapters.

The *Testamentum* indicates the number of widows, as well as presbyters, deacons, and subdeacons: "twelve presbyters, seven deacons, fourteen subdeacons will be designated in the church, and the widows having priority will be thirteen."[50] Even though the widow is mentioned

---

[47] A collection copied from a Syriac manuscript of the seventh to ninth centuries, which, however, can be certainly dated to the fifth century. The Syriac text with Latin translation has been published by I. Rahmani, *Studia syriaca*, fasc. 3: *Vetusta documenta liturgica* (Sharfè, 1908).

[48] Ibid., 90.

[49] The Syriac version with Latin translation has been published by I. Rahmani, *Testamentum Domini nostri Iesu Christi* (Moguntiae, 1899).

[50] Ibid., 1:34,4, *Loc. cit.*, 82–83.

after the subdeacon, she is treated differently. While the ordination of a subdeacon, as well as that of a lector, consists in a simple appointment, in the case of a widow the bishop pronounces on the chosen [woman] a prayer that has a structure similar to that used for the deacon and the presbyter.

The widow's rank is clearly shown by the place she takes in church near the bishop. During the offering of the sacrifice, in fact, widows take their seats with members of the clergy in the sanctuary: the bishop at the center, the presbyters to his right and left, near these the deacons to the right, and the widows to the left, then the lectors and subdeacons.[51] Widows take Communion together with the clergy, after the deacons, before the lectors and subdeacons.[52] As well as the bishop, presbyter, and deacon, a widow is ordained after having been "chosen," a term that indicates an election following examination.[53] To be chosen she must have been a widow for a long time and, "to have been asked to remarry many times, and refusing on account of her faith."[54]

The widow's duties show that she had a rather extensive pastoral responsibility toward women: teaching what is suitable to catechumens, instructing uneducated women, encouraging those women who wish to live as virgins, gathering women to pray together, correcting those women who misbehave, visiting women who are ill,[55] anointing women at baptism and covering them with a veil, so that the bishop does not see their nudity,[56] ensuring that women entering the church are not dressed in an alluring manner.[57]

However, what characterizes a widow in the first place is her way of life, the outcome of her renunciation, prayer, and ascesis.[58]

---

[51] Ibid., 1:23,1, *Loc. cit.*, 36–37.

[52] Ibid., 1:23,14, *Loc. cit.*, 94–95.

[53] The comparison with the other members of the clergy leads us to think that the people had a part in the election. Cf. R. Gryson, *op. cit.*, 115.

[54] *Testamentum*, 1.40.1, *Loc. cit.*, 94–95.

[55] Ibid., 1:40, *Loc. cit.*, 96–97.

[56] Ibid., 2:8, *Loc. cit.*, 128–31.

[57] Ibid., 2:4, *Loc. cit.*, 118–19.

[58] The priority of the way of life over the function appears clearly in the prayer of ordination the bishop pronounces over the widow, while she prays with lowered eyes at the foot of the altar. He asks the Lord to grant the elected woman the power to keep the precepts given to her as a rule, and to support the burden she has decided to bear (ibid., 1:41, *Loc. cit.*, 98–99).

The *Testamentum* also mentions deaconesses, but their grade is far more inferior to that of widows.[59] The only function this work attributes to deaconesses is bringing communion to pregnant women unable to go to Church on Easter day.[60]

3.4 Other Evidence

Starting from the mid-fifth century, a series of documents from the region of Edessa demonstrates that with the progressive disappearance of adult baptism deaconesses' powers are restricted, and little by little their ordination ends up being reserved for the superiors of female monasteries.[61]

Between 532 and 534 the "holy fathers," Eastern bishops in exile in Antioch, answering questions coming from areas in the East (most probably from Jacobite communities in contact with the Churches of Persia), testify that the *hegumenia* [superior] of a monastery was a deaconess, and in the absence of the deacon she distributed the sacred mysteries.[62] Moreover, they report that on the occasion of her ordination the bishop confers the *orarion* (the diaconal stole) on a deaconess, as he does for the deacon.[63]

Some years later, in 538, John bar Qursos, bishop of Tella Mauzelat, not far from Edessa, in replying to the questions asked him by the priest Sargis, confirms that the deaconess may distribute the Eucharist to children

---

[59] Their place in the church is by the door (ibid., 1:19, *Loc. cit.*, 27–29); during the offering of sacrifice, they are in the sanctuary, after the lectors and subdeacons (ibid., 1:23, *Loc. cit.* 36–37); likewise, in the diaconal litany they are mentioned after the lectors and the subdeacons (ibid., 1:35, *Loc. cit.*, 86–87);

[60] Ibid., 2:20, *Loc. cit.*, 142–43.

[61] We find a proof in can. 62 of the *Ordinationes* by Rabula, bishop of Edessa, translated to French by F. Nau, *Les canones et les résolutions canoniques*, Ancienne littérature canonique syriaques, 2 (Paris, 1906), 89: "Ne laissez pas les religieux aller aux réunions ou autres lieux sans les prêtres, ni les religieuses sans les diaconesses."

[62] *Chapitres qui furent écrit de L'Orient, leur questions furent présentées aux saints Pères et elles reçurent les reponses suivantes*, can. 9, in F. Nau, *Ancienne littérature syriaques*, 3 (Paris, 1909), 40: "La coutume qui existe en Orient, que les supérieurs de monastère soient diaconesses et partagent les mystères à celles qui sont sous leur pouvoir, sera conservée partout où il n'y a qu' une diaconesse, s'il ne se rencontre pas de prêtres ou de diacre dans l'endroit où l'on partage les mystères; mais si l'on trouve dans leur voisinage un prêtre pur ou un diacre, elles ne les donneront pas."

[63] Ibid., can. 11, *Loc. cit.*, 40.

under the age of five years, she can enter the sanctuary in the absence of the priest and of the deacon, wash the sacred vessels, pour the wine and the water into the chalice, read the Gospel and the other Scriptures to an assembly solely of women.[64]

Between 683 and 708, James of Edessa, questioned by the priest Addai, who was probably dealing with some demands, denies the deaconess permission to intinct at Communion. Indeed, she has been ordained not to serve at the altar but to serve women who are ill. Consequently, she can only tidy the sanctuary and light the lamp. If she is in a monastery she can take the sacred mysteries from the tabernacle and distribute them to her sisters. However, she can neither take these from the altar, nor place them on the altar, nor touch the altar. She anoints adult women at the moment of baptism, visits with ill women, and cures them.[65]

3.5 The Chaldean Rite of Ordination of a Deaconess

The most ancient rite of ordination of a deaconess in the Chaldean Church is found in five pontificals of the sixteenth century, copied more or less around the same time.[66] The rite, apart from the chants and

---

[64] Answers numbers 33, 36, 38, 42 in F. Nau, *Ancienne littérature canonique syriaque*, 2 (Paris, 1906), 16–18.

[65] In J. Mayer, *Monumenta de viduis, diaconissis virginibusque tractantia*, Spicilegium Patristicum 42 (Bonn, 1938), 53–54.

[66] The Questions on the sacraments by Catholicos Jsho'yab I, in the sixth century, the Synod of Mar George I, and the Arabic canons of Nicaea of the seventh century recommend making deaconesses, but they do not give indications on the rite [of ordination]. The anonymous work, *Expositio officiorum Ecclesiae*, attributed to George of Arbela, but in reality of the ninth century, only briefly mentions deaconesses: subdeacons exercise the role of the angels of the parable, appointed to separate the wheat from the chaff; "among women also has been chosen the order of deaconesses and of they who close the doors, because all Adam's progeny is one, even though it includes a diversity of fertility and of natural faculties" (Latin text in CSCO 76 [Connolly 31]). The *Liber Patrum*, composed between the twelfth and the fourteenth centuries, after treating the patriarch, the priests, the deacon, also mentions deaconesses and their function in the baptism of women, in terms very similar to those used by the patriarch Jsho'Yab I in the XXII Questions on the sacraments (Syriac text and German translation in G. Dietrich, *Die nestorianische Taufliturgie in Deutsche übersetzt unter Verwertung der neusten handschriftlichen Funde historisch-kritisch erforscht* [Giessen, 1903], German text pp. 96–99): "(deaconesses) administer the sacrament of baptism of women because it is not proper for the priest to see the nudity of women. Therefore deaconesses must anoint the

preliminary prayers, is comprised of six prayers. The second prayer is common to all ordinations, and it recalls the Byzantine formula "The divine grace," but applied to the bishop: "May the grace of our Lord Jesus Christ, which at any time grants what we need, be always with us." The third is taken from the ordination of deacons: "We present to you these servants, that they may be chosen deaconesses in the Holy Church, and we beseech you: may the grace of the Holy Spirit be upon them and make them perfect for the ministry for which they are presented to you." The central prayer, during which the bishop lays his hand on the head of the elect [woman], reads thusly:

> Lord, God powerful and omnipotent, you have created everything with the power of your Word and keep under your order everything you have created; you have looked favorably upon men and women equally, to give them the grace of the Holy Spirit. You, Lord, in your mercy choose now also this [female] servant here present for the work of the diaconate [*diakonia*], and grant her in your mercy the grace of the Holy

---

women and baptize them with water. The priest must only put his hand through the window or behind the curtain and sign the candidates; deaconesses perform the baptism and the anointing." Then the *Liber patrum* adds a passage of the treatise *Gli ordini di Cristo*, regarding deacons: "Our Lord has accomplished the function of the diaconate, when he washed his apostles' feet on Easter day": I. M. Vosté, *Liber Patrum*, Codificazione canonica orientale, Fonti, series 2, folder 16 (1940), 34. Ebedjesu bar Berika, metropolitan of Nisibe (d.1318), the last scholar of the Nestorian Church, briefly refers to deaconesses, but he speaks of their ordination. While the other cheirothonias are accomplished in the holy church, in front of the altar, "deaconesses, being women, receive their ordination in the church, but only in front of the door leading to the gates" (*Collectio canonum synodicorum* VI, can. 1 in A. Mai, *Scriptorum veterum nova collectio*, book 10, part 1 [Rome, 1838], 111–12). The oldest Chaldean pontifical that has reached us is the Syriac manuscript 38 of Berlin, of 1496, but this contains only the ordination of the lector, of the subdeacon, of the deacon, of the priest and the dedication of the altar. Neither is the ordination of a deaconess recorded in the handwritten pontifical manuscript Vat. syr. 66 of 1529, copied from a manuscript of 1276. So the first known rite is that found in the handwritten pontifical of 1556, Vat. syr. 45–46. The rite is almost identical in four other handwritten pontificals still of the sixteenth century: Vat. Borgia, syr. 21; the manuscript of Cambridge University Add. 1988; the codex of Mosul, library of the Chaldean Patriarcate. The text of Vat. syr. 45–46, to which J. Assemani refers, *Codex liturgicus Ecclesiae universae*, book 13 (Roma, 1766), is found, translated into French, in A. G. Martimort, *Les Diaconesses*, *op.cit.*, 159–63; Martimort also uses the variations in the Cambridge and Mosul codexes.

Spirit, that unblemished she may serve before you with a pure heart and good conscience, keeping irreproachably all the strength of morality. That she may educate the women, teach them chastity and good works and that she may receive from you her good end, her reward.

As we can see, the deaconess is assigned to service before God and to the task of educating women: such is the typical ministry of an *hegumenia*, in any case of widows according to the *Testamentum* and Titus 2:3-5. The pontifical makes a point of distinguishing the ordination of a deaconess from that of the deacon: "The bishop prays laying his hand on her head, not as for a *cheirotonía*, rather as for a blessing." The rubric is repeated at the end with other clarifications on the role of a deaconess:

A deaconess does not have access to the altar, because she is a woman, but only to the oil of chrism. Her function is to pray from memory, leading the nuns during the liturgical service, and at the end of the prayers to say aloud, together with the nuns, Amen; to anoint women who come to be baptized and to lead them under the hand of the priest, because men are not allowed to anoint a woman, even though they do that at the present time, while a priest must not look at a woman.

This last comment shows that the service of a deaconess in baptism had already fallen into disuse. The rite as a whole supposes that deaconesses are by now heads of monasteries of nuns.

We get the same impression from the testimony of Yahya ibn Jarir, who at the end of the eleventh century in the *Book of Guidance* affirms:

In ancient times deaconesses were ordained: they had the function of attending to adult women, so that these did not disrobe before the bishop. But when the religion spread and it was decided to administer baptism to infants, this function was abolished.[67]

4. In Western Syria

4.1. The Council of Nicaea

The first explicit evidence of the existence of deaconesses in the region of Western Syria is found in canon 19 of the Council of Nicaea of 325. This canon refers to the followers of Paul of Samosata, who professed

[67] G. Kouri Sarkis, *Le livre du Guide de Yahya ibn Jarir*, Or Syr 12 (1967): 303–18, French translation of chapters 29 (the structure of the church), 30 (the resurrection), 31 (the priesthood), ibid., 319–54; 421–80.

an erroneous trinitarian doctrine, and the canon establishes that they among his followers who are part of the clergy, if found without error, after being re-baptized are ordained by the Catholic bishop. The canon specifies that this prescription is valid also for deaconesses and adds: "We have mentioned deaconesses who have been admitted to this rank, because they do not have any *cheirotonía*, so that they must be considered entirely among the laity."[68]

From the text it seems that the council is not aware of a rite of ordination for deaconesses.[69]

4.2 The *Apostolic Constitutions*

The questions left open by the Council of Nicaea find an answer in the *Constitutiones Apostolorum*. Written around 380 in Antioch or in Constantinople, they represent the widest canonical and liturgical collection of antiquity.[70]

The comparison between the *Apostolic Constitutions* and its sources is very instructive for the problem of deaconesses, because it demonstrates the evolution that occurred between the third and fourth centuries.

While the *Didascalia* mentions deaconesses only once, the *Apostolic Constitutions* often mention them.[71] Also, their role is expanding when

---

[68] Text of the canon in H. T. Bruns, *Canones apostolorum et conciliorum veterun selecti* (Berolini, 1839), 1:19.

[69] R. Gryson, *Le ministère des femmes, op. cit.*, 86–87, and A. G. Martimort, *Les diaconesses, op.cit.*, 100–101 interpret thusly. On the contrary C. Vagaggini, *L'ordinazione delle diaconesse*, 156–60, maintains that the final subsection of the canon presumes the existence of two types of deaconesses: they who having received the laying on of hands belong to the clergy and must be treated as all other members of the clerisy, and they who not having been ordained must be considered as lay persons and therefore must not be re-ordained.

[70] I use the classic edition of F. X. Funk, *Didascalia et Constitutiones Apostolorum* (Paderborn, 1905), which draws a parallel between the text of the *Constitutiones* and the old Latin version of the *Didascalia*. In fact, the first six books of the *Apostolic Constitutions* are a reworking of the *Didascalia*; the seventh book in its first part is an enlargement of the *Didachè*, and its second part is a compilation of prayers and rules for the instruction of catechumens and baptism. The eighth book, from the *Traditio Apostolica*, has among other things a ritual for the various ordinations and for the Eucharistic liturgy, this latter called "Clementine." At the end of this book are found eighty-five canons entitled *Canons of the Apostles*.

[71] The term used is ἡ διάκονος, in the parallel passages of the second and third books of the *Didascalia*, ἡ διακόνισσα in the chapters proper to the *Constitutiones*, and in the eighth book [of the *Didascalia*].

compared with that of widows, whose importance is progressively diminishing[72] and who are no longer to be considered as part of the clergy.[73] The deaconess must be either a pure virgin or a widow who was married only once.[74] The task of a deaconess is to assist ill or disabled women in their homes.[75] She can be entrusted with carrying messages of the bishop and also with other services.[76]

[72] Widows in the *Constitutions*, as in the *Didascalia*, appear as persons assisted by the Church because of their precarious material condition. Since they live from the gifts offered to God, together with the clerics they are prefigured by the Levites of the Old Testament. They are like the altar (*Const.*, II, 26.8, *loc. cit.*, 105). Among widows some are instituted and constitute the order of widows (III, 1.1-2, *loc. cit.* 183). The minimum age to be admitted to the order is sixty years, as in 1 Timothy 5:9, while in the *Didascalia* it was fifty. Unlike in the *Didascalia* they are not denied the right to speak of truths beyond the basic truths (III, 5.3-6, *loc. cit.*, 189–91). This is explained by the conversion of educated women, who with their speech and example had contributed to spread the faith. They must not speak only in public: "We do not allow women to teach in the church, we only allow them to pray and listen to the masters" (ibid., III, 6.1-2, *loc. cit.*, 191). The *Constitutions* do not assign to the widows prayer, fasting, and the imposition of the hand on [anointing] sick people anymore. Moreover, the text is more severe and strict regarding baptism, which it considers specifically as a priestly act (III, 10.1, *loc. cit.*, 201). They [the widows] who performed baptism would incur a considerable risk: "For we do not recommend this; it would be rather dangerous, even contrary to the law and impious. In fact, if the head of the woman is the man, and he is the one designated for priesthood, it would be unjust overturning the order of nature, to abandon the head for the body's extremities. . . . It is the ignorance of the Greeks that leads them to ordain woman priests for female deities." The text demonstrates that there had to be women who claimed priestly rights, on the basis of what was customary within the pagan religion. But the *Constitutions* reply to this by recalling the argument in the *Didascalia*: had Christ judged it right he would have been baptized by his mother and would have sent along with the apostles the women to baptize (ibid., III, 9.1-4, *loc. cit.*, 199–201).

[73] Where the *Didascalia* says that neither the bishop, nor a deacon, nor a widow should utter any curse (III, 11.5, *loc. cit.*, 208), the *Constitutions* correct that: "neither the bishop, nor the presbyter, nor the deacon, nor any other member of the clergy" (ibid., III, 15.5, *loc. cit.*, 209).

[74] Ibid., 6.17.4, *loc .cit.*, 341.

[75] Ibid., III, 16.1, *loc. cit.*, 209.

[76] Ibid., III, 19.1, *loc. cit.*, 215. From the typology of the Holy Spirit the *Constitutions* draw a double consequence: as the Paraclete does not do or say anything alone, rather he glorifies Christ by doing his will, likewise the deaconess must not do anything without the deacon, who is the type of Christ; as it is impossible to believe in Christ without being instructed by the Holy Spirit, likewise no

With regard to their liturgical role, besides their service in the administration of baptism, deaconesses greet women coming to the assembly and seat them.[77]

Their role is inferior to that of a deacon: as with the deacon, the deaconess does not bless, does not baptize, does not offer the oblation, and moreover she "does not perform any of the things done by presbyters and deacons; she solely guards the doors and assists presbyters and deacons in the administration of baptism for reasons of decency."[78] In particular, she does not assist the bishop at the altar, nor does she distribute Communion.

Within the assembly deaconesses have the first place among women, and together with the clergy they take part in the distribution of offerings.[79]

They receive ordination through the laying on of hands and prayer of the bishop, in the presence of the presbyters, the deacons, and the deaconesses. The prayer of ordination has structure and contents analogous to those of the other ordinations. It recalls the Old Testament prophetesses, Mary, Deborah, Hannah, and Hulda, as biblical paradigms, as women filled with the Holy Spirit, and guardians of the doors of the temple. It also recalls that the only-begotten Son of God was born of a woman and asks for the chosen woman the gift of the Holy Spirit so that she may worthily fulfill the ministry with which she is entrusted.[80]

---

woman must go to see the bishop or the deacon without the deaconess (ibid., II, 26.6, *loc. cit.*, 105).

[77] Ibid., II, 58.4-6, *Loc. cit.*, 169–71. The *Constitutions* say nothing about the possibility of a deaconess not being present during the administration of baptism. The ministry of a deaconess seems quite diffused, therefore it is not deemed necessary to justify. Cf. *Didascalia* III, 12.2-4 and *Const. Apost.* III, 16.2, *Loc. cit.*, 209–11.

[78] Ibid., VIII, 26.6, *Loc. cit.*, 531.

[79] Ibid., VIII, 31.2, *Loc. cit.*, 532–34.

[80] "O, Eternal God, Father of our Lord Jesus Christ, creator of man and of woman, you who have filled with your Spirit Miriam and Deborah, Anna and Hulda, you who have not deemed it unworthy that your only begotten Son be born of a woman; you who instituted women as guardians of the holy parts of the tent of the covenant and of the temple; You, even now, look upon this [female] servant of yours elected to the diaconate; grant her the Holy Spirit and purify her from all sins of the flesh and of the spirit: so that she might fulfill the task entrusted to her for your glory and for the glory of your Christ; with Christ and with the Holy Spirit glory and adoration be to you forever and ever" (ibid., VIII, 20.1-2, *Loc. cit.*, 525).

Notwithstanding the diversity of tasks, nothing identifies a difference in value between this ordination and that of male clerics. Moreover, this rite is recorded immediately after the ordination of a deacon and before that of a subdeacon and of a lector.

4.3 Civil and Ecclesiastical Legislation in the Fifth and Sixth Centuries

The situation revealed by the civil and canonical legislation of the fifth and sixth centuries is not unlike that attested to by the *Apostolic Constitutions*.

First of all, Canon 15 of the council of Chalcedon (451) remained as an object of reference and discussion in the ensuing centuries up until the time of Latin Scholasticism: *Diaconissam non esse mulierem ordinandam ante annum quadragesimum, et eam cum accurata examinatione.*[81] If she marries after receiving the laying on of hands and having served in the ministry for a while, she must be excommunicated. We note that in this canon her ordination occurs with the laying out of hands (*cheirotonía*) and that the age is considerably younger than the sixty years usually required, perhaps as a consequence of the discussions and of the different disciplines in existence among Churches.

In fact, a law issued by emperor Theodosius on June 21, 390, still prescribed that [a woman] could not be admitted among the deaconesses before her sixtieth year, according to the apostolic precept of 1 Timothy 5:9.[82] Justinian in 535 would then lower this age limit to fifty years, and then in 546 to forty.[83]

A deaconess was considered as belonging to the clergy, as is also evident from the Justinian legislation. In Novella 3 of March 16, 535, addressed to Epiphanius, the patriarch of Constantinople, to counter the consequences of the movement of clerics, Justinian determines the number of clerics assigned to each church. In particular, regarding the cathedral of Saint Sophia, there could be no more than 60 presbyters, 100

---

[81] I. D. Mansi, *Sacrorum Conciliorum nova et amplissima collectio* (Florentiae, 1759–1798), VII, 364.

[82] *Codex Theodos.* 16.2, fn. 27, in T. Mommsen and P. Meyer, eds., *Theodosiani libri* XVI (Berolini, 1905), I/2, 843–44. This same law forbids a deaconess to tie her family assets to a church or a cleric or a poor person. The second part of the law was abolished on August 23 of that same year, due to protests against it (ibid., 16.2-28, *loc. cit.*, 844).

[83] *Novella* 6.6, in R. Schoell and G. Kroll, eds., *Corpus iuris civilis*, III (Berlin, 1928), 44; *Novella* 123.13, ibid., 604.

deacons, 40 deaconesses, 90 subdeacons, 110 lectors, 25 cantors, totaling 425 clerics, and also 100 porters.[84] Moreover, deaconesses are equated to clerics in many regards: they receive an ordination when they start in their function;[85] this ordination is not absolute, since a deaconess, like other clergy, is assigned to one church;[86] after ordination the deaconess is obliged to keep perfect continence, an obligation derived from her ordination;[87] as with clerics, deaconesses receive their sustenance from the Church (this is why Justinian limits the number of clerics assigned to each church) and they enjoy the *privilegium fori*.[88]

Not much about her functions can be expected to be found in civilian legislation. But we know that deaconesses exercise a ministry in the celebration of baptism and "are present at the other holy functions usually performed during the sacred mysteries."[89]

4.4 Greek Deaconesses between the Fourth and the Sixth Centuries

The conclusions reached by the studies on the liturgical and canonical sources are confirmed by historical documents that have recorded the existence of a certain number of deaconesses.

Olympia, deaconess of Constantinople, stands out among them all. She was a rich and noble young woman who, widowed at a very young age, was ordained by the patriarch Nectarius and was a friend and correspondent of John Chrysostom, who wrote seventeen letters to her.[90] She built a monastery next to the cathedral, where among others her mother Elisantia

---

[84] *Novella* 3.1, ibid., 21. As it is evident, the forty deaconesses are included among the 425 clerics.

[85] The term χειροτονία (*cheirotonía*) appears at least eleven times in the *Novella* 6.6, ibid., 43.

[86] *Codex Justin.*, 1.3-53 (Krüger) 37.

[87] *Novella* 6.6; *Loc. cit.*, 35.

[88] *Novella* 123.21, *Loc. cit.*, 609–11. [*Privilegium fori* is the clerical privilege to be tried before an ecclesiastical judge even in civil and criminal cases.]

[89] *Novella* 6.6, *Loc. cit.*, 44.

[90] For Olympia, cf. Palladio, *Dialogus de vita s. Joannis Chrysostomi*, 11.16.17, in PG 47:358-C; 56A–58A; 60A–61D; ID., *Histoire Lausiaque*, ed. C. Butler, in TS VI, 2, 1904; *Vie d'Olympias*, in *Jean Chrysostome, Lettres á Olympias. Vie anonyme d'Olympias*, ed. A. M. Malingrey, SCh 13/bis, 406–49; Sozomeno, *Historia Ecclesiastica*, 8.9.1-3, GCS 50:361–62; and above all, C. Militello, *Donna e Chiesa. La testimonianza di Giovanni Crisostomo* (Palermo, 1985), 21–47, which gathers and critically examines all the existing records.

and her sisters Marina and Palladia, also ordained deaconesses, entered. Before departing in exile, John Chrysostom first greeted the bishops in the sacristy, then summoned Olympia and the other deaconesses to the baptistery, and there bid them farewell, urging them to continue loving the Church by submitting themselves to his successor.[91] We know that Olympia received Marina after her baptism,[92] catechized countless women who had not been believers, distributed her belongings to the poor,[93] sheltered and hosted them in her house.[94] Moreover, John Chrysostom's biographer, Palladio, affirms that she "served the blessed Nectarius, archbishop of Constantinople, who even 'obeyed her' in church matters."[95] While in exile, John Chrysostom asked her help on issues regarding bishops and Churches.[96]

Another deaconess in Constantinople at the time of Chrysostom was his aunt, Sabiniana.[97]

Many years before that, in Eleutheropolis, Bishop Cleophas had ordained the deaconess Susanna, who suffered martyrdom during the persecution of Julian the Apostate.[98]

The council of Constantinople (360) deposed Elpidius, bishop of Setala in Upper Armenia, because he admitted the excommunicated Nectaria to the diaconate.[99]

In 370, when Dionisia brought her son Euthymius the Great to Otreio, bishop of Metilene in Lower Armenia, he made him a lector and ordained her deaconess of his Church.[100]

Among the correspondents of Theodoret of Cyrus were three deaconesses: Axia, Casiana, and Celerina. To the latter Theodoret recalls his christological doctrine and asks her to work for the true faith and for peace in the Church.[101]

---

[91] Palladio, *Dial*, 10, PG 47:35.

[92] *Vie d'Olympias*, 10.15-16, *Loc. cit.*, 427.

[93] *Histoire Lausiaque*, 56.2, *Loc. cit.*, 150.

[94] John Chrysostom, *ad Olymp. ep.* 8.10a, SCh 13/bis, 427.

[95] This news is confirmed by Palladio, *Dial.*, 17, PG 47:61: "I know that even the blessed Nectarius held her in high consideration and followed her advice in regard to the management of the church."

[96] Cf. C. Militello, *op. cit.*, 33–39.

[97] John Chrysostom, *ad Olymp. ep.* 6.1, SCh 13/bis, 130; Palladio, *Histoire Lausiaque*, 47, *Loc. cit.*, 129.

[98] B. Bagatti, *Alle origini della Chiesa*, II (Città del Vaticano, 1982), 27.

[99] Sozomeno, *Historia ecclesiastica*, 4.24,16, GCS 50:181.

[100] Cyril of Schytopolis, *Vita di Sant'Eutimio*, TU 49.2.10-11.

[101] Theodoret of Cyrus, *Lettres*, SCh 40:118; 98:62–64; 111:18–20.

These accounts—as well as from epigraphical evidence[102]—do not give information on the status and the functions of deaconesses. We know, however, that a certain number of deaconesses headed monasteries: in addition to Olympia and Elisantia were Lampadia, a friend of Macrina the Young, Teodula in Egypt, Martana, friend of Eteria, Manaris, deaconess in Gaza.[103]

4.5 The Byzantine Rite for the Ordination of a Deaconess

The rite of ordination for a deaconess in the Church of Constantinople is found in the Codex Barberini Greek 336 of the eighth century, and, except for some variants in the rubrics, in a series of codici up to the fourteenth century.[104]

The ordination takes place at the end of the anaphora, as with the deacon, while the subdeacon is ordained during the Liturgy of the Word.

She who is to be ordained is brought before the bishop in the sanctuary, like those to be ordained to the episcopacy, the presbyterate, and the diaconate (unlike for other lower orders). The bishop pronounces, over the chosen woman, who is bowing, the formula: "The divine grace," tracing three signs of the cross. This formula is used by all Eastern Churches, it is therefore prior to the division among the Churches, and together with the epiclesis it is considered as essential for the ordination of a bishop, a presbyter, and a deacon. The bishop then says the prayer:

> Holy and omnipotent God . . . you have given the grace of the effusion of the Holy Spirit not only to men, but also to women. . . . [L]ook upon this servant of yours and call her to the work of your diaconate. Copiously grant upon her the gift of your Holy Spirit, keep her in the right faith, that following your blessing she may fulfill her ministry in an irreproachable way of life.

---

[102] Many tomb inscriptions record the names of deaconesses, although without telling us anything about their functions. Noteworthy is that of Sophia, deaconess of Jerusalem, "bride of Christ" and "second Phoebe," as well as that of Theodora, buried in Pavia on July 22, 539. R. Gryson, *op. cit.*, 149.

[103] R. Gryson, *Le ministère, op. cit.*, 148–49.

[104] J. Morinus, *Commentarius de sacris ecclesiae ordinationibus*, 2nd ed. (Antwerpiae, 1695), I:56–57, 65:80–81, reports the texts of the Barberini codex, of the Grottaferrata codex (Gb.I) of the twelfth to thirteenth century, and of a Vatican codex of the twelfth century. E. D. Theodoru, Ἡ χειροτονία ἡ χειροφθεσία τῶν διακονισσῶν, "Θελογία," 25 (1954): 578–81, reviews seven codici, among them the Parisian codex Cosilin gr. 213 and the Athenian codex Ethn. Bibl. 662, of the eleventh and twelfth/thirteenth centuries, respectively, are very interesting for their rubrics.

The diaconal litany then follows, praying "for N. just ordained deaconess, that the benevolent God may grant her an unblemished and sinless diaconate."

Meanwhile the bishop, laying his hand on the head of the woman to be ordained, pronounces the epiclesis. He beseeches the Lord, who does not reject but rather receives into the order of ministries women who devote themselves to God and want to serve properly in God's holy abodes, grant the grace of the Holy Spirit to his servant who wishes to perform the office of the diaconate, as he granted the grace of the diaconate to Phoebe (cf. Rom 16:1-2), whom he called to the work of the ministry. The bishop asks that she may persevere unblemished in the holy temples.

The bishop then places the *orarion* around her neck, under the *maphorion*, bringing the edges to the front.

At the same time, the deacon resumes the litany of the anaphora. After the deaconess has partaken of the holy Body and Blood, the bishop gives her the holy chalice: she takes it and places it on the altar.[105]

This rite shows how in the Byzantine tradition the female diaconate is equated to the male diaconate, even though the functions are somewhat more restricted. She is not at the altar, does not move the *ripidion*, does not present the chalice to those taking Communion, does not chant the litanies, but she serves within the holy abodes and she perseveres without reproach in the holy temple.[106]

4.6 The Disappearance of Deaconesses

With the disappearance of the baptism of adults the female diaconate went on to lose its most important trait: anointing and assisting women during their baptismal rites. Deaconesses, then only *hegumene* in monasteries, tend to disappear altogether.

There are evidences for this in Syria and in Constantinople around the end of the twelfth century.

---

[105] Cf. the description of the ordination rite of Matthew Blastares in J. Goar, *Euchologion sive rituale Graecorum* (Venetiis, 1730), 2, 219.

[106] This leads A. G. Martimort, *op. cit.*, 155, to conclude that notwithstanding the apparent similarities, a deaconess was not a true deacon, rather something similar to the *hegumenia* [superior] of a monastery. Completely opposite are the conclusions of C. Vagaggini, in *L'ordinazione delle diaconesse nella tradizione greca e bizantina*, a.c., 183.

In the Syrian pontifical of Michael the Great, patriarch between 1166 and 1199, immediately after the rite of ordination for a deacon, under the title "Ordination of a deaconess" we read:

> The cheirotonía or ordination was once also performed for women. For this reason the rite for women was found in ancient manuscripts. In fact, at one time deaconesses were necessary mainly for the baptism of women. . . . But given that this ended a long time ago within the Church, due to the fact that those baptized are baptized at birth or as infants, . . . we have not transcribed this rite, even though this is found in numerous books which are accurate and copied carefully and to perfection.[107]

As for Constantinople, according to Anna Komnene, although the emperor Alexius I (1081–1118), in addition to his other graciousness toward the Church, was still well disposed to the work of deaconesses,[108] around the end of the twelfth century the famous canonist Theodore Balsamon says that their ordination is outdated. Discussing canon 15 of the Council of Chalcedon he writes:

> What is dealt with in this canon has passed into disuse. Today we no longer ordain deaconesses, even though some belonging to the community of ascetics are unlawfully called deaconesses.[109]

And we cannot rule out that here and there the ordination survived.

5. Female Ministries in Egypt

R. Gryson concludes his overview of widows and deaconesses by affirming that Patristic and Alexandrian writers of the third century left no information concerning a ministry performed by women of their time.[110]

---

[107] I. M. Vostè, *Pontificale iuxta ritum ecclesiae Syrorum occidentalium, id est Antiochiae*, versio latina (Città del Vaticano, 1941–1944), 201–2. The oldest manuscript is the Vat. syr. 51 dated 1172.

[108] Anna Comnena, *Alexiade*, XV: 7,8 trans. B. Leib (Paris, 1945), III, 217.

[109] Balsamon, *Scholia in Conc. Chalced.*, PG 137:441. The lack of knowledge is even greater around 1335, when Matthew Balstares wrote his alphabetical *Sintagma* of the canons: "There was once the order of women deacons, and another order, of widows . . . but today the ministry of deaconesses at the time of the Fathers is unknown to us" (*Sintagma*, letter Γ, PG 144:1173–76).

[110] R. Gryson, *op. cit.*, 64. Clement and Origen in their exegetical commentaries refer to the texts where St. Paul speaks of deaconesses, but they never seem to be aware of the actual situation in their Church.

However, in the fourth century the *Ecclesiastical Canons of the Holy Apostles*, written in Egypt,[111] recommend the institution of three widows for each community (two to pray for those in difficulty and to identify their needs, the other to assist ill women), along with three presbyters and three deacons.[112]

While the first two widows are types of prophetesses like Anna, the daughter of Phanuel (cf. Luke 2:36), the role of the third is one of those assigned to deaconesses in the *Didascalia*.[113]

The other canonical sources of the Alexandrian Church seem to completely ignore the existence of a feminine ministry, even though in some, due to the influence of Syriac documents, deaconesses are mentioned.[114]

---

[111] In addition to the original Greek, earlier versions in Latin, Syriac, Copt, Arabic, and Ethiopic have been conserved. The apostles are imagined gathered in council, making decisions according to the precept received from the Savior: "Divide the provinces by casting lots, regulate their division, the authority of bishops, the sees of presbyters, the assisting tasks of the deacons, the formation of lectors, the irreproachableness of widows, and all that is necessary to establish the Church." T. Schermann, ed., *Die allgemeine Kirchenordnung, frühchristiche Liturgien und kirchliche Überlieferung* (Paderborn, 1914), 13. Canons 15–21 give rules on the institution of bishops, presbyters, deacons, lectors, and widows.

[112] *The Ecclesiastical Canons of the Holy Apostles*, 20.1, *Loc. cit.*, 28.

[113] Among the required qualities, besides a predisposition to good service (*eudiaconos*), the other two are those that in 1 Timothy 3:8 are essential for deacons: "She should be of good service, moderate in all things, should inform presbyters on what is necessary, should avoid ill-gotten gains, should be moderate with wine in order to remain awake for the night services and accomplish other good deeds for which she might be asked, because these treasures of the Lord are good" (ibid). Canons 24–28 mention again the subject of a feminine ministry, but to rule it out: John specifies that "when the Lord instituted the Eucharist he did not allow women to stand with us," that is to say, to "celebrate" (according to R. Gryson, *op. cit.*, 84), or to "perform a diaconal service" (according to A. G. Martimort, *op. cit.*, 84f.). Were there perhaps women in Egypt who at the time of the composition of the *Canons* claimed a right to such service? The author condemns this claim: the Lord did not allow any woman to stand next to the Apostles during the last supper: "The weak will be saved by means of the strong."

[114] The *Canons* of Hippolytus, composed in Alexandria between 336 and 340, ignore deaconesses, even though they describe baptism and insist on baptismal nakedness. Cf. R. C. Coquin, *Les Canons d'Hyppolyte*, éd. crit. de la version arabe, introduction et traduction française (Paris, 1966) (PO 31:2). The Synod of the Apostolic Fathers who laid out the direction of the Church, kept in Coptic, both Sahidic and Bohairic, Arabic and Ethiopic, in its Sahidic version rules out the ordination of deaconesses, while it seems that the Arabic and Ethiopic versions

The same holds true of liturgical sources that,[115] apart from the *Eu-chologion* by Serapion, are rather recent and ignore the baptism of adults and the consequent problem of female nudity.

One exception is a rite found in the Ethiopian *Synodos*, which, in describing the baptism, specifies: in the case of a man, he must be anointed by a deacon or a priest; in the case of a woman, she will be anointed by a faithful [woman] who has remained a virgin.[116]

Finally, at the end of the thirteenth century an Arabic compilation of canons by Tâdj Al Riyâsa Abou Isaac ibn al Fadl Allah contains in the rubric for the rite of initiation: "They are then undressed and at least men turn toward the East, to be baptized. As for women, deaconesses instead undress them behind the curtain and cover them with a loose cloth."[117]

This same rubric is in the *Testamentum Domini*, which precedes it, except for the fact that, instead of widows, deaconesses are mentioned, perhaps due to the influence of the *Didascalia Araba*, which comes next.

These texts, which do not seem to have been used by the Alexandrian Churches, demonstrate at least a desire for a feminine ministry tentatively founded on a tradition that was apparently atypical of this Church.

---

knew of the existence of deaconesses, sub-deaconesses, and [female] lectors. However, mention of sub-deaconesses and [female] lectors is certainly a mistake of the compiler, while mention of deaconesses is explained by the text's literary dependence on the *Constitutiones Apostolorum* VIII, 28.6. Similar is the cases of the Arabic and Ethiopic *Didascalia*, adaptations of the first seven books of the *Constitutiones Apostolorum*, which refer to the texts where deaconesses are mentioned and abbreviates them: J. M. Harden, ed., *The Ethiopic Didascalia* (London, 1920), 95–96. In A. G. Martimort's opinion, *op. cit.*, 93, such prescription had no influence on the local institutions either in Egypt or Ethiopia.

[115] The *Great Euchologion* of the White Monastery, of the tenth century, even though based on the eighth book of the *Constitutiones Apostolorum* and the 1647 Tuki *Pontifical* do not speak of deaconesses. Equally, neither the *Ordinance of Priesthood* of the first half of the thirteenth century, nor *The Precious Pearl in Ecclesiastical Sciences*, by Juhanna ibn abî Zakariâ ibn Sibah, of the fourteenth century, nor the *Liturgical Ordinance of Gabriel V* (1409–1427), considers the ordination of deaconesses. Cf. A. G. Martimort, *op. cit.*, 93–95.

[116] H. Diesing, *Der äthiopische Text der Kirchenordung des Hippolyt* (Göttingen, 1946), 105.

[117] A. Baumstark, *Eine ägyptische Mess-und Taufliturgie vermutlich des 6. Jahrhunderts*, OC, 1 (1901), 41.

In recent times, within the Coptic Church the establishment of a ministry of service for the Church, the parishes and other ecclesial bodies, improperly named the diaconate, is a sign of such a need.[118]

6. Deaconesses in the Other Eastern Churches

6.1 In the Armenian Church

Apart from the deaconess Nectaria, unlawfully ordained by the bishop Elpidius of Setala, and Dionisia, the mother of S. Euthymios, ordained by Otreius,[119] we have no other names of deaconesses from Armenia.

Nonetheless, they surely existed, and it seems that during the celebration of baptism they claimed a more prominent role than that acknowledged for their colleagues in the Syriac and Byzantine Churches, against which the Synod of Sahapivan reacted in 444.[120]

However, it seems that, as in the other Churches, in Armenia deaconesses also ended up as simple *hegumene* in monasteries, reading the Gospel during the Divine Office.

Nevertheless, as late as the twelfth century the *Liber processualis* by Mxit'ar Goš (1130–1213), speaking of the monasteries of strict enclosure, mentions deaconesses and anachronistically assigns the task of baptizing adult women to them:

> *Sunt et mulierum diaconissae ordinatae chirotonia ad praedicandum mulieribus et legendum evangelium, ne ingrediatur ibi vir et ne illa extra conventum mulierum egrediatur; et quando sacerdotes baptismum conferunt adultis*

---

[118] Cf. *Chronique*, "Proche Orient Chrétien," 22 (1972), 190. G. Giamberardini in *Il prete per gli uomini di oggi*, ed. G. Concetti (Rome, 1975), 129; G. Viaud, *La liturgie de Coptes d'Egypte* (Paris, 1978), 85; with a remark by G. Martimort, *op. cit.*, 97, fn. 111.

[119] Cf. fn. 100.

[120] "Il faut faire le baptême avec crainte de Dieu et que le femmes, au moment du baptême, n'osent pas se tenir auprès des prêtres, comme certaines ont l'habitude de le faire audacieusement et de baptizer avec eux, mais qu'elles prient à leur place," in V. Hakobyan, *Kanonagirk Hayoc*, I (Erevan, 1964), 377–78, translated by A. Renoux in A. G. Martimort, *op. cit.*, 178, fn. 70. The prohibition is repeated by the Council of Dvin of 527, and again by Catholikos Nerses II (548–557): "Et que les femmes n'osent pas se tenir auprès des prêtres, mais les diacres les serviront. Et les femmes prieront à leurs place, et ne coopéreront pas avec les prêtres, tenant la place des diacres comme nous l'entendons dire" (ibid., 485, *Loc. cit.*, 179, fn. 72).

mulieribus, adveniunt diaconissae piscinam et abluunt aqua mulieres, et sacerdos ungit intra velamen.[121]

The rite of ordination is found in the manuscript of St. Lazarus 199 (323) in Venice, of 1216. A. Renoux discovered it also in the sixteenth-century Maštoc' or Erevan pontifical of Erevan, copied from a ninth-century manuscript. After chanting Psalm 44, the bishop says the following prayer:

> Gracious and merciful Lord, you have created all things with your word, with the Incarnation of your only Begotten Son you have made man and woman equal in holiness. You have deemed it good to grant the grace of the Holy Spirit not only to men but also to women. In the same way, now choose this [woman] servant of yours for what is necessary for your holy Church and grant her the grace of the Holy Spirit, so that she is guarded by pure justice, by mercy, and by the compassion of your Christ, to whom together with you, omnipotent Father, and the life-giving and freeing Holy Spirit glory pertains.[122]

The prayer is very spare. It does not evoke any biblical model, nor does it illustrate the tasks of the deaconess; rather, it only states the equality of man and woman founded on the mystery of the Incarnation before the gift of the Holy Spirit.[123]

---

[121] In G. Amaduni, *Disciplina armena* II. *Monachismo, Studio storico-canonico e fonti canoniche* (Venezia, 1940), 140.

[122] The French text is translated by A. Renoux, in A. G. Martimort, *op. cit.*, 181.

[123] There are close ties between the Armenian and the Georgian liturgies. An important source of the latter, Tiflis ms. 86, after the liturgy of Saint James, reports a rite of ordination. The liturgy contains three prayers for the ordination of a deaconess. The second prayer reproduces the prayer found in the two Armenian rites mentioned above. The first prayer evokes exemplary figures of the Old and New Testaments: "O Lord, God of Hosts, you have commanded Miriam, sister of Moses, first among all women, to invoke you; you have granted Deborah the grace of prophecy; in the new covenant by means of your Spirit you have ordained deacons to have only the Word, to be moderate with wine (1 Timothy 3:8), but to teach with good will so as to be an example of every good thing; grant to promote your servant to such a dignity, so that she anoints with oil those who come to holy baptism, leads them to the holy fountain, becomes a deaconess in your Church according to the order of Phoebe, whom the apostle ordained as a [female] minister in Cenchrae, give her the gift of convincing and instructing with vigilance young women to fulfill their duties, grant her the grace of expressing everything in your name, so that in serving you worthily and without sin she may dare to intercede in the hour chosen by your Christ." Finally, the third prayer says: "Omnipotent Lord, you have adorned your church with the

6.2 In the Maronite Church

The Maronite liturgy, of Syrio-Antiochian origin, with Syrian and Eastern influences, was heavily Latinized from the time of the 1215 union with the Roman Church; hence, there are practically no sources prior to the fifteenth century. The attempt made by the patriarch Stefano Douaïhî (1670–1704) to reform the liturgy according to original Maronite tradition was opposed by the Latinizing current. Therefore, we understand why the Pontifical and its rites ignore the ordination of deaconesses.

However, during the famous Synod of Mount Lebanon of 1736, the deliberations of which were approved by the Holy See, canon 2 of part 3, *de ministris, presbyteris et praelatis*, specifically deals with the problem of the female diaconate: *Diaconissae apud nos sunt quae vel perpetua virginitate servata, vel secundis repudiatis nuptiis, castitatem dicant et ministeriis quibusdam ecclesiasticis, episcopi benedictione accedente, devoventur.*[124]

The Synod text enumerates the tasks of deaconesses: guarding the doors reserved for women within the church, undressing women who are to receive baptism, anointing them with oil before baptism and with the chrism after it, washing and burying dead women, teaching the first principles of the faith and the rite of baptism to women who are coming to the faith, mediating between the women and the bishop or the presbyter, verifying a woman's virginity when there is question, caring for nuns in monasteries and of the holy objects kept there.[125]

Even though we must agree with Martimort in considering as anachronistic many of the tasks here attributed to deaconesses, and even though the text as a whole is a composite collection,[126] we must acknowledge that

---

ministry of the diaconate and have filled the multitude of Churches with the grace of the Holy Spirit, grant, O Lord, to promote to this grade of the ministry of the diaconate your [female] servant here, and grant her to accomplish with respect and sanctity this noble ministry. Receive and validate her vow, grant her the strength to persevere." The text is found in C. Conybeare and O. Wardrop, *The Georgian Version of the Liturgy of St. James*, ROC, 19 (1914), 165, trans. to French by A. G. Martimort, *op. cit.*, 181–82. The sources of these prayers are unknown. It is possible to think of an origin from Jerusalem, from which both the Georgian and Armenian liturgies drew inspiration, although such hypothesis is prevented by the fact that, at this stage of the research, the Church in Jerusalem does not seem to have provided a ministerial baptism reserved to women.

[124] Mansi, 38, 163.

[125] *Op. cit.*

[126] A. G. Martimort, ibid., 176–78.

the Synod reveals a clear awareness of the need for a female diaconate and of what should be its main tasks.

7. The Female Ministry in the Western Churches

7.1 *The Roman Church*

Like the *Traditio Apostolica*, the letter of Pope Cornelius to Fabian of Antioch, which in 251 or 253 considers the ministries of the Church of Rome, completely ignores the existence of a female ministry.[127]

As we have seen, Ambrosiaster over a century later knows of the existence of deaconesses, although he attributes their institution to the Cataphrygians, that is, to Montanists.

Pelagius proves to be more informed some decades later: he knows there are deaconesses in the East and considers them a residual of the apostolic era.[128]

A century later we find Pope Gelasius I's decretal to the bishops of Sicily and Southern Italy condemning the admission of women to altar service, which was advanced in certain Churches: *Nihilominus impatienter audivimus, tantum divinarum rerum subiisse despectum, ut feminae sacris altaribus ministrare firmentur, cunctaque non nisi virorum famulatui deputata sexum, cui non competunt, exhiberi.*[129]

It is not clear whether this text is about the diaconate or the presbyterate as G. Otranto maintains in his thorough study of it.[130] The text certainly proves that the Churches with closer relations to the East were influenced by the East, even as regards the acceptance of a female ministry, which was fiercely opposed in Rome where the different Eastern discipline was indeed known.

---

[127] Eusebius, *Storia Ecclesiastica*, 6.43.11, SCh 41:156. We can compare this list to the admonition of the *orationes solemnes: Oremus pro omnibus episcopis, presbyteris, diaconibus, acolythis, exorcistis, lectoribus, ostiariis, confessoribus, virginibus, viduis et pro omni populo sancto Dei*; P. De Clerk, *La prière universelle dans les liturgies latines anciennes*, LQF 62 (Münster, 1977), 136–39.

[128] Pelagius, *in Rom. 16:1*, PLS 1:1178; in *1Tim* 3:11, PLS 1:1351.

[129] Gelasius, *Ep.* 14.26, in A. Thiel, ed., *Epistolae Romanorum Pontificum genuinae* (Brunsbergae, 1868), 376.

[130] G. Otranto, *Note sul sacerdozio femminile nell'antichità in margine ad una testimonianza di Gelasio I*, in *Le abbazie nullius. Giurisdizione spirituale e feudale nelle comunità femminili sino a Pio IX*. Congresso della Società di Storia patria per la Puglia, sezione di Conversano, Corpus Historicum Corpanense 1982, 65–88.

7.2 Churches in Gaul

The same attitude of refusal is initially found within the Churches of Gaul, where perhaps, under the influence of Montanist communities, there were a series of attempts to introduce a female ministry. Thus in 936, the bishops gathered in council at Nîmes, learned that in some places the practice of conferring upon women the diaconal ministry had been introduced, and condemned this inasmuch as it was contrary to Church discipline and to reason: *Illud etiam a quibusdam suggestum est, ut contra apostolicam disciplinam, incognito usque in hoc tempus, in ministerium feminae, nescio quo loco, leviticum videantur adsumptae: quod quidem, quia indecens est, non admittit ecclesiastica disciplina, et contra rationem facta, talis ordinatio distruatur: providendum ne quis sibi hoc ultra praesumat.*[131]

Fifty years later the first council of Orange is more specific: deaconesses must not be ordained, and if any deaconess has been ordained she must not be considered different from simple laity.[132]

To suppress at an early stage any attempt to surreptitiously introduce such a ministry, toward the end of the fifth century the *Statuta Ecclesiae antiqua,* apparently by Gennadius of Massilia [Marseille], specify that women can neither teach men nor baptize in the liturgical assembly, although the text acknowledges a catechetical ministry reserved to widows and women religious preparing women for baptism.[133]

---

[131] Can. 2, in CCL 148:50. Likewise, in Spain the practice of ministry by women deacons or lectors was considered peculiar to heterodox sects, perhaps Priscillianists, as Can. 1 of the Council of Zaragoza of 380 shows; this warns Catholic women not to take part in such gatherings under the pretext of learning or exercising a ministry: *Ut mulieres omnes catholicae et fideles a virorum alienorum et coetibus separantur, vel ad ipsas legentes aliae studio vel docendi vel discendi conveniant, quoniam hoc apostolus iubet. Ab universis episcopis dictum est: anathema futuros qui hanc concilii sententiam non observarint* (J. Vives, *Concilios visigóticos e hispano-romanos* [Barcelona-Madrid, 1963], 16). Spain would continue to ignore deaconesses even when it came under the influence of Western liturgy, as shown by the *Liber Ordinum,* which only mentions of the blessing of virgins and widows.

[132] Council of Orange, Can. 25, CCL 148:84: *Diaconissae omnimodis non ordinandae. Si quae iam sunt, benedictioni quae populo impenditur capita submittant.*

[133] *Mulier, quamvis docta et sancta, viros in conventu docere non praesumat* (*Statuta Ecclesiae antiqua,* c. 99, Mansi, III, 959); *mulier baptizare non praesumat* (ibid., c. 100; *Loc. cit.,* 959); *viduae et sanctimoniales, quae ad ministerium baptizandarum mulierum eligintur, tam instructae sint ad officium, ut possint apto et sano sermone docere imperitas et rusticas mulieres, tempore quo baptizandae sunt, qualiter baptizatori interrogatae respondeant et qualiter accepto baptismate vivant* (ibid., c. 12, *Loc. cit.,* 952).

However, even at the beginning of the sixth century and notwith-standing prohibitions and anathemas, three bishops of North East Gaul, Licinius of Tours, Melaine of Rennes, and Eustochius of Angers, in a letter to the presbyters of Lovocato and Cathierno, must strongly intervene to condemn the Montanist practice of allowing those women called "conhospitae" to approach the altar during the eucharistic celebration, to take the chalice and distribute the Blood of Christ.[134] These bishops attributed the practice to a certain Pepodius (hence the "Pepodians").

The practice condemned at Nîmes and Orange spreads nonetheless, and from the sixth century onward juridical texts and documents at-test to the existence of deaconesses in Gaul and later also in Italy, even though they are either widows who had received a special blessing or the wives of deacons.

The Council of Epaone in Burgundy in 517 reiterates the prohibition of the council of Orange: *Viduarum consecrationem, quas diaconas vocitant, ab omni regione nostra penitus abrogamus, sola eis paenitentiae benedictione si converti ambiunt, imponenda.*[135]

As the text of this canon shows, deaconesses are widows who have received a liturgical consecration, something not allowed within the Latin Church, which since the fourth century recognized the *velatio virginis*. The council reaffirms the Western custom, explaining that for widows the only blessing possible is that of beginning penance as a convert.[136]

---

[134] J. Friedrich, *Über die Cenones der Montanisten bei Jeronymus*, in J. Mayer, *Monumenta de viduis, diaconissis virginibusque tractantia, o.c.*, 46: *Viri venerabilis Spatari relatione cognovimus quod . . . quasdam tabulas per diversorum civium capan-nas circumferre non desinatis et missas ibidem adhibitis mulieribus in sacrificio divino, qua conhospitas nominastis facere praesumatis; sicut erogantibus vobis eucharistiae illae vobis positis calices teneant et sanguine Christi populo administrare praesumant. Cuius rei novitas et inaudita superstitio non leviter contristavit, ut tam horrenda secta quae intra Gallias numquam fuisse probatur, nostris temporibus videatur mergere, quam patres orientales pepodianam vocant, pro eo quod Pepodius auctor huius schismatis fuerit, mulieres sibi in sacrificio divino socias habere praesumperit, praecipientes: Ut quicumque huic errori voluerit inhaerere, a communione ecclesiastica reddatur extraneus. Qua de re caritatem vestram in Christi amore pro ecclesiae unitate et fidei catholicae imprimis credidimus admonendam obsecrantes, ut, cum ad vos nostrae pervenerunt paginae litterarum, repentina de praedictis rebus emendatio subsecuta.*

[135] Council of Epaone, Can. 21, in CCL 148/A, 29. While here the woman deacon is a consecrated widow, in Can. 20 of the Council of Tours of 567, in CCL 148/A, 184, the wife of a deacon is called deaconess.

[136] The Latin tradition is affirmed by Pope Gelasius I in his Epistle 14:13, cited above: *Viduas autem velare pontificum nullus attentet, quoniam quod nec auctoritas*

In some Churches, imposing the blessing of penitence on widows of high rank had to have seemed humiliating. They therefore thought of following what had been done in Constantinople for Olympia: a diaconal ordination for widows who publicly professed Christian life, something that was regularly condemned by councils, such as the Council of Orléans in 533, which, leaving aside they who had already been ordained as long as they who lived in chastity, prohibits imparting such a blessing in the future.[137]

But just as the council of Orléans issues these canons, we find two names of deaconesses: the daughter of Saint Remigius, Bishop of Reims (d.533), Ilaria, assigned a bequest in her father's will,[138] and Saint Radegund, who at the death of her husband Clothar I, after repeatedly requesting [to become a deaconess], clothes herself in the monastic habit and receives diaconal consecration from Saint Médard, Bishop of Noyon: *manu superposita consecravit diaconam.*[139]

7.3 Deaconesses in Italy between the Seventh and Eighth Centuries

Around the middle of the seventh century, historical and liturgical documents attest to the existence of deaconesses in Italy in the strictest sense of the word. In fact, while in the Gregorian Sacramentary of the time of Honorius I (625–638) only the *consecratio virginum*[140] is found, the Trent and the Gregorian Hadrianean sacramentaries contain a prayer *ad diaconam faciendam.*[141] The prayer is the same as that preceeding the ordination of a deacon.[142] However, it is placed after the prayer *ad clericum faciendum* and *ad barbam tondendam*, and before the prayer *ad ancillas*

---

divina delegat, nec canonum forma praestituit, non est penitus usurpandum; eisque sic ecclesiastica sunt ferenda praesidia, ut nihil committatur illicitum, in A. Thiel, *Epistolae Romanorum Pontificum, op. cit.,* 369–70.

[137] Council of Orléans, Can.17: *Feminae quae benedictionem diaconatus hactenus contra interdicta canonum acceperunt, si ad coniugium probantur iterum devolutae, a communione pellantur; Can.18: Placuit etiam, ut nulli postmodum feminae diaconalis benedictio pro conditionis huius fragilitate credatur,* in CCL 148/A, 197.

[138] *Testamentum sancti Remigii Remensis episcopi,* CCL 117:477.

[139] Fortunatus of Poitier, *Vita sanctae Radegundae,* 12, in MGH, Auctores antiquissimi, 4.2.41.

[140] J. Deshusses, ed., *Le sacramentaire Grégorien. Ses principales formes d'après les plus anciens manuscrits,* I, Spicilegium Friburgense 16 (Fribourg, 1971), fn. 51.

[141] Ibid., fn. 994.

[142] Ibid., fn. 31.

dei velandas and *ad abbatem faciendum vel abbattisam,* that is to say in the context of the monastic or paramonastic rites, and it remained such in the Latin liturgical books that followed.

This innovation proves that in the regions where the Gregorian Sacramentary was used the need for deaconesses or their usefulness was felt, probably under Byzantine influence that was strong in Italy in the seventh century, especially in the liturgical sphere. An actual example of a deaconess proves this. The *liber pontificalis Ecclesiae ravennatensis* by the abbot Agnello attests that when Sergius, a married layman, was made a bishop in 773, he consecrated his wife a deaconess, and she remained such until her death.[143]

In Rome the existence of deaconesses is incidentally attested to at the end of the eighth century. On November 29, 799, when Leo III, after suffering many ordeals, triumphantly returned to Rome accompanied by Charlemagne, he was welcomed at the Pons Milvius by the clergy, nobility, senate, army, and by the whole Roman people together with the nuns, the *deaconesses* and the women of the aristocracy.[144]

7.4 The Testimony of the Liturgical Books

The intention of harmonizing the ancient Roman liturgy with the traditions and adaptations introduced in Franco-German regions within the Roman Church is recorded in liturgical books compiled from the ninth century onward.

The Romano-German Pontifical, compiled in the abbey of Saint Alban near Meinz around the mid-tenth century, contains the rite *ad diaconam faciendam.*[145]

The initial rubric, certainly inspired by Byzantine liturgical books, explains that the deaconess would receive the *orarium* from the bishop and from that moment on, when she goes to church, she must always wear it around her neck under her mantle with its edges hanging on both sides. Her consecration occurs between the *Alleluia* and the chanting of the gospel, like that of the deacon. The litany of the saints is sung and ended with the *Exaudi,* while the elect [woman] prostrates before the altar. The *ad modum praephationis* follows, the prayer *Deus qui Annam*

---

[143] In PL 106:725.

[144] L. Duchesne, ed., *Liber Pontificalis,* II, 6.

[145] C. Vogel, R. Eleze, *Le Pontifical Romano-Germanique du dixième siècle,* I, ST 226 (Città del Vaticano, 1963), 54.

filiam Phanuelis, which exalts the dignity of the Christian widow, mentioning the tasks assigned to her in 1 Timothy 5:3-16 and Titus 2:3-5, and asks for her: *inter coniugatas tricesimum, cum viduis sexagesium fructum. Sit in ea cum misericordia districtio, cum libertate honestas, cum humanitate sobrietas. Opus tuum die ac nocte meditetur, ut in die vocationis suae talis esse mereatur qualem illam per spiritum prophetiae esse voluisti.* After the imposition of the *orarium,* the deaconess takes the veil from the altar and puts it on while singing the antiphon: *Ipsi sum desponsata,* as in the *consecratio virginis;* then the giving of the ring and crown follow.

The Romano-German Pontifical spread throughout Europe from the end of the tenth century, and in Rome it was as well for the ordination of deaconesses, which seems to have been frequent, so much so that the pope authorized the suburbicarian bishops[146] to perform the ordination on his behalf, until the Pontifical of Gregory VII.

The pontifical, in the section titled *Missa ad diaconam consecrandam* records, although in a different order, the entire formulary of the Romano-German Pontifical.[147]

In the twelfth century, the rite is again found in the Pontificals of Troyes[148] and Engelbzerg,[149] and in the thirteenth century in the Pontifical of Poitiers,[150] as well as in the Pontifical of Guillaume Durand, who likely reports it to document it; in fact, he prefaces it with the following

---

[146] Four Decretals of the eleventh century authorize suburbicarian bishops to perform this rite. At least three times the bishop of Porto is granted the privilege of holding in Trastevere *omnen ordinationem episcopalem tam de presbyteris quam diaconibus vel diaconissis seu subdiaconibus, ecclesiis vel altaribus* [Benedict VIII (1018), PL 139:1621; John XIX (1022), PL 141:1121; Leo IX (1049), PL 143:602]. In 1026 John XIX authorizes the bishop of Silva Candida (Santa Rufina) to hold *consecrationem ecclesiarum, altarium, sacerdotum, diaconorum seu diaconissarum totius civitatis Leoninae* (PL 141:1130) in the Leonine City.

[147] M. Andreieu, ed., *Le Pontifical Romain au Moyen-Age,* I, ST 86 (Città del Vaticano, 1938), 169–70. There are no indications concerning rubrics, therefore we do not know if the deaconess received the stole. The verse of the Alleluia, *Amavit eam Dominus et ornavit eam stola,* leads us to suppose so.

[148] Ms. 4 of the Cathedral of Troyes, f. 121v, in V. Leroquais, *Les Pontificaux manuscrits des bibliothèques publiques de France* (Mâcon, 1937), II, 400.

[149] Engelberg, Abbey Library, ms. 54, f. 90v-93, in B. Gottwald, *Catalogus codicum manuscriptorum qui asservantur in bibliotheca monasterii OSB Engelbergensis,* (s. l.) 1891, 92.

[150] Ms. 39, f. 1-4v of the Municipal Library of Poitiers, V. Leroquais, *Les Pontificaux, op. cit.,* 257. Contrary to what the editor maintains, this is the case of the consecration of a deaconess.

annotation: *Diaconissa olim non tamen ante annum quadragesimum, ordinabatur hoc modo.*[151]

In the sixteenth century, the rite is found without Durand's annotation in the Pontifical of Perugia, which concludes with the rubric: *Deinde tradat ei episcopus librum evangeliorum et det ei potestatem legendi evangelium ad vigilias et incipiendi horas in ecclesia.*[152]

Two centuries earlier, the scholar Rolando Bandinelli, the future Pope Alexander III, maintained that diaconal ordination confers upon women the ministry of proclaiming the gospel during the liturgy.[153]

But in the fifteenth century, with the Pontifical of Giovanni Barozzi, bishop of Bergamo, a deaconess is given a book of homilies instead of the Book of the Gospels, maintaining the formula: *Accipe potestatem legendi evangelium cum omelia in Ecclesia Dei. In nomine Domini.* However, the author adds that at that time deaconesses are not usually ordained, and in a monastery it is usually the hebdomadary who proclaims the gospel during the night Office.[154]

Finally, in the 1497 Roman Pontifical, once the book of homilies was substituted by the breviary, what remained of the diaconal ordination was incorporated in the *consecratio virginis*, with the following rubric:

> *Et quia in nonnullis monasteriis est consuetudo quod loco diaconissatus qui in quibusdam antiquis pontificalibus habetur, virginibus consecratis datur facultas legendi officium et incipiendi horas canonicas in ecclesia, convenienter fit hoc modo.*

The presentation of the breviary follows, with the words: *Accipe potestatem legendi officium et incipiendi horas canonicas in Ecclesia. In nomine Domini.*[155]

---

[151] M. Andrieu, *Le Pontifical Romain au Moyen-Age*, III: *Le Pontifical de Guillaume Durand* ST 88 (Città del Vaticano, 1940), 411.

[152] Vatican Library, Chigi codex C.V. 148, cf. M. Andrieu, *Le Pontifical Romain au Moyen-Age*, III, 253. The *Ordo* of Durandus is found on f. 35v, the new *Ordo* on f. 45v.

[153] *Antiquitus diaconissas, id est evangeliorum lectrices, in ecclesiis ordinari moris fuisee dubium non est* (F. Thaner, ed., *Summa magistri Rolandi* [Innsbruck, 1874], 121).

[154] Vatican Library, cod. Vat. lat. 1145, f. 59v, cf. M. Andrieu, *Le Pontifical Romain au Moyen-Age*, III: 223.

[155] L. Hain, *Repertorium bibliographicum in quo libri omnes ab arte typographica inventa ad annum MD . . . recensentur* (Stuttgart, 1826–38), no. 13287.

This text has come to us today[156] almost unchanged, by means of the Tridentine Pontifical, which continues to mention deaconesses, demonstrating the tendency of the Latin Church to understand the life and works of women religious as diaconal service, and their profession as a substitute for their ordination.

Conclusion

1. In the larger Church, historic evidence regarding the exercise or claims of exercise of priestly functions by women is very rare and difficult to interpret—evidence concerning an instituted lectorate, acolytate, and subdiaconate are likewise nonexistent, even though actually these functions were always exercised by women—therefore, the problem of a female liturgical ministry recognized within the Church is essentially identified with the question of the diaconate.

Because second-century data are extremely scarce we cannot legitimately deduce that the female diaconate arose only in the third century and therefore not in continuity with the New Testament. The Patristic fathers, even those belonging to Churches that denied women access to the diaconate, with the exception of Ambrosiaster, in their commentaries do not doubt that Romans 16:1-2 and 1 Timothy 3:11 refer to true deaconesses. After all, given the attachment to tradition concerning ministry, if Churches had had the slightest suspicion that the female diaconate was not founded in apostolic practice they would have never, ever, introduced such an innovation, which was sharply opposed to the surrounding culture and the heritage of Judaism.

On the contrary, it is likely that such a mentality, together with the fact that female ministry was claimed by heterodox sects as menacing not only the orthodox faith but even the constitution of the Church, represented an obstacle to the continuation and evolution of the female diaconate.

The New Testament roots of the female diaconate, after all, are attested to by Byzantine, Armenian, and Georgian liturgies, which recall Romans 16:1-2 and 1 Timothy 3:11 in describing the function of a deaconess.

2. The functions of the female diaconate are rather far-reaching, depending on various eras and regions. They range from anointing adult women before and after baptism, catechizing them before and receiving

---

[156] I have examined the Regensburg edition of 1891, 84–95: the above-mentioned rubric is found on p. 95.

them after baptism, pastoral care of ill women (including their anointing), preparing deceased women for burial, guarding of the church doors, monitoring of the liturgical assembly, praying for the Church, presiding at liturgical prayer and proclaiming the gospel within female religious communities in the absence of the presbyter and the deacon, distributing the Eucharist to women and children, even up to accomplishing delicate missions on behalf of the bishop.

3. At least beginning with the *Didascalia Apostolorum* and the *Apostolic Constitutions*, that is, from the beginning of the third century, this ministry in various churches was conferred with a liturgical rite, which in the East involves the formula "The divine grace"—considered essential for the episcopate, presbyterate, and male diaconate—the laying on of hands, and an epicletic prayer that recalls biblical paradigms of the Old and New Testament, preferably prophetesses, and invokes the outflowing of the Holy Spirit on the elect [woman], so that she may worthily accomplish her ministry, as well the imposition of the diaconal stole (*orarion*), and in Constantinople also of the sacred chalice with the Blood of Christ.

The facts that the recalled paradigms are different in regard to the male diaconate and that women do not have access to the altar because of sexual taboos inherited from Judaism, more than from the Old Testament (the notion of pure and impure in connection to blood)—and perhaps because of a certain distrust in the ability of male ministers to look upon women with a simple and chaste eye—does not prevent us from considering the female diaconate equal to the male diaconate; after all, throughout the centuries, the tasks concerning the latter underwent variations no less numerous and profound, passing from catechesis to the itinerant proclamation of the gospel, to important administrative functions within the local Church, to delicate diplomatic assignments at the service of the bishop and of the Church, and finally, for almost a thousand years, to simple cantor of the gospel during a solemn Mass and to extraordinary minister of the Eucharist.

Even though it would be anachronistic to apply sacramental categories proper to Latin theology from Scholasticism onward to previous eras and diverse environments, nothing in the rites and prayers for the ordination, at least in some Churches, demonstrates a different theological consideration of the diaconate conferred on women.

4. With the end of the first millennium and the cessation of adult baptism, the female diaconate loses its fundamental task, which was linked to the baptism of women, and its unrestrained decline begins. The deaconess is reduced to the *hegumenia* of a monastery, where she presides

over the Liturgy of the Hours, proclaims the gospel, reads the patristic homily, has custody of the sacred species, and distributes Communion to ill women.

The female diaconate died out without having been suppressed; on the contrary, according to some evidence, it seems it never disappeared within certain Churches. The male diaconate, reduced to chanting the gospel during solemn Mass, did not suffer the same fate solely because it was considered an obligatory step on the path to the presbyterate and the episcopacy.

Throughout the centuries, however, attempts to revive the female diaconate have not been lacking, more due to the urgency of pastoral needs than the consideration of the dignity and vocation of women. In fact, its restoration, already accomplished in the Anglican Church and some Reformed Churches, will be one of the topics of the planned pan-orthodox council.

5. Different in many aspects is the history of the Latin Church, which initially ignores and strongly opposes the female diaconate, perhaps because of the identification of claims for a female ministry with membership in or adherence to second generation Montanist sects that undermined the hierarchical structure of the Church, more than as a consequence of encratic tendencies that consider women with suspicion or even negatively.

Knowledge and influence of the Eastern Churches between the seventh and the eighth centuries, recognizable even in the name of the stole found in liturgical sources (*orarium*), would help to overcome these hesitations. But by then the diaconate of women was in serious decline even in those Churches, due to the cessation of adult baptism.

The diaconate would be considered no more than a blessing on virgins or widows who consecrated their lives to God's service so as to enable them to proclaim the gospel during the Liturgy of the Hours and to preside over them within female religious communities and finally to accomplish God's work on behalf of and in the name of the whole Church, or also to exercise the power of jurisdiction within monasteries.

And the imposition of the stole in some monasteries would remain as testimony to what the female diaconate in the Church was or might be able to be.

Translated by Carmela Leonforte-Plimack with Phyllis Zagano

5

The Deaconess in the Byzantine Tradition

Cipriano Vagaggini

I have been asked to express my opinion about the possibility that the Church, if it judges it appropriate, would be able to confer on women the sacrament of order in the diaconal grade. I have been requested[1] in particular to bear in mind the position A.G. Martimort has taken on this issue in his work *Les diaconesses; essai historique* (Ed. liturgiche, Rome, 1982). It is said that this work leads many to maintain that the Church cannot admit women to the diaconal order. To try to clarify the above-mentioned issue, I will consider only the ordination of deaconesses in the Byzantine tradition, as I did in my 1974 article, "L'ordinazione delle diaconesse nella tradizione bizantina" (*Orientalia christiana periodica* 40 [1974]: 145–87). In that article I maintained, and I still maintain today, that the competent authority of the Church, if it judges it appropriate, can admit women to the sacrament of order in the diaconate. The essential principals of my position are the following.

1) We know well the rite of the Byzantine tradition for the ordination of deaconesses. The oldest codex we have for this rite is the eighth-century Barberini Codex Gr. 336, known as the Barberini Euchologies. Then, with some slight variations in the rubrics, the same rite appears in a series of codices until the fourteenth century. As far as our issue is concerned, what has to be particularly noticed in this rite, apart from other details, is above all the fact that the ordination of deaconesses occurs and can occur only within the sanctuary (the *bema/vima*, behind the iconostasis), at the foot of the altar. According to the Byzantine rite, ordination within the sanctuary only occurs (and today this is still the case) for the ordination of the bishop, the presbyter, the deacon, and the deaconess. Ordination

"La diaconessa nella tradizione greca e bizantina," *Il Regno* 32 (1987): 672–73.

[1] An historical-liturgical contribution offered upon request to the synod fathers. —*Il Regno* Ed.

to any other order, such as subdeacon, acolyte, etc., has always taken place, and even now takes place, outside the sanctuary—today, usually at the threshold of the entrance door to the sanctuary, but still outside of it.

2) Has this liturgical fact a precise significance? For a long time historians have not asked themselves this question. Instead, all things considered, the answer is given in the clearest manner by Theodore of Mopsuestia (born in Antioch c. 350 and died in Mopsuestia, Cilicia, in 428). He says, with regard to 1 Timothy 3:8-15:

> It is worth adding that we should not be surprised if (Paul) mentions neither subdeacons nor lectors. In fact, these are outside of the grades in the ministry of the Church: created later because of the needs that had to be attended to by others (ministers) for the good of the great number of believers. Therefore, the law does not allow them to receive the *cheirotonia* (= imposition of the hands) in front of the altar because they do not minister the mystery; but lectors perform the readings and the subdeacons, inside [the sanctuary], take care of what is needed for the service by the deacons, as well as attending to the lights in the church. This is because only presbyters and deacons perform the ministry of the mystery—the former fulfilling their priestly office, the latter administering the sacred things. (See *Theodori ep. mopsuest. in ep. B. Pauli comm.* [Cambridge, 1880], vol. II, pp. 132–34, and my article p. 182.)

The text demonstrates that Theodore bears witness to the theological conviction that within the whole of "sacred orders" there exists a fundamental distinction between the group comprising bishop, presbyter, and deacon, on the one hand, and the group comprising lector and subdeacon, on the other hand; and this distinction has its ritual expression in the ordinations, in the fact that the first group is ordained at the foot of the altar within the sanctuary-*vima* and the second not. The distinction, according to Theodore, has its origin in the fact that [those in] the first group (bishop, presbyter, deacon) are of apostolic origin and the others are not. Theodore does not speak about deaconesses in this context, but he knows them well and deems them of apostolic origin, as also did at that same time John Chrysostom and Theodoret of Cyrrhus (see my article, p. 183, footnote 2). The same is supposed in the Byzantine rite for the ordination of deaconesses, where the deaconess Phoebe, of whom St. Paul speaks in Romans 16:1-2, is mentioned.

According to this view we should say the following: first, in the perspective of the Byzantine church, as handed down in its rituals (*euchologi*) from the eighth century onward, the ordination of deaconesses is considered, together with the presbyterate and the diaconate for men, what today we call a real sacrament (of diaconal order), and not a sacramental, much less a sort of blessing of a more or less ascetic type. It is pure fantasy to insinuate that it is only a sort of blessing for the purpose of an ascetic life. Second, by virtue of this sacrament, the order which deaconesses receive is what today we would call a major order, the last one of the group formed by the order of bishops, the order presbyters, and that of deacons. To say that in the Byzantine rite of that time the feminine diaconate is something thoroughly different from the diaconate of men (Martimort, p. 155) is ambiguous and misleading. What is this thoroughly different thing? In reality, of course without saying that in the Byzantine tradition the diaconate of women was simply the same as the diaconate of men (here Martimort restates the obvious), we must say that in that tradition the diaconal order included two grades, one male and one female, with a very different range as far as their liturgical functions were concerned, but both of a strictly sacramental nature and as major orders.

3) At this point the question arises regarding the specific functions to which women who received the aforementioned feminine diaconal sacrament were entitled and ordained to. It is ambiguous and misleading to say that: "As long as the Byzantine tradition was kept alive it did not assign any liturgical duty to deaconesses" (Martimort, p. 250). Instead, in this area it is necessary to make two affirmations.

The first is that in Byzantium they were convinced that diaconal ordination *per se* allowed women to perform precise duties, even of a liturgical nature. In this sense the evidence of the civil-canonical legislation in the *Novella* of Justinian 6.6 (535) is explicit. In this *Novella* the deaconesses' duties are described in sum as follows: "*To serve during sacred baptisms and be present in the other secret things that are customarily performed by them in the sacred mysteries.*" In this affirmation is included at least the liturgical task of anointing women's bodies during the conferring of baptism (which took place by immersion). This duty was well known throughout the previous Eastern tradition, as is shown, for example, by the *Didascalia* III, 12 (third century), by the *Apostolic Constitutions* III, 16.2-4 and VIII, 28.6 (fourth century), by St. Epiphanius (PG 42:744–45; *circa* 375), by Severus of Antioch (*Letter* 62, *circa* 519–538).

The second affirmation is the observation that, notwithstanding the above-mentioned general and theoretical conviction, one notices on the practical level a tendency by which the liturgical functions of deaconesses in the Byzantine rite were effectively performed by men deacons or presbyters. In fact this situation did not preclude the possibility for the deaconesses to perform the liturgical duties mentioned in the *Novella* of Justinian 6.6, but rather rendered that possibility purely theoretical. And this carried with it the major disadvantage that the office of deaconesses, in itself truly a sacrament, tended to become purely theoretical and honorary.

4) At this point one might argue that in today's church the idea of reestablishing the ordination of deaconesses, following the path we have traced so far, is false, because these deaconesses would in practice have no function, especially no liturgical function, in the life of the church today, as there is no longer baptism by immersion. The answer is that the situation has largely changed in the life of the present church, and as far as the extent of the tasks, even the liturgical tasks, of women the situation is also outdated. It is known, in fact, that today there are many cases, especially in third world countries, but not only there, where there are women who by indult in practice perform all the tasks, even of a liturgical nature, that a parish priest can perform, except to say Mass and to confess. And, let us not forget that Benedict XIV, when he approved *in forma specifica* (i.e., as a pontifical law) the Lebanese Maronite synod of 1736 allowed deaconesses of that rite (who at the time were usually abbesses of monasteries) among other things to give "extreme unction" to their nuns (See Mansi 38, col. 163–64).

If that is the case, one senses the legitimacy and urgency for competent authorities to admit women to the sacrament of order of the diaconate, and to grant them all the functions, even the liturgical functions that, in the present historic moment of the church, are considered necessary for the greater benefit of believers, not excluding—as I personally maintain— if it is judged pastorally appropriate, equality between the liturgical functions of men deacons and women deacons.

Translated by Peter J. Houle, Carmela Leonforte-Plimack, and Phyllis Zagano

6

The Ordination of Deaconesses in the Greek and Byzantine Tradition

Cipriano Vagaggini

PREMISES

1) Purpose

The current problem of "feminine ministries" is not about the theological possibility of a "ministry" generally given to women. Rather, it is the problem of their "ordained" ministry and of the nature of that ordination (sacrament or not?), of its duties and of its relationship with other ordained ministries, especially the subdiaconate, diaconate, and presbyterate. We will only consider the problem of the possibility of an ordained women's diaconate.

This study seeks to make a historical contribution to the problem. It will not attempt to rewrite, not even in summary form, the general history of the institution of deaconesses and its relationships to those of widows and virgins.[1] In this history we only want to bring to light any data that can be used in resolving the aforementioned problem. There-

"L'ordinazione delle diaconesse nella tradizione greca e bizantina" by Cipriano Vagaggini was published in *Orentialia christiana periodica* 40 (1974): 146–89.

[1] For this general history there are now two foundational works that take into account earlier research and provide the bibliography. For the history of the deaconesses, and of their relationship to the widows, virgins, and abbesses, from their rise in the Church to their disappearance: A. Kalsbach, *Die altkirchliche Einrichtung der Diakonissen bis zu ihrem Erlöschen, Römische Quartalschrift. 22 Supplementheft* (Freiburg I/B, 1926). The author then provided a later summary in the article "Diakonisse" in *Reallexikon für Antike und Christentum 4 (1959): 917–28.* For the period through the sixth century, and though it is with regard to the Greek and Latin tradition, the historical problem was recently taken up again by R. Gryson, *Le ministère des femmes dans l'Église ancienne* (Grembloux, 1972). There is also a useful collection of texts, though it has not yet been completed: J. Mayer,

fore, we will analyze the data that are directly or indirectly liturgical, in my opinion more than has been done thus far.[2] From the point of view that we are proposing, there are two truly interesting ecclesiastical traditions: the Greek Byzantine and the Syriac (Nestorian, Monophysite, and Maronite). The Latin tradition seems to me to be much less valuable for our purpose. Basically, in this field there is neither an Egyptian nor an Armenian tradition.

2) The manner of presenting the question

Today we are impelled to ask the question in the following manner: was the ordination, χειροτονία [*cheirotonia*] of deaconesses conceived of as a sacrament or as a sacramental; as a major order or a minor order? However, this approach to the question presupposes many things that are characteristic of later Western theology: (1) the technical difference between a sacrament and a sacramental; (2) the distinction between major and minor orders and in which grouping each of the orders is placed; (3) the opinion that the minor orders (including the subdiaconate) are, or were, only sacramentals and not sacraments.[3]

All of this presents problems for which there are no simple solutions. Historically, it is known that the technical distinction between a sacrament and a sacramental, along with the assertion that the number of sacraments is seven, came about in the West only in the twelfth and thirteenth centuries. Without denying that earlier, both in the East and in the West, one can find some initial reflections that tend to distinguish between μυστήρια and μυστήρια, *sacramentum* and *sacramentum*, order and order: these are only a matter of initial signs that go in different directions and that lead to different lists.

Monumenta de viduis, diaconissis virginbusque tractantia (Florilegium Patristicum, fasc. 42) (Bonn, 1939).

[2] These deal more directly with the ordination of deaconesses: *Die Geschichte der Diakonissenweihe,* in *Eine heilige Kirche* 21 (1939): 57–76; E. D. Theodorou, Ἡ «χειροτονία» ἤ «χειροθεσία» τῶν διακονισσῶν ["He Cheirotonia e cheirothesia ton diakonisson"], in Θεολογία [Theologia] (Review of the Holy Synod of the Greek Church, Athens) 25 (1954): 576–601; 26 (1955): 57–76.

[3] For a panorama of the history and the current status of the aforementioned questions, see, for example, *DTC, Sacramentaux* XIV I (1939): 465–82. See there also *Ordre* XI 2 (1932): 1298–1309, especially 1308–9 and 1380–81: the position of medievals and moderns on the problem of whether the minor orders are sacraments or only sacramentals.

From a theoretical point of view, today one usually says: the sacraments were instituted by Christ or by the Apostles and they function *ex opere operato*; the sacramentals were instituted by the Church and they function *ex opere operantis (Ecclesiae)*.[4] However, it is not shown how, for example, marriage as a sacrament was instituted by Christ or by the Apostles. Rather, the washing of the feet, according to John 13:1-15, was instituted by Christ, who instructed his Apostles to do likewise; but the Church has considered this to be only a sacramental. Some among the so-called sacramentals (benedictions and constitutive consecrations) were considered to have effects *ex opere operato*.

As far as the sacrament of Order is concerned: it is well-known that the major scholastics commonly considered minor orders to be sacraments also. Subsequently, such was denied because it was said that the minor orders appear only later in Church history and in a varied and changing manner in different regions. However, marriage as a sacrament also appears later. Commonly, both modern and ancient exegetes do not consider "the seven" in Acts 6 to have been what were later called the "deacons." From the viewpoint of the institution by the Apostles, the deaconesses are in no worse a state than the deacons or than the monarchial episcopate (Rom 16:1-2; Phoebe; 1 Tim 3:11 as interpreted by many ancient and modern authors; the testimony of Pliny the Younger in 111–13: see Kirch, *Enchiridion* n. 30).

Methodological conclusion: when seeking to discern the nature of the ordination of deaconesses in the ancient documents, one must guard against presupposing *a priori* the distinctions of medieval and modern theology between sacrament and sacramental, with major orders equaling sacraments, minor orders equaling sacramentals.

As the starting point for our research we will take the *Didascalia Apostolorum*, the original Greek text of which is said to have been written in Syria in the middle of the third century. My reason for doing so is that among the documents that we have today, it is in the *Didascalia* that deaconesses appear for the first time not only as a group clearly distinct from the "established" widows and virgins but also as a ministry of the local Church, whose pastoral and liturgical task is clearly determined as being parallel to the ministry of the deacons, albeit with more restricted roles. The text does not yet speak of the "ordination" of the deaconesses;

[4] See, for example, *DTC, Sacramentaux*, pp. 470–75. To my knowledge, the expression *Opus operantis Ecclesiae* was made official for the first time in an official document in the encyclical of Pius XII *Mediator Dei* from 1947: AAS 39 (1947): 532.

however, had it not existed, the *Didascalia* established the premises for it. Moreover, the author insists in such a way as to persuade every bishop of the usefulness and necessity for each of them to have deaconesses in their Churches [dioceses], leaving the sense that it is a question of an institution, I would say, not necessarily new to the Church, but certainly not very widespread. (See III 12, 2.)

I

THE *DIDISCALIA* (mid-third century):

THE DIACONATE OF WOMEN

LITURGICAL AND PASTORAL MINISTRY TO WOMEN.

1) The Foundational Texts[5]

a) II 26, 3-8: with the central passage 6. Context: Lay people must give a tenth, as well as the first fruits, to the bishops, presbyters and deacons, widows and orphans: just as in the Old Testament the Israelites gave them to the High Priest, the priests, and the Levites:

> II, 26, 3. These (the bishops) are your high priests; what the Levites once were are now the deacons,[6] the presbyters, widows, and orphans. 4. For you the high priest is the Levite bishop: he is your teacher, and, after God, your father who regenerates through water; he is your prince and he is your chief, and your powerful king. And may he who reigns in place of God be honored like God, since the bishop presides over you as the image of God (*in typum Dei*). 5. On the contrary, the deacon is there as an image of Christ; therefore, may he be loved by you. 6. May the deaconess be honored by you as image of the Holy Spirit. 7. May also presbyters be considered by you as images of the Apostles. 8. Consider the widows and the orphans as images of the altar.

b) III 12-13. In my opinion, all of 13 must be considered as referring equally to deacons and deaconesses: something that is not noted often enough.[7] It emerges in 12,1, as the general theme of 12 and 13, as well as in 13,1, as the particular theme of all of 13. In each text the author speaks equally about deacons and deaconesses. Context: 12: it is extremely useful

---

[5] F. X. Funk, *Didascalia Apostolorum*, 2 vols. (Paderborn, 1905, reprinted 1962).

[6] It is certain that according to the author the word "the deacons" includes deaconesses. See below II 26,6 as well as III 13 bearing in mind 13,1-2 and 12,1.

[7] Gryson, *loc. cit.*, 75–79 does not take into account *Did*. III 13,2-7 for deaconesses.

and practically necessary that every bishop have in his Church not only deacons but also deaconesses, for the ministry to women; 13: deacons and deaconesses, each within his or her area, must be at the service of the bishop with regard to the faithful and they must act with zeal and solicitude, with full agreement between them, as "two bodies in one soul."

III 12: Therefore, bishop, make[8] permanent workers of justice (διακόνους) who may help your people for life. Elect and make deacons from among your people those whom you like:[9] the man so that he might take care of the many things that are necessary,[10] and the woman for ministry among women. There are things for which you may not send a deacon to women because of the pagans; however, you will send deaconesses. 2. Also, for many other things a woman deaconess is required. First, when women step down into the water (for baptism); when they step down it is necessary that they be anointed with oil by the deaconess. When you cannot find a woman especially a deaconess, the man who is baptizing must anoint she who is being baptized. But where there is a woman present and especially a deaconess, decency requires that women are not seen by men. Except for the laying on of the hand you anoint only the head, as in the past priests and kings in Israel were anointed. 3. Likewise, when you impose your hand, anoint the head of they who are being baptized, whether they be men or women. After that, when you baptize, or when you authorize deacons or presbyters to baptize, the deaconess as we have already said, anoints the women, but a man pronounces the invocation ἐπίκλησις of the Godhead. And when she who has been baptized emerges from the water, the deaconess receives her, teaches, and instructs her about how the seal of baptism must be kept intact in chastity and holiness. 4. Therefore we say that the ministry of the woman deaconess is highly desirable and utterly necessary because even the Lord Our Savior was served by women who served him and they were Mary Magdelene and Mary the daughter of James, and the mother of Joseph and the mother of the sons of Zebedee.

---

[8] The Greek has προχειρίζου. προχειρίζω means: to place before, present, choose, establish in an office, order. At least since the eighth century, it is a technical term for ordination. See Lampe's dictionary; the Greek index of the *Apostolic Constitutions*; J. Hanssens, *La forme danse les ordinations du rit grec*, in *Gregorianum* 5 (1924): 236–39.

[9] δοκιμάζεις = you have tried and chosen.

[10] In the *Didascalia*, the male deacon has a very significant place in the life of the local Church and which overshadows that of the presbyters. Eye, agent, and right arm of the bishop, his duties are very extensive above all in the pastoral, charitable, administrative field. See, for example, II 28; 30; 31; 32,3; 34,3, 37,6; 42,1; 44 (important); III 8,1,4.

The deaconess will be necessary to you in other things, so they might enter the households of pagans where you cannot enter where there are believing women and to attend to those women who are ill and to bathe those who are recovering from illness.

III 13: Deacons should model their behavior on that of bishops and they should be more active than bishops. They should not love dishonest profit and they should be diligent in their ministry. Their number should be sufficient according to the number of faithful in the church so they may attend the elderly women who are ill, to brothers and sisters who are sick, so they may accomplish their ministry with dispatch. The woman will take care of women; the deacons, being a man, will take care of men and, when ordered by the bishops he should be prepared and quick in moving for the ministry and the service. 2. Therefore may each one know about his or her own task and carefully fulfill it with concern. And you should be on one mind, as two bodies with one soul, so you will understand how large the diaconal ministry is. 3. As the Lord said in the Gospel: "whoever wishes to become great among you shall be your servant, and whoever wishes to be first among you shall be your slave; just as the Son of Man did not come to be served, but to serve, and to give His life a ransom for many." Likewise, you deacons should do the same and when it is necessary in your ministry you will give your life for your bothers. Do not doubt this, because even our Lord did not hesitate when he served us as it was written in Isaiah: "To justify the righteous, performing well as service for many." 4. Therefore if the Lord of heaven and earth served us and bore everything for our sake, how much more must we do the same for our brothers; because we are all his followers and we have been given the same tasks as Christ. Also, in the Gospels you will find how it is written that our Lord girt himself with a cloth and took water from the basin while we were all seated; he washed our feet and wiped them with a cloth. 5. In so doing he demonstrated brotherly love so that we also may do the same to each other. If therefore the Lord did that, you, deacons, do not hesitate to do likewise to the powerless and the sick because you are the workers of truth, encouraged by the example of Christ. May you then serve with love, not complaining or doubting, because in so doing you act according to the ways of men and not of God and at the end of your life you will be rewarded according to your ministry. 7. Therefore you deacons must visit all those who are in need. Let the bishop know about those who are distressed; you must be his soul and mind, ever strong and always obedient to him.

2) The Foundational Data

a) *The diaconal ministry in the Church includes two branches: one masculine and the other feminine, for pastoral ministry to women.* The author's idea is to persuade the bishop that, for adequate diaconal service in his

Church, he needs not only men deacons but also women deacons. For the author, this diaconal ministry in the Church includes two branches: one male and one female (III 12,1-2; 13,1). This is so that such a ministry be an adequate service as much for men as for women (III 13,1-2). As a result, the author treats the male and female diaconates in a parallel way. Nevertheless, the work of the deacon in the Church, even if it generally exercised with regard to men, is much more extensive than that of the deaconess. The duties of the deaconess are restricted to ministry for women, and in cases in which natural decency or decency required by customs and environment would not easily allow the bishop, presbyter, or deacon to approach them.

b) *The liturgical work of the deaconess* is related to the baptism of women. According to the *Didascalia*, the person who is baptized, whether woman or man, is baptized completely naked and, even before baptism, is anointed with oil all over his or her body. The bishop anoints the person's head (III 12,2). However, as for women, it is indecent that they be seen naked by a man, and therefore the deaconess performs the remaining anointings. But only "a man" and not the deaconess, pronounces "the names of the invocation of the Godhead" over those same women who are then baptized. Women who thus baptized come out of the pool are then "received" by the deaconess, who is also responsible for instructing them about the obligations to preserve in chastity and holiness the seal of baptism received. It is well-known that these two tasks, receiving the baptized and further instructing them, subsequently developed into the role of godfather and godmother.

c) *The pastoral work of the deaconess to assist women.* The *Didascalia* is far from focusing on the liturgical work of ecclesiastical ministries. Indeed, above all, it deals with their general pastoral work. For deaconesses, it is the visiting of and charitable help for Christian women who are sick or in need. The *Didascalia* signals, above all, the case of Christian women in domestic settings where there are still pagans (III 12,1.4113,1) and concerning whom, for that reason, the bishop was unable to send a deacon. From the advice of III 13, simultaneously given to the deacon and deaconess, one can glimpse the practical importance and great extent that this diaconal ministry of visiting and assisting the needy had in the ordinary life of the church. It is a task that should be fulfilled with the greatest solicitude and charity, under the direct responsibility of the bishop, whom the deacon or deaconess must notify about particular cases (III 13,1.7. *Cf.* II 30; 31): without doubt this is because he might make arrangements to distribute the alms of the Church (*Cf.* II 2,4; 25,2;

27,4; III 4,1-2). In this task, whoever carries out the diaconal ministry must function as the soul and mind of the bishop (III 13,7). The text reiterates for both the deacon and the deaconess what was said of the deacon alone in II 44.

d) *Limits of the work of the deaconess: no allusion to any Eucharistic work; prohibition against women teaching and baptizing.* There is no hint in the *Didascalia* to the way in which deaconesses were appointed and no hint of any of their tasks in the celebration of the Mass or concerning the Eucharist. In III 6,9, in the context of a discussion about widows, the author prohibits not only widows from teaching and baptizing, even if "constituted," but women in general.

A pagan wishing to be catechized by a widow, especially concerning the incarnation and passion of the Lord (III 5,3-6) must be referred to the rectors of the Church. In order to teach such doctrines, one must do so with authority (*firmiter prout decet*). If a pagan heard them explained by a woman, the effect, the author seems to say, could run contrary to what the Christian woman would wish (III 5,6). "It is neither right nor necessary therefore that women should be teachers, and especially concerning the name of Christ and the redemption, fruit of His passion. You, women, and especially you widows, have not been appointed to teach" (III 6,1-2). The reason for this affirmation: Christ did not send women to teach:

> . . . for Our Lord Jesus Christ, our teacher has sent forth us, the Twelve, to teach the people and all nations. With us there were some women disciples: Mary Magdalene, Mary the daughter of James, and the other Mary; but he did not send them forth with us to teach the people. Had it been necessary that women teach our Lord would have commanded them to teach together with us. (III 6,1-2)

According to the *Didascalia*, women must not baptize: "We do not approve of a woman baptizing, or that one should be baptized by a woman, for it is a transgression of the commandment, and a great peril to she who baptizes and to he who is baptized" (III 9,1). The author speaks cautiously: we do not approve; it is against the law; it is dangerous. He goes no further. Was the author thinking of what is defined in modern categories as certainly illicit and probably invalid? In any case, the negative position against women baptizing was certainly common in antiquity.[11]

---

[11] Tertullian, *De bapt.* 17 PL 1:1328–29; *De praescrip.* 41 PL 2:68. After the *Did.*, besides the *Apostolic Constitutions* which emphasize, too, the negative position as

What is the reason for this prohibition?: "If in fact women had been permitted to baptize, our Lord and Teacher Himself undoubtedly would have been baptized by Mary His mother, whereas He was baptized by John, like others of the people" (III 9,2).

Naturally, there remains the problem of the objective value of this argument, as well as of the argument referenced above about the prohibition against women teaching. But one finds an abundance of these arguments in the subsequent tradition. However, one understands how with similar premises, the author of the *Didascalia* certainly wanted deaconesses to anoint women at the moment of baptism, but he did not allow them actually to baptize them, reserving this task for a man.

e) *The rank of deaconesses: probably, among the "dignities," after the deacons and subjected to them, but before lectors and subdeacons.* Here one cannot go beyond likely conclusions. With regard to *agape*, *Didascalia* III 28 distinguishes within the Church the laity from the *dignitates* (ἀξιώματα: II 28,5). Among the *dignitates*, there appear in the very same text: the bishop (priest, pastor), presbyters, deacons, and the lector. The *Didascalia* only mentions the subdeacon in II 34,3 in a context that does not discuss "dignity." But if one pays attention to the great importance that the author gives to deaconesses in the life of the Church, and to the fact that he considers their ministry to women as parallel to the deacons' ministry to men, even if less extensive (III 12-13), one gets the impression that, for him, deaconesses occupy a place in the community that is clearly superior to that of lectors and subdeacons, who are mentioned only once, and in a wholly incidental manner.

Didascalia II 26,3-7 says that while one must honor the bishop as the image of God and the deacon as the image of Christ, the deaconess must be honored as the image of the Holy Spirit and the presbyters as the images of the Apostles. This text is partly explained by *Didascalia* II 28: the bishop is the image of God, the mouth of God (II 28,2-9); the deacons are images of Christ, because, just as one cannot draw near to God without Christ, likewise the laity must approach the bishop through the deacon:

> . . . the laity should have great confidence in the deacons so that they do not continually bother the prince (= bishop); rather through the ministers, that is to say the deacons, they should point out to him what they want; in fact, no one may go to the omnipotent God except through

---

the *Did.*; the same negative attitude is found again in Epiphanius (*Haer.* 79.3 PG 42:744) and in Basil with regard to lay people in general (*Ep.* 188 can. 1 PG 32:668).

Christ; therefore everything the laity wants to do first should be made known to the bishop through the deacons and only after be done. (II 28,6)

The presbyters are the images of the Apostles because they are the council of the bishop and the curia of the Church (II 28,4). The statement that the deaconess is the image of the Holy Spirit seems to contain the idea, later explained by the author of the *Apostolic Constitutions* II 26,5-6: because just as the Holy Spirit is the Spirit of Christ and does nothing without his desire, so, too, the deaconess must not do anything without the consent of the deacon; and just as it is not possible to believe in Christ without the Holy Spirit, so women must approach the deacon or the bishop through the deaconess.[12]

II

FROM THE DIDISCALIA TO THE APOSTOLIC CONSTITUTIONS (end of the fourth century): THE FACT OF THE *CHEIROTONIA* ORDINATION OF DEACONESSES AND ITS IMPLICATIONS FOR THEIR RELATIONSHIPS TO THE "CLERGY" AND THE "PRIESTHOOD."

Canon 19 of Nicaea, a text by Basil, and some texts by Epiphanius serve our purpose here.

1) Canon 19 of Nicaea and the *cheirotonia* ordination of deaconesses

This canon speaks explicitly of deaconesses, of their χειροθεσία [*cheirothesia*, ordination], of their relationship to the laity in the Church. But the meaning of this text is highly debated.[13] In order to facilitate the commentary, we will number the sentences. We will provide the Greek

---

[12] These expressions have implications in the area of trinitarian doctrine, which is not a topic to be explored here. However, before the Council of Nicaea, "subordinationist" expressions or images such as is found in *Didache* II 26 were not meant to signify anything other than that in the economy of salvation, in everything, Christ does the will of the Father and the Holy Spirit: "he will not speak on his own authority but whatever he hears he will tell you . . . because he will receive what is mine and he will announce it to you" (John 16:13-14), and he is given to human beings only by Christ, to whomever Christ wishes and in whatever measure he wishes.

[13] History of the interpretation in Kalsbach , *loc. cit.*, 46–49. For Gryson's interpretation, see Gryson, *loc. cit.*, 86–87.

text only of the last sentence, the meaning of which is controversial. Its precise translation will be the aim of the discussion.

> 1. Regarding the Paulinists who later took refuge in the Catholic Church, the view has been established that they must be rebaptized. 2. If any of them had previously been part of their clergy and if they appear to be blameless and irreproachable, after having been baptized they should be ordained (χειροτονείσθωσαν) by the bishop of the Catholic Church. 3. If, however, after an inquiry they are deemed unfit, they must be deposed. 4. Likewise, with regard to the deaconesses (ώσαύτως δὲ καὶ περὶ τῶν διακονισσῶν) and generally with regard to those who are counted among the clergy, the same rule will be kept. 5. ʿΕμνήσθημεν δὲ τῶν διακονισσῶν τῶν ἐν τῷ σχήματι ἐξετασθεισῶν, ἐπεὶ μήτε χειροθεσίαν τινὰ ἔχουσιν, ὥστε ἐξάπαντος ἐν τοῖς λαϊκοῖς αὐτὰς ἐξετάζεσθαι.[14]

With regard to the fifth sentence, two recent scholars: Kalsbach and Gryson believe that the Council makes a general affirmation that is valid for all deaconesses and in all cases: that is to say, those deaconesses did not receive *cheirothesia*, ordination, and therefore always belong to the laity.

Other authors, ancient, from the seventeenth century, and modern, though with different shades of meaning, believe that the fifth sentence refers to one group of deaconesses and the fourth sentence to another group. They believe that the Council establishes that only those belonging to the group denoted in the fifth sentence do not receive *cheirothesia*, ordination, and therefore that they belong to the laity. But they maintain that, with regard to the deaconesses in the fourth sentence, the Council claims, first, that among the Paulinists they had already received *cheirothesia*, ordination, and they belonged to the clergy. Second, the Council allows that some of these deaconesses, having been rebaptized and having entered the Catholic Church—if they are found worthy—might eventually be ordained with the imposition of hands by the Catholic bishop and be numbered among the Catholic clergy, according to the general rule for Paulinist clergy, as explained in sentences 2 and 3.

---

[14] The text presents just one textual question. In sentence 4, following Pope Gelasius, some Latin sources read: διακονῶν rather than διακονισσῶν (see Hefele-Leclercq, *Hist. des conc.* I/I p. 616), against the other Greek sources. This reading appears too strongly as a correction in order to avoid the problem of the text and that of the supposed contradiction. In sentence 5 we maintain, along with the majority of editors, μηδέ instead of μήτε but it does not seem that the variation is significant because the terms also allow for an identical meaning.

In my opinion, the first solution is untenable. The fundamental reason is that such an interpretation introduces a contradiction between sentences 4 and 5. In fact, in any case, sentence 4 first affirms that the deaconesses of whom it speaks of are part of the clergy. In fact, it says "likewise about the deaconesses and, generally, about those who are included in the canon." Now, in the canons of Nicaea, to be included in the canon either means or implies clerical status,[15] while in the above-mentioned interpretation, the text is made to say that each and every deaconess must simply be included among the laity.

Moreover, the same interpretation contradicts sentence 4, insofar as this sentence affirms that, for the deaconesses of whom it speaks, the same rule must be observed as that established in the preceding context for the ex-Paulinists who had clerical status within that sect: these latter, in order to be admitted to the Catholic clergy first had to be rebaptized and then, if previously found worthy, receive *cheirotonia*, ordination, by a Catholic bishop. If, however, they were found unworthy, they were to be deposed. In my opinion, it is arbitrary to restrict the sense of "equally" (ὡσαύτως), as did Kalsbach and Gryson, in sentence 4 regarding deaconesses, as if it is meant to refer only to that part of the canonical rule of the Council according to which the ex-Paulinist clergy found unworthy were to be deposed, but excluding the other part, so that those found worthy could be ordained by the Catholic bishop and admitted to the Catholic clergy. Gryson[16] believes that the aforementioned restriction must be accepted because, he says, otherwise one cannot explain why, in sentence 5, the canon says that deaconesses (Gryson means any deaconesses) do not receive ordination and therefore are always lay. However, the objection is precisely whether or not sentence 5 refers to all deaconesses.

Now, this sentence 5, from a philological point of view, perfectly allows for a meaning that does not imply that it is a matter of each and every deaconess but only of a certain group among deaconesses: this removes every contradiction between sentences 5 and 4. The boundaries of the fifth sentence allow it to be translated in the following way:

---

[15] Can. 17: many who "are within the canon" give themselves to usury. If, from now on, any of them does this again "that one is deposed from the clergy and removed from the canon." See also the beginning and end of can. 16.

[16] *Loc. cit.*, 87.

Moreover,[17] we have dealt[18] with those deaconesses,[19] even if[20] they do not have *cheirothesia*, ordination, establishing that[21] they are to be counted among the laity.

Therefore, the text becomes understandable without any contradiction with regard to the preceding text and the whole canon appears to be logically constructed. The first sentence affirms the general rule that all Paulinists (trinitarian heretics) who want to enter the Catholic Church must be rebaptized. Sentences 2 and 3 apply in particular to those ex-Paulinists who, within that sect, were part of the clergy. They presented the particular problem of whether, after they had been rebaptized, they could be admitted to the Catholic clergy. The synod states that an inquiry is to be made: if they are found worthy, the Catholic bishop may give them holy orders (and thereby admit them to the Catholic clergy). If, on the other hand, they are found unworthy, he must depose them from the clerical status that they had among the Paulinists. Sentence 4 determines that the preceding norm applies to deaconesses as well, and to other Paulinists who were included in the canon, that is, those who were clergy. These "others" are at least the subdeacons and the lectors.[22] Among these deaconesses and other clergy, one can presume that they had received

---

[17] δέ (ἐμνήσθημεν δέ) can have an adversative sense (rather, on the contrary), or continuous (at the same time, and then, more, besides).

[18] ἐμνήσθημεν: first-person plural aorist middle of μιμνήσκω or of μνάομαι (which in different tenses have the same form): The meaning: 1. "to think" in general; 2. "to remember"; "to mention" 3. "to deal with"; "to take care of." It can suggest a request or a command.

[19] τῶν διακονισσῶν τῶν ἐν τῷ σχήματι ἐξετασθεισῶν = of those deaconesses who are found within the schema, that is, in the habit, state, rank.

[20] ἐπεί: can mean: 1. a concept of time: when, after, while; 2. a sense of the cause of something: why, the motive for something; 3. a sense of consequences: therefore, so. 4. a concept of limitation: even though, nevertheless.

[21] ὥστε: consecutive conjunction (so that, in order to) with the infinite as the desired or possible outcome. It is often used with verbs that convey a desire, command, or decision. It occurs frequently in the structure of the canons of Nicaea (8;14;15;13;17): in the event that these or those situations occur, it determines or establishes that . . . ὥστε. In sentence 5 such volition or judgment can be implied in the verb ἐμνήσθημεν or in an implied verb, such as: we have dealt with deaconesses and decided that . . .

[22] From can. 3 it is clear that for the Council of Nicaea, the clergy, besides the bishops, presbyters, and deacons, also included other male categories.

the Paulinist *cheirothesia*, ordination. In the canons of Nicaea *cheirothesia*, ordination, is the same as *cheirotonia*, ordination.[23]

Next, in sentence 5, the synod analyzes another particular case: that of deaconesses who were such without having received *cheirothesia-cheirotonia*; the synod determines that such deaconesses, in any case, should simply be considered laity.

Therefore, the Council is aware that not all deaconesses received *cheirothesia*. But does it presume this only among the Paulinists, or also among the Catholics? Certainly, at least among the Paulinists. From the text one cannot exclude that, according to the Council, the same thing occurred among the Catholics.

Against the interpretation we have explained Kalsbach makes one objection: backing such an interpretation, he says, causes the unverifiable hypothesis of the existence of two types of deaconesses: ordained and not ordained. One can respond, first and foremost, that it is not a matter of a hypothesis but of a fact implied by the same text and without which the text is incomprehensible because it is contradictory.

If one then analyzes the historical context before and after Nicaea, one can notice the following. It is impossible to resolve the question of whether in the *Didascalia* the deaconesses were or were not considered part of the "clergy." But the author certainly considers them to be more important in the Church than the lector who, nevertheless, for the author, belonged to the "dignities." We also know that the *Didascalia* is urging the bishops to resolve to institute a female diaconal ministry in their Churches [dioceses]. This implies that such was not the usual practice. Moreover, the author does not speak of the liturgical ordination of deaconesses but rather presents their ministry as parallel, even if more restricted, to that of the deacons. All of this leads to the conclusion that it is not a rash hypothesis to think that, between the first half of the third

---

[23] One cannot verify that the *cheirothesia* in sentence 5 is a different liturgical act than the *cheirotonia* in sentence 2 and in canons 4, 8, 9, 15, 16. In the ancient documents *cheirotonia* and *cheirothesia* are not infrequently synonyms. Such is the case, for example, in the Council of Chalcedon can. 6: *Sacramentario di Serapione* n. 28 and n. 1 (Funk, ed., *Didiscalia* II p. 190). See C. Vogel, *Chirotonie et chirothésie. Importance et relativité du geste de l'imposition des mains dans la collation des orders*, in *Irénikon* 45 (1972): 7–21; 207–39. Other documents go on to expressly distinguish between *cheirotonia* and *cheirothesia*. See, for example, in *Apostolic Constitutions* VIII 28,2-3. Therefore it must be that the distinction between *cheirotonia* and *cheirothesia*, if it exists, results every time from individual documents.

century and the end of the fourth, that is, between the *Didascalia* and the *Apostolic Constitutions*—where deaconesses appear clearly as members of the clergy and are ordained with the laying on of hands—there was a period of transition: a period in which the practice of ordaining deaconesses and considering them clergy gradually spread but was not necessarily imposed everywhere simultaneously. In this way, the position of the Council of Nicaea, as we have interpreted it, appears normal and logical as evidence, indeed, of such a state of things.

Moreover, as can be seen below with regard to Basil and Epiphanius, still around 374 and among the same Catholics, in Cappadocia deaconesses were not part of the clergy and therefore were not ordained with the laying on of hands. Rather, according to Epiphanius, they were certainly part of the ἐκκλησιαστικὸν τάγμα below the subdeacons and lectors but before exorcists and, according to Gryson,[24] probably received ordination with the laying on of hands. Therefore, it is not an unwarranted hypothesis to suggest that the Nicene legislation in itself and as it was interpreted around 374 allowed for both possibilities.

Finally, in the interpretation offered by Kalsbach and Gryson, it remains an enigma how, from the *Apostolic Constitutions* and subsequently, the usual Greek and Syriac custom, comprised of the great councils such as Chalcedon and Trullo, let alone civil legislation, could have accepted deaconesses who had been ordained and made part of the clergy without ever justifying the contradiction—if they ever did—of the Nicene canon.

The above at least demonstrates that the later tradition was not aware of contradicting a canonical rule of the Council of Nicaea, opposing the ordination of deaconesses and the fact of counting them among the clergy. The author of the *Apostolic Constitutions* in no way gives the impression of innovating anything in canonical practice.

2) Epiphanius of Salamis's understanding of the division of the ministries into two groups: "Hierosyne" [Priesthood] and "after the Hierosyne." The deaconess is not part of the "Hierosyne."

Among the information that we have about deaconesses in the fourth century before the *Apostolic Constitutions*, let us note the following.

From Letter 199 of St. Basil to Amphilochius—the so-called canons of St. Basil[25]—from 375 one can see that for him the deaconess is bound to

---

[24] *Loc. cit.*, 134.
[25] Can. 44 PG 32:370.

remain continent. If she is guilty of violating her "consecration" to a life of chastity, she is bound to do penance and is only to be readmitted to communion after seven years if, in the meanwhile, she has proven herself to be living a chaste life. This demonstrates that for Basil deaconesses are not part of the clergy. Indeed, in antiquity, for a grave fault, clergy were demoted to the laity, but never permitted to do public penance, according to the principle that someone must not be punished twice for the same fault (*Ap. Const.* VIII 47,25).

In the writings of Epiphanius of Salamis one finds a great deal of information about the existence, functions, obligations, and position of deaconesses in the Church.

With regard to the proper ministry of deaconesses, Epiphanius says that this ministry pertains to women when required by decency: "Whenever a woman's body must be undressed, so as not to be seen by men in the sacred duties. . . ."[26]

Deaconesses must either be married to only one man, observing continence, or they must be widows who were only married once, or perpetual virgins. These are the same obligations imposed on bishops, presbyters, deacons, and subdeacons.[27]

According to Epiphanius, deaconesses were certainly "constituted" (καθίστημι).[28] But how? It is likely, but not certain, that Epiphanius was familiar with the ordination of deaconesses by the laying on of hands.[29]

---

[26] *Haer.* 79,3 PG 42:744–45. See also ibid., *Exposit. fid.* 21 PG 42:824–25.

[27] See *Expos. fid.* 21 PG 42:824–25.

[28] Ibid., 824C.

[29] In a letter preserved in Jerome's Latin translation, Epiphanius defends himself against John of Jerusalem—considered by him to be adhering to the "Origenist heresy"—of having ordained (*ordinavimus, ordinavi*) someone a deacon and then presbyter and then having sent him to Palestine to a monastery: *fratrum, et fratrum peregrinorum, qui provinciae tua nihil debuere* (CSEL 54, 396, 4-5). Then, he adds, it seems in order to defend himself from the accusation of having "ordained" deaconesses and likewise sending them to Palestine: *numquam autem ego ordinavi diaconissas et ad alienas misi provincias neque feci quidquam ut ecclesiam scinderem* (ibid., 398, 11-13). The fact that in that letter the Latin uses the same word *ordinavi* for presbyters, deacons, and deaconesses could indicate that the original Greek also used a single term. But one cannot be entirely sure, even if it is likely, that the term was χειροτονέω [ordain] or not, for example, the simple καθίστημι [constitute or appoint]. In the fragments of the Latin translation of Hippolytus completed more or less in the same period as Epiphanius (last quarter of the fourth century, according to Botte): *ordinare* translates as χειροτονεῖν in

The newest thing Epiphanius says is about the relationship between deaconesses and ἱερωσύνη [hierosyne, priesthood]. In Contra Haereses (374–377), Epiphanius says that the highest level (τάξεις) in the Church is comprised of the ἱερωσύνη: "it is like the mother and parent of the other levels."[30] To the ἱερωσύνη belong: bishops, presbyters, deacons, and subdeacons. "After the ἱερωσύνη" are: lectors, deaconesses, exorcists, interpreters, buriers, doorkeepers, and all those upon whom it is incumbent to maintain good order in the Church.

One will note that this is an attempt to distinguish Church ministers according to two neatly divided groups: something more or less analogous to what elsewhere and later was called major and minor orders.

For Epiphanius, therefore, deaconesses are not part of the ἱερωσύνη; it is not for them to exercise clerical functions (ἱερατεύειν).[31] Nevertheless, they belong to the ἐκκλησιαστικὸν τάγμα [ecclesiastical rank].[32] The expression seems to be a general term that covers both ἱερωσύνη or ἱερατικὸν τάγμα [priestly rank],[33] as well as what Epiphanius lists in the Expositio fidei after ἱερωσύνη. Nevertheless it is not clear whether in Epiphanius's use of the term ἐκκλησιαστικὸν τάγμα is the same as κλῆρος or κληρικοί [clergy].[34]

Among the fathers Epiphanius is the one who predominantly developed the argument against the ἱερωσύνη of women in contrast to the practice of some Montanist sects and of the Collyridian sect.[35] He states that among the Montanists: "There are women bishops, presbyters, et cetera because, they say, indeed in Christ there is no difference; neither male nor female."[36]

---

n. 2 p. 4; n. 7 p. 20. At the beginning of n. 8 p. 22 where the Latin has ordinatur (the deacon) Sahidic Coptic has κατίσθαι; but the Sahidic text does not seem to be accurate. Finally, the same n. 8, ordinatur resonates with χειροτονεῖν.

[30] Haer., Exposit. fid. 21 PG 42:821–25.

[31] Haer. 79, 3 PG 42:744.

[32] Ibid. 79, 4 PG 42:745.

[33] Ibid. 75, 7 PG 42:513C.

[34] Rather, it is clear in can. 6 of Chalcedon (451). In Epiphanius and contemporary and earlier authors (see κληρικοί in Lampe's dictionary) the terminology is not univocal, nor are the conclusions about κλῆρος and κληρικοί and the foundations on which they are based. The "clergy" sometimes includes: bishops, presbyters, deacons (Haer. 68, 3 PG 42:189A); sometimes presbyters, deacons, "and others" (ibid. n. 2 PG 42:185A); sometimes they simply seem to be opposed to "laity" or the "crowd" (τάγμα: ibid., col. 186D–188A); sometimes it also seems to include ascetics and "virgins" (ibid., n. 4, col. 189C.).

[35] Haer. 49 and 79 PG 41:880–81; 42:740–56.

[36] Haer. 49,2 PG 41:881A.

Epiphanius's arguments against these abuses amount to the following: 1. the fact that in the Hebrew Bible, the New Testament, and the Christian tradition there is no female priesthood. 2. The main issue is the fact that Christ did not make Mary a priest, nor did he give her the task of baptizing, which he certainly would have done and should have done if he had wanted women priests in the Church. 3. Women are fragile, weak, and rather unintelligent. 4. He turns to some biblical passages: Gen 3:16; 1 Cor 11:8; 14:34; 1 Tim 2:14.

Epiphanius's statements about the role of the deaconess with regard to the ἱερωσύνη raise the problem, among others, of what exactly the concept of ἱερωσύνη is for the bishop of Salamis. Here one wonders in particular about the basis for his assertion that the subdeacon belongs to the ἱερωσύνη and that the lector does not belong to it.[37] It is certainly not because of less "sacred" duties. The subdeacon in the Eastern tradition is rather the equivalent of the acolyte in the Western tradition. One might consider their commitments to continence.

Why isn't the deaconess in the ἱεροσύνη at least equal to or even above the subdeacon? According to Epiphanius himself, her duties pertaining to the baptism of women are, shall we say, more sacred, because they are more sacramental than those of the subdeacon or lector. Also, with regard to continence, the commitments of the deaconess are equal, if not greater than, those of the bishop, presbyter, deacon, and subdeacon. These questions are not resolved by Epiphanius.[38]

III

THE *APOSTOLIC CONSTITUTIONS* (end of the fourth century): THE DEACONESS AS AID TO THE DEACON WITH REGARD TO WOMEN, BUT, AS FOR THE IMPORTANCE OF MINISTRY, SHE IS CLOSER TO THE DEACON THAN TO THE SUBDEACON OR LECTOR, EVEN HAVING THE SAME *CHEIROTONIA*.

---

[37] One can note this in connection to the case of the canons of the Council of Laodicea (343–381). These do not speak of deaconesses. However, the ecclesiastical groups are divided in this way: 1. the ἱερατικοί (ἱερατικὸν τάγμα): presbyters and deacons (the bishop seems to be outside of the list); 2. the others τῆς ἐκκλησιαστικῆς τάξεως = ὑπηρέται [attendants], lectors, singers, exorcists, ushers; 3. the τάγμα τῶν ἀσκητῶν [rank of ascetics]; 4. the laity. See canons 24, 27, 36, 41, 42, 54.

[38] Other information about deaconesses around the end of the fourth century and before the *Apostolic Constitutions* provides some details that are of general interest for the history of the institution. However, they do not offer any new information about our theme. See Gryson, *loc. cit.*, 135–42; 146–50.

Apart from the virgins and widows, the *Apostolic Constitutions* often speak about deaconesses.[39] Then, comparing texts that, in this field, the *AC* have in common with the *Didascalia* and those which they have independently, one can see the difference between the two. The *AC* fundamentally follow the route of the *Didascalia*, but in it the female diaconate appears as a self-evident, common institution in the region for which the *AC* were written, with some details that are more precise compared with the *Didascalia*, especially with a clear rite of *cheirotonia* [ordination] that is accompanied by a precise text.

1) Liturgical functions of the deaconess: baptism of women and the welcome and oversight of women in the liturgical assembly

In the *Didascalia* the function of deaconesses is above all to help the bishop or the presbyter in the baptism of women, because of decency.[40] While it rests with the bishop to anoint the head of every person being baptized, man or woman, by laying his hand on the person's head, and it rests with the deacon to anoint the forehead, and it is the task of the deaconess to anoint the woman's whole body. But only the bishop or the presbyter says the words of invocation (ἐπίκλησις) in which, in order to baptize, he names the Father, Son, and Holy Spirit.[41]

After baptism, the deacon "receives" the men, the deaconess the women.[42]

Compared with the *Didascalia* the *AC* entrust deaconesses with an additional active task in the liturgical gathering: that of welcoming the women who enter the Church, monitoring the respective doors, especially taking care of strangers and the poor and assigning everyone a place if necessary; the deaconess must behave like a ναυστολόγος, that is, as we might say today, like a *steward* or *stewardess* of a ship: work that they share with the porters or even with the subdeacons and deacons.[43]

---

[39] II 26,3-6; 57,10; 58,6; III 8,1; 11,3; 16; 19; VI 17,4; VIII 19-20; 21,2; 28,6-8.
[40] III 16,2,4; VIII 28,6.
[41] III 16,2-4.
[42] III 16,4. The *Apostolic Constitutions* drop what the *Didiscalia* added at this point: it is the task of the deaconess to "receive" the baptized women, and educate and teach them that the seal of baptism cannot be broken, but it must be kept intact in chastity and in holiness. (*Did.* II. 12,3).
[43] See II 57,10; 58,6; VIII 20,1; VIII 11,11.

2) Insistence on and new arguments about the limits of the work of deaconesses

One of the constant concerns of the AC is to define carefully the respective duties of individual ministries.[44] The AC reiterate and emphasize what the *Didascalia* said about the prohibition of women in general "to teach in the Church."[45] By no means did the Lord send women to preach (εἰς τὸ κήρυγμα). It also adds a new argument: "if the man is head of the woman (1 Cor 11:13) it is not right that the rest of the body should govern the head."[46]

This same argument, as well as others, helps the author of the AC to reinforce everything that the *Didascalia* had said about the general prohibition against women baptizing. If it was dangerous and illegal according to the *Didascalia*, for the AC it becomes nothing less than "impious."[47] Why? Here are the reasons:

> 2. If, in fact, "the man is the head of the woman" and the man is elected for the priesthood (προχειρίζεται εἰς ἱερωσύνην), it is not right to disregard the order of creation (δημιουργίαν), and abandon the source (ἀρχή) from which it is derived in favor of the body. In fact, the woman is the body of the man, is taken out of his side and is subjected to him from whom she is derived for the procreation of children. For it is said, in fact, "He shall rule over you." The man is the source (ἀρχή) of the woman and is therefore her head. 3. If as above, therefore, we do not allow women to teach how would it be possible to allow them against nature (παρὰ φύσιν), to fulfill priestly actions (ἱερατεῦσαι)? This is the mistake of the impiety of pagans and not Christ's law: to ordain women priests (ἱερείας χειροτονεῖν) to the goddesses. 4. Had it been necessary to be baptized by women our Lord certainly would have been baptized by his Mother and not by John; or, as he sent us (the Apostles) to baptize, he would have sent together with us women for the same purpose. On the contrary, he never ordered this in any way and he did not hand it down in writing since he knew both the necessities of nature (τὴν ἀκολουθίαν τῆς φύσεως), and the requirements of decency because he is the creator of nature and the legislator of the natural order.[48]

---

[44] See III 10-11; VIII 28,46.
[45] III 6.
[46] III 6,2.
[47] III 9,1.
[48] III 9,1-4.

In comparison with what one reads in the *Didascalia,* what is noteworthy above in the *AC* is the insistence on a new argument: that because of φύσις and δημιουργία, by nature, women are inferior to man and the head of the woman is man, since she was formed from man and made so that he might have children. Now, the author supposes, to teach and to baptize means to exercise superiority. Therefore, these acts are contrary to the nature of woman.

It is also worth noting the reference to the connection between female priesthood and female divinity among the pagans.[49]

However, for the author of the *AC,* baptizing is an act reserved for the bishop or, with the permission of the bishop, for the presbyter. Not only is it impermissible for laypeople to do it,[50] it is not even permissible "for other clergy . . . such as lectors, cantors, porters, attendants (ὑπηρέται), only for bishops and presbyters with the help of deacons."[51]

As a matter of fact, the *AC* have an entire paragraph that seeks to delimit neatly the respective liturgical duties of the bishop, presbyters, deacons, deaconesses, and subdeacons.

> VIII 28, 2: A bishop blesses (εὐλογεῖ), he is not blessed; he lays on hands (χειροτονεῖ), offers [the sacrifice] (προσφέρει), receives the blessings (εὐλογίαι)[52] from the bishops but not from the presbyters; the bishop removes every cleric who deserves to be removed, except for a bishop, whom he cannot remove by himself. 3. The presbyter blesses (εὐλογεῖ), is not blessed, he receives the blessings εὐλογίαι from the bishop or from another presbyter, he extends his hand for the blessing, but he does not impose his hand for the ordination (χειροθετεῖ, οὐ χειροτονεῖ); he does not remove his inferiors, but he excommunicates them if they are liable to such a punishment. 4. The deacon does not bless (εὐλογεῖ); does not issue the blessing εὐλογία, but he receives it from the bishop or from the presbyter;[53] he does not baptize, he does not offer the sacrifice (προσφέρει); but when the bishop or the presbyter have offered the sacrifice he distributes the Eucharist to the people but not as the priest does (ἱερεύς), rather, because he is the servant (διακονούμενος) of

[49] The same fear seems to be underlying in everything Epiphanius says about the Collyridians, *Haer.* 79 PG 42:740–56.

[50] III 10.

[51] III 2,1.

[52] The εὐλογία is what remains of the offerings presented by the faithful for the Mass, which is not consecrated. See VIII 31,2.

[53] However, according to VIII 31,2 the deacon distributes the εὐλογίαι by order of the bishop or the presbyter.

the priests.[54] 5. It is not permitted to anyone among the other clerics to perform what pertains to the deacon. 6. The deaconess does not bless (εὐλογεῖ) and she does not do anything that is done by presbyters and deacons, but it pertains to her to guard the doors and to minister to presbyters in the baptism of women for the sake of decency. 7. The deacon excommunicates the subdeacon, the lector, the cantor, the deaconess if necessary in the absence of the presbyter. 8. The subdeacon is not permitted to excommunicate the lector, nor the cantor, nor the deaconess, nor the cleric, nor a lay person. In fact, they are ministers (ὑπηρέται) to the deacons.

In VIII 46 one notes again clearly how the author of the *AC* was very concerned about the matter of the precise delimitation of hierarchical tasks, especially in the liturgical field. One can see that this insistence has a polemical emphasis, specifically against the tendency of some deacons to overstep the boundaries of their ministry in order to assume presbyteral functions. Canon 18 of Nicaea had already strongly challenged this tendency.

3) The extra-liturgical duties of the deaconesses: to assist women and to be their mediators to the bishop and the deacon.

How, with regard to the work of the deaconess, the *Didascalia* places the primary emphasis on offering assistance to believing women, especially those who are ill and in need.[55] *AC* III.19, which describes the zeal and spirit that must animate the "deacons" in the aforementioned ministry, is addressed equally to deacons and deaconesses in a way that is more explicit and insistent than in the *Didascalia*.

> Let the woman (deaconess) be zealous in taking care of women and let both (deacon and deaconess) be zealous in carrying messages, in traveling away from home, in assisting, in serving, as Isaiah said of the Lord: the righteous one will be justified because he has well served the many. (*Is* 53, 11). Let everyone then recognize his or her proper task, let each accomplish it with zeal, with one mind, with one soul, knowing what is the reward of their service [as deacons and deaconesses.][56]

---

[54] The other duties of the deacon in the Mass are described in VIII 6-15; at vespers and morning prayer in VIII 35,2-39.

[55] III 16,1; 19,1-7.

[56] III 19,1-2.

And so, the rest of the discourse is addressed both to deacons and deaconesses, no less than the recommendation to do everything under the direction of the bishop: "you deacons must visit all those who are in need of a visit and you must report to your bishop about those who are afflicted, since you must be his soul and his mind."[57] All of this considerably emphasizes the parallelism of the deacon for men and the deaconess for women in charitable extra-liturgical ministry as messengers and instruments of the bishop.

Moreover, in the *AC* there appears another extra-liturgical ministry of deaconesses: serving as mediators and accompanying women when they need to speak with the deacon or the bishop: "And as we cannot believe in Christ without the teaching of the Holy Spirit, so let no woman address herself to the deacon or bishop without the deaconess."[58]

4) Deaconesses are clearly part of the clergy

This is certain for the *AC* VIII 31,2: "the deacons, at the behest of the bishop or of the presbyters, distribute to the clergy the offerings that remain from the mystical oblations: to the bishop, four parts; to the presbyter, three parts; to the deacon, two parts; and to the rest of the sub-deacons, or readers, or singers, or deaconesses: one part."

Deaconesses are ordained by *cheirotonia* just as is the bishop, the presbyter, the deacon, the subdeacon, and the lector. Neither virgins, nor widows, nor exorcists receive *cheirotonia*, ordination.[59]

On the rank of the deaconess among the other clergy one observes the following: according to the *AC* VIII 28,2-8, especially 7 and 8, the deaconess is clearly included, along with the subdeacons, lectors, and cantors, among the attendants (ὑπηρέται) of the deacon. The deaconess as attendant of the deacon in ministry to women also emerges from II 26,6. Here the statement of the *Didascalia* that the deaconess is the image

---

[57] III 19,7.

[58] II 26,6. The bishop is the image of the Father, the deacon of Christ, the deaconess of the Holy Spirit.

[59] In the extant text of the *Apostolic Constitutions* the subdeacon is noted only once in book 8, which, on the other hand, is not familiar with the porters who appear in books 2, 3, and 6. While the *Didascalia* is familiar with the subdeacon, books 2, 3, and 6 of the *Apostolic Constitutions*, mention the ὑπηρέται, unknown to book 8 (since VIII 28,8 does not seem pertinent). In conclusion: in terms of the name, function, and rank of subdeacons, porters, and the ὑπηρέται, there does not seem to be unity in the *Apostolic Constitutions*.

of the Holy Spirit is explained in this way: while the bishop is the image of the Father, the deacon is the image of Christ: because as Christ served the Father and did nothing without him, so, too, the deacon serves the bishop and may do nothing without him. The deacon ess is the image of the Holy Spirit: "because she neither says nor does anything without the deacon, just as the paraclete neither says nor does anything alone, except to glorify Christ, he abides by his will."

One cannot obtain a firm answer for the further question of whether deaconesses who have the rank of clergy according to the *AC*, come right after deacons, subdeacons, or even after the other clergy.[60]

5) What is the nature of the *cheirotonia* ordination of deaconesses in the *AC*?

a) *The cheirotonia ordination of deaconesses*. The *AC* VIII 28,1-3 distinguish very neatly χειροτονία, χειροθεσία, εὐλογία. Only the bishop can do all three of these. The presbyter can do the second and the third, but not the first. The deacon (and even more so for those after him) cannot do even the third. *Cheirotonia* is the same as ἐπίθεσις τῶν χειρῶν (*AC* III 10,2; VIII 46,9), that is to say: a laying on of hands with physical contact. *Cheirothesia* is an extension of the hand without physical contact with the one being blessed (*AC* VIII 37, 4.39, I). The εὐλογία seems to be a simple prayer or formula for benediction that can also be done without the extension of hands over the one involved, since the author of the *AC* insists that the deacon is permitted to do "neither *cheirothesia*, nor εὐλογία, neither minor nor major" (VIII 46,11. Cf. III 10,1).

The deaconess is made through *chierotonia*, that is to say by ἐπίθεσις τῶν χειρῶν [laying on of hands] strictly reserved only for the bishop (VII 19,2; III 11,3).

During this rite the "presbyter, the deacons and the deaconesses" must be present (VIII 19.2).

---

[60] A series of texts place the deaconesses right after the deacons and before the subdeacons; above all in the order in which the various ordinations are presented: bishops, presbyters, deacons, deaconesses (VIII 19), subdeacons, and lectors. VIII 2-8 has: bishop, presbyter, deacon, deaconess, subdeacon; in III 11,3 it says "we do not allow the presbyter to ordain with the laying on of hands (χειροτονεῖν) neither deacons nor deaconesses, lectors, ὑπηρέται, cantors, nor doorkeepers." But in other texts deaconesses are named after all of the male members of the clergy: II 26,3; VI 17,1-4; VIII 28,7-8. See especially VIII 31,2-3.

The following is the blessing that the bishop says over the deaconess:

> O, Eternal God, Father of our Lord Jesus Christ, creator of man and of woman, you who have filled with your Spirit Miriam and Deborah, Anna and Hulda; you who have not deemed it unworthy that your only begotten Son be born of a woman; you who instituted women as guardians of the holy parts of the tent of the covenant and of the temple; You, even now, look upon this [female] servant of yours elected to the diaconate; grant her the Holy Spirit and purify her from all sins of the flesh and of the spirit: so that she might fulfill the task entrusted to her for your glory and for the glory of your Christ, with whom and with the Holy Spirit, glory and adoration be to you and forever and ever.

Therefore, the above is substantially a prayer that the deaconess might receive the gift of the Holy Spirit in order to fulfill worthily the ministry of the diaconate that was entrusted to her. However, other than door-keeping, what this ministry consists of does not emerge. But, as usually occurs in the liturgy—as with Hippolytus' *Apostolic Tradition*—the ministry of deaconesses is seen against the background of salvation history: inasmuch as one reads in the Old Testament and New Testament about instances in which the movement of God, now done in the Church, in its own way appears to be ongoing. In the Old Testament, the aforementioned prayer refers to the prophetesses and to the female doorkeepers in the tent of the Covenant and the temple (Exod 38:8; 1 Sam 2:22). For the New Testament, recall that the Son of God did not find disdain in being born of a woman.

One could wonder why the prayer makes no mention of the case of Phoebe (Rom 16:1-2), nor of 1 Timothy 3:11, nor numerous other and important liturgical and extra-liturgical tasks that the *Apostolic Constitutions* also identify with the deaconess. On the whole, the theology of this prayer is poorer than the theology that results from the picture of the deaconess illustrated in the *Apostolic Constitutions*. This possibly confirms that the aforementioned prayer is not an innovation on the part of the author of the same *Constitutions*.

b) *Comparison between the* cheirotonia *[ordination] of deaconesses and other ministers.* We have already observed above that the author of the *AC* distinguishes clearly between the *cheirotonia* of deaconesses and the "constitution" of virgins and widows. These latter do not receive *cheirotonia*; they do not belong to the clergy. Virginity and widowhood, for the *Apostolic Constitutions*, are not ministries but ascetic and spiritual states of life (VIII 24.25). Not even the exorcist receives *cheirotonia*; it is a charism in the modern sense, not a ministry (VIII 26).

There is no agreement among the extant text of the *Apostolic Constitutions* in the number of the ministers who are subordinate to the subdeacon, nor of the reality of whether these do or do not receive *cheirotonia*. In books II–VII the ministers are: the bishop, presbyter, deacon, deaconess, attendant (ὑπηρέτης), the cantor (ψάλτης, ᾠδός, ψαλτῳδός), the usher (πυλωρός).[61] According to III 11,3, all of these receive the *cheirotonia* that is reserved only for the bishop: "we do not allow presbyters, but only bishops to give *cheirotonia* (χειροτονεῖν) to the deacons, or the deaconesses, or the lectors, or other attendants, or cantors or ushers; this is the rule (τάξις) and ecclesiastical harmony."

On the other hand, in book VIII, the list is: bishop, presbyter, deacon, deaconess, subdeacon (ὑποδιάκονος, which seems to be the same as the ὑπηρέτης of earlier books), and lector. They all receive *cheirotonia* (VIII 16-22). The ushers no longer appear in book VIII. The deacons, deaconesses, and subdeacons now guard the doors (VIII 11,11; 20,1). Rather, the same book frequently speaks about cantors (10,10; 12,43; 13,14; 28,7-8; 31,2; 47,26.43.69). And it is certainly the case that also in book VIII, the cantors are clergy distinct from lectors (VIII 31,2; 47,26). But here it does not speak of ordination, let alone the *cheirotonia* of cantors.

The above is further evidence of the nature of compilation of the extant text of the *AC*, which is not always consistent.

Between the *cheirotonia* of the deaconess and that of the bishop, presbyter, deacon, subdeacon, and lector in book VIII of the *AC*, one cannot find any difference with regard to the minister (bishop), the act of the laying on of hands and the general structure of the prayer that accompanies it. In that respect, it would not make sense, with regard to book VIII, to distinguish between major orders and minor orders among the aforementioned ministers, or even between sacraments and sacramentals.

However, it is important to guard against, with the typical Western mentality, the *a priori* belief that if one cannot find any distinction among the various *cheirotonia*, ordinations, in regard to the aforementioned points, the question is thus resolved in the sense that, in reality, such a distinction was not made. One cannot rule out, *a priori*, that such a distinction came to be perceived and expressed in other circumstances of the same rite.[62]

---

[61] The order of these is not always the same. III 2,1 has: lector, ψάλτης, usher ὑπηρέτης. In III 2,3: deacon, deaconess, lector, ὑπηρέτης, cantor, usher.

[62] From a text by Theodore of Mopsuestia (350–428), we know that it was prohibited to ordain subdeacons and lectors in front of the altar, as instead one was supposed to do for the bishop, presbyter and deacon. See below and pages 136–37.

In fact, in the text of the *AC* itself, one must attend to the following points: The bishop is ordained by two or three other bishops in the presence of the presbyterate and the ministry of the deacons (VIII 4,6; 47,1). The presbyter is ordained only by the bishop in the presence of the presbyters and deacons (VIII 16,2). The deacon is ordained by the bishop alone in the presence of the presbyterate and the deacons (VIII 17,2). The deaconess is ordained only by the bishop in the presence of the presbyterate, deacons, and deaconesses (VIII 19,2). The subdeacon and the lector are ordained by the bishop alone, but nothing is said about the presence or absence of the presbyterate, deacons, deaconesses, sub-deacons, or lectors (VIII 21.22). This detail should capture our attention. We know, in fact, from the earliest euchologies (eighth through eleventh centuries) that the ordination of subdeacons and lectors, in contrast to that of bishops, presbyters, deacons, and deaconesses, was done in the *diakonikón*, that is to say the sacristy, and not in public in front of the altar in the sanctuary. The fact that it was not done in the sanctuary in front of the altar, as occurred, rather, for the bishops, presbyters, and deacons, is testified to be a law by Theodore of Mopsuestia, a contemporary of the *AC*.[63] Therefore, there is legitimate suspicion that there is a trace of this same law in the *AC* when in the ordination of subdeacons and lectors the text is silent about the presence of the presbyterate, deacons, subdeacons, and lectors. Equally, there is legitimate suspicion that when the *AC* direct the ordination of the deaconess to occur in front of the presbyterate, deacons, and deaconesses (VIII 19,2), the text presupposes that such ordinations be done in public and at the foot of the altar within the sanctuary, as those of bishops, presbyters, and deacons. However, even with regard to the presence of the presbyterate, deacons, and deaconesses, the ordination of deaconesses in the *AC* appears to be assimilated more with that of the presbyters and deacons than with that of the subdeacons and lectors.

Furthermore, one must pay attention to the extent and importance of the ministerial work that was assigned in each respective *cheirotonia*. Now, according to the *AC*, the work of the deaconess is certainly inferior to that of the deacon, even if parallel to the same, because she is the aid of the deacon in ministry to women. But her work is much higher than that of the subdeacon and lectors, even if the deaconess, as a woman, did not read Scripture in the public assemblies. From this point of view,

[63] See below and pages 136–37.

the *cheirotonia* of deaconesses in the *AC* appears even closer to that of the deacon than to that of the subdeacon.[64]

Regarding the obligations of celibacy and continence, the *AC* require more from the deaconess than from the other clergy, presbyters and lower. According to the *AC* VI 17,1-4 the deaconess must be a "pure virgin or otherwise a monogamous widow, faithful and honorable" (VI 17,4), while after ordination the attendants (ὑπηρέται), cantors, lectors, and doorkeepers may still marry. According to *AC* VIII 47,26 the only clergy who can still marry after their ordination are the lectors and cantors, but no longer the subdeacons. Presbyters, deacons, and subdeacons were not permitted to marry after ordination, but if married they could continue to live regularly in matrimony (II 2,3; VIII 47,5.51).

IV

THE BYZANTINE TRADITION AFTER THE *AC*: DEACONESSES WITHIN THE CLERICAL SYSTEM WITH *CHEIROTONIA* OF THE SAME KIND AND MEANING AS THE *CHEIROTONIA* OF THE DEACON, NOTWITHSTANDING THEIR MORE RESTRICTED POWERS—AS THEIR ORDER BECOMES MORE AND MORE SOLELY HONORIFIC—AND THE IMPOSSIBILITY OF THEIR BEING ADMITTED TO THE PRESBYTERATE.

For our topic, the Byzantine tradition after the *AC* is particularly interesting.[65] Here in the Greek tradition the position of the deaconesses,

---

[64] From a theoretical point of view it will be noted that the fact of being a helper to the deacon and of having less extensive duties than he is not an argument against the nature of sacrament of the female diaconate. The presbyter, too, is a helper to the bishop with duties less extensive than his and the deacon is the helper of the bishop and presbyter. Even in the New Testament, presbyterate and diaconate appear by divisions and subdivisions of the duties of an initially unique and full ministry: the apostolate.

[65] The principal documents for our information are: the Council of Chalcedon, the second Council of Trullo from 692, the civil nomocanonical law, historical information and various epigraphs. According to the surveys done by Kalsbach (pp. 55–56), the documents attest to the diffusion of the institution of the deaconesses after the fourth century for the following Greek Orthodox provinces: Antioch, Syria to Northeast Antioch, Cappadocia, Seleucia to Calycadno, Pontus, Caria, Phrygia and Pisidia, the Hellespont, Armenia Minor (Roman province), Jerusalem (but there, at the end of the sixth century the institute had disappeared). For

which becomes clearer on many levels as evidenced from the *AC*, reaches its greatest development before its definitive decline between the eleventh and twelfth centuries.

1) Conditions, obligations, tasks of deaconesses and their place among the clergy

Deaconesses could be elected either from the laity—provided that they were virgins or monogamous widows—or from among the constituted virgins, canonical widows, or even from simple nuns or abbesses. In fact, in Byzantine history, the deaconesses were often nuns or abbesses. At least around the eleventh century that was the custom.[66] However, the diaconate of women, as such, was clearly distinct from the aforementioned states of life.

According to the Theodosian Codex of 390,[67] the deaconesses had to be at least sixty years old, in reference to 1 Timothy 5:9. Canon 15 of the Council of Chalcedon in 451 determined that they be no younger than forty.[68] Justinian's *Novella* 6,6 of 535 said they should be about fifty.[69]

Byzantium there is ample documentation in ecclesiastical and civil law and in various other historical sources (Kalsbach, pp. 64–68). In the Byzantine Church the institution of the deaconesses continued until at least the end of the twelfth century. See Kalsbach, p. 65, n. 10. Texts by the canonists T. Balsamon (1140–1195) and M. Blastares from 1335 in Mayer, *loc. cit.*, pp. 63–64, 58–59, 65–66. In Theodorou, *loc. cit.*, Θεολογία (1954), a text by Anna Comnena on the care that her father Alexius I Comnenus (1081–1118) took of the deaconesses. See on p. 580 the rubrics of euchologion between the eleventh and fourteenth centuries.

[66] See, for example, the rubric of the Parisian Coisliniano 213 of the eleventh century (and also of the twelfth- or thirteenth-century Codex Athenian *Ethn. Bibl.* 662) introduces the rite for the ordination of deaconesses: "Order for the *cheirotonia* of the deaconess, who must be at least forty years old, a pure virgin and, according to the practice that is now in force, a great *schema* [highest ranking] nun (μονάζουσα μεγαλοσχημῶν)." See Theodorou, Θεολογία (1954), 580. M Blastares attests likewise around 1355, referring to ancient texts. See Mayer, *loc. cit.*, 580. See also Kalsbach, *loc. cit.*, 54–55, 67–68.

[67] XVI 2,27. See Mayer, *loc. cit.*, 16. Around the same period Theodore of Mopsuestia rejected this interpretation of 1 Tim. 5:9. See H. B. Swete, *Theodori M. in ep. B. Pauli Com.* (Cambridge, 1882): 158–59.

[68] See Mayer, *loc. cit.*, 28.

[69] Ibid., 35.

For those who attempted matrimony after their ordination, church law called for excommunication; the civil law of Justinian decreed the death penalty.[70] According to the general law established by canon 6 of the Council of Chalcedon,[71] "absolute" ordinations of deaconesses were not permitted; each time they had to be ordained for a specific church, or *martyrion* or monastery. From Justinian (527–565) to Heraclius (610–640) the Great Church of Hagia Sophia in Constantinople had forty deaconesses.[72] For their ecclesiastical service (ἐκκλησιαστικὴ ὑπηρεσία), they were financially supported by the respective Church.[73]

In Justinian's *Novella* 6,6 from 535, their tasks were described in this way: "to serve at sacred baptisms and to be present at other secret things, they customarily perform in the venerable mysteries."[74] But what are these "other secret things that they customarily perform in the venerable mysteries"? Much later, the canonist T. Balsamon (1140–1195), attesting that, in his time, there was no longer an ordination of deaconesses, says that when they existed "they [the deaconesses] also had a proper place (βαθμὸν) inside the sanctuary (βῆμα)."[75] Another late author, of the fourteenth century, M. Blastares (c. 1335), reports on the tasks of deaconesses who, according to the opinion of some, when they existed, "were authorized to enter near the holy altar and who, alongside the deacons, performed the tasks of the deacons."[76] However, aside from the responsibility for the baptism of women, the aforementioned statements are not confirmed in the documents.[77]

---

[70] Council of Chalcedon Can. 15 (See Mayer, *loc. cit.*, 28). Justinian, see Mayer, *loc. cit.*, 35–37; 38; 39.

[71] See *Conciliorum Oecumenicorum Decreta* p. 66.

[72] *Novella* 3,1 of 535 (Mayer, *loc. cit.*, 34–35); Fozio, *Syntagma* 30 (ibid., 63).

[73] *Novella* 123,30 of 546 (Mayer, *loc. cit.*, 38).

[74] Mayer, *loc. cit.*, 36.

[75] See Mayer, *loc. cit.*, 64. The same author adds that, in his time, deaconesses were still ordained (προχειρίζω therefore = order) in Constantinople, but that they did not have access to the βῆμα, but: "In many things they attend to ecclesiastical work (ἐκκλησιάζω) and they direct the gatherings in women's convents."

[76] Mayer, *loc. cit.*, 66.

[77] In the Byzantine period, one no longer finds mentioned, as a duty of deaconesses, to look after the doors of the Church at least to allow women to enter—the duty about which the *AC* speak and which in Pseudo Ignatius (fourth–fifth centuries; *Ad. Antioch* XII 2: see Mayer, *loc. cit.*, 33) stands out as a hallmark of deaconesses. Rather, the duty of looking after the doors appears specific to the

Furthermore, as the baptism of adults gradually ended, the institution of deaconesses also became less common, and where it still continued for some time, it became purely honorific, granted to women of high rank or to nuns and abbesses of monasteries.[78]

Deaconesses, clearly considered part of the clergy along with presbyters, deacons, subdeacons, lectors, and cantors, come right after the deacons in the official lists in which the individual ranks of the clergy are named.[79] It was believed that having received "holy ordination" (τὴν ἱερὰν χειροτονίαν), they constituted a "holy order" (ἱερὰ τάξις) and were part of the ἱερωσύνη.[80] According to the Justianic legislation, among these same clerics, besides deaconesses, the group of ἱερωσύνη always seems to have included only presbyters, deacons, and subdeacons.[81]

---

subdiaconate in the related rite of ordination. See the texts published by J. Morinus, *Commentarius de sacris ecclesiae ordinationibus*, 2nd ed. (Antwerp, 1695), 1:58, 66, 68, 75, 79. See also J. Goar, *Euchologion*, 2nd ed. (Venice, 1730), 203.

[78] See Kalsbach, *loc. cit.*, 68–69.

[79] *Novella* 3,1: Mayer, *loc. cit.*, 34–35. In this official list the doorkeepers are also named, but as a group that is clearly distinct from the clergy. See also Kalsbach, *loc. cit.*, 67–68.

[80] Justinian's *Novella* 6,6 (Mayer, *loc. cit.*, 37). In the *Novella* 123,30 (Mayer, *loc. cit.*, 36) the ministry of the deaconess is called ἱερὰ διακονία [sacred service]. With regard to the obligation of deaconesses not to marry after ordination, it says "It is a necessity that all of the venerable deaconesses who are ordained (χειροτονεῖν), from the moment of *cheirotonia*, be cautioned . . . that they, too, must fear God . . . and fear and be ashamed of falling from the holy order (τῆς ἱερᾶς ἐκπεσεῖν τάξεως) knowing that if they ventured to be ashamed of the ordination (*cheirotonia*) or to abandon that holy ordination (τὴν ἱερὰν χειροτονίαν) or to choose, in any case, another, wicked way of life, they will be subject to death. . . . If, in fact, in the ancient laws, those who, because of their deceit, were called virgins (= vestals), they were subject to death if they had become corrupted: how much more must we require the same punishment with regard to chastity for those who have true knowledge of God, so that they safeguard what suits nature and respect that which is required for priesthood (τό τε ὀφειλόμενον τῇ ἱερωσύνῃ τηροῖεν)" (*Novella* 6,6).

[81] According to the lexicon by Lampe, in ancient Christian literature, ἱερωσύνη as it applies to Christians, means: 1. the bishops (*AC* II 34.4; Council of Sardis canon 10); 2. the presbyterate; 3. the major orders in general (Epiphanius, *Expos. fidei* 21 PG 95:296A; Theodoret, Phil., I. i. GCS 3,445; Pseudo Dionysius *EH* I. i. [PG 3:372B]). While, for Epiphanius, the ἱερωσύνη means only bishop, presbyter, deacon, and subdeacon (see above and notes 30–34) and the deaconess is excluded, the Justinian legislation includes the deaconess, but it does not seem to admit lectors and cantors. In fact, if the inability to marry after ordination

Consequently, the deaconesses were placed under a special nomocanonical law, as were the clerics.[82]

2) The Byzantine rite for the *cheirotonia*, ordination, of deaconesses and its significance in relationship to the other *cheirotonia*, ordinations

This deals with the rite initially established in the Greek Barberini Codex 336 called the "Barberini Euchology," of the eighth century, and then, with some slight variations in the rubrics, from a series of codices up until the fourteenth century.[83]

a) *The rite and the texts.*

> *Prayer for the ordination* (χειροτονία) *of deaconesses. When the holy anaphora has ended and the doors (of the sanctuary) have been opened, before the deacon says "remembering all of the saints. . . ," the one who is to be ordained* (ἡ μέλλουσα χειροτονεῖσθαι) *is brought to the pontiff [bishop] who says in a loud voice "the divine grace. . . ."* [84] *Meanwhile she bows her head and the pontiff [bishop] places his hand on her head and, making three crosses, says the following prayer:*

> O holy and omnipotent God, who have sanctified the woman through the birth in the flesh of your only begotten Son our Lord: you who have given the grace and poured out your Holy Spirit not

---

is required of the ἱερωσύνη, this obligation even according to the canons of the Apostles (*AC* VIII 47,26), did not bind the cantors and lectors. If that is true, only in a later period does the idea that subdeacon and lector are also part of the ἱερωσύνη assert itself within the Byzantine tradition. In the euchologion said to be that of Allazio (Morinus, *loc. cit.*, I. p. 87B; and Goar p. 197) the lectorate is called: "the first rank within the ἱερωσύνη."

[82] Primarily the quoted regulations of Theodosius and Justinian. See Mayer, *loc. cit.*, 15–16; 34–40.

[83] In Morinus, *loc. cit.*, the Barberinian texts are transcribed, as well as the *Grottaferrata* codex (*Gb. I* twelfth–thirteenth centuries) and a twelfth-century Vatican codex. (Morinus I pp. 56–57; 65; 80–81). In Theodorou, Θεολογία (1954), 578–81, there is a review of seven codices. The most interesting for the rubrics is from the Parisian Coislinian codex (Coislin. gr. 213) from the eleventh century (and the Athenian *Ethn. Bibl.* 662 from the twelfth–thirteenth centuries). See also Goar, *loc. cit.*, 218–19.

[84] The complete formula: "The divine grace, which always heals what is weak and replaces what is flawed, promote (προχειρίζεται) [name] to deaconess. Therefore we pray for her, that the grace of the most Holy Spirit might descend upon her."

only to men but also to women: You, even now, O Lord, look upon this servant of yours and call her to the work of your diaconate and send forth in abundance the gift of your Holy Spirit. Keep her in the true faith and may she fulfill everything in her ministry (λειτουργίαν) in an irreprehensible way of life according to your approval because to you, Father, Son, and Holy Spirit, are due all glory, honor, and adoration, now and forever, world without end. Amen.

And after the Amen, one of the deacons prays in this way:

In peace let us pray to the Lord (*Response*: Kyrie eleison).

For heavenly peace and for the well-being of the whole world, let us pray to the Lord.

For the peace of the whole world, let us pray to the Lord.

For our archbishop N., for his priesthood, for his preservation, peace, health, and salvation and for the work of his hands, let us pray to the Lord.

For N. who is now being made a deaconess (ὑπὲρ τῆς νῦν προχειριζομένης διακονήσσης τῆσδε),[85] for her salvation, let us pray to the Lord.

That the merciful God may grant her an immaculate and irreproachable diaconate, let us pray to the Lord.

For our devout emperor who is loved by God.

So that we may be freed from every danger and need, let us pray to the Lord.

Help us, save us, have pity on us and guard us with your grace, O God.

While the deacon is saying this prayer, the bishop laying his hand on the hand of she who is to be ordained (τῆς χειροτονουμένης), *prays in this way:*

Lord and Ruler, who does not reject women who dedicate themselves and who wish to serve properly in your holy dwellings, but receive them in the order of ministers (ἐν τάξει λειτουργῶν): grant your Holy Spirit to this servant of yours who wishes to dedicate herself to you and to fulfill the office (χάρις) of the diaconate, as you granted the grace (χάρις) of the diaconate to Phoebe whom you called to the work of ministry (λειτουργίας). Grant her, O Lord, to persevere without sin in your holy temples, to conduct herself properly, and especially care for her continence and make her perfect as your

---

[85] τῆσδε is missing in Goar's text. See Theodorou, Θεολογία (1954), 576. For the sense of προχειρίζω see above p. 104, n. 8.

servant so that even she, when she is before Christ's tribunal she may receive the just reward for her conduct; for the mercy and the goodness of your only begotten Son through whom you are blessed.

After the response "Amen," the bishop places the diaconal stole (ὡράριον) around her neck, under her veil (μαφόριον), bringing forward the two ends. Then the deacon who stands at the ambo says:

"remembering all the saints, etc."

After the deaconess has received the Body and Blood of Christ, the archbishop gives her the holy chalice; she receives it and places it on the altar.[86]

Now let us see what can be learned about the meaning of the *cheirotonia*, ordination, of deaconesses from the texts and rites and from the general context for the ordination of other ministers.

b) *Cheirotonia in the ordination of deaconesses as in the other ordinations.* The ordination of deaconesses is called *cheirotonia.* During the two prayers the bishop "places his hand on her head" (ἐπιθέτεσει τὴν χεῖρα, ἔχει τὴν χεῖρα . . .).

A particular tradition in the canonical and didactic documents of the Greek and Byzantine Church explicitly distinguished *cheirotonia* and *cheirothesia*: attributing only to *cheirotonia* what today we call ordination and considering *cheirothesia* as an εὐλογία or blessing.[87]

---

[86] Among the information about the rite for the ordination of deaconesses that might come from non-liturgical sources, that of M. Blastares from about 1335 is interesting. It attests that, according to the ancient codices on the deaconess: "one does everything that one does on the deacons with few exceptions." She is led to the sacred altar and covered with the veil (μαφορίῳ) been said: 'Divine grace, which always heals what is weak,' she does not genuflect on either knee, but only bows her head. The pontiff [bishop] places his hand on her head and prays that she might be able to fulfill without fault the work of the deaconess, observing chastity and honesty in her conduct, safeguarding the holy temples; but he does not permit her to serve in the pure mysteries or to handle the *ripidion* (= the small liturgical fan that the deacon is appointed to wave slowly over the chalice after the consecration), as does the deacon. After this the pontiff [bishop] places the deacon's stole (ὡράριον) around her neck, under the veil, bringing it back around across the chest. At the time of Communion, the pope shares with her the sacred mysteries, after the deacon. After this she receives the chalice from the hands of the Pope, however she does not distribute it, but places it right away on the holy altar." (See in Mayer, *loc. cit.*, 58–59.)

[87] See the brief documentation of this fact in Vogel, *Chirotonie*, 7–12. "The ritual distinction between *cheirotonia* for the orders and *cheirothesia* for subordinate

In reality, from the fact that the ordination of deaconesses is called *cheirotonia* and that the gesture that accompanies it is an ἐπίθεσις of the hand, one cannot conclude anything about the nature of such an ordination compared with that of other ministries. According to the texts published by Morinus[88] of the seven ancient euchologies which have in a way more or less the complete series of "ordinations," one can see that: for the bishop, presbyter, deacon, and subdeacon, as well as for the deaconess, the title of the rite is *cheirotonia* and the gesture is ἐπίθεσις of the hand; the same is true for the lector, except that twice in the title προχείρησις is mentioned instead of *cheirotonia*; the "ordination" of the abbot is called προχείρησις (which can mean: promotion) and four out of five times it has the ἐπίθεσις of the hand.

Regarding the title *cheirotonia* and the act of the laying on of the hand, the ordination of the deaconess might be related as much to that of the deacon (presbyter and bishop), as to that of the subdeacon and lector.

The same must be said if one considers the general content of what is asked of God for the ordinand in the ordination: it is always about the gifts of God, of the Holy Spirit, which allow the one being ordained to carry out well the duties of his or her ministry.

From other features, however, the Byzantine ordination of deaconesses is clearly distinguished from that of the subdeacons and lectors—and

---

functions of the clerical course of advancement was done gradually only from the eighth century and following and appears clearly only in the juridical documents or of a didactic nature. . . . After Zonaras (c. 1150) and Balsamon (1140–1195)— and despite some hesitation in these two important commentators—*cheirotonia* and *cheirothesia* stabilize: the first term remains reserved for the laying on of hands done by the bishop to the presbyter and deacon; the second indicates the gesture of blessing for the creation of subordinate functionaries. . . . However it suffices to open the liturgical books, especially the Euchologion in order to observe that the cultic language did not follow the juridical or didactic diversification about which we have spoken. The term *cheirotonia* applies as much (in the sequence of the Euchologion) to the ordination of the deacon, presbyter, and bishop as much as to the laying on of hands by which means the bursar of a monastery, the lector, cantor and subdeacon are introduced to their functions. The laying on of hands—whether called *cheirotonia* or *cheirothesia*—is, in the East, part of the ritual for *all* levels of the hierarchy, even of the subordinates, contrary to the Latin custom" (ibid., 10–12).

[88] I .p. 54–102. One notices, however, that the final euchologion, by Allazio also noted by Morinus, *loc. cit.*, 85, seems to represent not the Byzantine tradition, but the Greek Melkite Antiochene and Syrian Churches.

all the more from that of the other "dignities," such as that of the arch-deacon, abbot, etc.—and is related to that of the deacons, presbyters, and bishops.

c) *Ordination at the foot of the altar* within the sanctuary is obligatory for deaconesses just as it is for the bishop, presbyter, and deacon, and it is prohibited for the subdeacon and lector.

According to the oldest euchology, the eighth-century Barberini Codex (*Codex Barb. gr.* 336), and that of twelfth-/thirteenth-century *Grottaferrata Gb I*, the ordination of the subdeacon is done in the διακονικόν, that is, the sacristy.[89] The later euchologies say that the ordination of the subdeacon is done "either in the diakonikón, or in front of the great doors of the temple."[90] The great doors of the temple seem to be those at the entrance of the Church, in the back, facing the altar. According to Goar,[91] the ancient Venetian editions of the euchology say that when a subdeacon is ordained: "the Pontiff [bishop] is on the throne in the exterior vestibule, where he vests for the liturgy." The text of the ordination published by Goar[92] says that in ordaining a subdeacon the Pontiff [bishop] "sits by the beautiful door," that is, again it seems, at the entrance door to the nave. With re-gard to the current custom, I myself have assisted more than once at the ordination of subdeacons done at the *solea* of the central door that leads to the sanctuary, but always outside the sanctuary itself. I would not be able to say whether such is the general custom, nor when it was introduced.

This is how this matter evolved: in the ancient Church, at least until the eleventh or twelfth century, the place for ordination of the subdeacon was the sacristy, thus the ordination was semi-private in nature. And then it moved: either into the atrium of the Church; or inside the Church, but in the back next to the entrance doors; and finally, to the main door of the sanctuary. However, it always remained and still remains carefully outside of the sanctuary.

The same occurred and still occurs for the ordination of the lector or cantor.

From this point of view, Byzantine ordinations are divided into two groups: those that occur at the foot of the altar inside the sanctuary:

---

[89] Morinus I, *loc. cit.*, 74, 79; Goar, *loc. cit.*, 204.

[90] Coislinian codex of the eleventh century (Coisl. gr. 213). See Morinus, *loc. cit.*, 68, 74. See also pp. 79, 87.

[91] Goar, *loc. cit.*, 204.

[92] Goar, *loc. cit.*, 203. Also, *The Euchologion* (Rome, 1873), 130.

bishop, presbyter, deacon, deaconess; and those that do not occur at the foot of the altar and are outside the sanctuary: subdeacon, lector, cantor, as well as "ordinations" to other "dignities" (archdeacon, abbot, etc.).

At this point two questions arise: (1) when can one document this distinction; (2) did it have a clear theological significance in the Byzantine ecclesiastical tradition?

Here there is a fundamental and so far as I know unstudied text by Theodore of Mopsuestia (born in Antioch c. 350, and died in Mopsuestia in Cilicia in 428, contemporaneous with the AC and with John Chrysostom) that in my opinion can help. With regard to 1 Timothy 3:8-15, Theodore says:

> It is worth adding that we should not wonder why (Paul) mentions neither subdeacons nor lectors. In fact, they are not grades of the Church (τῶν γὰρ τῇ τῆς ἐκκλησίας λειτουργίᾳ βαθμῶν ἔξωθεν μᾶλλον οὗτοί εἰσιν): they were created subsequently because of the necessities that were to be fulfilled by other ministers for the good of the many faithful. Therefore the law does not allow them to receive the *cheirotonia* before the altar (ὅθεν οὐδὲ νενόμισθαι αὐτοὺς πρὸ τοῦ θυσιαστηρίου τὴν χειροτονίαν δέχεσθαι) because they do not minister to the mystery; rather the lectors do the readings and the subdeacons within [the sanctuary][93] take care of what is needed for the service of the deacons, and also take care of the lighting of the church, because only the presbyters fulfill the ministry of the mystery. The first ones fulfill their priestly office, the second ones minister to the sacred things.[94]

[93] The Latin version from the sixth century (see subsequent note) says "*intra diaconicum.*"

[94] *Theodori episcopi mopsuestiani in ep. B. Pauli Commentarii*, ed. H. B. Swete (Cambridge, 1882), 2:132–34. The text is preserved in its whole in an African Latin version from the sixth century. Until the mark + it also has the Greek text from the series of excerpts. The Latin text was noted in the East in the ninth century. Rabanus Maurus cites it (*Enar. In ep. Pauli*, lib. 23 *In ep. I ad Tim* cap. 3 PL 112:607C–D) and also Amalarius who attributes it to Ambrose, *Liber officialis* II 6 n.2 (ed. Hanssens II 213–14). Note: the same practice, around the same period, seems to be confirmed by a passage from the Council *ad Quercum* from 403, in which, among the other accusations made against John Chrysostom, the thirteenth was: that "he had ordained presbyters and deacons without being at the altar" (See Hefele-Leclercq, *Hist. des conc.* II/I p. 144). It says nothing about the ordinations of lectors and subdeacons, probably, indeed, because these were not done at the altar.

From this text one can see that the theory that is later defended by Symeon of Thessalonica[95]—aside from his terminology, which opposes *cheirotonia* and *cheirothesia*—through which he distinguishes between two groups of ordinations based on those that take place at the foot of the altar in the sanctuary or those that are done outside the sanctuary: this has deep, solemn roots in the Greek liturgical and didactic tradition, which attached to that distinction a precise theological concept.

Theodore of Mopsuestia is very familiar with deaconesses and appreciates them as an apostolic institution, as did John Chrysostom and Theodoret of Cyrrhus[96] around the same period, and as the Byzantine ordination rite presumes when it calls to mind Phoebe. However, these authors do not provide details about how and where the ordinations of deaconesses were done, nor do they compare them to the ordinations of the subdeacon and lector.

Nevertheless, it is true that the Byzantine tradition, as attested by the euchologies distinguishing between the ordinations that are done in the sanctuary and those that are done outside, and placing the ordination of deaconesses in the first group, equates that ordination with that of the deacon, even though the deaconesses' powers are more restricted, and they are not allowed to serve at the altar during the celebration of the Mass.

d) *The moment of the ordination of deaconesses*, when it occurs within the Mass,[97] is at the end of the anaphora before the prayers in preparation for the distribution of Communion. That is precisely the moment at which the ordination of the deacon also occurs. The subdeacon is ordained in the first part, the didactic part of the Mass. Even here one can see that the ordination of deaconesses is comparable to that of the deacons and not to that of the subdeacons.

---

[95] *De sacr. ord., loc. cit.,* 56 PG 155:361–63. "There are two ordinations outside of the βῆμα, those of the lector and subdeacon. There are others, as well: those of the officials, the delegate or the candle-bearer. . . . However, the noble ordinations (ἐξαίρετοι = main, chief, most important) are done inside the βῆμα."

[96] For Theodore of Mopsuestia: *In 1 Tim* 3:11 (ed. Swete II, pp. 128–29; 158–59). For John Chrysostom, *Hom. In. ep. ad Rom* 30:2 PG 60:663C–664A; *In I Tim II*, I PG 62:553D. For Theodoret of Cyrus: *In I Tim.* 3:1 PG 82:809A; *In Rom* 16:1-2: Phoebe PG 82:217D.

[97] According to a rubric from the codex *Barberini gr. 336* (see Morinus, *loc. cit.*, I p. 80 C-D) the ordination of deaconesses, as with that of the deacons, can also occur in the so-called Mass of the Presanctified, and so it is done before Communion.

e) *The formula: "the divine grace . . ."* The structure of the prayers said over the deaconess during her ordination is wholly the same as that of the deacon: the initial formula included: *the divine grace. . . .* In the Byzantine rite this formula, in contrast with what occurs in the Syriac tradition, is used only in the ordination of the bishop, presbyter, and deacon but not in that of the subdeacons or other ministers or officials.

This is an additional serious argument which indicates that the *cheirotonia*, ordination, of deaconesses in the Byzantine tradition was considered to be of the same nature and significance as that of the deacons, presbyters, and bishops and that it was not comparable to that of the subdeacon, nor was it considered a simple benediction.

In fact, recent studies[98] have demonstrated, above all, the antiquity of the formula, also confirming the assertions made by Symeon of Thessalonica. The fact that it is used in a nearly identical way within all of the Eastern rites, makes one presume that it already existed before the separations, particularly before 431, since the formula is also used by the Nestorians. Second, these studies have demonstrated the importance of the formula in the Eastern rites in the way they conceptualize ordination itself. According to later Latin models, one should probably say that, for the Eastern Churches, the formula "the divine grace . . ." was, at least originally, an indispensable part of the basic formula of the sacrament, along with the two epicletic prayers that usually follow. Therefore, the fact that, in the Byzantine tradition, such a formula is not used for the subdeacon and for the lector, is a further argument to say that that tradition considered the ordination of the subdeacon and lector to be of a different nature and to have a different significance than the ordination of the deaconess and deacon.

f) *The diaconal orarion is* given to the deaconess by the bishop at the end of her *cheirotonia* rite. But the deaconess wore a veil that covered her head and also her shoulders: the μαφόριον.[99] The diaconal stole was placed around her neck, under the veil, in a way that the two ends hung in front of her chest; the deacon, on the other hand, wore the stole on the left shoulder in a way that the one end hung in front and the other in back. This feature also relates the deaconess to the deacon, because

---

[98] J. M. Hanssens, *La forme sacramentelle dans les ordinations sacerdotales du rit grec*, in *Gregorianum* 5 (1924): 208–27; 6 (1925): 41–80. B. Botte, *La formule d'ordination: "La grâce divine" dans les rites orientaux*, in *L'Orient syrien* 2 (1957): 285–96. E. Lanne, *Les ordinations dans le rite copte*, ibid., 5 (1960): 81–106.

[99] See Morinus, *loc. cit.*, I p. 179 n.14.

the diaconal stole is the sign, *par excellence*, of the deacon and his ministry. Even long ago ecclesiastical law explicitly prohibited subdeacons, lectors, and cantors to wear the orarion, the specific sign of the diaconal ministry.[100]

g) *The chalice.* After ordination the deaconess received Communion right after the deacons.[101] There is no reason to doubt that she received Communion in the same way as the deacons: inside the sanctuary, first receiving the host from the bishop in her hands, and then drinking from the chalice that he offered her. After this, as also occurred with the deacon, she received the same chalice from the hands of the bishop. The difference, however, was that the deacon received the chalice in order then to distribute it to the communicants outside of the sanctuary, at the entrance of the holy door: the deaconess, instead, once she received the chalice went to place it on the altar.

This is an ambiguous act, as part of a compromise to indicate a status above that of the subdeacon (who always received Communion outside of the sanctuary and without the ability to hold the chalice with the blood), but not equal to the status of the deacons: even if apparently more akin to the status of the deacon than of the subdeacon.

With the aforementioned gesture of the chalice, the Byzantine tradition hints somewhat at the idea, without bringing it neatly to a conclusion that in later Latin models, one could name as a certain *potestas* of the deaconess *in eucharistiam*. It is noteworthy that the Nestorian and Monophysite traditions largely carried this concept forward since the fifth/sixth centuries, clearly granting the deaconesses also the power to distribute Communion to women and children in certain circumstances, in the absence of the presbyter or deacon.[102]

Conclusion

In conclusion, for our purpose we must first of all observe that in Christian antiquity there were different beliefs and tendencies distin-

---

[100] Council of Laodicea, canons 22 and 23 transmitted to the *Corpus Juris dist*. 23 chapters 27 and 28. See, for example, Hefele-Leclercq, *Hist. des conc*. I/2 p. 1012.

[101] See explicitly codex *Coisl. gr. 213*. See Theodorou, Θεολογία (1954), 580 (see also 581), and also M. Blastarès: cited above.

[102] See the texts in Mayer, *loc. cit.*, p. 33, ll. 2-3 (*Testamentum Domini*); p. 52, ll. 22-25 (Severus of Antioch, c. 465–538); p. 53, ll. 2-3; 3-7 (John of Tella, c. 483–538); p. 54, ll. 2-3 (James of Edessa, d. 578).

guishing between ministry and ministry, ordination and ordination, with regard to the nature and significance of the respective orders or ranks.

1. *The Apostolic Tradition* of Hippolytus (c. 210) is the first extant document that talks about the way in which bishops, presbyters, deacons, widows, lectors, virgins, and subdeacons were established—it ignores deaconesses—and their respective tasks as well as their *raison d'être* in the Church. Now, with regard to the meaning and ways in which each of these were constituted, Hippolytus in the *Tradition* makes a clear distinction between two groups of male ministers: bishops, presbyters, and deacons on one side; lectors and subdeacons on the other, while widows and virgins appear there as ways of life and not as ministries. From the point of view of ritual, for Hippolytus, the difference between these two groups is that only the bishops, presbyters, and deacons receive the laying on of hands while he asserts persistently that the lector (n. 11) and the subdeacon (n. 13) cannot receive it. In n. 10 of the text edited by Botte,[103] after having said that one must not lay hands on the widow because "she does not offer the oblation (προσφορά) and does not have the λειτουργία," he adds as a general principal: "*cheirotonia* is given only to the cleric (κλῆρος) in view of the λειτουργία." The λειτουργία here seems to mean the service focused on the altar, which the bishop, presbyter, and deacon perform and the lector and subdeacon cannot perform.

The Western tradition after Hippolytus always not only makes a distinction, like Hippolytus, between two groups—bishop, presbyter, deacon and lector, subdeacon—but, besides, and always, as with Hippolytus, it makes the aforementioned distinction on the ritual basis of the presence or absence of the laying on of hands. This, at least until the time when, in the West, the opinion spread that also in the constitution of the bishop, the presbyter, and the deacon the *traditio instrumentorum* or the anointing, respectively, played a role.

2. On the other hand, in the Eastern tradition, *cheirotonia*, ordination, was conferred not only on the bishop, presbyter, deacon, and deaconess but also on the lector and subdeacon. In the Antiochene tradition, it is even used for the installation of "offices," ὀφφίκια, as with the bursar and the archdeacon, for the head of the monastery, etc. In this tradition, therefore, the distinction between the "orders" is not made on the basis of the laying on of hands. In the tradition of the Byzantine euchologies, a distinction between *cheirotonia* and *cheirothesia*, which appears in the

---

[103] Pages 30–31 in Botte.

eighth century and following, is not even understood by many authors. It stabilizes only after about the middle of the twelfth century: as if it were only the presbyter and deacon ordained by *cheirotonia*, whereas the ministers who were inferior to them would be ordained by *cheirothesia*, the equivalent of what today we call a simple blessing.[104]

Nonetheless, the ancient Greek tradition sometimes sought to establish, and did establish in another way, a distinction among groups of ministers on the list: bishop, presbyter, deacon, deaconess, lector, subdeacon.

3. Epiphanius of Salamis[105] distinguished the ministers who belong to the ἱερωσύνη: bishops, presbyters, deacons, subdeacons, and those who do not belong to it and only come *after* the ἱερωσύνη: lectors, deaconesses, exorcists, interpreters, undertakers, and doorkeepers. However, one cannot know with certainty what Epiphanius meant by ἱερωσύνη, nor why, for example, the subdeacon belongs to it but neither does the deaconess nor the lector.

4. Theodore of Mopsuestia[106] is a witness to an ecclesiastical law that does not allow either lectors or subdeacons, and much less other offices, to be ordained at the foot of the altar inside the sanctuary and infers that the reason for this is that "they were established subsequently" and "they do not minister the same mystery"; therefore "they are instead outside of the ranks of Church ministry." With this, Theodore is a witness to the theological thinking that there exists a distinction between the bishop, presbyter, deacon group on one side, and the lector, subdeacon group on the other, and that such a distinction has a ritual expression in the fact that the first ones are ordained at the foot of the altar inside the sanctuary and the second ones are not. Theodore does not talk about deaconesses in this context, though he is familiar with them and understands them to be an apostolic institution. One might also suppose that the *Apostolic Constitutions* (same region, Syria, and the same period as Theodore), speaking with great clarity about the *cheirotonia*, ordination, of deaconesses and saying that this occurs in the presence of the presbytery, the deacons, and deaconesses (VIII 19,2), presumes with this that it occurs in public, and presumably in front of the altar in the sanctuary, as opposed to ordination of the subdeacons and lectors (VIII 21.22), which took place

---

[104] See above pp. 133–35.
[105] See above, para. II n. 2.
[106] See above, para. IV n. 2 c, pp. 136–37.

in the διακονικόν.[107] Later, Simeon of Thessalonica affirmed the principle: "noble (or principal) ordinations are done inside the βῆμα."[108]

5. From the moment that one documents the Byzantine tradition of euchologies (seventh/eighth centuries) and until the pertinent rites were transcribed in those texts (fourteenth century), deaconesses always appear to have been ordained at the foot of the altar inside the sanctuary in clear and deliberate juxtaposition to what was done in the ordination of lectors, subdeacons or other "offices." Other ritual details for the Byzantine ordination of deaconesses go along the same lines: the moment of ordination, the use of the formula "the divine grace . . . ," the orarion, Communion after the deacons from the hands of the bishop in the sanctuary, the fact of receiving from the bishop the chalice that the deaconess then went to place on the altar.

With all of this, it seems to me certain that in the history of the undivided Church the Byzantine tradition maintained that by nature and dignity the ordination of deaconesses belonged to the group of bishops, presbyters, and deacons and not to the group of lectors and subdeacons, and even less to that of the other offices or dignities that came to be established ritually outside of the sanctuary.

6. If one accepts what has been said thus far, one must also acknowledge the following conclusion: theologically, in virtue of the use of the Byzantine Church, it appears that women can receive diaconal ordination, which, by nature and dignity, is equated to the ordination of the deacons, and not simply to that of the subdeacons or lectors, and much less, to use the terminology of today, to that of some lesser ministry constituted by what today one would call a simple benediction.

7. It is nevertheless true that in the same Byzantine tradition the liturgical work of the deaconesses was far more restricted than that of the male deacons. But it is also true that, in the same custom of the Church today, from this perspective, the situation is already largely obsolete with regard to the distribution of Communion and many other tasks. It is noteworthy that today there are cases in which, by indult, women do almost everything that can be done by the clergy, except say Mass, hear confessions, and do the anointing of the sick.[109] It is also true that the an-

---

[107] See above, para. III n. 5 b.

[108] See above, p. 137.

[109] The fact of not having granted women the permission to perform anointing of the sick is connected to the Western idea, scholastic and later, that sees in such anointing above all a type of addition to penance for the remission of sins,

cient tradition of the Church unanimously denied women the possibility of entering the priesthood. Such was affirmed with different arguments, the value of which it is the place of theology to reflect on at each occasion.

Translated by Amanda Quantz, Carmela Leonforte-Plimack and Phyllis Zagano, with Robert F. Taft and Valerie Karras

---

and excessively relegates to secondary status the idea of the rite as a means of obtaining from God healing from the illness, an idea that rather is primary in many ancient sources. However, in the ancient Eastern tradition, it appears more than once that, among the duties of the deaconess, providing anointing of the sick to women was included. There is no historical basis on which to interpret this anointing without a doubt to a sacramental in the modern sense, in juxtaposition to a sacrament. As often repeated, such a distinction, both in the East and Latin West before scholasticism, was anything but clear. In the anointing of the sick, among the historically documented ways to do the anointing, in the Greek tradition the most ancient seems to be that of anointing the whole body, in particular, the parts that are ill (testimony of Theodulf in the eighth century ms. of Sinai 960, from the thirteenth century: see J. Dauvillier, *Extrême Onction dans les Eglises orientales*, in *Dict. De Droit Can.* V (1953): 731–33). Now the general custom explained by Epiphanius (*Haer.* 79.3 PG 62:744D–745A) was that one had to expose a woman's body every time in the rite and for reasons of fittingness, the deaconess intervened. See also J. Danielou, *Le ministère des femmes dans l'église ancienne*, in: *La Maison-Dieu* 61 (1960): 94. For the Syrian Monophysite Church there is the testimony of James of Edessa (d. 578): see Mayer, *loc. cit.*, 53–54; of Bar Hebraeus (1226–1286): see W. De Vries, *Sakramenthentheologie bei den syrischen Monophysiten* (Rome, 1940), 220. The Maronite tradition is summarized by the Lebanese synod of 1736, distinctively approved by Benedict XIV in 1741. Of the deaconesses: "officia sunt, ut muliebri hoestati ac pudore in ecclesia consulatur . . . .3. ut chrismate vel oleo nuda earum corpora tam in baptism et confirmatione, *quam in extrema unction ungant*, defunctas etiam lavent et sepeliant. . . . Quamvis autem diaconissarum officia, quoad sacramenta baptismi, confirmationis et extremae unctionis jam diu cessarint, quum non amplius totius corporis unctiones fiant: durant tamen quoad dicatas Deo in sacris coenobiis virgines, quibus abatissae praeficiuntur. Abatissae enim diaconissarum benedictionem accipiunt, et munia omnia quae illis in conciliis sunt concessa exequuntur." Mansi 38 col. 163–64. Moreover, it is the case historically that in the ancient Church the faithful often provided themselves with the anointing of the sick, with the oil blessed by the priest for this purpose, and again, this does not demonstrate that it was considered only a "sacramental." See Dauvillier, *op. cit.*, 725–89.

7

A View of the Past and Future of Feminine Ministries within the Church

Reflections about a Book by Roger Gryson*

Philippe Delhaye

I. A Current Issue

The 1971 Synod has received bad reviews, but time will tell us only in the long run whether it really deserves the criticisms aimed at it or whether the dissatisfaction comes, in part or completely, from a lack of communication or from a campaign by certain pressure groups.[1] In any event, one will not be able to accuse the Synod of having studied timeless issues. Reports by the representatives of the episcopal conferences clarify the present aspects of such burning questions as priesthood and justice.

Among these "hot points" is that of the "feminine ministries in the Church," raised on behalf of the Canadian episcopate by Cardinal Flahiff,

"Rétrospective et prospective des ministères féminins dans L'Eglise," *Revue théologique de Louvain* 3 (1972): 55–75.

* R. Gryson, Le ministère des femmes dans l' Église ancienne, coll. Recherches et Synthèses - Histoire, 4 (Gembloux, Duculot, 1971). [Roger Gryson, The Ministry of Women in the Early Church, trans. Jean Laporte and Mary Louise Hall (Collegeville, MN: Liturgical Press, 1976).]

[1] In *Figaro*, Monday, 8 November 1971, 15, M. Jean Bourdarias acknowledged that the door was only half-opened by Father Thomas, press delegate for the French Language: "Thanks to him journalists knew what was discussed in the synod, but in reality it was difficult for them to know what was really occurring. . . . The question is to know if it could be different," he adds. "By half opening the door of this closed council, the Pope has taken the risk of seeing the noise from outside interfering on the proposals inside. He has also taken the risk of seeing those outside misunderstanding what was happening."

archbishop of Winnipeg.[2] He did not directly speak of a priesthood of women, as certain sensational newspapers have made him say with a misunderstanding that, very often, more complicates this thorny issue. He was rather thinking of a diversification of the ministries of teaching, of the apostolate, and of action of so much discussed today, and of opening these ministries to women: "At the same time that new ministries appear, in response to the new needs of an evolving society, under the action of the Holy Spirit, can we already foresee what new ministries will be more suitable for women, their nature, their gifts and their training, in today's world of which *Gaudium et spes* speaks so eloquently?"[3]

This debate brought before the Synod a demand that has been around for several years and that starts from two different perspectives. One of these maintains the Church does not do justice to women and does not allow them to "serve" as they might. John XXIII saw the wish for a female advancement as a sign of the times,[4] as Sister Valentine Buisseret recalls in her booklet: *La femme et l'avenir de l'Église.* "Now—she declares elsewhere—it is unquestionable that, with regard to the condition of women, the disparity is still quite great between ecclesiastical institutions and the increasing role of women in the evolution and structures of modern society."[5]

We can add to this tendency one of the propositions of *Concilium*'s Congress in Brussels (12–17 September 1970): "We must denounce the discrimination practiced against women within the Church and within society as well. It is time to seriously envisage the place of women in the ministries."[6] But much earlier—toward the end of the Council—were the Rome lectures by a theologian of a completely different orientation,

---

[2] This text is published in *Doc. cath.*, v. 68 (1971): n. 1596, 988–89.

[3] Ibid., 988.

[4] This text of *Pacem in terris* may be read in *Doc. cath.* v. 60 (1963), no. 1398, col. 520.

[5] Sister Valentine Buisseret, a missionary Dominican of Fichermont, *La femme et l'avenir de l' Église. Address aux Pères du Synode* (Bruxelles, 1971), 16, here I refer to 2–3.

[6] *Concilium*, n. 60 supplement, Congrès de Bruxelles, 162. This motion gained 143 of 178 votes, while the highest approval was 157 for Proposition 3, and the lowest 142 for Propositions 9 and 10. A more striking "free motion" on the status of women had been proposed by the Canonist Msgr. Jean-Marie Aubert, professor of Catholic theology at Strasbourg, but this seemed to duplicate the text prepared by the organizing committee. Perhaps in this way the motion avoided rejection, as with Father Detry's Proposition on the liberalization of the Church.

Father Daniélou.[7] In fact, with great courage he had taken a position in favor of the ordination of women, when, at the same time, *L'Osservatore Romano* published a series of articles very severely judging this possibility.[8]

Another point of departure is within the discussion on priesthood, linked to the movement for a more "horizontal" view of ministry.[9] Insofar as the difference between the common priesthood of the faithful and the ministerial priesthood[10] becomes blurred, we do not see how women could be excluded from the latter. Since 1963, the Dutch Jesuit Haye van der Meer, a disciple of Rahner, showed the psychological reversal implied by the change he seeks.[11] As has been seen in the case of the priest, the

---

[7] Even more recently, during an interview with *Express* (16–22 June 1969), Cardinal Daniélou has stated one should not exclude the possibility of priestly ordination for women. The magazine attributes the following words to Daniélou: "I know a considerable number of young women who do not understand why they are and will remain excluded from priesthood. I am dean of the faculty of theology in Paris. I have an increasing number of women in my courses. And St. Paul's three reasons opposing the priesthood of women do not seem convincing at all. According to him, women could not speak in public: today, with microphones the problem is solved; women were not made to lead: but today women are heads of companies; and finally, women were not 'public persons': now, women in the twentieth century have a public role. One should examine where lie the true reasons preventing the Church from considering the priesthood of women."

[8] These articles of G. Concetti were published in *L'Osservatorio Romano* (8, 9, 11, 12 November 1965).

[9] Proclaiming St. Teresa of Avila a Doctor of the Church (27 September 1970), Paul VI recalled that through baptism women take part in the common priesthood. On the other hand, the Holy Father clearly differentiated this latter from ministerial priesthood, which is closed to women; cf. *Doc. cath.*, v. 67 (1970): n. 1572, 908.

[10] It is relatively odd to find, in recent publications, that the same authors struggle for the suppression of the law of celibacy, for the priestly ordination of women (upon whom celibacy would without doubt be imposed), for the involvement of clergy in politics, and for an "existential" dependence of the priesthood in relation to a community.

[11] J. Hayes Van der Meer, *Priestertum der Frau?*, coll. *Quaestiones disputatae*, 42 (Fribourg-Br.-Bâle-Vienne, 1969). This work becomes again "relevant" because it has been published in Italian, *Sacerdozio della donna* [this time without a question mark] (Brescia, 1971). The argument has been questioned by F. X. Remberger, *Sacerdozio della donna?* [here with a question mark!], in *Teologia del presente* 1. (1971): 35–42.

representative of God before an assembly of the faithful and all people, van der Meer said, it was fairly normal to choose only men because they naturally evoke the image of the Father. But now that above all we ask the president of an assembly to come from it and to represent it before God, women can fulfill this function as well, if not better. Some have said that a woman could not pronounce the words of Christ over the bread: "This is my body." But today this is irrelevant; it is presidency, an evocative presence of the assembly before God that is required. Israel is the bride of Yahweh, the Church the bride of Christ. How could a woman not hold this role? This same aspect of the problem is shown by the comparisons that can be drawn with the positions of other Christian Churches.[12] The Eastern Orthodox Churches are absolutely intransigent on this subject, and remain faithful to a sacred concept of the presbyterial ministry. On the contrary, some Reformation Churches consider their pastors principally as animators or preachers; therefore they see no reason to deny this role to women. Because the Reformed Church of France admitted the female pastorate during its 58th Synod (1–3 May 1965), Pastor Roux noted that in this manner the distance between Catholics and the Reformed was enlarged, but that the ecumenical argument was irrelevant "since there is no agreement between Catholics and Protestants on the nature of the ministerial priesthood."[13]

One sees that the problem of feminine ministries is one that must be faced directly, in a systematic way, no matter one's convictions, because it is raised insistently and trying to avoid it is pointless. Even if one determines that one must reply "no," one must know how to formulate this "no," which arguments to use, and how to refute objections. In his October 11, 1971, communication to the Synod, Cardinal Flahiff relayed the express wish on behalf of the Canadian episcopal conference to soon establish "a mixed commission (that is, of bishops, priests, lay men and women, religious men and women) in order to study deeply the issue of feminine ministries within the Church." The Synod did not have to make a firm decision on this because it is a consultative body, but, at the end of October, one can say that the synod members generally favored

---

[12] The Ecumenical Council of the Churches has published a booklet that takes into consideration the diversity of the points of view: *De l'ordination des femmes* (Genève, 1964). A critical analysis of it has been done by the Father Charles Boyer in *L'Osservatore Romano*, weekly selection in French, 30 April 1965.

[13] One finds echoes of these debates in the article that Gallay has dedicated to them in *La Croix* of 2–3 May 1965.

the creation of such a commission. The commission will have to examine many sides of the issue, especially those found in Scripture and Tradition. Gryson's book, which I propose to examine here and about which present my own evidence and thoughts, represents an essential ingredient for this research. In fact, the book provides an exhaustive textual analysis, developed according to the same critical methods and presented with the same clarity as Gryson's work on the origins of the ecclesiastical celibacy. It is not easy to sum up such a dense study; at least we can accept some conclusions and highlight the justifications that have led to his essential points.

II. The Place of the Women with Christ and the Apostles

While Jewish women did not have any place in the cult of the temple or in the activity of the rabbis, Jesus willingly surrounded himself with women who followed him and helped him in his preaching. They would be faithful to the point of standing at the foot of his cross with John alone. They would also be the first witnesses of the resurrection.[14] The text of Luke 8:1-3 is particularly significant: "Afterward he journeyed from one town and village to another, preaching and proclaiming the good news of the kingdom of God. Accompanying him were the Twelve and some women who had been cured of evil spirits and infirmities, Mary, called Magdalene, from whom seven demons had gone out, Joanna, the wife of Herod's steward Chuza, Susanna, and many others who provided for them out of their resources." Throughout the synoptic texts we find mention of these feminine groups, within which Mary Magdalene is always mentioned as first. The Gospel of Matthew speaks of her and of Mary, mother of James and Joseph, as well as of the mother of the sons of Zebedee (Matt 27:56) where she is shown in the company of the "other Mary" (Matt 28:1). The Gospel of Mark mentions these women many times: Mary Magdalene and Mary, the mother of James (the younger) and of Joseph and Salome (Mark 15:40); Mary Magdalene and Mary, the mother of Joseph (Mark 15:47); Mary Magdalene and Mary, the mother of James, and Salome (Mark 16:1). In the Gospel of Luke, following the list in 8:2-3 just mentioned, we find three female witnesses to the resurrection: Mary Magdalene, Johanna, and Mary, the mother of James (Luke 24:10). John gives more detail on the group of women present at Calvary:

---

[14] Gryson has dedicated the first chapter of his book to the study of New Testament texts.

"Standing by the cross of Jesus were his mother and his mother's sister, Mary the wife of Clopas, and Mary of Magdala." (John 19:25). Moreover, the family ties take on a greater importance in Acts (1:14), because this book shows the Apostles remaining in prayer "together with some women, and Mary, the mother of Jesus, and his brothers."[15]

During the initial preaching of the Good News, many women appear next to the Apostles, assisting them in their work, and endowed with an active and sometimes decisive role. Mary, the mother of John-Mark, hosts the meetings of the Christian assembly of Jerusalem in her house (Acts 12:12); Lydia, trader in purple, helps Paul and his companions in their apostolate (preaching and baptizing) in Thyatira (Acts 16:15).

The greetings at the end of the Pauline epistles recognize the apostolic activity of several women. Romans (16:1ff.), for example, mentions Phoebe, "deaconess (*diakonos*; 16:1) of the Church in Cenchreae"; Priscilla (16:3), whose name precedes that of her husband Aquila (as in Acts 18:26; 2 Tim 4:19); a Mary (Rom 16:6), Thryphena, Tryphosa, Persis (Rom 16:12); the mother of Rufus (16:13), Nereus and his sister (16:15).[16] The praises

---

[15] We know that the first two chapters of Acts are the basis of religious reforms in the twelfth century. They saw at that time, in the first pages of Acts, the ideal of the *vita apostolica* comprised poverty and contemplation. Robert of Arbrissel (d. 1117) who founded the order of Fontevrault taking from Benedictine customs furthers the interpretation. He says that in the Cenacle, Mary was the center and soul of the assembly; she took precedence over the Apostles. The ideal religious community is therefore one in which an abbess, taking the role of Mary in the Cenacle, governs two communities, one of women, the other of men. The men religious have only a prior as leader, and depends on the abbess for governance and action. *Cf.* M. Heimbucher, *Die Orden und Kongregationen der katholischen Kirche*, 3rd ed., v. 1 (1933), 327–29; *Histoire de L'ordre de Fontevrault*, by the men religious of Sainte-Marie-de-Fontevrault-de-Boulaur, vol. 3 (Auch, 1911–1915). Regarding the "feminist" attitude of Robert of Arbrissel and the relations of his movement with that of "courtly love," we shall see the brief but clarifying comments of Henri-Irénée Marrou in *Les troubadours*, 2nd ed. (Paris, 1971), 165–71, who relies on the great work by Bezolla, *Les origines et la formation de la littérature courtoise en Occident*, vol. 5 in book 4, coll. *Bibliothèque de l' École Pratique des Hautes Études*. Section Histoire-Philologie fasc. 286, 313, 319, 320 (Paris, 1944–1962).

[16] S. John Chrysostom, among others, interprets in the light of these cases S. Paul's advice to women to be discreet. Priscilla is named before Aquila, her husband, because she has more influence than he. She instructed Apollos (Acts 18:26). Many women transmitted the evangelical message to their husbands and children (1 Cor 7:13-16). This shows, S. John Chrysostom concludes, that women are able to hold a teaching role in the Church but "not that which falls

sung for certain names are indeed striking, as well as the title *diakonos* given to Phoebe in relation to a church near Corinth. Without doubt, the critics emphasize that the term *diakonos* took a long time to pass from the general meaning of service and ministry to that of deacon in the ecclesiastical sense.[17] But regarding Romans 16:1, Kittel in his dictionary maintains that the semantic evolution is already there: "The designation of Phoebe as *diakonos* of the community of Cenchreae comes at the point where the charism starts to become the basis of the mission, the function."[18] At the end of the process, we see 1 Timothy (3:11) sets comparable conditions for recruiting women as deacons: "Women, similarly, should be dignified, not slanderers, but temperate and faithful in everything."

Moreover, this charism-ministry of the diaconate is not the only one benefitting women of early Christianity.[19] In addition, according to Acts 21:9, the four daughters of the "deacon" Philip are mentioned regarding the charism-ministry of prophecy, in connection with Paul's staying with that family. Besides, Paul does not forbid women from praying or prophesying in public in Christian assemblies (1 Cor 11:4-5) and stops asking them to do away with wearing a veil. Do we need to recall this? The prophet, in the biblical sense of the word, is neither solely nor necessarily the one who announces the future, but, as the epistle itself says

---

within priestly function" (R. Gryson, *Le ministère*, 135–42, 80–85 English). In this interpretation we can see it is not due to the force of the [male] voice; the solution of the microphone, advanced by some, as I mentioned above, does not meet the true problem.

[17] Regarding the ecclesial meaning and the evolution of the ministries, see L. Ott, *Le sacrement de l'Ordre*, trans. M. Deleporte, in *Histoire des Dogmes*, book 4, *Sacrements*, fasc. 5 (Paris, 1971); A. Lemaire, *Les ministères aux origines de l'église*, coll. *Lectio Divina*, n. 68 (Paris, 1971), is unfortunately too focused solely on the criteria of vocabulary.

[18] A. Oepke, γυνή, in Kittel, *TWNT*, I, 776–90. This sentence is quoted by Gryson 24, 4 English.

[19] Throughout his work, Gryson shows how the question of feminine ministries has been complicated by confusion between the deaconesses and the widows. Certainly, over the years, it is the rare case where widows are presented as members of clergy (Tertullian and *Testament de Notre Seigneur*); but widows *per se* do not receive an ordination; they enter by "nomination" a religious state of life (prayer, fasting, good works) and are financially aided by the Churches. Such is also the image given them by the apostolic texts: Acts 6:1; 1 Timothy 5, 3:16. I wonder why Gryson has not included J. Viteau, *L'institution des diacres et des veuves*, in *RHE*, book 22 (1926), 513–37, in his bibliography. It is true that he had to make a difficult choice.

(1 Cor 14:3-4), "one who prophesies does speak to human beings, for their building up, encouragement, and solace . . . builds up the church."[20]

If Christ and the apostles show themselves welcoming women to an extent that goes far beyond Jewish and pagan customs, it is even more significant to note their exclusion from the group of the seventy-two sent by him (Matt 10:1-15) as well as from the group of the Twelve who, after having been chosen and instructed, are entrusted with the universal mission to "make disciples . . . , baptizing . . . , teaching them to observe all that I have commanded you" (Matt 28:16-20). This mission, which is at the same time a service and a power, will be passed on to the bishops and the presbyters of the first communities. No place would be made for women. The early Church, as Hamman wittily notes, "was predominantly female, as it would be in the bourgeois society of the nineteenth century."[21] It gave women an importance and a freedom far greater than Judaism and paganism. Nonetheless, we are constantly confronted by the fact that Gryson has noted in his chapter, and above all in his conclusion: "The main obstacle is that, even though there were among Jesus' disciples women who, according to all evidence, possessed the qualities needed to accomplish this mission, he did not mandate women to preach the gospel with apostolic authority."[22] The Hellenistic Christian environment would not have been amazed to see women-priests, because their cults had them. Did they transfer the institution to their new religion? They did not, as we shall see following Gryson, they remained faithful to the apostolic options: women are able to assume ministries of a diaconal kind; they are excluded from the episcopate and the presbyterate.

---

[20] But then, one would say, how should one understand verse 34 of chapter 14 of the same epistle: "women should remain silent in the churches"? Gryson (*op. cit.*, 27–29, 6–7 English), in agreement with many exegetes of the Patristic epoch, reckons that this text simply asks women not to whisper/chat and not to comment among themselves the word of the preacher. For that they should wait to be back in their homes; verse 25 says in fact: "If they want to be instructed on some points, they should ask their husbands at home." Another reply of Gryson is even more radical and consists in seeing in these verses 34-35 "an interpolation external both to the authentic text of chapter 14 and to Paul's thought" (28, 6 English). Which are the arguments? Many important manuscripts reject these verses at the end of chapter 14; these [verses] "interrupting the rest of the ideas, since verse 36 logically follows verse 33." "Many lexicographic and syntactic details are unusual in Paul's vocabulary and style, such as the formula 'as even the law says.'"

[21] A. Hamman, *La vie quotidienne des premiers chrétiens* (Paris, 1971), 62.

[22] Gryson, *op. cit.*, 177, 113 English.

III. The Norm of the Ancient Church in the East

A. Diaconate and Feminine Ministries

It is not easy to know if the first centuries of Christianity included women engaged in a *"diakonia"* or an ecclesial diaconate. On the contrary, in the great liturgical and canonical compilations, the *Didascalia of the Apostles* (third century) and the *Apostolic Constitutions* (fourth century), deaconesses appear to be members of the clergy who receive an authentic ordination conferred by the laying on of hands and the prayer of the bishop. Here is the text quoted by Gryson:

> O Eternal God, the Father of our Lord Jesus Christ, the Creator of man and of woman, who replenished with the Spirit Miriam, and Deborah, and Anna, and Huldah; who did not disdain that your only-begotten Son should be born of a woman; who also in the tabernacle of the testimony, and in the temple, did ordain women to be keepers of your holy gates,—now also look down upon this you servant who is to be ordained to the diaconate, and grant her the Holy Spirit and cleanse her of all stains of flesh and spirit, that she may worthily discharge the work which is committed to her to your glory, and the praise of your Christ, with whom glory and adoration be to you and the Holy Spirit forever. Amen.[23]

For which functions are these deaconesses ordained? In itself, their liturgical ministry is reduced to taking part in women's baptisms and in the anointing this ceremony includes. In addition, they are a necessary intermediary between women and male ministers, bishops, priests, and deacons, even in all that concerns the apostolate or the exercise of charity. The *Constitutions* also speak of their carrying messages, of welcoming women in the Church, and of "even more services" which the text does not specify.

The *Testament of Our Lord Jesus Christ*[24] has a somewhat different vocabulary, because it favors ordained widows over deaconesses, but if we

---

[23] Gryson, *op. cit.*, 107–8, 62–63 English. The names mentioned are those of the sister of Moses and of other prophetesses of the Old Testament. Guarding the doors—which would correspond to the deaconess's role of welcoming women—refers to Exodus 38:8: "The bronze basin, with its bronze stand, was made from the mirrors of the women who served at the entrance of the tent of meeting." They are also mentioned, but in derogatory terms, in 1 Sam 2:22 (in Hebrew).

[24] This work was published in the second half of the fifth century, probably in a monophysite environment in Syria. *Cf.* Gryson, *op. cit.*, 92–101, 53–58 English.

go beyond the words, we also find here important feminine ministries and an ordination by the laying on of hands. These women ministers take their place with the clergy behind the curtain that hides the eucharistic offering from the people; they take communion after the deacons and before the subdeacons and lectors. Their ministry is extensive: they teach women catechumens, instruct uneducated women, encourage women who want to live as virgins or in chastity, and gather them for prayer, and rebuke those who misbehave. These ordained women visit ill women and anoint women at baptism. These measures passed from the liturgy into civil law. The legislation of Byzantine emperors, especially of Justinian, codified the status of deaconesses. The clergy of Holy Wisdom (often called Saint Sophia) comprised 425 members, including forty deaconesses; they enjoyed the same privileges, especially the *privilegium fori*, and received their economic support from the Church.[25] We see Gryson's emphasis on the importance of this aspect in the ancient life of the Church when he writes: "From a doctrinal point of view, since for several centuries a large portion of the church[26] followed this practice without raising a theoretical problem, it is perfectly conceivable to confer on women a diaconal type of ministry."[27]

B. Exclusion of Women from the Presbyterate and the Episcopate

If the Christian East has been shown to be generous regarding feminine diaconal ministry, it refused to admit women to the eucharistic

---

[25] Gryson, *op. cit.*, 122–27, 71–74 English.

[26] One may wonder why feminine diaconal ministries existed almost exclusively in the East. Gryson does not explain this. Hamman advances a hypothesis. In the East, women were confined, so that only other women could attend to them in certain situations. In any case, relations between male ministers and Christian women would soon look suspicious if female ministers were not intermediaries and witnesses. In the West, women were freer; they could more easily be in touch with male ministers (*La vie quotidienne des premiers chrétiens*, p. 83). We see here how ambivalent the reference to sociocultural circumstances can be. Usually, in fact, the existence of feminine ministries is explained by women's emancipation rather than by their removal from public responsibilities. On the other hand, historians, perhaps a bit hastily, reject the female diaconate in the West, unless the notion of West is ambiguous. In this regard Congar recalls certain cases of feminine ministry and jurisdiction: "Like the abbesses of Kildare in the Irish monastic system and, in general, the abbesses of double monasteries, or those of Las Huelgas in Castile."

[27] Gryson, *op. cit.*, 177, 113 English.

ministry, to public preaching, and to governance of the Christian people, as did the entire Christian Church of that time.

This is certainly not for lack of imagination! In fact, several Christian heterodox sects gave great importance to women prophetesses-apostles, primarily the Gnostics, the Nicolaitans, the Naassenes.[28] The Cataphrygians[29] mention appearances of the Christ as a woman and, as a result, ordained women bishops and priests. St. Epiphanius, St. Augustine, and, later, St. John Damascus would class these practices in their catalogues of heresies. Other sects tried to legitimize the assignment of sacred functions to women, referring to the greatness of Mary's role in the redemption. St. Epiphanius replies that Mary herself was not a priest. Otherwise Jesus would have been baptized by her and not by John.[30] In the fourth century, the Priscillianists took hold in the West and wished to introduce the feminine priesthood there. Western bishops reacted strongly, for example, at the Council of Nîmes in 394.[31] Pope Gelasius protested against the fact that "women discharged altar service" and "performed all the other things which have been assigned solely to the ministry of men."[32]

Why? By whom? It seems that the ancient Church essentially dreams of a criterion it considers decisive and normative: the attitude of Christ and of the Apostles. It wishes to reproduce as much as possible the way, the attitudes, and the views of the Lord Jesus. Now, if Jesus, in the anachronistic simplification of the *Didascalia of the Apostles*, "was served by women deacons, Mary of Magdalene, and Mary, the daughter of James and mother of Joseph, and by the mother of the sons of Zebedee, and with other women,"[33] he never, let us note, entrusted women with missions of official teaching, sacramental [ministry], or pastoral governance.

The *Ecclesiastic Canons of the Apostles*, which were compiled at the beginning of the fourth century in Egypt, imagine a discussion of the Twelve about the feminine eucharistic ministry. The issue is to know if a

[28] Gryson, *op. cit.*, 39, 15 English.
[29] Gryson, *op. cit.*, 131, 77 English.
[30] Epiphanius of Salamis, *Contre les hérésies*, 79, 3:1-2. Gryson (*op. cit.*, 133, 78–79 English) notes that this issue appeared also in the *Didascalia of the Apostles* and in the *Apostolic Constitutions*, as we shall see.
[31] Gryson, *op. cit.*, 162–63, 100–101 English. It is highly probable that the opposition to the feminine diaconate by a major part of the Western churches is due to the fear of seeing it as a first step toward claims about the presbyterate.
[32] Gryson, *op. cit.*, 168, 105 English.
[33] Gryson, *op. cit.*, 76, 41–42 English.

woman would be able to make "the oblation of the Body and the Blood" of the Lord. The answer is negative with reference to the Last Supper: Jesus did not associate women with the oblation he asked the Twelve to perpetuate. One must now be content with limiting women to ministries of another type, especially "comforting those who are in need."[34]

The reformulation of the *Apostolic Constitutions*, the *Didascalia*, would add other functions to this *diakonia*, as we mentioned above, but they would maintain the prohibition of kerigmatic and sacramental functions, calling to the example of Christ: "Jesus the Christ, when he sent us, the Twelve, to instruct people and all nations did not send women to preach, even though they were not lacking." "If one had to be baptized by women, without doubt the Lord himself would have been baptized by his mother and not by John."[35]

Around the same period, St. Epiphanius of Salamis (c. 315–403) refutes the heretics who had ordained women bishops and priests, referring to the way Christ acted. If in the economy of the New Testament, access to priesthood had been open to women, no one would be more worthy of this dignity than the Virgin Mary. But women were not allowed to either baptize or preach. The same is true for the women who were around Jesus and the Apostles. The Twelve were all men; the succession of bishops and presbyters linked to them counts only men.[36]

IV. Future

If history has its intrinsic value, if the revelation of Scripture and Tradition are normative for the faith and for the life of the Church, it is nonetheless legitimate and necessary to confront these with the questions of the present and of the future. This is what I wish to undertake, or at least to outline here, as I am convinced of the necessity of taking sides, yet without trying to attract a following. In a sense, the problem of the ministry of women goes beyond its own importance and brings into focus a problem of theological hermeneutics. Let us try to list the issues.

A. A first problem is posed with regard to the feminine *diaconate*. Certainly one should not try to "do archeology" and look to revive a feminine diaconate such as the one the Christian East has long known. Gryson

[34] Gryson, *op. cit.*, 83–84, 46–47 English.
[35] Gryson, *op. cit.*, 97–98, 55–57 English.
[36] Gryson, *op. cit.*, 133, 78–79 English.

says rightly: "it is not certain that the restoration of the feminine diaconate today would make much sense, unless we give it a new content than
the content of the diaconate in the past."[37] The functions with which deaconesses and widows had been entrusted in antiquity do not have much
significance or usefulness today. Likewise, the theological relevance of
the continuity with the ancient feminine diaconate has another importance. Through it the Church of today would link itself to the life of the
apostolic Church, to those founding moments when the Twelve acted
because of the *exousia* of Christ. A restored feminine diaconate today
could be reshaped in many ways; in any event it would be in continuity
with the apostolic practice of which the Epistle to the Romans and the
Pastoral Epistles, among others, are testimonies. Maybe some people
would be more sensitive to the issue of the "practice of the Church" (*ex
praxi Ecclesiae*) regarding the third and fourth centuries rather than to the
biblical guarantors (both Scripture and Tradition). But it seems to me,
from Gryson's study, that the Churches of the third and fourth centuries
clearly did not believe they were authorized to create anything new;
they wished to be faithful to the tradition of Christ and the Apostles.
The commentaries of Origen and of St. John Chrysostom on the text of
Romans concerning the deaconess Phoebe are particularly significant.
These Churches were convinced they followed a traditional path when
counting women among the clergy and entrusting them with certain
specific sacred ministries.[38] "Be part of the clergy"! This proposition

---

[37] Gryson, *op. cit.*, 177, 113 English.

[38] Perhaps it is helpful—amid the present verbal confusion—if I specify the
sense in which I here use the two terms of ministry and clergy. I mean by ministry the mission and the qualification of a person who, through hierarchical
ordination, is entrusted with certain sacred functions in connection with the
action of the Church, the "sacrament of salvation." The clerical state does not
in itself necessarily imply a ministry, as we see in the present discipline for
tonsured men who have not yet received any minor order. It marks being set
apart, the difference between *kleros* and *laos* (from which comes "laic") through
a willingness to dedicate oneself to some sacred tasks (even non ministerial)
and it implies some privileges. The theology and law of the thirteenth century
reserved the power of jurisdiction solely to clerics, although one can imagine
this borderline case: the cardinals elect a lay person as pope: at that moment, he
does not have any jurisdiction. This lay pope receives tonsure; at that moment
he receives all the powers of Peter. Vatican II, as did the ancient Church, rejects
such an hypothesis and deems that only entrance into the episcopate could give
the elect these powers. In the sociological language of today, the clergy are no

might appear to be a challenge in a time when one demands the end of the clergy in a sociological sense.[39] To be part of the clergy in the Middle Ages simply meant having received tonsure and not being subject to secular justice. This *privilegium fori* was at that time so desired that, in certain regions, a third of the boys were tonsured, without a thought in the world of entering into the ministry. The 1917 code reform reserved tonsure for future priests, but it still had to overcome some customs and opposition. Today, the controversy about the "clerical state" is about a segregation or a separation regarding secular life. In itself, the controversy does not aim at the ministries themselves, so much so that one can ask: would opening the clerical state to women be of any use? I do not think so, save in the disappearance of the relatively recent rule of law that reserves to clerics all ecclesiastical jurisdiction. In the Middle Ages and in modern times, many abbesses had power of jurisdiction, as Congar has reminded us. If a reform of this kind may be useful in certain countries, why hesitate to carry it out? Moreover, generally, as the Third World Congress for the apostolate of the laity wished, one should hope "that qualified women should be consulted regarding revision of canons concerning women, so that feminine dignity is fully recognized and women are given greater possibilities in the service of the Church."[40]

This service would be precisely one or another ministry that the Church would create and that could rightly culminate in the diaconate. The adaptability of this order that comes from the apostolic life is certainly great, as Church history demonstrates. Nearly everywhere is the hope that hierarchy officially joins forces with those men and women who have specific responsibilities in ecclesiastical life, in such a manner that they are linked to the ministerial priesthood at least like distant participants.

In the article mentioned above, Congar gives these examples: "ordinary catechetical services, religious education, relationships with *Action Catholique*, missionary work, secretaries or parish assistants, charitable services of the Church taken on as a permanent vocation, starting a community of work with a specific testimonial character, different services pertinent to pre-evangelization or evangelization and taken on as a

---

longer defined by vocation, even less by privileges, rather by a willing separation from the other faithful.

[39] This idea is found in many contributors to the special issue of *Esprit*, entitled *Réinventer l'Église?* (39) n. 408, Nov. 1971.

[40] Cf. *Doc. cath.*, 64 (1976) n. 1504, col. 1883.

vocation, etc."[41] Certainly, these services can be provided by lay persons, but is this not the case for most part of the tasks assigned to permanent deacons by Vatican II?[42] As emphasized by the Vatican decree concerning missionary activity *Ad Gentes*, a diaconal ordination provides these ministries with a greater connection to the action of the church and assures some sacramental graces.[43]

B. The question presents itself in a thoroughly different manner regarding the *presbyterate* and the *episcopate*, which imply presiding over the assembly, confecting Eucharist, the remission of sins, and pastoral ministry. In a sense one can say that the crux of the question is posed thusly: does the attitude of Christ and of the Apostles constitute a definitive norm for the Church?

a) A first kind of answer to this question may be to find in the research the intrinsic reasons, valid since the beginning of the Church, which are invariable and therefore will be definitively binding. An argument of this sort is what manuals once called a *ratio theologica*, an argument of a theological origin or of convenience, which has as its function justification of a statement or stance regarding revelation. This kind of argument is found since the patristic era, as Gryson has abundantly shown. It continued among canonists and scholastic theologians, for example, in the *Summa Theologica* of St. Thomas, *Supplementum*, q. 39, art.1. It is mainly around this text that post-Tridentine theologians have gathered their observations:[44] for them a woman is not made to lead, to manage, to preside. This way of arguing has often been advanced in pessimistic and discourteous terms. It can be formulated in a question about the role of women. This is what Cardinal Suenens did recently in replying to journalists: "The priesthood of women is certainly worthy of study.

---

[41] Y. Congar, *Le diaconat dans la théologie des ministères*, in *Vocations* (April 1966): 21. Let us specify that in 1966 Congar envisaged less the idea of a female diaconate than that of "minor orders."

[42] *Lumen Gentium* 29. I think especially of the administration of baptism, distribution of the Eucharist and of viaticum or communion to the sick, of the administration of sacramentals. As is known, the *Institutio generalis* of 3 April 1969 already allows women to read during Mass.

[43] *Ad Gentes* 16.

[44] By reading the commentaries on this Thomistic text (especially G. Vasquez, *Commentarium in tertiam partem sancti Thomae*, disputatio 254) one gets the impression that the question has not advanced much. One can better understand the urgency for psychological and sociological studies (underlined by Gryson, *op. cit.*, 177, 113 English) to clarify this aspect of the problem.

It is still to be seen whether women have a complementary or identical role to men, whether there is not an enriching diversity between the ministry of Jesus and that of Mary. In the Gospels, there is not the least contempt for women. The priesthood, moreover, is divided into many functions and the Church knew genuine deaconesses. If I have some reasons against priesthood [of women]," concludes the Cardinal, "I do not have any reasons in favor of it yet."[45]

b) Another way of thinking looks for a solution to the problem within the "power of the Church." Some say if apostolic power accepted women for priestly ordination, we would recognize the legitimacy of this decision. If the Church does so, it is because it has the power. This attitude joins that of certain theologians of the school of Gardeil and Chenu: the pope or the council can define a dogma if the whole Church accepts it. We have sometimes presented the definition of the assumption in this manner. I confess, it is very difficult for me to enter into this system of thought. First of all, I would like to know how the pope and the bishops would be able to know what can be defined as a dogma or established as a ministry. On the other hand, even for dogmas like the assumption, the magisterium looks for at least an indirect and implicit reference to revelation, especially concerning what it tells us about the sanctity of Mary and the glorification of Christ. Vatican II has much insisted on the idea that the magisterium of the Church is not able "to invent" new religious truths. It has as its norm revelation contained in Scripture and Tradition: "This magisterium is not above the word of God, rather it serves it, teaching only what was transmitted, because by God's mandate, with the assistance of the Holy Spirit, it listens to this Word with love, guards it devoutly, and also presents it with fidelity, and draws from this unique deposit of faith, presenting all that is to be believed as being revealed by God."[46] This reference to Christ and the apostles is certainly the worry of many of those who wish to reiterate the issue of feminine ministries. Byrne spoke in this sense at the Synod, on October 22, 1971: "Women must not be excluded from any service in the Church, to the extent that the exclusion would be sheltered by a *questionable interpretation of Scripture* (my emphasis), by male prejudices, or by a blind attachment to traditions purely human that perhaps draw their origin from the social situation of women in other eras."[47]

---

[45] *La Libre Belgique*, 12 February 1970.
[46] *Dei Verbum* 10.
[47] Cf. *Doc. cath.*, vol. 68 (1971): 1597, 1041.

c) Then, here we are faced again with an "indisputable" interpretation of Scripture, of the decisions taken by Christ and the Apostles. Numerous people would say today: Christ and the Apostles could not act differently, they had to adapt to the ideas of their time concerning the inferiority of women. Others would go further and blame the Apostles themselves of similar prejudices. Contemporary psychological and sociological evolution has removed an obstacle to the fundamental equality of men and women in Christ, and especially in the "common priesthood." Let us go further, some say, let us draw conclusions from the cultural change and extend the equality between men and women to the ministerial priesthood.

It is odd to see some Anglican bishops and theologians deny this sort of consideration. They say Christ and his followers did not hesitate to innovate in fields where public opinion imposed its solutions, for example, in matters of divorce. Christ and the Apostles gave women a place that Judaism did not grant to them. "The Gospel, and the Church that announces it, have not hesitated to moderate the authoritarian character of the attitude of Israel toward women and to move away from the habits of the society within which the Church was born. The masculine character of Christian priesthood must therefore have deeper motives than simple conservatism or a lack of esteem for the feminine nature."[48] In a more general manner, the argument of Scripture and Tradition is presented in this document: "[Women priests] would be contrary to the tradition of the Church since the time of the Apostles. If one affirms that the tradition is wrong, one should prove either that the Apostles were unfaithful to the will of Christ, supposing he wanted women to enter the priestly ministry; or that Christ himself was wrong in not declaring such was his intention, supposing that he wanted women to be able to enter priestly ministry. Now, the two propositions are unsustainable. It is therefore perfectly legitimate to say that it is in the nature of things—and here, in the nature of the church of Christ—to exclude women from sacred orders."[49]

d) It was awkward to find that this sort of assertion is held among some members of the Reformed Church, less responsive than Catholics and Orthodox to the argument of tradition. We find here an option for a "historical faithfulness" which, as far as I am concerned, I would willingly support.

[48] The text of this report has been published in *Church Times* (December 16, 1966) and translated in *Doc. cath.*, 64 (1967): 1488, col. 363–68.
[49] Cf. *Doc. cath.*, ibid., 363.

The development of "human sciences" leads us to better understand the importance of sociocultural factors and, in a sense, their universal presence in our world of theological and rational thought. When Yaweh speaks to his people through Moses and the prophets he pours out his message, his "communication," enlightening a conscience that grasps some truths, some values, in a new manner, without freeing itself entirely of its habits of thinking and living. Christian revelation cannot thoroughly escape this law of the psychological environment. It is the condition itself of an authentic incarnation that theologians have always recognized by distinguishing more or less skillfully "the divine" and "the human" in Christ himself, trying to establish the laws of a hermeneutics of the sacred books, speaking of "divine law" and of "ecclesiastical positive law" regarding Christian frameworks. The modernist and anti-modernist struggles had already highlighted this double aspect of things; it is in regard to these that Jean Guitton himself spoke of the "law of mentalities."[50] When a "word of God" is understood, heard, proclaimed by a man, it transcends history in itself, but it inserts itself into a mentality that has its own geographical and historical coordinates. For example, God asserts himself through the prophets as judge, defender of morality, rewarding pure hearts and chastising those who do evil to others or "before" him. But the prophets, and moreover the people of God, do not have a clear idea about a hereafter that would allow the reestablishment of justice. Therefore they risk thinking of the action of God as only pertaining to earthly existence. They interpret all adversity as a punishment, all happiness as a reward. Only some prophets sense the distortion of revelation, like Ezekiel and the author of the book of Job.

Similarly, one can recall the words of John XXIII opening the sessions of Vatican II: "One thing is the deposit of faith itself, that is, the truths contained in our venerable doctrines, and another thing is the form under which these truths are formulated, although they keep the same sense and scope."[51]

Clearly, this sociocultural inclusion of faith is found at many levels. It seems to me one must at least distinguish two types. The first is extrinsic and marginal, even though it is linked to the structures of language and of society: it allows the word of God, which transcends history, to express

---

[50] J. Guitton, *Portrait de M. Pouget* (Paris, 1957).

[51] John XXIII, *Discours prononcé lors de l'ouverture solemnelle du Concile* (11 October 1962), in *Vatican II. Les seize documents concilliares*, ed. P.-A. Martin (Montreal and Paris, ed. Fides, 1967), 587.

itself, to be developed, to come true, all without ceasing to be the word of God and to transform itself in a simple fact of history. In the field of morals, I would think of mentioning as an example the Pauline kerygma on conscience or on faith, hope, and charity. Another kind of sociological influence is deeper, perhaps intrinsic, in the sense that it accepts a societal fact as something which is not questioned and which limits itself to giving a Christian interpretation. These would be the counsels of St. Paul about the "good use" of slavery, considered from each perspective, that of the masters and that of the victims of this alienation.

In the case of ministries in the New Testament, the "divine idea" is the transmission of a word, a gift of sanctification, a mission of governing the people of God (Matt 28:16-20). It is this Christ wished to give to his twelve disciples, it is this that the Apostles understood to live and organize. Why and how deny that this ministerial mission diversifies itself in three levels, that it relates itself to the twelve patriarchs of Israel, that it is unrelated to the *episcopoi* and the *presbyteroi* of the Greek synagogues and communities? The institution of deacons and deaconesses is in itself the apostolic adaptation of the concept of Christian service entrusted to a steward who, while providing aid to the principal ministries, is given powers and responsibilities. Therefore, there is clearly a socio-cultural environment of Christian ministries, but this is contingent and external with regard to the divine mission itself. Because this had been chosen by Christ and the Apostles, it must perpetuate itself as means God wanted for his action. On the other hand, what is first of all socio-cultural is the introduction of these ministries in different milieux and in different eras. The first *presbyteroi-episcopoi* can be heads of families, engaged in a profession, to whom the Apostles have entrusted the presidency and governance of a community. They can also, like Timothy and Titus, perpetuate Paul's way of life as an itinerant preacher entirely devoted to his mission. The priests of the fourth century have a thoroughly different role and life in Gaul, where bishops are rare, and in Africa, where each city is the seat of a diocese. Deacons can "be little" priests as St. Jerome maintains and as one sees in the Middle Ages, or they can be only secondary collaborators. The image of the priests may be "monastic" in the twelfth century, "religious" after the Council of Trent, close to secular life in rural environments during the Middle Ages and in the industrialized centers of our day. Within this diversity, the scales of value, the exercise of powers and ministries can considerably vary. However, beyond these historical and cultural vicissitudes remains the fundamental idea that the priest announces the Gospel and actualizes the priestly powers of Christ.

As far as I am concerned I do not think that the Church would have the right to modify this, no more than calling into question the fundamental structure of the ministries: episcopacy, presbyterate, diaconate.

Perhaps one can clarify this point of view of historical accuracy by applying it to the Eucharist. One would legitimately think that if Christ had become incarnate in China, he would not have chosen the bread and wine that were common foods in the Mediterranean basin and were part of the Jewish Passover, which Christ renewed going beyond it; without a doubt he would have preferred rice and *saké*. But because this historical choice, in itself minor, was made, the Church is bound and it cannot replace bread with rice, even when it changes the cultural milieu. History shows us that the powers of the Church regarding sacraments are very extensive; they have taken on different forms throughout the centuries. But the Church has never arrogated unto itself a creating power in this domain, as the Council of Trent recognized with the formula "salva illorum [sacramentorum] substantia" (Denz.-Sch., 1728).

In this perspective, I would have no difficulty admitting that if Christ and the Twelve did not entrust women with any mission of an apostolic type (episcopacy, presbyterate), then that relates to their milieu and time. Nothing tells us that they were duped by a supposed inferiority of women, but one can also speak of a certain Pauline anti-feminism. The reasons grounded or not for the opinions taken are of little importance. These are no less a norm and a limit for a Church that wants to remain faithful to what the Lord did. This perspective does not link the exclusion of women from the episcopacy and the presbyterate to some more or less questionable opinions concerning women's "nature"; rather it is linked to the historical conditions that have constituted the historical reality of the Church.

Having said that I do not claim at all that my argument would become faith. I only demand the right to express my conviction without forgetting the advice of St. Paul: *unusquisque in suo sensu abundet* (Rom 14:5).

Translated by Carmela Leonforte-Plimack and Phyllis Zagano

8

Were There Deaconesses in Egypt?

Ugo Zanetti

In an article published in this journal some years ago, Professor G. Otranto stated that, according to the various authors who had studied the issue, "in the ancient Church . . . the only function allowed (for women) . . . was the diaconate in the East, except in Egypt";[1] that same year the study by Monsignor Martimort appeared, of which its fourth chapter, "Il n'y a pas eu de diaconesses en Égypte et en Éthiopie," demonstrated through texts that these two churches did not seem to have known the female diaconate in antiquity.[2] Even so, Martimort, who is not an orientalist, obviously had to refer to existing translations; some years ago, I noted that one of the points he had made was flawed because of an unfortunate interpretation: following a question posed by Professor Otranto, I would now like to offer some observations on this topic.

Indeed, Monsignor Martimort had good reason to emphasize the importance, for his proof, of the "Euchologions that authentically represent the customs of the churches in Egypt" (p. 94) and in particular of the "Great Euchologion of the White Monastery, of the tenth century[3] [which] has reached us in a state quite fragmentary and scattered, so much so that the section regarding ordinations is missing; nonetheless, we find, in the intercessory prayer of the anaphora, the standard mention of bishops [etc.]. . . . There is no mention of deaconesses" (ibid.). This latter detail is to be challenged.

"Y eut-il des diaconesses en Égypte?," *Vetera Christianorum* 27 (1990): 369–73.

[1] Giorgio Otranto, "Note sul sacerdozio femminile nell'antichità in margine a una testimonianza di Gelasio I," in *Vetera Christianorum* 19 (1982): 341–60 (cf. p. 343).

[2] Aimé Georges Martimort, *Les diaconesses. Essai historique, Bibliotheca "Ephemerides Liturgicae,"* Subsidia, 24 (Rome, 1982), chap. IV, pp. 73–97.

[3] E. Lanne, *Le Grand Euchologe du Monastère Blanc, Patrologia Orientalis* 28, 2 (Paris, 1958).

In fact, in the commemoration of the departed, after the remembrance of bishops, priests, deacons, subdeacons, lectors, cantors, monks, porters, and "σπουδαῖοι," we read:[4]

NEϨΟΡΓΙϹΤΗϹ ΝΕ ΤΕΓΚΡΑΤΕѰΕ ΜΜΟΟѰ·
ΝΡΕϤΔΙΑΚΟΝΕΙ Ν̄ ϹϨΙΜΕ ΝϹΙΟѰΡ ΜΠΑΡΘΕΝΟϹ · ΝΧΗΡΑ

The translation used by Msgr. Martimort gives: "the exorcists (ἐξορκιστής) those who abstain from (ἐγκρατεύειν) the use of women (διακονεῖν), the eunuchs, the virgins (παρθένος), the widows (χήρα) . . ." It is quite obvious that the translation of διακονεῖν as *use* is quite strange; without doubt, when this edition was published, the question of the female diaconate was somehow obscured by circumstances, so the translator could not arrive at the only translation grammar authorizes:

> "the exorcists, they who practice continence (ἐγκρατεύειν), women who exercise the diaconate (διακονεῖν), the eunuchs, the virgins (παρθένος), the widows (χήρα) . . ."

Perhaps the repetition of *they who practice continence* and the *eunuchs* might seem to be a duplication, a problem easily avoided when we consider the words in their absolute sense, since *they who practice continence* do so freely, which is not the case for eunuchs; in any case, it seems to me beyond doubt that we must differentiate *they who practice continence* from the group that follows (which, moreover, is separated in the manuscript by a period). The last can have only one meaning, since what we read in Coptic: *ᵉn-ref-diakoni ᵉn-shime* might be translated literally in Latin as *diaconizantes feminae* or, in Greek, as αἱ διακονοῦσαι.

In fact, we then find the plural article (*n-*), the prefix of agency (*ref-*), the verb διακονει (which, like all borrowed Greek verbs in Coptic, is frozen in the singular imperative), the conjunction -*n*- and finally the word *shime*, which means "woman" or "female" (γυνή or θῆλυς).[5] With

---

[4] P. 300 (and [36] of the fascicle) = p. 61 of the manuscript, lines 19-21; I follow spelling and punctuation of this edition. All the nouns that follow are direct object complements of the verb "remember" in line 13; they are applied to "those who have left this life . . . the bishops, the priests, [etc.]."

[5] Cf. W. C. Till, *Koptische Grammatik (Saïdischer Dialekt)*, *Lehrbücher für das Studium der orientalischer Sprachen*, 1 (Leipzig, 1955): paras. 114 and 117, pp. 67–68; and W. E. Crum, *A Coptic Dictionary* (Oxford, 1939), col. 385a. The fact that the word must be understood here as an adjective is evident, among other things, because it has remained unchanged, while the noun "woman" is one of those terms that in Coptic has a proper form for the plural.

regard to the omission of θηλεῖαι (or of γυναῖκες) in my translation, one must know that, in the cited Coptic text, the only function of the word "women" is to mark the feminine of the name of agency, which does not have its own form for this;[6] since the Greek participle is declined, the word "women" or "female" is here superfluous.

They who have doubts concerning my translation will have to consult the Sahidic Coptic version of book VIII of the *Apostolic Constitutions*, at a passage also quoted by Martimort,[7] which translates as: "But, for what concerns subdeacons (ὑποδιάκονος) and lectors (ἀναγνώστης) and women deacons (διάκονος), we have already said that they must not be ordained (χειροτονεῖν)"; now, the word translated as "women deacons" is exactly ⲛ̅ⲇⲓⲁⲕⲟⲛⲟⲥ ⲛ̅ⲥϩⲓⲙⲉ, where the first *n-* is the article, and the second is a conjunction between the noun *diakonos* and its adjective *shime*, so that it would be more exact to translate it literally as *female deacons*, the equivalent of *diaconesses* in French.

Returning to the prayer of intercession found in the Great Euchologion of the White Monastery, the reader will perhaps ask why it does not use the feminine noun corresponding to the Greek διακόνισσα. The reason is simple: since it does not have a proper word for that (as for the pair king-queen), the Coptic language can only note the feminine [case] through the singular definite article; for the plural or the indefinite it must apply the adjective "female" to achieve the same result.[8] In this way we find, within the Coptic translation of the letter sent by Severus of Antioch to the deaconess Anastasia, ⲁⲛⲁⲥⲧⲁⲥⲓⲁ ⲧ̅ⲇⲓⲁⲕⲱⲛ = Ἀναστασία ἡ διάκονος.[9] But in the text of the *Apostolic Constitutions* cited above, the Coptic translator could not write simply ⲛ̅ⲇⲓⲁⲕⲟⲛⲟⲥ, which inevitably would have been understood as meaning "the deacons," not "the deaconesses," and therefore he was obliged to specify: "the female deacons."

To avoid any misunderstanding, one point remains to be clarified. In the Great Euchologion of the White Monastery, the Coptic verb ⲇⲓⲁⲕⲟⲛⲉⲓ

---

[6] Till, *op. cit.*, para. 146, p. 75; see below for the forms of the feminine.

[7] *Op. cit.*, p. 89 (and fn. 73). In Coptic what is quoted here is canon 66 in the series of *Canones ecclesiastici*, ed. P. de Lagarde, *Aegyptiaca* (Göttingen, 1883), at p. 277. For the bibliography, cf. *CPG* 1732 (M. Geerard, *Clavis Parum Graecorum*, I, = *Corpus Christianorum*, p. 222, n. 1732): Canons 63 and following are taken from book VIII of the *Apostolic Constitutions*.

[8] This juxtaposition is not at all contrary to the Coptic, as is easily seen in the examples given by Till and Crum (see fn. 5 above).

[9] M. Chaîne, ed., *Une lettre de Sévère d'Antioche à la diaconesse Anastasie*, in *Oriens Christianus*, n.s. 3 (1915): 32–58, here at p. 36. Cf. *CPG* 7070 (12).

is found two more times, in the sense of *to serve*: p. 290 = [26] = p. 28 of the manuscript, l. 23 [we say to God: "You served me (διακονεῖν) for my salvation"], and on p. 318 = [54] = p. 106 of the manuscript, l. 15 [we pray for "they who serve (διακονεῖν) the needs of the saints"].[10] In my opinion, this in no way questions the interpretation proposed for *the women who exercise the diaconate*; in fact, not only does the passage that interests us list ecclesiastical states, among which a deaconess would seem more appropriate than a simple zealous Christian woman (which the deaconess can also be!), but, above all, the verb ⲆⲓⲀⲔⲟⲚⲉⲓ is used as an intransitive verb, without any object complement, which obliges us to give it a technical meaning: *exercise the diaconate*.

Of course, the issue would have been simpler—and this note would not have been necessary at all—if the euchologion simply read *the female deacons*, like in the version of the *Apostolic Constitutions*. This is not the case: is it because they did not like to speak of *deaconesses*? This remains to be studied. We should also study—but this goes far beyond my purpose—to what extent the acephalous anaphora in which this mention of *women who exercise the diaconate* is found[11] mirrors an Egyptian use rather than a Syrian practice. Indeed, the arguments proposed by Msgr. Martimort seem to well demonstrate that the term *deaconess* was hardly frequent in Egypt.[12] This paper is only to highlight the fact that, contrary to what we thought, the notion of a female diaconal ministry was not thoroughly lacking.[13]

Translated by Carmela Leonforte-Plimack and Phyllis Zagano

---

[10] The edition translates in a more literary manner: "you have healed" and "they who provide for the needs of the saints."

[11] Pages 61–63 of the manuscript = pp. 300–304 of the edition and pp. [36–40] of the fascicle; this anaphora is not identified in the introduction, p. 227 = p. [13] of the fascicle, and it is not treated individually in A. Hänggi and I. Pahl, *Prex eucharistica, Spicilegium Friburgense*, 12 (CH-Fribourg, 1968), 134.

[12] But the term was indeed more frequent than we sometimes think: in addition to the examples quoted here and to those of Martimort himself, we must add at least the three uses in Ethiopian found in the following footnote.

[13] It is not within the scope of my intent to resume this issue. However, it is useful to draw the attention of researchers to two Eastern publications published after Martimort's: R. Beylot, *Testamentum Domini éthiopien* (Louvain, 1984) (the word *deaconess* is found on pages 197, 200, and 204 of the French translation, accessible to everyone); and M. Kristin Arat, "Die Diakonissen der armenischen Kirche in kanonischer Sicht," in *Handes Amsorya* 101 (1987): 153–89 [*Festschrift 1887–1987*: jubilee issue of journal of the (Armenian) Mekhitarist Fathers of Vienna, Mechitaristengasse, 1070 Wien].

9

The Liturgical Function of Consecrated Women in the Byzantine Church

Valerie A. Karras

[Although the ordained order of deaconesses vanished in the Byzantine Church, some women continued to fulfill, either informally or formally, various liturgical functions in public church life. The author examines[1] the art-historical and textual evidence of three groups of women: noblewomen who participated as incense-bearers in a weekly procession in Constantinople; matrons who helped organize and keep order in a monastic church open to the public in Constantinople; and the possibly ordained order of myrrhbearers in the Church of Jerusalem.]

Women continued to play active and ecclesiastically recognized liturgical roles in the processions, vigils, and services of the Byzantine Church even during and after the decline of the ordained female diaconate by the late twelfth century.[2] The Byzantine Church, following historical

"The Liturgical Function of Consecrated Women in the Byzantine Church," *Theological Studies* 66 (2005): 96–116.

[1] This article is developed from a chapter of the dissertation, Valerie A. Karras, "The Liturgical Participation of Women in the Byzantine Church" (PhD diss., The Catholic University of America, 2002), 136–63.

[2] It is impossible to date precisely the disappearance of the ordained female diaconate, but Theodore Balsamon, canonist and patriarch-in-exile of Antioch, writing from Constantinople in the late twelfth century, claimed that the office had devolved into an honorary title for certain nuns (Theodore Balsamon, *Scholia in concilium Chalcedonense*, in PG 137:441) and that deaconesses had no access to the altar (*Responsa ad interrogationes Marci* 35, in PG 138:988). By contrast, the ordination rite preserved in eighth-century to eleventh-century *euchologia* (books with collections of liturgical services) describes the ordination of the female deacon in a manner virtually identical to that of the male deacon, including or-

Christian tradition,[3] excluded women from the ordained orders of the presbyterate (priesthood) and the episcopate based on an anthropology of separate and unequal roles for the sexes,[4] and grounded biblically in the Pauline prohibition against women speaking in church (1 Cor 14:34), and particularly on the deutero-Pauline injunction against women teaching (1 Tim 2:11-12), the latter argued as a result of woman's role in the Fall from grace in the Garden of Eden. The argument from 1 Timothy 2

---

dination at the altar during the liturgy and reception of the Eucharist there at the hands of the bishop. The eighth-century *Barberini euchologion*, the earliest extant, is published in *L'eucologio Barberini Gr. 336 (Ff. 1–263)*, ed. Stefano Parenti and Elena Velkovska, Bibliotheca Ephemerides Liturgicae, Subsidia, vol. 80 (Rome: C.L.V.—Edizioni Liturgiche, 1995), 185–88; the ordination rite for female deacons from the Grottaferrata G.b.I. manuscript (also known as the Bessarion Codex) is published in the seventeenth-century *Euchologion sive rituale Graecorum*, ed. Jacobus Goar, reprint 1960 (Graz: Akademische Druck-U. Verlagsanstalt, 1730), 218–22. For a fuller discussion, see Valerie A. Karras, "Female Deacons in the Byzantine Church," *Church History* 73 (June 2004): 272–316, especially 309–14.

[3] Although scholars such as Giorgio Otranto of the University of Bari, Italy, have argued on the basis of limited epigrammatic evidence that women were ordained to the priesthood and episcopacy in the early Christian Church, their views have not won wide acceptance within the academic community. Giorgio Otranto, "Note sul sacerdozio femminile nell'antichità in margine a una testimonianza di Gelasio I," *Vetera Christianorum* 119 (1982): 341–60; Giorgio Otranto, "Il sacerdozio della donna nell' Italia meridionale," in his *Italia meridionale e Puglia paleocristiane*: Saggi storici (Bari: Edipuglia, 1991), 95–121. An English translation of the former article appears in Mary Ann Rossi, "Priesthood, Precedent, and Prejudice: On Recovering the Women Priests of Early Christianity," *Journal of Feminist Studies in Religion* 7 (Spring 1991): 75–94. See my evaluation of the arguments of Otranto and others in Valerie A. Karras, "Priestesses or Priests' Wives: *Presbytera* in Early Christianity," *St. Vladimir's Theological Quarterly* 51, nos. 2–3 (2007): 321–45. I have not had the opportunity to review the evidence and analysis presented in a forthcoming book on this subject, *Ordained Women in the Early Church*, ed. and trans. Kevin Madigan and Carolyn Osiek (Baltimore: Johns Hopkins, 2005).

[4] "Au total, dans ces brefs textes canoniques, l'exclusion du sacré apparaît plus comme un aspect de la répartition sexuelle (et inégale) des fonctions que comme une incapacité liée à la faiblesse féminine, qui serait, de la sorte, comparable aux prohibitions du droit impérial" (Joëlle Beaucamp, *Le statut de la femme à Byzance [4e–7e siécle]*, vol. 2, Les pratiques sociales, Trauvaux et mémoires 6 [Paris: De Boccard, 1992], 285). Similarly, Beaucamp asserts that "[l]'affirmation d'une répartition des rôles sociaux entre les deux sexes, si elle est moins fréquente que la référence h la faiblesse féminine, semble plus prégnante" (ibid., 289).

was used, for example, by the late fourth-/early fifth-century archbishop of Constantinople, John Chrysostom, specifically to justify the exclusion of women from the priesthood.[5]

However, the biblical injunctions against women speaking and teaching were not, even in apostolic times, interpreted as a complete exclusion of women from all liturgical and pastoral functions, including charismatic preaching and ecclesiastical offices. For example, the context of 1 Corinthians 14:34 clearly indicates that the "speaking" that was prohibited to women was of the question-and-answer variety, since the following verse instructed women to ask their husbands at home if they needed to know something. That the injunction was contextual is further supported, only three chapters earlier (1 Cor 11:5), by Paul's directing women who prophesy to cover their heads. "Prophesying" was, of course, public preaching, particularly on moral issues, and the office of prophet was a charismatic office of the early Church.[6] As for 1 Timothy, chapters 3–5 outline the qualifications and responsibilities of various clergy or officials in the church community. Among those discussed by the writer of the pastoral epistle are two groups of women: Widows (1 Tim 5:1-16) and female deacons (1 Tim 3:11).[7] The consecrated,

[5] Chrysostom declared that "the divine law excluded women from this ministry. . . . Topsy-turvy . . . 'the followers lead their leaders'—bad enough, if they were men; but they are women, the very ones who are not even allowed to teach. Do I say 'teach'? St Paul did not allow them even to speak in church" (*On the Priesthood* 3, 2 [PG 48:633]; English translation in John Chrysostom, *Six Books on the Priesthood*, trans. Graham Neville [Crestwood, NY: St. Vladimir's Seminary, 1984], 78).

[6] The literary evidence and single epigraphical example of female prophets in early Christianity are presented and discussed in Ute E. Eisen, *Women Officeholders in Early Christianity: Epigraphical and Literary Studies*, trans. Linda M. Maloney (Collegeville, MN: Liturgical Press, 2000), 63–87.

[7] Dispute continues over the meaning of the phrase "[the] women likewise." However, the placement of this phrase, in the very middle of the section on the diaconate, mitigates against interpreting it as a reference to the wives of deacons, particularly since no such reference to wives (or "women" in general) appears with respect to the episcopacy. See Martimort, *Deaconesses*, 20–22, for a summary of the problems of interpretation. Kyriaki Karidoyanes FitzGerald reads it as a reference to female deacons, arguing in part on the basis of patristic interpretations of the passage (*Women Deacons in the Orthodox Church: Called to Holiness and Ministry* [Brookline, MA: Holy Cross Orthodox, 1998], 5–6, 9–10).

or "enrolled" (1 Tim 5:9), order of Widows[8] disappeared, judging from the lack of extant evidence, sometime after the middle of the sixth century.[9] In their lifestyle, their spirituality, and their pastoral and liturgical roles, though, they provided important links to two other women's orders on the rise from the late third or early fourth centuries: female monasticism and the ordained order of female deacons.[10] Moreover, the liminal nature of the Widows—"enrolled" or consecrated, and with certain liturgical functions, but not ordained[11]—prefigured the nature of consecrated or enrolled women serving similar functions in the Byzantine Church.

[8] The most complete study on this consecrated order of older women is Bonnie Bowman Thurston, *The Widows: A Woman's Ministry in the Early Church* (Minneapolis: Fortress Press, 1989); other studies include Steven L. Davies, *The Revolt of the Widows: The Social World of the Apocryphal Acts* (Carbondale: Southern Illinois University, 1980); and Dennis MacDonald, "Virgins, Widows, and Paul in Second Century Asia Minor," in *SBL 1979 Seminar Papers*, vol. 1, ed. Paul Achtemeier (Missoula, MT: Scholars, 1979), 169–84. Roger Gryson discusses Widows as well as other orders (*The Ministry of Women in the Early Church*, trans. Jean Laporte and Mary Louise Hall [Collegeville, MN: Liturgical Press, 1976]). My article follows the practice of several scholars in distinguishing, through the use of capitalization, between a generic "widow" (a woman whose husband has died) and a "Widow" (a woman who belongs to the consecrated order by that name).

[9] Justinian's Code provides specific penalties for the rape of women belonging to female ecclesiastical orders, including Widows. CJ 1,3,53; 9,13,1; in Joélle Beaucamp, *Le statut de la femme à Byzance (4e–7e siècle)*, vol. 1, *Le droit imperial* 119. Section 3 of the statute deals with virgins and nuns, section 4 with deaconesses, and section 5 with virgins, nuns, and others, including Widows. However, by this time, there is no longer any evidence of Widows serving liturgical or specifically mandated pastoral functions. It is likely that the order had already died out earlier in many places.

[10] Susanna Elm, "Vergini, vedove, diaconesse: alcuni osservazioni sullo sviluppo dei cosidetti 'ordini femminili' nel quarto secolo in Oriente," *Codex Aquilarensis* 5 (1991): 77–90. Much of this material is re-presented in Susanna Elm, *"Virgins of God": The Making of Asceticism in Late Antiquity* (New York: Oxford University, 1994), chap. 5, *"Parthenoi*, Widows, Deaconesses: Continuing Variety," 137–83. See also Thurston, *Widows*, 114–15.

[11] At least one exception to this rule appears in the Syrian community that was the source of the *Testamentum Domini*, a fifth-century document adapted from the third-century *Didascalia Apostolorum*. This church order gives an ordination rite for Widows, who rank higher than deaconesses in this particular community and actually seem to be the equivalent of deaconesses in other church orders, such as the *Apostolic Constitutions*. See *Testamentum Domini nostri Jesu Christi*,

In the early Christian period, the various ordained and consecrated orders and informal roles that women played in church life reflected a variety of needs and concerns, including: (1) performance of pastoral and liturgical activities serving the needs of women in the community, particularly those needs created by the restrictions of Eastern Mediterranean societies that segregated and secluded women;[12] (2) recognition of women's historical contributions to the ministry of Christ and to the apostolic Church;[13] and (3) formal ecclesiastical acknowledgment of the contributions of contemporary women, especially those with money and influence.[14] Many of these needs and concerns, such as the baptizing of adult women converts and the conveying of the Eucharist to the homes of housebound women, were met through the order of the female diaconate. With the apparent demise of that order, these continuing needs and concerns had to be met in other ways.

In the Byzantine period, there were women who usually bore some sort of formal ecclesiastical title and who were organized more or less formally into consecrated or ordained orders. These consecrated women functioned in public settings, either associated with the metropolitan church or, in one case, with a *male* monastery that provided for liturgical participation by the faithful, both male and female, of the surrounding neighborhood. All of these ecclesiastical women have one thing in com-

---

ed. and trans. Ignatius Ephraem II Rahmani (Mainz: Kirchheim, 1899; reprint Hildesheim: Georg Olms, 1968), 95–99.

[12] Female deacons particularly served these functions in the areas of baptism of adult women and the conveying of the Eucharist to the homes of ill women. These liturgical and pastoral duties are discussed in a number of studies of the female diaconate in addition to those already cited, including J. G. Davies, "Deacons, Deaconesses and the Minor Orders in the Patristic Period," *Journal of Ecclesiastical History* 14 (1963): 1–15; A.-A. Thiermeyer, "Der Diakonat der Frau," *Theologische Quartalschrift* 173 (1993): 226–36. Earlier works on the female diaconate include Jan Chrysostom Pankowski, *De diaconissis* (Regensburg [Ratisbonae]: George Joseph Manz, 1866); and A. Kalsbach, *Die altkirchliche Einrichtung der Diakonissen bis zu ihrem Erlöschen* (Freiburg im Breisgau, 1926).

[13] Eisen provides an inscription, probably from the fourth century and from the Mount of Olives, that refers to a woman deacon named Sophia as "a second Phoebe," clearly a reference to Romans 16:1 (*Women Officeholders*, 158–60).

[14] Using as an example the wealthy noblewoman and patron of John Chrysostom, the deaconess Olympias, Susanna Elm asserts that "special recognition for services rendered—irrespective of whether or not a woman fulfilled the prerequisites laid down by the bishops themselves . . ." (Elm, *Virgins of God*, 182).

mon: they reflect the Byzantine Church's recognition that the various needs of a mixed community require the pastoral and liturgical participation of women as well as men.

My article examines three "orders" or groups of women active in Constantinople or in Byzantine Jerusalem in the tenth through thirteenth centuries: (1) a trio of women whose unique contributions to the orthodoxy of the Church were recognized by their special participation as incense-bearers in the most important and well-known weekly liturgical procession in Constantinople; (2) a quartet of women who assisted in the public liturgical functions of a men's monastery in Constantinople; and (3) an order of women in the Church of Jerusalem called the *myrophoroi* (myrrhbearers).

Processional Incense-Bearers

Although active liturgical roles for women were ecclesiastically prescribed and thus recognized in the forms of titles and specific consecrated or ordained orders for the other two groups of women examined in this article, such does not appear to be the case in this instance. A fresco[15] preserved in a monastery church in the Epirote city of Arta in northern Greece depicts a weekly procession in Constantinople, providing an interesting piece of artistic evidence of the rare processional role of a few select women based on their personal, historical connection with certain important ecclesiastical events in the late thirteenth century.

The Arta monastery of the Panaghia Vlachernitissa, originally a male monastery, was converted to a women's monastery sometime before AD 1230. A few decades later, the monastery church, most likely constructed originally in the tenth century, was expanded into a three-domed and three-aisled basilica and decorated with Byzantine frescoes and other artistic and architectural elements.[16] Among the thirteenth-century decorations of the convent church extant today are a sculpted marble *templon*, a mosaic floor, and, most outstandingly, a unique fresco, preserved in fragmentary form on the southernmost arch on the west side of the narthex, depicting the procession (or litany) of the famous icon

---

[15] A photograph of the processional fresco from the monastery church of the Panaghia Vlachernitissa, Arta, Greece, is provided in *Women and Byzantine Monasticism*, ed. Jacques Y. Perreault (Athens: Canadian Archeological Institute, 1991), pl. 2 fig. 9.

[16] *The Oxford Dictionary of Byzantium*, 3 vols., ed. Alexander P. Kazhdan et al. (New York: Oxford University, 1991), 1.191–92.

of the Theotokos *Hodegetria* in Constantinople.[17] The weekly Tuesday procession of the city's palladium through the capital is described in numerous sources, both Byzantine and foreign, over a period of at least three centuries, with the earliest accounts dating to the twelfth century.[18]

The fresco is remarkable for two reasons. First, it is unusual to find depicted in a church a historical religious ceremony, particularly an outdoor procession. Most frescoes depict scenes from the life of Christ, the Theotokos, and the saints. Benefactors are occasionally shown with Christ or a patron saint, but usually set against a gold background, i.e., outside of any historical or social context. Second, the occasional religious events that are depicted in icons and frescoes, such as the ecumenical councils, generally do not contain women. The icon depicting the final restoration of the icons following the Council of Haghia Sophia in AD 843 is an exception because the Empress Theodora is shown, but she herself convoked the council; moreover, it is Patriarch Methodios who takes center stage, not Theodora. Myrtali Acheimastou-Potamianou theorizes that the reason for the unusual iconographic subject in this monastery church far from Constantinople, and in particular the prominent presence of three women at the forefront of the procession, has to do with the connection of the monastery's patron to two significant synods held in the Vlachernae church in the capital and in Adramyttion, and to the "celebrity" status attached to the mother of the patron, who opposed the emperor, her own brother, for the sake of the orthodoxy of the Byzantine Church.

[17] Myrtali Acheimastou-Potamianou has published several articles on this monastery church. For a detailed discussion of this processional fresco, see "The Basilissa Anna Palaiologina of Arta and the Monastery of Vlacherna," in Perrault, *Women and Byzantine Monasticism*, 43–49. Acheimastou-Potamianou ("Basilissa Anna Palaiologina," 48) dates the fresco, both stylistically and in terms of content (see below), to the late thirteenth century. The fresco is explicitly identified as a representation of the *Hodegetria* procession in an inscription which reads: "ē chara tēs yperagias th(eoto)kou / tēs o[dē]getrias tēs en tē/Konstantinoupolei" (ibid., 46).

[18] Acheimastou-Potamianou, "Basilissa Anna Palaiologina," 44; R. Janin, *Les églises et les monastères*, La géographie ecclésiastique de l'empire byzantin, vol. 3 (Paris, 1953, 1969, 1975) 203ff.; George P. Majeska, *Russian Travelers to Constantinople in the Fourteenth and Fifteenth Centuries*, Dumbarton Oaks Studies 19 (Washington, DC: Dumbarton Oaks Research Library and Collection, 1984), 16, 36, 138, 362–66; A. Vasiliev, "Pero Tafur, a Spanish Traveler of the Fifteenth Century and His Visit to Constantinople, Trebizond and Italy," *Byzantion* 7 (1932): 106ff. Majeska notes that the icon was also brought to different locations in the city, including the Great Church of Haghia Sophia, the Pantocrator Church, and the imperial palace (*Russian Travelers*, 364).

In 1274,[19] the Byzantine emperor Michael VIII Paleologos for political and military reasons submitted himself formally to the pope and the Church of Rome at the Second Council of Lyon, and promised that the Byzantine Church would immediately follow his steps by reuniting itself with Rome as well. Instead, the Byzantines, clergy and laity alike, vociferously rejected the agreement. Michael's attempts to win forcibly the approval of his Church and Empire led him to persecute and imprison those opposed to the union, including his own sister, Irene-Eulogia. Epiros, with Arta as its functional capital, had been independent of Constantinople since the Latin conquest of 1204 and hence became a haven for opponents of Michael's policies who were fleeing potential imprisonment.

When Michael died in 1282, his son Andronikos reversed his father's religious policies, immediately releasing those imprisoned by Michael, such as Irene-Eulogia. A game of "musical chairs" ensued, with the patriarchal throne as the prize, that pitted John Bekkos, a pro-unionist elected under Michael, against Joseph, who both succeeded Bekkos and preceded him (Joseph had resigned earlier, under Michael, in protest of the union). Finally, the following year, Gregory II of Cyprus was elected as the new patriarch, in part thanks to the Bishop of Kozyle in Epiros, who was serving as ambassador to Constantinople for the Despot of Arta, Nikephoros.[20] Not coincidentally, Nikephoros's wife, Anna Kantakouzena Palaeologina, was the daughter of the recently released Irene-Eulogia. Also not coincidentally, the new patriarch, Gregory, convoked in April 1283, at the Church of the Vlachernae in Constantinople, a synod that condemned Bekkos and deposed all unionist bishops; later that same year another synod met in Adramyttion, cementing the victory of the anti-unionists.[21] Pachymeres records that Irene-Eulogia, her daughter Anna, and her other daughter, Theodora, were in attendance.[22]

---

[19] For a fuller discussion of these events, see J. M. Hussey, *The Orthodox Church in the Byzantine Empire* (New York: Oxford University, 1986), 220–49.

[20] Acheimastou-Potamianou, "Basilissa Anna Palaiologina," 43.

[21] Gregory would hold another synod the following year which condemned the Latin Church's addition of the *Filioque* to the Creed, while articulating a more nuanced understanding of the relationship between the Son and the Spirit. See Aristeides Papadakis, *Crisis in Byzantium: The Filioque Controversy in the Patriarchate of Gregory II of Cyprus (1283–1289)* (New York: Fordham University, 1983; reprint, Crestwood, NY: St. Vladimir's Seminary, 1996), for a detailed exposition of Gregory II of Cyprus and his theology.

[22] George Pachymeres, *De Michaele et Andronico Palaeologis libri tredecim*, Corpus Scriptorum Historiae Byzantinae, ed. Immanuel Bekker et al. (Bonn, 1835), II,

Acheimastou-Potamianou finds the confluence of these events significant evidence of the probable rationale for the depiction of the procession of the Theotokos *Hodegetria* and the prominent place given to three
women in that procession on the wall of the monastery church in Arta:

> There is no doubt that at this time the established Tuesday procession
> in Constantinople took on greater magnificence and meaning. We may
> firmly state that the pious Eirene-Eulogia, a "celebrity" following her
> imprisonment, could not have failed to take part, along with her two
> daughters, in the procession of the icon of the Hodegetria, the palladium
> of the Capital, either in one or more of the Tuesday processions or in
> a special litany of the icon conducted to celebrate the events that had
> taken place. The memory of the ceremony in Constantinople in which
> the three ladies participated is, perhaps, preserved in the fresco of the
> Vlacherna monastery. Very likely, the recent death of Eirene-Eulogia
> in 1284 while Anna Palaiologina was still in Constantinople prompted
> the selection of this particular scene with its emotional charge. The
> representation of the litany in the women's monastery of the Vlacherna,
> the burial church of the family of the despots, was probably intended
> as a memorial service for the mother of Anna, and served to immor-
> talize Eirene-Eulogia with her two daughters at a propitious time in
> the position of Orthodoxy, on behalf of which she had struggled with
> such great zeal.[23]

Thus, an important liturgical procession in Constantinople remarkably
included women in a visibly prominent role. It was unusual for women
to play an active role in liturgical processions since the Byzantine practice
of secluding women, especially upper-class women, meant that they
were discouraged even from appearing in public outside of church and
at important events such as funerals.[24] Matrons would have had more

---

59; cited in Acheimastou-Potamianou, "Basilissa Anna Palaiologina," 45. Acheimastou-Potamianou also notes that a fresco of the two councils, which appears
on the west side of the south arch, depicts two women in attendance (they are
wearing the traditional head-and-shoulder covering of Byzantine noblewomen
known as the *maphorion*). She suggests that this might be an iconographic attes-
tation supporting Pachymeres' account of the presence of these women at the
anti-unionist councils (ibid., 47–48).

[23] Ibid., 45–46.

[24] On the seclusion of women in Byzantine society, see Michael Angold, *Church
and Society in Byzantium under the Comneni, 1081–1261* (New York: Cambridge
University, 1995), 426; Alice-Mary Talbot, "Women," in *The Byzantines*, ed. Gug-
lielmo Cavallo, trans. Thomas Dunlap, Teresa Lavender Fagan, and Charles

freedom than young, unmarried women, who were much more rigorously secluded, so it was probably not unusual for married women to participate in the weekly procession. Nevertheless, to have such a visibly public and active role was extraordinary. Even the deaconesses of the Great Church in Constantinople do not appear to have taken part in the elaborate procession that occurred during the part of the Divine Liturgy known as the Great Entrance. Thus, Eirene-Eulogia and her daughters Anna and Theodora were honored in this striking way as women of wealth and privilege who exhibited strong and self-sacrificing dedication to the Byzantine Church.

Part of the unusual public nature of their participation is represented in their holding some sort of liturgical vessels. Unfortunately, the poor state of preservation of the fresco and the small size of the figures makes it unclear what exactly the women are holding in their hands.[25] It is likely from their shape that the objects held by the two women in front of the third are either incense burners, as Acheimastou-Potamianou believes,[26] or pyxes (incense holders).[27] Their holding either of these vessels would further underscore their prominent liturgical position in the procession. Moreover, their role as incense-bearers would also recall the myrrh-bearing women of the Gospels, who remained steadfast in their loyalty to Jesus Christ. Thus, these women's dedication was recognized by the Byzantine Church's placing them prominently in an important procession, and doing so in a manner that equated them with the

---

Lambert (Chicago: University of Chicago, 1997), 117–43, at 132. Michael Psellos, an eleventh-century writer and imperial official, claimed that his mother lifted the veil from her face for the first time at her daughter's graveside. While this is likely rhetorical hyperbole, it nevertheless is useful as a gauge of the ideal behavior of a noblewoman in the Byzantine period. See José Grosdidier de Matons, "La femme dans l'empire byzantin," in *Histoire mondiale de la femme*, ed. Pierre Grimal (Paris: Nouvelle librairie de France, 1967), 28.

[25] A detail of the fresco focusing on the women and the vessels they are holding may be found in Perreault, *Women and Byzantine Monasticism*, pl. 3 fig. 12.

[26] Ibid., 45. Alternatively, he suggests the women may be holding lamps.

[27] The domed shape of the vessels may indicate that they are incense-burners. However, it is also possible that they are pyxes. Some were decorated with images of the myrrhbearing women, and incense was one of the contents they might hold, as evidenced by the Council of Narbonne in AD 589. See W. F. Volbach, *Elfenbeinarbeiten der Spätantike und des frühen Mittelalters*, 3rd ed. (Mainz, 1976), nos. 89–106 and 161–201a; cited in the "pyxis" entry in *The Oxford Dictionary of Byzantium*, 3:1762.

apostolic women of Scripture. Interestingly, their liturgical participation linked them to another group of women who also deliberately imaged these same women recorded in Scripture: namely, the myrrh-bearers of the Church of Jerusalem, who will be described later after the graptai.

The Graptai of the Pantokrator Monastery

As already noted, although the order of Widows and later the order of deaconesses died out in the Byzantine Church, the pastoral and liturgical needs that they met continued to exist. One group of women who partially met those needs served, curiously, at the male monastery of the Pantokrator in Constantinople.

The monastery of Christ the Almighty (Pantokrator) was founded by either the Byzantine emperor John II Komnenos or his wife, Irene, in the 1130s.[28] An interesting feature of the monastery was its triple church: three physically connected churches built at different times and dedicated, respectively, to Christ Pantokrator (south), the Theotokos *Eleousa*, or "Merciful" (north), and the Archangel Michael (center). A hospital and an old-age home were also attached to the monastery.[29]

As with Byzantine women's monasteries, so too the Pantokrator monastery followed the principle of seclusion or *abatos*,[30] that is, it did not admit members of the opposite sex into the monastic foundation proper: "Women will not enter the monastery and the monastery will be a forbidden area for them, even if they are distinguished ladies and are adorned by a devout life and a noble birth."[31] Because the clergy needed

---

[28] The *typikon* (rule) of the monastery is dated to October 1136; see Paul Gautier, "Le typikon du Christ Sauveur Pantocrator," *Revue des études byzantines* 32 (1974): 1–145. An English translation of the *typikon* and an introduction are provided in "Pantokrator: Typikon of Emperor John II Komnenos for the Monastery of Christ Pantokrator in Constantinople," trans. Robert Jordan, in *Byzantine Monastic Foundation Documents*, ed. John Thomas and Angela Constantinides Hero, with the assistance of Giles Constable, vol. 2 (Washington, DC: Dumbarton Oaks Research Library and Collection, 2000), 725–81.

[29] Jordan, "Pantokrator," 725.

[30] Alice-Mary Talbot, "Women and Mt Athos," in *Mount Athos and Byzantine Monasticism*, ed. Anthony and Mary Cunningham Bryer (Aldershot, Hampshire, 1996), 67–79; E. Papagianne, "Hoi klērikoi tōn byzantinōn gynaikeiōn monōn kai to abato," *Byzantiaka* (in Greek) 6 (1986): 77–93.

[31] Jordan, "Pantokrator," 749 sec. 18; Gautier, "Le Typikon du Christ Sauveur Pantocrator," 61, ll. 530–32.

for the sacramental life of the monastery could be found within it, a male monastery was, of course, able to exclude women far more than a female monastery could exclude men. Nevertheless, although a monastery needed a certain amount of seclusion from the world in order that its members could devote themselves to their spiritual practices, Byzantine monasticism was no more removed from the world than was medieval Western monasticism. As Rosemary Morris has remarked, monastic "contacts with the secular world were often close and frequent and, though monastic tradition might decree the opposite, complete seclusion—a life 'in the world but not of it'—was, in fact, rarely practiced."[32]

In fact, while never developing the mendicant orders that became prevalent in the West, neither did the Eastern Christian monastic tradition practice the complete seclusion found in Western cloistered orders, except in the most extreme type of anchorite (solitary) monasticism. From the beginnings of monasticism in Egypt and Palestine, there was a steady intercourse between monks and laypersons. Hospitality was a basic monastic virtue; the Basilian (and Macrinan) style of monastic life included charitable activities for the lay faithful in the neighboring community; and, as Morris has also noted, "central to the relationship between monks and laity was the role of the monk as spiritual guide."[33] This social, philanthropic, and spiritual monastic outreach was particularly true of coenobitic monasteries in urban areas, such as the Pantokrator in Constantinople. Its hospital, old-age home, and off-site sanatorium for lepers showed its founder's commitment to monastic philanthropy.

Pantokrator's spiritual leadership, too, was obviously important to its founder. The outermost church of the monastic complex, the Eleousa, served as a liminal area between the *abatos* of the monastery and the world outside the monastery walls,[34] providing spiritual nurture to the public with a regular calendar of services. The *typikon* (monastic rule) for the monastery mandated for the Eleousa church a large number of clergy, whose duties included celebrating for the people of the city a

---

[32] Rosemary Morris, *Monks and Laymen in Byzantium, 843–1118* (Cambridge: Cambridge University, 1995), 90.

[33] Ibid.

[34] Thus, for example, sec. 18 of the typikon forbids women's entering the monastery but makes the following provision: "But if some must enter, perhaps for the burial of their relations or their commemoration, they will not enter by the monastery gate but by the gate of the church of the Eleousa" (Jordan, "Pantokrator," 749).

weekly Friday night vigil, replete with a procession of banners into the church.[35] The section enumerating the clergy attached to the *Eleousa* listed a total of fifty clergy: priests, deacons, chanters, lamplighters, etc.[36] In addition to the fifty clergy, the section also mandated extra orphans to serve as alternate lamplighters when there were not enough "certified" orphans. Finally, completing the section on clergy, but excluded from the clergy count of fifty, was the founder's description of four women "with the rank of graptai":[37]

> We decree that four respectable women of propriety, mature in age and character and with the rank of *graptai*, should carry out their duties, two in one week and the other two in the next, and the four of them should be present on a Friday evening and watch over the church and what happens there. For we have decreed that these orphans and *graptai* should exist for this reason, that they should conduct the procedure of the meeting of the holy banners every week, carry out the service to those brothers who gather by refreshing them all with water, and see to the oversight of the church and the things connected with it.[38]

So, according to the *typikon*, people were needed to care for a monastic church that was open to the public on a regular basis, in order to offer visitors appropriate hospitality, and especially to ensure order during what was obviously a popular and well-attended weekly vigil. In earlier times, consecrated Widows or ordained female deacons would

---

[35] "On Friday of each week a vigil should take place with the night office when the banner of intercession with all the rest preceding and following it, together with all the clergy and people, will be invoked on the way by the members of the clergy of the *Eleousa* and will be met with all reverence and fitting honor and in faith brought into the church and all men and women, that is as many as follow these revered banners, will make an *ektenes* [litany or supplication], banners and people alike in the appropriate order, for the pardon and remission of our sins. *Kyrie eleison* [Lord, have mercy] will be repeated fifteen times for each banner and then they will go forwards again towards the holy tomb" (Jordan, "Pantokrator," 754–55, sec. 31). This service may have had a philanthropic aim as well and been intended primarily for poorer citizens since the *typikon* also stipulates that "those taking part will receive for their own consolation twelve *hyperpyra nomismata*." *Nomisma* means "coin," generally, but *hyperpyron* was used specifically for the standard Byzantine gold coin. See *The Oxford Dictionary of Byzantium*, 3:1490.

[36] Jordan, "Pantokrator," 754, sec. 30.

[37] The possible meaning of the title will be discussed later.

[38] Jordan, "Pantokrator," 754; Gautier, "Pantocrator," 77, ll. 785–90.

have served such functions as doorkeepers and maintainers of order.[39] However, as mentioned above, by the thirteenth century, both of these orders had disappeared from the Byzantine Church. Therefore, the emperor or empress, recognizing the pastoral and liturgical need, given the social segregation of the sexes in Byzantine culture mentioned earlier, for women as well as men to fulfill these tasks, appointed four women "with the rank of *graptai*" to serve the faithful visiting the monastic church throughout the week, rotating in teams of two on a weekly schedule, with all four *graptai* serving during the Friday evening vigil processions, which must have attracted a large crowd.

In fact, these *graptai* were the equivalent of deaconesses or Widows, in terms of both their eligibility requirements and their duties. With respect to eligibility, it is unclear whether the requirement that the *graptai* be proper or chaste (*semnas*) necessarily meant their being widowed, as were deaconesses and Widows, or virginal, as were deaconesses, but the general tenor is the same: the *graptai* had to be older women who were above reproach.[40] As to their functions, although there is no indication that they shared the sacramental duties connected to baptism and Eucharist that female deacons performed in earlier times, the duties of maintaining order and seeing to the needs of the faithful during church services were the same.

Were these *graptai* ordained? Were they considered clergy? There is no indication that they were ordained, and, since their duties had less to do with active participation in the liturgical services than with the peripheral liturgical duties of overseeing the banner procession at the Friday vigil and keeping order in the church, it is unlikely that they were ordained, particularly since, as previously mentioned, they were not included in the enumeration of the fifty clergy of the *Eleousa*. On the other hand, they were listed together with the clergy in that section and were counted as part of the clergy rather than as servants in the section that set forth

---

[39] For the doorkeeping and maintenance of order functions of the deaconess, see, e.g., the fourth-century *Apostolic Constitutions* II, 57 in Francis X. Funk, *Didascalia et Constitutiones Apostolorum* (Paderborn: Schöningh, 1905), 201.

[40] Enrolled Widows had to be at least sixty years old, according to 1 Timothy 5:9; the general qualifications in the Pantokrator *typikon* are reminiscent of this biblical passage. Deaconesses in the early church also had to be at least sixty years old originally, but the minimum age was later lowered to forty. See Karras, "Female Deacons," 274–75 and 294. Women in both orders could not have been married more than once and had to be of honorable reputation.

the remuneration scale for the various clergy.[41] So, why were the *graptai* listed with the clergy but not officially counted as part of them?

The answer may be twofold. First, the absence of ordained women by this time, due to the disappearance of the ordained female diaconate, may have led the founders and the capital's clergy to entertain not even the possibility of considering the *graptai* to be ordained, even to a minor order. Note, by contrast, that the certified orphans/lamplighters were listed as part of the clergy.[42] Second, the very title, the "rank" (*taxis*) or order of *graptai*, accorded them by the monastery's imperial founders may provide a clue. This term or office is unknown: it appears in no ancient, patristic, or Byzantine Greek lexicon, nor in any standard Byzantine reference works, such as the *Oxford Dictionary of Byzantium*. However, the literal sense of the term, "written," may relate these women to the Widows of the early Church as opposed to the female deacons. Although the writer of the First Epistle to Timothy uses a different word, *katalegesthō* (to count among, or to enroll), the meaning is identical: these were enrolled women who had an established pastoral, spiritual, and semi-liturgical church ministry and hence were supported by the church (or monastery, in this case), but they were not part of the clergy who participated more centrally in the liturgical services as celebrant, chanter, etc. Thus, they were indeed clergy in its broader sense but were consecrated as opposed to being ordained to either major or minor orders.

Myrophoroi—The Myrrhbearers

The Patriarchate of Jerusalem, although autocephalous ecclesiastically, in reality was very closely linked to the Byzantine Church throughout most of the middle Byzantine period, particularly in liturgical terms.

---

[41] "We decree that the clergy [*klerikous*] of this church should receive as their [cash] allowances and grain allowances the following: the leading priests should each receive fifteen *hyperpyra nomismata* and twenty-five maritime *modioi* of grain each, the four precentors six similar *nomismata* each and fifteen similar *modioi* of grain each, the eight orphans or lamplighters the same amount, the four *graptai* four similar *nomismata* each and twelve maritime *modioi* of grain each." Just below this, the *typikon* continues, "A weekly allowance should also be given to the servants [*douleutais*]" (Gautier, "Pantocrator," 77–79; "Pantokrator," 755, sec. 32).

[42] Beyond the difference in clerical categorization, it appears that the Comneni desired that their monastery adhere to the Hebrew prophetic injunction to care for the widows and orphans (the most vulnerable members of society) by providing them with salaried ministries.

The hymnography emanating from the monastery of St. Sabas outside Jerusalem, and certain liturgical practices, especially paschal ones, were exported to Constantinople and other places by pilgrims wishing to re-create the rituals of this most ancient and apostolic of churches.[43] By the turn of the first millennium, Jerusalem had an elaborate and well-established set of rites surrounding the celebration of Easter. One unique element of the Jerusalem rite, of which traces appear in other places (such as the incense-bearing women in the Arta fresco), is the order of *myrophoroi*, myrrhbearers, who participated in the Holy Saturday and Resurrection services of the Church of Jerusalem.

All four gospels[44] record that several female disciples of Jesus,[45] unlike the Twelve, attended his crucifixion and burial, and returned early on Sunday morning with myrrh and spices to anoint his body, only to find the empty tomb and hence become the first evangelists of the resurrection. These myrrhbearing women, or *myrophoroi* in Greek, were celebrated in the early Church for their courage and selfless devotion. The Eastern Church even gave Mary Magdalene the title *isapostolos*, or "equal to the apostles."[46] In the Byzantine period, the development of the *Pentecostarion*, the cycle of hymns for the period from Easter to All Saints (the week after Pentecost) included the special commemoration of the Myrrhbearers on the third Sunday after Easter. At approximately this same time, a special order of women developed in the Church of Jerusalem who were named after these female disciples of Jesus Christ.

---

[43] Pilgrims from both the Latin West and the Greek East brought back to their home communities descriptions of the Lenten and paschal rites of the Jerusalem church. These descriptions often led to the incorporation of certain Jerusalem rituals (particularly surrounding the crucifixion and resurrection) into the rituals of their own local and regional churches. One of the most famous of such pilgrims in late antiquity was the late fourth-century Spanish nun Egeria, who kept a diary of her pilgrimage to Egypt, Palestine, and Syria. *Éthérie. Journal de voyage*, ed. H. Pétré, Sources chrétiennes 21 (Paris: Cerf, 1948); English translation in *Egeria's Travels*, ed. and trans. John Wilkinson, 3rd ed. (Warminster: Aris & Phillips, 1999).

[44] Matthew 27:55–28:10; Mark 15:40–16:11; Luke 23:49–24:11; John 19:25–20:18.

[45] The number of women and their names vary in the accounts, but all include Mary Magdalene; the three Synoptic Gospels also list Mary the mother of James.

[46] The epithet *isapostolos* was given in the early Church to women such as Saint Thecla, companion to the Apostle Paul, and Saint Nina/Nino, apostle to the Georgians, as well as to men (e.g., Constantine the Great) who were deemed by the Church to have played an important role in propagating the Christian faith.

It is not known when exactly the order of *myrophoroi* developed in the Jerusalem Church; when they disappeared is equally unknown. They are not mentioned in early church documents relating to the paschal celebration in Jerusalem, including the detailed description given by Egeria in the late fourth century. However, there are numerous references to these women in a *typikon*[47] (liturgical rule) of the Church of Jerusalem, contained in a twelfth-century manuscript that apparently is a copy of an earlier work from the late ninth or early tenth century.[48] Egeria's diary and the dating of the original *typikon* on which the twelfth-century manuscript is based thus provide us with a *terminus post quem* of the fifth century and a *terminus ante quem* of the ninth century, since the *myrophoroi* were clearly an established order by the time the *typikon* was written. It is likely that they still existed in the thirteenth century when the extant manuscript was copied from the lost original, although it is also possible that they had become defunct by that time but still existed within institutional memory. Their disappearance thus may coincide with, or postdate by a century or so, the disappearance of the female diaconate in the Byzantine Church.

Unlike the confusion over the use of the term *myrophoroi* by certain Russian travelers describing the Great Church in Constantinople,[49] these

[47] Note that there are two distinct types of *typika*: monastic and liturgical (although a monastic *typikon* may include elements of a liturgical *typikon*).

[48] The text of this *typikon*, *Typikon tēs en hierosolymois ekklēsias*, is reproduced in A. Papadopoulos-Kerameus, *Analekta hierosolymtikēs stachyologias* [in Greek], vol. 2 (St. Petersburg, 1894), esp. 179–99. The manuscript dates to AD 1122, but in the prologue (p. iii) Papadopoulos-Kerameus argues that it is a copy of an earlier work from the late ninth or early tenth century, based on a prayer commemorating Patriarch Nicholas, whose patriarchate lasted from AD 932 to 947 (the two Latin patriarchs named Nicholas reigned several decades after the written date of the manuscript, so the commemoration cannot refer to either of them). The *typikon* provides the texts and rubrics (some of which may have been added in the twelfth century) for the liturgical services of the Church of Jerusalem. A summary of the material on the *myrophoroi* contained in the Jerusalem *typikon* can be found in Gabriel Bertonière, *The Historical Development of the Easter Vigil and Related Services in the Greek Church*, Orientalia Christiana Analecta 193 (Rome: Pontificum Institutum Studiorum Orientalium, 1972), 50 n. 108.

[49] I am indebted to George Majeska, who has brought to my attention that some Russian travelers to Constantinople, such as Anthony of Novgorod, mentioned "myrrhbearing women" who sang and who had a special place near the Great Church's "prothesis chapel," or *skeuophylakion*, which was located just outside the north door in the northeast bay. Despite Anthony's identification of them

women definitely cannot be identified with deaconesses, since that order is separately mentioned in the *typikon*'s description of the paschal services. Thus, the *myrophoroi* were a distinctive order unique to the Church of Jerusalem. Their liturgical functions are quite clearly spelled out in the Jerusalem *typikon*, and largely mirror, in a stylized and liturgical fashion, the activities of the biblical myrrhbearing women.

The Jerusalem *myrophoroi* began their liturgical service early on Holy Saturday morning, when they accompanied the patriarch and his clerical assistants, such as the archdeacon and chanters, to the Holy Sepulcher. The myrrhbearers were to clean and prepare the oil lamps in the Holy Sepulcher, chanting the canon and the liturgy of the hours while they worked. When they had finished cleaning and preparing the lamps, they chanted the "Glory to the Father" and a hymn in plagal second tone.[50] A deacon then would chant the litany, and the patriarch would lock the Holy Sepulcher after extinguishing the lamps.

It cannot be stated for certain whether the *myrophoroi* were included as part of the clergy in the vesper service and for the Divine Liturgy of St. James,[51] since they are not individually mentioned in the rubrics. However, it is likely that their inclusion should be inferred since, at the end of the liturgy, the *typikon* mentions that the myrrhbearers remained behind and reentered the Holy Sepulcher in order to cense and anoint it.[52] The Church of the Holy Sepulcher was then locked until the return of the patriarch and clergy early the following morning.

---

as myrrhbearers, however, Majeska believes that the reference is to the deaconesses of the Great Church, who, according to Constantine Porphyrogenitus, *De ceremoniis* 44 (35) were located in the "women's narthex." Majeska theorizes that the confusion of titles is due to the Russians' not having deaconesses; the title "myrrhbearer," however, was frequently used for women serving a wide variety of non-ordained functions in the Russian Church.

[50] See original text in Papadopoulos-Kerameus, *Analekta*, 179, ll. 5–11. The manuscript mistakenly uses the masculine plural on occasion rather than the feminine plural when referring to the *myrophoroi*. It is likely that the copyist was confused by the (masculine) second declension ending of the title for these women, although the term *myrophoroi* occurred commonly in Byzantine hymnography. The text of the hymn appears in the manuscript shortly before these rubrics.

[51] The patriarch presided over the second half of the liturgy from within the Holy Sepulcher, using the Holy Stone as an altar.

[52] See original text in Papadopoulos-Kerameus, *Analekta*, 189, ll. 11–14.

For Easter matins, the clergy, which apparently included the *myropho-roi*, gathered early in the morning at the patriarchate, in the *secreton*,[53] where they changed into white vestments before presumably returning to the Church of the Holy Sepulcher. Although the text does not give a full list of clerical orders included, the rubrics for the paschal matins service make it impossible not to understand the term "clergy" to include the myrrhbearers. Outside the church, the clergy chanted the Easter *apolytikion*,[54] "Christ is risen," several times as a refrain to psalm verses intoned by the patriarch, who then called out: "Open to me the gates of righteousness; I shall confess the Lord as I enter in," to which the arch-deacon responded with another "Christ is risen." Then,

> The doors of the church are immediately opened and the patriarch to-gether with the clergy enter the church, chanting the "Christ is risen." And the patriarch and the archdeacon immediately enter into the Holy Sepulcher, those two alone, with the *myrophoroi* standing before the Holy Sepulcher. Then the patriarch shall come out to them and say to them [the *myrophoroi*]: "Rejoice! [*or* Greetings!] Christ is risen." The *myrophoroi* then fall down at his feet, and, after rising up, they cense the patriarch and sing the *polychronion*[55] to him. They [then] withdraw to the place where they customarily stand.[56]

The matins service then proceeded normally with the chanting of the canon for Easter, the *exaposteilarion*, the praises (lauds), and the Easter *aposticha*.[57] Near the end of the service comes the final reference to the *myrophoroi*.[58] Following the deacon's chanting of the *epakousta*, there was

---

[53] *Secreton* means office or private room; perhaps this was the private office or vestry of the patriarch of Jerusalem.

[54] The *apolytikion* is the dismissal hymn(s) for vespers. It is chanted again toward the beginning of the matins service, and during the small entrance of the Divine Liturgy.

[55] The *polychronion* (literally, "many years") was a hymn of praise sung for either an emperor or a patriarch.

[56] See original text in Papadopoulos-Kerameus, *Analekta*, 190–91.

[57] Papadopoulos-Kerameus, *Analekta*, 191–99. The *exaposteilarion* is a hymn chanted at matins and connected to the particular gospel reading for that Sunday (there is a cycle of gospel readings for matins). The *aposticha* are a set of hymns normally done near the end of vespers; the paschal *aposticha*, however, are sung at matins through the Ascension.

[58] See original text in Papadopoulos-Kerameus, *Analekta*, 199.

a procession to the *bema*[59] with two of each clerical order: deacons, subdeacons, deaconesses, and *myrophoroi*.[60] The deacons held censers, the subdeacons and deaconesses held *manoualia*,[61] and the *myrophoroi* each carried a *triskelion*.[62] The two *myrophoroi* took up position one on each side of the Holy Sepulcher, censing throughout the second deacon's reading of the Gospel. At the end of the reading, the myrrhbearers entered the Holy Sepulcher and censed and anointed it.

It is clear that the activities of the *myrophoroi* in the liturgical services of Holy Saturday and Sunday mimicked those of the original myrrhbearing women: they were present at the tomb, they censed and anointed Christ—in the person of the patriarch—and the tomb, and they even re-created the myrrhbearing women's encounter with the angel(s), or the risen Christ, at the tomb early on Sunday morning.[63]

The *typikon* leaves many questions unanswered. For example, it is unclear whether there are a number of *myrophoroi* or only two. Since the rubrics at the end of the matins reads "the two *myrophoroi*" as opposed to "two of the *myrophoroi*," it is possible that there were only two in this order. However, only two of each order participated in the matins procession, so, for example, it also says "the two deacons," although there

---

[59] The *bema* was a type of raised platform or pulpit that was located in the center of the *solea*, the part of the nave immediately in front of the sanctuary and iconostasis.

[60] Papadopoulos-Kerameus, *Analekta*, 199. The text is not very clear as to the order of clergy in the procession since it treats the subdeacons together with the deacons and before the *myrophoroi* and deaconesses, but it also says that the *myrophoroi* follow the deacons. The probable order is deacons, *myrophoroi*, deaconesses, and subdeacons.

[61] The *manoualion* is a single candlestick used in processions. Peter D. Day, *The Liturgical Dictionary of Eastern Christianity* (Collegeville, MN: Liturgical Press, 1993), 180.

[62] The *triskelion* is a "portable lectern from which the Gospel may be read. It is so called because it is made up of three shafts, whereas the lectern, which is made of two shafts to form a large X-shaped structure, is called the diskelion" (Day, *Liturgical Dictionary*, 294).

[63] "In keeping with the principle of imitation of the activities described in the Gospel, the Jerusalem liturgy has the *myrophoroi* greet the patriarch when he emerges from the tomb after the entrance of Orthros and then incense and anoint the tomb after the Vigil Liturgy and again after the Gospel at the end of Orthros" (Bertonière, *Easter Vigil*, 50 n. 108). The patriarch may be understood either as Jesus, in the Johannine account, or as the one or two angels in the Synoptics (and John), but presumably he represents the risen Lord.

were undoubtedly more than two connected to the church. Therefore, it is possible that there were more than two *myrophoroi* attached to the Church of the Holy Sepulcher, although for practical reasons only two participated liturgically, at least for the Easter matins. In fact, given the Jerusalem Church's propensity to re-create the Passion events as closely as possible, it is likely that there were more than two *myrophoroi* since the gospel accounts generally list more than two women at the crucifixion, if not at the tomb itself.[64]

A second unanswered question concerns where the particular location[65] was within the church for the *myrophoroi* when they were not actively participating in the services. Bertonière finds the reference significant because it suggests that "their role was something of a permanent office."[66] This raises perhaps the most important unanswered question, namely, whether the *myrophoroi* were ordained. They probably would not have been considered a major order since (1) they do not appear to have had the type of sacramental functions associated with major orders,[67] and (2) they would not have fit into the threefold system of major orders, deacon(ess), presbyter/priest, and bishop, already well entrenched in church practice at least five centuries earlier. Therefore, either they were "consecrated" but not ordained, such as the Widows in the early Church, and probably the *graptai* already mentioned, or they were ordained to a special minor order of clergy, akin to the level of reader. This latter option seems more likely, given the myrrhbearers' important liturgical functions during the Easter services and the *typikon*'s assumption that they are part of the clergy.

Thus, although there is no ordination rite extant for the *myrophoroi*, either in the Jerusalem *typikon* or elsewhere, one may hypothesize that some sort of tonsure, or minor-order ordination (*cheirothesia*), was likely done for the *myrophoroi*, for two reasons. First, it would fit with the early and Byzantine Church's practice of clearly restricting liturgical

---

[64] Matthew and Mark name at least three women at the crucifixion but only two at the tomb early Sunday morning; Luke does not give the names of the women at the crucifixion but names three women at the tomb along with an indeterminate number of other women; and John gives the names of three women at the crucifixion but only Mary Magdalene at the tomb.

[65] Papadopoulos-Kerameus, *Analekta*, 191.

[66] Bertonière, *Easter Vigil*, 50 n. 108.

[67] E.g., deacons and deaconesses took the Eucharist to the sick and received it themselves at the altar; they also assisted in the baptism of converts.

functions to clergy, of either major or minor orders. Eirene-Eulogia and her daughters indeed participated in a liturgical procession, but it was an out-of-doors procession that was not part of a standard liturgical service. Laypersons traditionally did not participate in the worship of the Byzantine Church beyond the activities common to all the faithful; even chanters and readers were ordained as members of the minor orders of clergy. Second, as previously discussed, although the *typikon* gives no definition of the term "clergy," it is apparent from the rubrics at the beginning of the paschal matins service[68] that the term must include the *myrophoroi* since they enter the church with the patriarch and immediately stand at the entrance to the Holy Sepulcher while he enters it with the archdeacon. Thus, while the *myrophoroi* may have been consecrated by a simple prayer, it appears more likely from their functions as described in the Jerusalem *typikon* that they were in some way ordained to a type of minor order.

Conclusion

While early female church orders such as Widows and deaconesses vanished by the later Byzantine period, meager but important literary evidence demonstrates that women in the Byzantine Church, at different times and in different parts of the empire, continued to be specially designated for particular liturgical roles and were even ordained, consecrated, or "enrolled" into various orders. These roles or orders served one, or usually more, of three functions: (1) they honored certain women for their particular devotion to the church; (2) they provided a means for women faithful to be properly cared for during church services, while attending to the demands of social convention; and (3) they evoked the scriptural witness of the apostolic ministry of women to Jesus Christ.

Eirene-Eulogia and her daughters served in a semi-liturgical role that honored them personally by positioning them prominently in a popular weekly procession with the palladium of the city. Moreover, the nature of their liturgical role evoked the myrrhbearers of Scripture, who did not abandon their Lord at his crucifixion and who later went with myrrh and incense to attend to his body. The *myrophoroi* of the Church of Jerusalem explicitly imaged the myrrbearing women of the gospels during the Easter services at the Church of the Holy Sepulcher, re-creating in a stylistic and liturgical manner the actions of the biblical women for whom

[68] Papadopoulos-Kerameus, *Analekta*, 190–91.

their order was named. As for the *graptai*, they demonstrate that, even after the decline of the orders of Widows and female deacons, the need for a liturgical and pastoral ministry by and for women was recognized even in a male monastery, which responded by essentially re-creating the early order of Widows in these older, well-respected women "with the rank of *graptai*."

The existence of these various orders and groups of women in the Byzantine Church, as with their predecessors in early Christianity, reveals the ambivalence of a male-dominated ecclesiastical hierarchy toward the active liturgical participation of women as more than lay faithful. This ambivalence resulted from, on the one hand, theological notions of women's subordination to men combined with social conventions that limited women's activity to private, domestic space, and, on the other hand, the theological recognition of the spiritual equality of women combined with a pastoral desire to ensure that the Church met the full spiritual needs of its women faithful. Thus, women continued to be excluded from the leadership ranks of presbyters and bishops, and even the female diaconate disappeared with no formal indication in the extant literature of how, when, or why.[69] On the other hand, the service of women in formally recognized liturgical roles continued to fulfill a combination of needs and interests arising from such disparate factors as (1) a culture that imposed sexual segregation and the seclusion of women, (2) a desire to honor publicly and formally those who had contributed much to church life, and (3) the Byzantines' fondness for re-creating liturgically the important events in the life of Christ. Thus, while the theology and practice of the Byzantine Church disallowed the ordination of women to most major orders, its pastoral and liturgical concerns for its faithful, specifically for its women faithful, led to diverse and unique roles and orders for some women—as processional incense-bearers, wardens of a public vigil hosted by a male monastery, and liturgical representations of the myrrhbearing women who ministered to Christ.

---

[69] I have proposed that the disappearance of the ordained female diaconate in the Byzantine Church was connected to the rise in the middle Byzantine period of notions of ritual impurity associated with menstruation. See Karras, "Female Deacons," 309–14.

10

Remembering Tradition

Women's Monastic Rituals and the Diaconate

Phyllis Zagano

In 2002 the International Theological Commission wrote that "it per-tains to the ministry of discernment which the Lord has established in his Church to pronounce authoritatively" on the question of women deacons. This study discusses the ways by which ancient and contemporary cere-monies for women demonstrate the tradition of the ordination of women as deacons. It distinguishes between and among monastic profession, consecration of a virgin, and diaconal ordination, addressing in particular the ceremonials of Carthusian nuns.

When the International Theological Commission (ITC) published its research on the diaconate in 2002, it presented two conclusions: (1) the women deacons of history were not precisely identical to male dea-cons; and (2) the sacrament of orders clearly distinguishes among the priest, bishop, and deacon both in tradition and in the teaching of the magisterium. Therefore, the ITC wrote, "it pertains to the ministry of discernment which the Lord has established in his Church to pronounce authoritatively on this question," i.e., ordaining women as deacons.[1]

The ITC specifically noted distinctions between men and women dea-cons in the ancient church "evidenced by the rite of institution and the

"Remembering Tradition: Women's Monastic Rituals and the Diaconate," *Theological Studies* 72 (2011): 787–811.

[1] ITC, *From the Diakonia of Christ to the Diakonia of the Apostles* (Mundelein, IL: Hillenbrand Books, 2004), 109; translation of the official French document, "*Le Diaconat: Évolution et perspectives*," http://www.vatican.va/roman_curia /congregations/cfaith/cti_documents/rc_con_cfaith_pro_05072004_diaconate _fr.html. This and all other URLs referenced herein were accessed May 16, 2011.

functions they exercised."[2] Depending on limited examination of available texts, the ITC ignored some scholarship that supports the argument that women deacons were indeed considered as belonging to the same order as men deacons in antiquity, but also well after. For example, the ITC implies that the eighth-century ordination liturgies of the Barberini codex, which are virtually identical for men and women deacons, did not incorporate women into the order of deacon, arguing that the rituals were mainly for monastic women; and the ITC further asserts that the women so ordained exercised no liturgical ministry.[3]

Significant scholarly evaluation of historical evidence, however, combined with worldwide calls for the restoration of the tradition of women deacons, drives contemporary discussion relative to the formalization of ministry by women through ordination to the diaconate. Evaluation of the historical evidence of women deacons has at least two subsets: What did women deacons do? And, how were women deacons ritually acknowledged?[4]

This study investigates ritual. It does not enter into arguments about the precise functions of the women deacons of history except to acknowledge the fact that whatever they did was sufficiently "diaconal" in nature for them to be called deacons. Rather, this paper evaluates historical and current ceremonies for Cistercian and Carthusian nuns in comparison

---

[2] ITC, *Diakonia of Christ*, 109.

[3] Ibid., 23–24. See Valerie A. Karras, "Female Deacons in the Byzantine Church," *Church History* 73 (2004): 272–316, at 275.

[4] Some of the more recent work demonstrating the fact of women deacons includes: Roger Gryson, *The Ministry of Women in the Early Church* (Collegeville, MN: Liturgical Press, 1976), translation of *Le ministère des femmes dans L'Église ancienne*, Recherches et synthèses, section d'histoire 4 (Gembloux: J. Duculot, 1972); Aimé Georges Martimort, *Deaconesses: An Historical Study*, trans. K. D. Whitehead (San Francisco: Ignatius, 1986), translation of *Les Diaconesses: Essai Historique* (Rome: C.L.V.-Edizioni Liturgiche, 1982); Ute E. Eisen, *Women Officeholders in Early Christianity: Epigraphical and Literary Studies* (Collegeville, MN: Liturgical Press, 2000), translation of *Amtsträgerinnen im frühen Christentum: Epigraphische und literarische Studien* (Göttingen: Vandenhoeck & Ruprecht, 1996); Kevin Madigan and Carolyn Osiek, *Ordained Women in the Early Church: A Documentary History* (Baltimore: Johns Hopkins University, 2005); Gary Macy, *The Hidden History of Women's Ordination: Female Clergy in the Medieval West* (New York: Oxford University, 2007). The debate between Gryson and Martimort centers on whether ordained women received the sacrament of holy orders; the negative interpretation drives the ITC's 2002 document.

with known diaconal ordination ceremonies in an effort to recover some of the lost tradition of women deacons, distinguishing between and among monastic profession, diaconal ordination, and consecration of a virgin, which latter brings women into the order of virgins.[5]

Ordination ceremonies for women deacons are known from the early third century.[6] They preserve significant literary and epigraphical evidence of women deacons in many regions, often against pressure to end the practice of ordination of women as deacons.[7]

In the sixth century Radegund (ca. 520–586), queen and wife of Frankish King Clothar, insisted on being ordained deacon, and Caesarius of Arles (ca. 468–542) wrote his Rule for Virgins. Subsequently, women deacons existed regionally up to the twelfth century, and as late as the eleventh century popes allowed Western bishops to ordain women as deacons.[8] The orders of women under direct investigation here, the Cistercians and Carthusians, distinguished by adherence to their oldest

---

[5] Canon 604 of the 1983 Code of Canon Law provides for the "order of virgins."

[6] The third-century *Didascalia Apostolorum* does not present rituals but references women deacons as parallel to male deacons: The fourth-century Syriac *Apostolic Constitutions*, dependent on the *Didascalia*, gives the ordination rites for deaconesses, among others, and the consecration rite for virgins and widows, among others. See A. Vööbus, *The Didascalia Apostolorum in Syriac, I. Syr. 175 and 176* and *II. Syr. 179 and 180*, Corpus Scriptorum Christianorum Orientalium (CSCO) 401–402 and 407–408, trans. A. Vööbus (Louvain: Peeters, 1979), book 8:3–5, 16–26; *Les constitutions apostoliques*, 3 vols., ed., trans., intro., critical text, and notes Marcel Metzger, Sources Chrétiennes (hereafter SC) vols. 320, 329, and 336 (Paris: Cerf, 1985–1987), 3:138–48, 216–28; Engl. trans. "Apostolic Constitutions," in *Fathers of the Third and Fourth Centuries*, ed. Alexander Roberts and James Donaldson, *Ante-Nicene Fathers: The Writings of the Fathers down to A.D. 325*, vol. 7, repr. ed. (Peabody, MA: Hendrickson, 1994), 481–83, 491–93. Extant ceremonies include those found in the following mss.: Barberini gr. 336; Grottaferrata gr. Gb1, Vatican gr. 1872, and Coislin gr. 213.

[7] See esp. Eisen, *Women Officeholders in Early Christianity*; Madigan and Osiek, *Ordained Women in the Catholic Church*; and Macy, *Hidden History of Women's Ordination*.

[8] In 1018 Pope Benedict VIII gave the bishop of Porto the right to ordain women deacons, a right affirmed by Popes John XIX in 1025 and Leo IX in 1049. In addition to the works noted above, document collections regarding women deacons include: Josephine Mayer, *Monumenta de viduis diaconissis virginibusque tractantia*, Florilegium patristicum tam veteris quam medii aevi auctores complectens 42 (Bonn: Peter Hanstein, 1938); Heike Grierser, Rosemarie Nürnberg, and Gisela Muschiol, "Texte aus der kirchlichen Tradition und lehramtliche

known rules and usages, were founded in the reformist wave of the eleventh century.[9]

The initial hypothesis for this article is that the tradition of ordaining women to the office of deacon seems to have become connected to or subsumed within other monastic rituals, beginning with the early sixth-century Rule of Caesarius of Arles.[10] My working hypothesis is that where a bishop or priest is needed for a contemporary ceremony, the ceremony historically relates to ordination as it developed over centuries. Conversely, if a bishop or priest is not necessary to the ritual, that ritual more clearly relates to the permanent monastic profession to a stable community, which in the oldest traditions and the oldest orders is always made at the hands of the abbess or prioress, paralleling the process of incardination for secular clerics.

Other ceremonies extant today, specifically those for consecration of a virgin, reveal much about older traditions regarding women's service in the church. The Latin church has two rites for the consecration of a virgin: one for consecration lived in the world, and another for consecration combined with monastic profession. A third Carthusian rite for consecration of a virgin is *sui generis*.

Although the ritual for consecration to a life of virginity lived in the world has similarities to the diaconal ordination ritual, I here focus on three monastic ceremonies: for consecration of a virgin combined with monastic profession (Benedictine), for monastic profession alone (Benedictine, Cistercian, Carthusian), and for consecration of a virgin performed some time after monastic profession (Carthusian).

The similarities and distinctions between Cistercian and Carthusian traditions are illustrative of two major points of investigation: determining, first, whether roots of some Carthusian and Cistercian ceremonial traditions are planted in those for the diaconate and, second, whether

---

Dokumente," in *Diakonat: Ein Amt für Frauen in der Kirche—Ein frauengrechtes Amt?*, ed. Peter Hünermann et al. (Ostfildern: Schwabenverlag, 1997).

[9] While Cistercians are a Benedictine reform order, Carthusians are formally *sui generis*, although various women's convents, including some Benedictine convents, joined the order after the first convent of Prébayon joined the Carthusian order.

[10] Caesarius of Arles, *Regula ad virgines* in *Codex regularum monasticarum et canonicarum . . .*, 6 vols., ed. Lucas Holstenius and Marian Brockie (1759; Augsburg: Veith, 1957), 1:354–62 (1759 ed.). See also Maria Caritas McCarthy, *The Rule for Nuns of St. Caesarius of Arles: A Translation with a Critical Introduction* (Washington, DC: The Catholic University of America, 1960).

monastic profession is wholly within the ceremonial purview of the abbess or prioress. Following on this second point, it appears the abbess or prioress admits the professing nun to what vestigial diaconal functions and rights remain within the abbey or monastery, specifically to liturgical functions and rights proper to a nun of the abbey or monastery (but not proper solely to the abbess or prioress). For example, when the Cistercian nun makes solemn profession with benediction or consecration as a nun, she receives the cowl from the abbess and with it certain liturgical rights. However, when the Carthusian nun receives the consecration of a virgin (typically four years after solemn profession) she receives the stole, maniple, and cross from the presiding cleric, along with certain liturgical rights. In both cases the woman superior presides over the monastic profession, the Cistercian abbess or the Carthusian prioress receiving the individual nun permanently into the monastic community. But the Carthusian consecration of a virgin is performed by a cleric, usually a bishop.

In Cistercian and Carthusian usages, consecration (or benediction) of a virgin or nun and solemn monastic profession are distinct. However, the ceremonies bespeak two, or possibly three, events: (1) solemn monastic profession as member of a stable monastic community; (2) personal profession of vows within that community; and (3) consecration as a virgin or nun.

I posit that vestiges of the ceremony of ordination as deacon were incorporated into ceremonies of monastic profession, and that personal profession of solemn vows and consecration of a virgin have overcome and displaced diaconal ordination, which remains a well-remembered part of women's monastic life in the Orthodox churches. The following discussion moves from monastic profession and the Rule of Benedict, to the Rule of Caesarius of Arles, to the ordination of women deacons, to the consecration of virgins, to Cistercian ritual and tradition, and finally to Carthusian ritual and tradition. Each section contributes to the supposition that the tradition of women deacons has been lost, but not forgotten, in the Latin church.

Monastic Profession and the Rule of Benedict

Monastic profession offers a pathway to distinguish among the other ceremonies under investigation. The older tradition of women's monastic profession presents the abbess as chief celebrant of the profession liturgy. Only Benedictine ceremonials that included consecration of a virgin as part of monastic profession required the celebrant to be a cleric, usually a bishop.[11] That the ordinary celebrant for consecration of a virgin is a bishop may indicate that ceremony's relationship to sacrament. When the consecration of a virgin is not included in the profession ceremony, the priest or bishop plays a different role. Benedictines—at least those in Eichstätt, Germany, as Collins reports—dropped the consecration of a virgin at least by the early nineteenth century; thereafter only the abbess presided at profession ceremonies.

That the Rite of Consecration to a Life of Virginity exists today as separate and distinct from the rite of monastic profession, even though it can be combined with monastic profession, supports the notion of relation of consecration of virgin to the roots of ordination—but not entirely because Benedictine choir nuns (but not lay sisters) received the cowl at profession, not at consecration of a virgin,[12] and the monastic profession was later joined to the ritual of consecration of a virgin.[13] Hence certain questions arise: Does the cowl have liturgical significance? Is it related to the diaconal stole? Or is it related to the alb, which according to current liturgical instructions is to be worn by all adult ministers at liturgy? Or is it a combination garment, serving as both alb and stole? Or, is it neither? In any event, the cowl is presented within the ceremony, after profession is made.

The further question naturally arises: What then comprises monastic profession, and what are its symbols? For Benedictines, the importance of the vows is explained in the Rule of Benedict (ca. 530). The novice promises "stability, fidelity to monastic life, and obedience in the oratory in presence of the whole community, and in writing. He states his promise in a document drawn up in the name of the saints whose relics are there, and of the abbot, who is present" (RB 58.17-19).[14] The novice lays his or her profession document on the altar and prostrates at the feet of each member of the community, following which he or she is considered a full member of the monastic community.

---

[11] Mary Collins, "Sisters Professing Sisters: Retrieving a Lost Tradition," *American Benedictine Review* 47 (1996): 284–309.

[12] Mildred Anna Rosalie Tuker and Hope Malleson, *Handbook to Christian and Ecclesiastical Rome*, 4 vols. in 3 (London: Adam and Charles Black, 1900), 3:76.

[13] Ibid., 3:109.

[14] Benedict, *The Rule of St. Benedict in English*, ed. Timothy Fry et al. (Collegeville, MN: Liturgical Press, 1981). This edition is known as *RB 1980*. There is a threefold aspect to the one promise in Benedictine monastic profession, not three separate vows. In fact, "promise," not "vow," is used.

The ceremony of monastic profession is understood first and foremost as the ceremonial donation of one's life to God through the aegis of the monastic way of life, as accepted by the abbess or abbot in the name of the community. The details of that monastic life—Benedict's interpretation of the model of the Christian community at the time of Jesus—are continually worked out according to individual times and traditions in which the community exists. The monastic profession presented in the Rule of Benedict does not include specific vows of poverty, chastity, and obedience, but rather promises of obedience, stability, and conversion. The later concept of the evangelical counsels has been subsumed into monastic profession, but the counsels are not specifically stated. Common life assumes poverty in terms of common ownership of temporal goods; obedience to the community as represented by the abbess further supports that life; and conversion is in fact the entire project. But what about chastity? Specifically, although Benedict may have assumed that members would be celibate, why do monastic profession ceremonies—historically at least—include consecration of a virgin for women? Is this ceremony what remains of diaconal ordination and consecration of a virgin from the earliest days of the church? Have the two ceremonials been conflated? If so, why?

The Rule of Caesarius of Arles

Benedict's Rule is preceded by many others, including that for women by Caesarius of Arles, bishop of Arles from 502 until his death in 542; his influence in Gaul was second only to that of Gregory of Tours (ca. 538–595), archbishop of Tours from 573 to 595.

Pope Symmachus (papacy 498–514) accorded Caesarius special approbation of his episcopal authority by awarding him a pallium—at the time worn only by the pope and metropolitans connected to the Holy See—and authorized the wearing of the dalmatic by Caesarius's deacons.[15] Caesarius's particular status—he had deacons, by then an order surviving primarily in Rome and other major sees—would also allow him to create a means of organizing women for his local church, even in the face of growing patriarchal resistance to ministry by women.

The rule Caesarius wrote for women (ca. 512–534), often called a "rule for nuns," is actually titled *Regula ad virgines*. It follows earlier descriptions

---

[15] See McCarthy, *Rule for Nuns* 5, citing Caesarius of Arles, *Opera omnia nunc primum in unum collecta*, 2 vols. in 3, ed. Germain Morin (Namur, Belgium: Maredsous Abbey, 1937–1942), 2:9–10, 12–14.

of the necessary work of the "wise virgin" in terms remarkably similar to those used to describe the diaconal charism then and now.

Many interpretations of the wise virgin's lamp oil analogy (Matt 25:1-13) preceded Caesarius's writings. For Origen, the oil symbolized piety; for Athanasius, good works; for Basil, virginity; for John Chrysostom, almsgiving; and for Evagrius, charity and mercy.[16] Given the contemporary understanding of the diaconal charism and charge to ministry of the word, the liturgy, and charity, one might assume diaconal roots as in patristic understandings that the "wise virgin" spent her life in piety, good works, virginity, almsgiving, charity, and mercy. Might Caesarius's interpretation be a contraction of these ministries restricted to within the cloister?

Caesarius's Rule depends in large part on Augustine's, as well as on the *Regula monachorum* and *De institutis*, and may have influenced the later Rule of Benedict as well as the *Regula Tartensis*.[17] Caesarius's Rule established a means for women who wished to devote their lives to God in a dangerous age for unmarried women bereft of respected ways for unattached women to earn a living.[18] One can assume that women's diaconal ministry outside the cloister during this period, particularly by never-married women or by widows, would be unseemly and unsafe. One can further assume that a married woman would be busy with the affairs of her own household, and, since the church as a whole had moved away from house assemblies, that ministerial avenue for women would have closed.

We know from epigraphical and literary sources that women deacons faded as church structure grew in the West; evidence of their existence

---

[16] See Rosamond Nugent, *Portrait of the Consecrated Woman in Greek Christian Literature of the First Four Centuries* (Washington, DC: The Catholic University of America, 1941), 75–77.

[17] The definitive study of Caesarius's Rule is McCarthy, *Rule for Nuns*, which presents the Rule in Latin and English translation. See also, Caesarius, *Regula ad virgines*, in *Codex regularum*, 1:354–62, and in Migne, PL 67:1105–20.

[18] "Thus Caesarius very probably built up the body of his cloister regulations in response to the all-too-evident needs of the women of his diocese who, attempting to live a life of virginity, were frequent victims of attack due to the wildness of the times. . . . He saw that he must legislate for economic security for his monastic foundation because the society from which his nuns came provided no means of livelihood for unmarried women" (McCarthy, *Rule for Nuns*, 60–61, citing Arthur Malnory, *Saint Césaire, évêque d'Arles, 503–543* [Paris: Emile Bouillon, 1894]).

diminishes beyond the sixth century even though they are known to have existed as late as the twelfth century.[19] As earlier individual official relationships between bishops and widows, virgins, and women deacons faded into history, monastic life was the only safe means for women's complete self-donation to the things of God and to ministry.

As a sixth-century diocesan bishop, Caesarius had available liturgical formulae both to ordain a woman as deacon and to ratify the virgin's permanent consecration, but he evidently wanted to provide permanently for their livelihoods and security. In today's terms, Caesarius was establishing an institute of consecrated life within his diocese, and he eventually obtained papal sanction for the foundation to be exempt from local episcopal authority.[20] What he did, in fact, was establish an exempt independent monastery of women.

Caesarius's Rule gathers together several different traditions of monastic life: those of the Lérins tradition, of John Cassian, and of the Rule of Saint Augustine.[21] Caesarius accepts in his Rule provision for widows and "those who have left their husbands" to enter the monastery.[22] He also allows young girls—of six or seven years of age—to be admitted[23] and directs that "all shall learn to read."[24]

We must recall, however, that Caesarius's rule is not called "a rule for nuns" but, rather, "a rule for virgins," its title transformed in historical consciousness to a rule for *monachas*, female monks or nuns. Therein lies the distinction. Neither a life of consecrated virginity, nor a charitable life of widowhood, nor a ministerial life of a woman deacon is identical to monastic life. The commonality of the distinct vocations is that each was lived by women in the early church. Societal limitations would restrict (but not eliminate) women from entering eremitic life, and anchoretic life for women was rare. Widows of means might still be able to live their

---

[19] See, e.g., Eisen, *Women Officeholders in Early Christianity.*

[20] "Diocesan bishops, each in his own territory, can erect institutes of consecrated life by formal decree, provided that the Apostolic See has been consulted" (c. 579, 1983 Code of Canon Law). McCarthy (*Rule for Nuns*, 66) references the bull of exemption.

[21] The Abbey of Lérins founded on an island off the coast of southern France in the early fifth century by Saint Honoratus was quite influential in the fifth, sixth, and seventh centuries. See Adalbert de Vogüé, *Les règles des Saints Pères*, 2 vols., vol. 1, *Trois règles de Lérins au Ve siècle* (Paris: Cerf, 1982), 21–26.

[22] Rule no. 5, McCarthy, *Rule for Nuns*, 172.

[23] Rule no. 7, ibid., 173.

[24] Rule no. 18, ibid., 174.

charitable lives outside monastic settings with or without ordination as deacons. Somewhat later, some (recall Radegund) might insist on ordination as deacon before establishing monasteries of women.

But in the Arles of Caesarius's time, virgins who sought a life of prayer and service were unprotected. Hence, Caesarius sought to organize women who would live the charism of the "wise virgin" in a monastery headed by his sister. We do not know if he ordained her or any others as deacon, but there would have been ceremonial recognition of her creation as abbess.

Caesarius's Rule could appear to be for never-married women, but he allows the once-married to take up monastic enclosure. In one of his sermons he notes "there are three professions in the holy Catholic Church: there are virgins, widows, and also the married. . . . Good virgins, who want to be such not only in body but also in heart and tongue, are united to holy Mary with the rest of the army of virgins."[25] Like Augustine before him, Caesarius does not elevate virginity above widowhood or marriage and recognizes these three states as ways of living the Christian life in relation to God. That is, the state of virginity is a status, not a job description, any more than is the state of widowhood or the state of marriage. However, recalling the diaconal charisms attached by the Fathers of the Church to the "wise virgin," the task of being a "wise virgin" in the widest sense seems more that of the woman deacon.

As noted above, others have demonstrated as probable that women in all three states—virgins, widows, and the married—could have served as deacons. The changing nature of the ecclesial assembly, however, may have restricted the abilities of widows and married women to serve, and the never-married would be in an uncomfortable position without institutional protection of their state, independent of their wish or willingness to serve diaconal functions on behalf of the assembly.[26] In fact, Caesarius's barbarous times offered no safety for women alone, or even in groups, and the creation of a monastery was in itself a perilous endeavor.

Therefore, as McCarthy indicates, Caesarius is the first to lay down a concrete plan for organizing women's sheltered lives; he followed

---

[25] Caesarius, *Sermo* 6.35, as translated by McCarthy, *Rule for Nuns*, 59 n. 51. Caesarius compares virgins to Mary, widows to Anne, and the married woman to Susanna. See *Sermo* 6 in *Caesarius Arelantensis, Sermones*, 2 vols., *Corpus Christianorum Series Latina* 103–4, ed. D. G. Morin (Turnhout: Brepols, 1953), 1:30–36, at 35.

[26] Caesarius gives thirty as the minimum age for diaconal ordination and delineates the deacon's eleemosynary duties. See *Sermo* 1, *Sermones* 1:11.

John Cassian (ca. 360–435), who had earlier concluded that unmarried women could live a dedicated life only within cloister.[27] Caesarius made their cloister absolute and permanent, endowing the foundation, the monastery of St. John, with property from his diocese.[28] Theoretically, an exempt monastery would be free of financial constraints and episcopal interference, and so Caesarius further ensured the internal integrity of the cloister by forbidding any persons beyond approved clerics from entering the enclosure and oratories, a concept taken from the Lérin tradition's Rule for Monks.[29]

If women of Caesarius's monastery were ordained, it is unlikely women not of the monastery were ordained as deacons, especially since local Gallic synods from 396 to the mid-sixth century attempted to outlaw the practice.[30] Caesarius's preferred episcopal status would permit him to do two things: disallow women deacons outside his monastery and include them within it.

Independent of the internal practices in Caesarius's monastery, ceremonies for consecrations of virgins, deaconesses, and widows existed and survived outside the monasteries well after this time.[31] Since

---

[27] McCarthy, *Rule for Nuns*, 60.

[28] Ibid., 59. See also Caesarius of Arles, *Sermons*, 3 vols., trans. and intro. Mary Magdeleine Mueller (New York: Fathers of the Church, 1956–1973), 1:xi. Caesarius was at first stymied in his attempts to endow the monastery, but he eventually succeeded in circumventing church law, which forbade alienating ecclesiastical property for the purposes of endowing a monastery. See W. E. Klingshirn, "Caesarius's Monastery for Women in Arles and the Composition and Function of the 'Vita Caesarii,'" *Revue Bénédictine* 100 (1990), 441–81, at 456–59.

[29] Rule nos. 36–37, McCarthy, *Rule for Nuns*, 182–83. Caesarius founded his convent in either 512 or 513, recapitulating his Rule and affixing his signature to it. Various scholars calculate the dates differently. The first known printed edition of Caesarius's Rule was published in 1621 by E. Moquot, SJ, as an appendix to a life of St. Radegund who, we must recall, received ordination as deacon before she founded her own monastery at Poitiers between 552 and 560, using Caesarius's Rule. "Abbandona il marito, si fa ordinare diaconessa, forzando con autorità di regina le resistenze del vescovo Medardo" (Baudonivia and Paola Santorelli, *La vita Radegundis di Baudonivia* [Naples: M. D'Auria, 1999], 34).

[30] Eisen (*Women Office Holders in Early Christianity*, 184–85) notes that the 396 Synod of Nîmes forbade a "*ministerium faeminae leviticum*," and several later synods—Orange (441), Epaon (517), and Orléans (533)—forbade the ordination of women as deacons.

[31] Cassian Folsom relates that Roman, Gallicanized-Roman, and pure Gallican ceremonies are found in the Romano-Germanic Pontifical composed between 950

a premise here is that extant diaconal ceremonies followed women into monasteries, I need to examine known ceremonies for the ordination of women deacons before continuing with monastic ceremonies.

Ordination of Women Deacons

Many of the extant liturgies for the ordination of a woman as deacon are from the Eastern church, which maintains a more complete official memory of the tradition than does the Western church. To this day, women—typically monastic women—are ordained or may be ordained to the diaconate in a few Eastern churches, recovering their traditions.[32] There is substantial evidence of ancient ordination rituals for women deacons, including manuscripts in the Vatican Library.[33] Overall, the earliest significant manuscript evidence of the ordination of women as deacons is from the fourth-century *Apostolic Constitutions*, which, for all their difficulties, give evidence of liturgical practices of the early church.[34] The prayer for the ordination of a woman as deacon from the

___

and 962 in the Benedictine abbey of Mainz. See Folsom, "Liturgical Books of the Roman Rite," in *Handbook for Liturgical Studies*, 5 vols., ed. Anscar J. Chupungco (Collegeville, MN: Liturgical Press, 1998), 1:245–318, at 298.

[32] See Phyllis Zagano, "Catholic Women's Ordination: The Ecumenical Implications of Women Deacons in the Armenian Apostolic Church, the Orthodox Church of Greece, and Union of Utrecht Old Catholic Churches," *Journal of Ecumenical Studies* 43 (2008): 124–37; Zagano, "Grant Her Your Spirit: The Restoration of the Female Diaconate in the Orthodox Church of Greece," *America* 192, no. 4 (February 7, 2005): 18–21.

[33] For example, the eighth-century Barberini gr. 336 manuscript, also known as the Nicolai Manuscript, or as the Euchologion of St. Mark, published in a definitive Greek/Italian version by Stefano Parenti and Elena Velkovska, eds., *L'Eucologio Barberini Gr. 336*, 2nd ed. (Rome: C.L.V.-Edizioni Liturgiche, 2000); the eleventh-century Bessarion Manuscript, also known as Grotta Ferrata, gr. Gb1, the Patriarchal *Euchologion*, or as the George Varus Manuscript, a definitive version of which is in Miguel Arranz, *L'Eucologio constantinopolitano agli inizi del secolo XI* . . . (Rome: Gregorian University, 1996), 153–60. There are other manuscripts, some of which appear to have been copied from one or both of these manuscript sources, such as Vatican Manuscript gr. 1872, translated into Latin by Jean Morin, in *Commentarius de sacris ecclesiae ordinationibus* (1695; Farnborough: Gregg, 1969), 78–81. This work includes several other manuscripts, including Barberini gr. 336.

[34] In fact, the *Apostolic Constitutions*, book 8, includes the Clementine Liturgy, the most ancient extant complete order of the rites for celebrating the Eucharist.

Apostolic Constitutions, like the later ritual from the Barberini codex, is nearly identical to that for a male deacon:

> 8.19. *Concerning a deaconess, I Bartholomew make this constitution: O bishop, thou shall lay thy hands on her in the presence of the presbytery and of the deacons and deaconesses, and say:*
> 8.20. Eternal God, Father of our Lord Jesus Christ, Creator of man and woman, who filled with the Spirit Miriam and Deborah and Anna and Hulda; who did not disdain that your only-begotten Son should be born of a woman; who also in the tent of the testimony, and in the temple appointed women to be guardians of your holy gates: now look upon this your servant who is being appointed for ministry, and give her the Holy Spirit and cleanse her from every defilement of body and spirit so that she may worthily complete the work committed to her, to your glory and the praise of your Christ, through whom [be] glory and worship to you in the Holy Spirit for ever. Amen.[35]

Other manuscripts present other evidence. In the Byzantine tradition, for example, the woman to be ordained is presented to the bishop, who lays his hands on her head and recites a prayer similar to the one above, further asking God: "Bestow the grace of your Holy Spirit also on this your servant who wishes to offer herself to you, and fill her with the grace of the diaconate, as you gave the grace of your diaconate to Phoebe whom you called to the work of ministry."[36]

Prayers specifically for women deacons from still other manuscripts follow similar patterns within the ordination ceremony. Three prayers for the benediction of a woman as deacon (there is no gender in the Georgian language) refer to her as "maidservant," a term more ordinarily connected with virginity.[37]

---

[35] Paul F. Bradshaw, *Ordination Rites of the Ancient Churches of East and West* (New York: Pueblo, 1990), 116. See *Apostolic Constitutions* 8.17 and 8.18 (Bradshaw, *Ordination Rites*, 115) for the prayer for the ordination of a deacon. The 2002 ITC document, *Le diaconat: Evolution et perspectives* (see n. 1 above), clearly recognizes that the prayer and imposition of hands mark admission to the diaconate. "Deaconesses took up their functions through an *epithesis cheirôn* or imposition of hands that conferred the Holy Spirit, as did the lectors" (ITC, *Diakonia of Christ*, 22).

[36] Bradshaw, *Ordination Rites*, 137–38, translating the Barberini gr. 336 manuscript (in *Commentarius de sacris ecclesiae ordinationibus*, 52–58).

[37] Ibid., 168–69, adapted from the tenth-eleventh-century manuscript Tiflis A86, in F. C. Conybeare and Oliver Waldrop, "The Georgian Version of the Liturgy of St. James," *Revue de l'Orient Chrétien* 19 (1914): 162–73.

The point here is not to referee the longstanding disagreement between those who argue that women were sacramentally ordained and those who disagree, but rather to evaluate the similarities between and among rituals for women, including those used for the ordination (or appointment) of a woman as deacon, and those used for men. There are indeed distinctions in the liturgies for men and for women. For example, in the East the male ordinand touches the altar with his forehead; the woman stands upright; the man receives the *Rhipidion*—a sacred fan—as symbol of his office, but the woman does not. Also in the East, the male distributes Communion, and the woman does not, although she self-communicates from the chalice. (It is generally understood that it was a duty of the woman deacon to bring Communion and otherwise minister to ill women.)[38] While the majority of these examples are from Eastern liturgies, they demonstrate how women deacons were understood locally and represent the common tradition of the whole Church, East and West.

In the West, from at least the third through the sixth centuries, there was significant discussion relative to the place and status of women in the church; whether widows, virgins, or deacons, and sources reveal some confusion as to who held what status and for what reason. At the end of the fourth century, Ambrosiaster vociferously complained about the possibility of women having liturgical ministry and authority, whereas Pelagius seems to have favored it. However, both Ambrosiaster and Pelagius see women deacons referred to in 1 Timothy 5:3-16, differing only on whether they are widows or virgins.[39]

Eastern rituals for ordaining men and women deacons are both termed "ordinations" (*cheirotonia*) and are performed in the presence of the assembly by the local bishop through the imposition of hands. The bishop declares his intent by asking for "Divine Grace," the ordinands are led to the altar, and both ordinations (of men and of women) take place within the sanctuary during the Eucharist. Further, the bishop invokes the Holy Spirit, recites two prayers (significant of major orders), and presents stoles (also significant of major orders) to both male and female *ordinandi*, who each self-communicate from the cup.

It seems strange to cite identical ceremonies as sacramental for men but not sacramental for women. Even without arguing for or against

---

[38] See Martimort, *Deaconesses*, 150–55.
[39] See Gryson, *Ministry of Women*, 92–99.

the sacramental character of these diaconal ordinations of women, we must recognize that they who were so ordained were either widows or virgins, or married women who practiced continence (had, in Caesarius's terms, "left" their husbands).[40] That is, they were already practicing continence required for ordination and would not be permitted to remarry. That the female diaconate remained a characteristic of the church in the East, and remains so predominantly as a monastic female diaconate in Orthodoxy to this day specifically for the purpose of assisting at liturgy and ministering to sick nuns of the monastery, further suggests that as it was suppressed into female monastic life in the West, its ceremonies combined with other monastic ceremonies or eliminated entirely.[41] It makes sense to retain women deacons in the East. The major distinction between the eucharistic liturgies East and West is that the East must have a deacon, not always easily available to a woman's monastery, while the West allows diaconal functions to be overtaken by the priest-celebrant.

If we look at the characteristics of contemporary diaconal ordination ceremonies, we find great continuity in the tradition, perhaps most obviously the inclusion of the litany of the saints, the invocation of the Holy Spirit, the public nature of the ordinations, and the required participation of the diocesan bishop. In fact, today the deacon is properly ordained only by the diocesan bishop, who alone imposes hands on the deacon.[42]

Consecration of a Virgin

As in ancient times, today the proper presider at the consecration of a virgin is the diocesan bishop.[43] The status of consecrated virgin does not immediately appear to be equal to the ministerial status of a deacon, although the ceremony appears to have the same roots as ceremonies for the ordination of deacons and priests.

While the consecrated virgin aspires to live as a spouse of Christ and not as a public minister of the church, her consecration places her in a particular relationship with the diocesan bishop. There are two current ceremonials for the Consecration to a Life of Virginity, one for such a life

---

[40] Ibid., 110.
[41] See Kyriaki Karidoyanes Fitzgerald, *Women Deacons in the Orthodox Church: Called to Holiness and Ministry* (Brookline, MA: Holy Cross Orthodox, 1998).
[42] See c. 1016, *Code of Canon Law*.
[43] See René Metz, *La consécration des vierges: Hier, aujourd'hui, demain* (Paris: Cerf, 2001), 87–89.

to be lived in the world, the other to be lived within monastic profession. The introduction to each rite states:

> The custom of consecrating women to a life of virginity flourished even in the early Church. It led to the formation of a solemn rite constituting the candidate a sacred person, a surpassing sign of the Church's love for Christ, and an eschatological image of the world to come and the glory of the heavenly Bride of Christ.[44]

Hence, the eschatological witness of celibacy is here recalled as independent of membership within a given monastic community. When lived in the world however, such contemporary consecrated virginity appears to be very much like the contemporary diaconate. The contemporary ritual describes a life reminiscent of the words of Origen, Athanasius, John Chrysostom, and Evagrius mentioned earlier: "They are to spend their time in works of penance and of mercy, in apostolic activity, and in prayer. . . . They are strongly advised to recite the liturgy of the hours each day, especially morning prayer and evening prayer."[45]

Are contemporary consecrated virgins living the diaconal charge and charism?[46] Were the consecrated virgins discussed by the Church fathers also deacons? Were the women who lived Caesarius's Rule for Virgins also deacons? The problematic distinctions between various commentaries, rituals, and historical substantiations regarding those for whom the rituals were used creates the conundrum under study here. History has retained evidence of widows, virgins, and women deacons. How can these women be distinguished in their distinct states and ministries? The broad brush might paint the picture thus: widows and virgins, including those who lived in monasteries, may also have been deacons, or not.

Widows were typically appointed to a life of prayer, although they engaged in some social services as well. Women deacons were also expected to lead lives of prayer as well as engage in ecclesial social services, catechesis, and especially in ministry to women. Widows living in the world often included women of means who knew how to run large

---

[44] "Rite of Consecration to a Life of Virginity," in *The Rites of the Catholic Church: The Roman Ritual Revised by the Decree of the Second Vatican Ecumenical Council*, 2 vols. (Collegeville, MN: Liturgical Press, 1991), 2:157.

[45] Ibid.

[46] The US Association of Consecrated Virgins reports approximately two hundred members included in a total of three thousand consecrated virgins worldwide. See http://www.consecratedvirgins.org/default.asp.

households and who (especially if they were also deacons, or able to become deacons) were those best prepared to head a monastery.[47]

In seeking the first historical evidence of women as deacons, however, we find references to their more direct ministries within ecclesial communities—assisting at baptisms, anointing the sick, catechizing the young, keeping order in the assembly, and carrying the sacrament to ill and homebound women—all of which point to a public ministry more directly connected, ultimately, to the diocesan bishop.[48] This is not to say that no widows were deacons, but rather to distinguish between their respective charisms: the one to prayer, the other to a more public ministry.

Similarly, consecrated virgins seem to have been of two modes, the one consecrated to a life of virginity with an emphasis on prayer, particularly liturgical prayer, and the other consecrated to a life of virginity that included public ministry, termed "apostolic activity" in the contemporary ritual. The former might be understood in today's terms as hermit, anchorite, or cloistered nun, whereas the latter might be understood in terms of apostolic religious life or secular lay ecclesial ministry.

In any event, we can infer from the very language used in its introduction that the contemporary ritual for the consecration of a virgin has at least some roots in the rituals for the creation of women deacons. Contemporary consecrated virgins are expected "to spend their time in works of penance and of mercy, in apostolic activity, and in prayer." And their prayer is to include what is normally recommended for deacons today: daily recitation of the liturgy of the hours, especially morning and evening prayer.

In fact, the life of consecrated virginity lived in the world appears remarkably similar to that of the deacon. The consecrated virgin is admonished to a life spent with the word, the liturgy, and charity. She is bound to the diocesan bishop, who presides at her consecration and who either in person or by his delegate is to meet with her annually. The obvious distinction between the contemporary consecrated virgin and the deacon is that the consecrated virgin has no public liturgical ministry other than those she may otherwise perform in her parish, i.e., serving as lector or as extraordinary minister of the Eucharist. She may

[47] Gryson (*Ministry of Women*, 110) finds the order of widows somewhat akin to a contemporary secular institute.

[48] Jean Daniélou, citing Epiphanius, includes anointing the sick: *The Ministry of Women in the Early Church*, 2nd ed. (London: Faith, 1974), 29; "Le ministère des femmes," *Maison-Dieu* 61 (1960): 94.

not be granted faculties for either preaching or presiding at baptism or marriage, all typically within the deacon's mandate. She is not a cleric.[49]

It must be emphasized that the question of status (consecrated virgin or widow) should not be confused with that of mandate for ministry (diaconate). That is, although the current rite for the consecration of a virgin indicates a certain expectation of "ministry" it is not direct commissioning to ministry and neither includes nor implies appointment to office or a granting of faculties. The rite for consecration of a virgin is primarily one of conferring status, of ratifying a state in life. The rite of ordination to the diaconate imparts a mandate for ministry.

It is clearly possible that ancient rites for consecrating virgins and for ordaining deacons were conflated to form the single rite extant in the West that can be used in two circumstances, alone or together with religious profession for nuns. It is important to note that specific language of the rite points to both the monastic profession and diaconal ordination rituals.

By returning to monastic ritual we can observe the possibility that several distinct events are conflated into one ceremony.

Cistercian Ritual and Tradition

The Cistercians were founded in 1098 by Robert of Molesme at Citeaux Abbey near Dijon, France, as a return to the original monastic Rule of Saint Benedict. Two canonically distinct orders follow the tradition of the Cistercian Order (OCist) and the Order of Cistercians of the Strict

---

[49] The ordinary means for entering the clerical state is through ordination to the diaconate. While lay persons, including women, can be delegated to perform formal baptisms and to witness marriages, they may never preach homilies at the Eucharist. Bishops cannot delegate preaching authority to nonclerics, except for Masses for children. Canon 767 restricts the homily to *sacerdoti aut diacono,* that is, to bishops, priests, and deacons. "The homily . . . must be reserved to the sacred minister, Priest or Deacon . . . , to the exclusion of the non-ordained faithful, even if these should have responsibilities as 'pastoral assistants' or catechists in whatever type of community or group. This exclusion is not based on the preaching ability of sacred ministers nor their theological preparation, but on that function which is reserved to them in virtue of having received the Sacrament of Holy Orders" (Vatican Congregation for the Clergy, On Some Questions Regarding Collaboration of Nonordained Faithful in Priests' Sacred Ministry [August 15, 1997], http://www.vatican.va/roman_curia/pontifical_councils /laity/documents/rc_con_interdic_doc_15081997_en.html).

Observance (OCSO). Here I limit my study to the nuns of the latter order, which is also known since 1892 as the Trappistines, referring to the reform begun by Armand de Rancé (1626–1700) at LaTrappe, Orne, France.

A great deal of scholarship has developed in the Benedictine tradition regarding chapter 58 of the Rule of Benedict, which understands monastic profession to include the affirmation of stability, conversion of life, and obedience according to the Rule. For my purposes, the operative question is whether monastic profession is a vow made to God or a promise made to the monastic community. Scholars—notably including Benedictine Richard Yeo—find monastic profession is the latter; that is, monastic profession is a solemn and absolutely binding promise to live according to monastic practices and the virtues of fraternal charity, patience, humility, poverty, and gentleness, made in God's presence and solidified by the self-surrender expressed by the placing of the written document (*petitio*) on the altar.[50] In Yeo's view, "monastic profession is properly seen as a species of religious profession,"[51] and the later singing of the *Suscipe* expresses the personal profession within the community.[52]

In Cistercian practice, the individual makes monastic profession in the hands of the abbot or abbess in chapter, where that tradition is preserved, as follows: "The Abbot/Abbess sits and receives his/her (miter and) staff. The one making profession stands before the Abbot/Abbess and reads the profession formula . . . goes to the altar to place on it the formula of profession, and to sign it upon the altar itself." A solemn profession that includes the solemn blessing or consecration of the monk/nun, however, takes place during a Mass celebrated by the abbot (for monks) or father immediate (for nuns), or his delegate, the diocesan bishop.[53] The nun to be professed stands before the abbess, as above, and makes her petition. Following the homily, the abbess interrogates her, inquiring as to her resolve. Then follows the prayer of the faithful and the litany

---

[50] Richard Yeo, *The Structure and Content of Monastic Profession: A Juridical Study, with Particular Regard to the Practice of the English Benedictine Congregation since the French Revolution* (Rome: Pontificio Ateneo S. Anselmo, 1982), 329–31. Yeo, tenth Abbot President of the English Benedictine Congregation, writes that the petition expresses a vow, but it is "anachronistic rather than incorrect to say that this vow includes vows of poverty, chastity, and obedience" (331).

[51] Ibid., 341.

[52] Yeo writes that the *Suscipe* ritualizes "the acceptance of the candidate by God [and] is linked up with incorporation into the community" (ibid., 333).

[53] The dual terms "blessing or consecration" could signify their ancient interchangeability.

of the saints. The litany of the saints marks the ceremony's relationship of the blessing/consecration within ancient (and contemporary) ordination ritual. After the litany, "the one making profession stands before the abbess and reads the profession formula written herself, as found in the Constitutions of the Order, or the Congregation, or the Monastery . . . goes to the altar to place on it the formula of profession, and to sign it upon the altar itself."[54] Following the rite of profession, the abbess invokes the triune God's blessing on the professed member, who lies prostrate.[55] It is only after these blessing/consecratory prayers that the cowl and black veil are presented to Cistercian nuns.

Which of these events is rooted in monastic membership? Clearly, the placing of the schedule (profession document) upon the altar and the profession at the hands of the abbess involve the stability, conversion of life, and obedience as expressed in chapter 58 of the Rule of Benedict, and as understood by Cistercians. But which of these is/are rooted in consecration of a virgin? Which may be rooted in ordination of a deacon, or perhaps subdeacon?

The key to searching out roots of diaconal ordination within Cistercian tradition is two-pronged: the abbess's blessing and invocations, and her presentation of the cowl. The cowl, while it is a uniquely monastic garment, is also a uniquely liturgical garment. Both options for the prayer read by the abbess at its imparting demonstrate the cowl's relationship to both the self-immolation of profession and to liturgical ministry:

> May the Lord clothe you in the new self created according to God in justice and holiness of truth: and may the ministry which we outwardly perform be realized inwardly through the gift of the Holy Spirit.

Or:

> Our brother/sister is now being clothed in the garment which the holy Fathers appointed to be worn by those who renounce the world as a sign of innocence and humility. May the Son of God who in his goodness put on the garment of our mortal nature, himself grant our brother/sister to be clothed in his very self.[56]

---

[54] "The Rite of Solemn Profession and the Blessing or Consecration of a Monk/Nun," *Cistercian Ritual*, trans. Carol Dvorak (privately printed, 2004), 84–85, available at http://www.ocso.org/index.php?option=com_docman&task=cat_view&gid=54&Itemid=86&lang=en.

[55] "Rite of Solemn Profession," 85.

[56] Ibid.

The cowl is worn only by those perpetually professed in the abbey. Temporarily professed nuns wear a cloak during liturgies. Perpetually professed nuns do not obtain the liturgical authority of the abbess, which includes imparting a blessing (at least at the conclusion of Vespers), reading the gospel during Sunday Vigils, and imparting the blessing or invocation upon the newly professed member, but they are full members of the chapter and may ordinarily serve as hebdomadary for the Liturgy of the Hours.

While the cowl is only worn by those fully professed, and only those fully professed have certain liturgical authority, another level of liturgical authority—that of the abbess—is simultaneously evident. The abbess presides at the Liturgy of the Hours, and, as mentioned above, imparts a formal blessing at the conclusion of Vespers. Does this reflect her ancestral history of deacon-abbess? In the West the tradition of deacon-abbesses was reflected, if not preserved, in Benedictine and Cistercian abbeys of Catalonia, whose abbesses wore the stole at liturgy.[57]

The ritual of presenting the stole to a woman and the circumstances of its wearing have long been the subject of scholarly debate. Aimé Georges Martimort's penultimate chapter in his *Deaconesses: An Historical Study* (1982, 1986) is titled "The Case of Carthusian Nuns." His comments are nearly an appendix to his long and detailed response to Roger Gryson's *The Ministry of Women in the Early Church* (1972, 1976), in which Gryson concluded:

> From a doctrinal point of view, since for several centuries a large portion of the Church followed this practice [of ordaining women as deacons] without raising a theoretical problem, it is perfectly conceivable to confer on women a diaconal type of ministry. Women deacons, then receive a true ordination, with nothing distinguishing it formally from the ordination of their male colleagues.[58]

Again, even without attempting to referee the "ordination" debate, or determine it one way or the other, it is obvious that rituals conferring status and implying ministry existed outside monasteries and were brought into them. No clear and perfect timeline or documentary history exists in any individual monastery or order from the ancient church to the present, but clues to the ways women handed down their rituals are sufficient to point toward their provenance. Carthusian nuns may provide the clearest link to the tradition.

[57] Martimort, *Deaconesses*, 240 n. 36.
[58] Gryson, *Ministry of Women*, 113.

Carthusian Ritual and Tradition

The Carthusians were founded by St. Bruno of Cologne, who began the first charterhouse in 1084 in the valley of the Chartreuse Mountains in the French Alps. Carthusians are hermits who share daily liturgical worship and have weekly communal meals and recreation. In 1145, nuns of Prébayon in Provence, France, asked to be received into the order, becoming the first Carthusian nuns. It was thought that women could not live as strict an eremitic life as men, and so women Carthusians lived a more coenobitical life until 1970 or so. Carthusian nuns now live a life nearly identical to that of the monks. There are currently two women's charterhouses in France, two in Italy, one in Spain, and a new foundation in South Korea.[59]

When Carthusian nuns receive the consecration of virgin, in a ceremony led by a priest or bishop, they are presented with the stole, maniple, and cross as well as the veil, ring, and crown.[60] Some scholars, including Daniel Le Blévec, argue that there is no connection between the Carthusian rite of consecration of a virgin and the ancient practice of ordaining women as deacons.[61] However, any position depends on minimal historical evidence.

Unlike Cistercians, Carthusians are not within the Benedictine family.[62] Although Carmelite and Benedictine monasteries of women did join the Carthusian order, of interest for my study is their provenance from

---

[59] See http://www.chartreux.org/en/frame.html.

[60] One Carthusian nun wrote to me to say that they receive the stole and maniple not as an ordination ceremonial but as a connection with "the tradition." Current usage provides for ceremonial presentation of the black veil, the ring, the stole, and the book of the divine office. See Nathalie Nabert, *Les moniales chartreuses* (Geneva: Ad Solem, 2009), 54–55.

[61] See Daniel Le Blévec, "La consécration des moniales cartusiennes d'après un pontifical romain conservé à Avignon" (Bibl. mun. 205), in *Die Geschichte des Kartäuserordens*, 2 vols., ed. James Lester Hogg (Salzburg: Salzburg Insititut für Anglistik und Amerikanistic, 1991–1992), 1:203–19. Martimort (*Deaconesses*, 235–40) notes that others support the connection between the Carthusian rite and diaconal ordination: Y. Gourdel, "Chartreux," in *Dictionnaire de spiritualité* . . . , vol. 2 (1953), col. 721; M. de Fontette, "*Recherches sur les origins de moniales chartreuses,*" in *Études d'histoire et de droit canoniques dediées à Gabriel Le Bras*, 2 vols. (Paris: Sirey, 1963), 2:1150–51; L. Ray and P. Mouton, "*Chartreuses (Règle des moniales),*" in *Dictionnaire de droit canoniques* . . . , vol. 3 (1942), cols. 630–32.

[62] Camaldolese, Vallombrosans, Sylvestrines, Celestines, Olivetans use or used the Rule of Benedict.

Poitiers and the Rule of Cesarius of Arles. One tradition is that Prébayon, the first woman's monastery to join the Carthusian order, was founded in 611 by Radegund's niece, Germilie.[63] Between 552 and 560, Radegund had founded and completed the construction of a convent near Poitiers, of which Prébayon appears to have been a daughter monastery.

Even though the Second Council of Orléans in 533 had ruled that henceforth no women would "receive diaconal benediction due to the frailty to her sex,"[64] it is generally agreed that Radegund—perhaps a virgin, or at the very least the uncooperative queen and wife of Frankish King Clothar—insisted on diaconal ordination for herself and obtained the same privilege for nuns of her monastery.[65]

Historical records on the Abbey of Prébayon are sparse, since it was destroyed by the Saracens in the ninth century and successive waves of destruction resulted in more losses. It has long been believed, however, that Radegund's niece Germilie brought the tradition of diaconal ordination with her to Prébayon, where it remained. Hence the ceremony of giving the stole, maniple, and cross to the Carthusian nun during the consecration of virgin would have come into the Carthusian order with the practices of the convent at Prébayon.[66] Since other local practices appear to mirror those of Prébayon,[67] the uneven pattern of convents joining the Carthusian order and others being founded anew supports both the maintenance of the older tradition and the confusion regarding its provenance. The pattern also supports the notion that the practice of ordaining nuns as deacons was widespread.

Like Benedictines, Carthusians receive a cowl, theirs signifying reception of a minor order. Nathalie Nabert writes that *"cuculle"* is the proper name within Chartres for the distinctive Carthusian scapular attached by bands of cloth on either side. Since 1291, Nabert writes, women

[63] Dom Augustin Devaux, "Premier chapitre pour une histoire des moniales chartreuses," in *Études et documents pour l'histoire des Chartreux, Analecta cartusiana* 208 (Salzburg: Institut für Anglistik und Amerikanistik, 2003), 1–42, at 4.

[64] Canon no. 18 seems directed at women outside the cloister, since its preceding lines declare excommunication for women deacons who "indulged again in marriage" (Gryson, *Ministry of Women*, 107).

[65] "D'ailleurs, les vierges et les autres chrétiennes vouées à la vie religieuse se retiraient dans les monastères, dont les abbesses recevaient parfois, telle sainte Radegonde, l'ordination des diaconnesses" (Fortunat, *Vita S. Radigundis* n. 12, Migne, PL 88:502), quoted in *Dictionnaire de théologie catholique*, 696.

[66] Le Blévec, "Consecration des moniales cartusiennes," 205.

[67] Devaux, "Premier chapitre pour une histoire," 40.

Carthusians, just as men, received the minor order of porter, the two bands on the cowl signifying that order.[68]

Hence the ceremony within the ceremony of consecration of a virgin at which the Carthusian nun receives the stole, maniple, and cross may provide the clearest contemporary window to the past. Each item—stole, maniple, and cross—signifies the clerical order of deacon.

The stole, a band of cloth worn by Carthusian nuns around the neck and hanging freely at the front, in the manner of Eastern women deacons, is today a distinctly liturgical garment of the deacon, priest, and bishop. However, in the East the deacon's stole finds earlier reference than those of priest and bishop; it is known in the fourth and fifth centuries.[69]

The maniple, a band of cloth worn on the left arm during Mass, dates to sixth-century Rome as an item given at ordination to the subdeacon— at that time a major order. It was solely a mark of major orders worn only during the celebration of Mass.[70]

The cross placed on the shoulder of the Carthusian nun as part of the consecration liturgy has its historical echoes in the present. The introduction to the ancient ceremony of the blessing and consecration of virgins in the Roman Pontifical of 1839 speaks of the great symbolism of the cross.[71] Perhaps echoing the tradition, the Sisters of the Assumption, founded in France in 1839 and whose apostolic ministry brought them into contact with "the world," once wore a white mantle with a violet cross on the shoulder in chapel.[72]

The ritual for the conferral of the stole, maniple, and cross to Carthusian nuns appears to be a ceremony within a ceremony, one that includes the litany of the saints common to ordinations. That is, the ordinary ritual for the consecration of a virgin begins and proceeds, but is interrupted by a uniquely Carthusian ritual of the presenting of the stole, maniple, and cross. The seventeenth-century Roman Pontifical at Avignon[73] clearly states that what follows is the old usage and custom

---

[68] Nabert, *Moniales chartreuses*, 29.

[69] Joseph Braun, "Stole," in *The Catholic Encyclopedia*, vol. 14 (1912), 301–2.

[70] Joseph Braun, "Maniple," in *The Catholic Encyclopedia*, vol. 9 (1910), 601–2. In the Greek rite the corresponding vestment is worn only by the bishop.

[71] Nabert, *Moniales chartreuses*, 95.

[72] F. M. Rudge, "Sisters of the Assumption," in *The Catholic Encyclopedia*, vol. 2 (1907), 6.

[73] In the Bibliothèque Municipale d'Avignon (ms. 205, chartreuse de Salettes, 1696–1697).

of Carthusian women: first, the maniple is placed on the right arm of the woman, then the cross on her right shoulder, and finally the stole around her neck.[74] The stole is not worn over one shoulder and tied at the side; rather it hangs around the neck to the front in the fashion of a Western priest.

After Communion in the Mass for the consecration of a virgin, the bishop invests those consecrated in their liturgical responsibilities, presenting them the breviary in a manner similar to the presentation of the Book of Gospels to a deacon: "Accipite librum, ut incipiatatis horas canonicas, et legatis officium in ecclesia."[75]

Several manuscripts, particularly those from the thirteenth to the seventeenth centuries, attest to the historicity of the Carthusian ceremony as it is celebrated today.[76] An interesting affirmation of the rite is contained in the decision of Philippe Howard, cardinal of Norfolk, who in 1687 decided on behalf of the Sacred Congregation for Rites that, while the ritual may have the appurtenances of the ordination of deacon, it was not such. Therefore, he wrote, the ritual could continue to be used, as it imperiled neither dogma nor discipline.[77] (Determining that it was not a diaconal ordination in the seventeenth century, however, does not deny its roots in such.)

Two contemporary writers, Dom Augustin Devaux and Daniel Le Blévec, argue against the relationship between the ceremonial presentation of the stole, maniple, cross, and breviary to Carthusian nuns within

[74] Le Blévec, "Consecration des moniales cartusiennes," 213.

[75] Ibid., 215

[76] See manuscripts in the following libraries: Bibliothèque municipale de Grenoble (ms. 324, chartreuse de Bertaud, XIIe siècle); Stadtbibliothek Darmstadt (ms. [H] 710, chartreuse de Bruges, 1450ca); Bibliothèque royale de Bruxelles (ms. 8245, chartreuse de Bruges, 1450ca); Bibliothèque nationale de France – Richelieu (ms. Latin 1437 et 1438, chartreuse de Gosnay, fin XVe-début XVIe siècles); Bibliothèque municipale de Douai (ms. 569, chartreuse de Gosnay, 2ème moitié du XVIe siècle); Bibliothèque municipale d'Avignon (ms. 205, chartreuse de Salettes, 1696–1697); Bibliothèque municipale de Charleville-Mezières (ms. 420, chartreuse de Gosnay, fin XVIIe siècle); Bibliothèque municipale de Lyon (site Part-Dieu) (ms. 861, chartreuse de Prémol, fin XVIIe siècle); and Archives départmentales du Nord, Lille (62 H 17, chartreuse de Gosnay, fin XVIe siècle).

[77] "Le maintien de l'usage cartusien ne mettait en péril ni le dogme ni la discipline" (Devaux, *"Premier chapitre . . . "* 31), citing *Analecta Juris Pontificii* 8.1286. *Rapport de Philippe Howard, Cardinal de Norfolk, sur le rit de la consécration des vierges chez les moniales chartreuses* (chartreuse de Prémol, 1687).

their ceremony of consecration of a virgin and any historical diaconal ordination. Devaux labors to disconnect Caesarius of Arles from Radegund, and Radegund from Prébayon, citing lack of sources. However, if the continuity of the tradition cannot be proven with manuscript evidence, then neither can its discontinuity. Devaux admits the dearth of sources and the repeated destructions of monasteries of nuns but attempts to prove a negative from the small number of known manuscripts. We do not know if there are undiscovered others, but we can be certain there were some—if not many—manuscripts destroyed. In fact, given the ingrained traction against the tradition of ordaining women, it is not difficult to speculate that certain manuscripts were purposefully "lost." In any event, extant manuscripts clearly demonstrate a ritual within a ritual that invests the newly consecrated virgin in stole, maniple, and cross.

Following Devaux, the later analysis by Le Blévec is of the seventeenth-century Avignon manuscript of the Carthusian nuns' ceremonial is aimed at solving what he deems "a difficult liturgical problem" because many historians connect Carthusian practice with the ordination of women as deacons.[78] That the ceremony of conferring the stole, maniple, and cross is unrelated to diaconal ordination Le Blévec aims to prove by arguing in part that the ceremony does not seem to have been identical in every Carthusian house in history. But it is already known that other traditions—notably Benedictine and Carmelite—joined Chartreux, bringing their own customs and usages into the order. These, especially the Carmelites, may not have had the diaconal ceremony in the first place. What Le Blévec does not address is the question he begins with. If the ceremony of conferring the stole, maniple, cross, and, later, breviary is not related to diaconal ordination, where did it come from and to what is it related?

Conclusions

Given the distinctions between and among monastic profession, personal vows, consecration of a virgin, and diaconal ordination, what do

---

[78] "L'usage de conférer aux moniales de 'l'ordre des chartreux, à l'occasion de leur consécration, l'étoile et le manipule pose quant à lui un difficile problème de tradition liturgique sur lequel se sont penchés depuis longtemps de nombreux historiens. La thèse traditionnelle fait remonter cet usage aux diaconesses de l'Eglise des premiers temps" (Le Blévec, "Consécration des Moniales Cartusiennes," 104–5).

the historical and current ceremonies under evaluation here tell about the lost tradition of women deacons? We know that women were ordained and served as deacons, and that their ordination and service faded in the West. If we could pinpoint a time when the female diaconate disappeared in the West, or at least in France, we might choose the mid-sixth century, around the time Caesarius's Rule was gaining sway, and various local synods in Gaul were routinely ruling against further creation of women deacons.[79]

Is the tradition of women deacons lost, or merely misplaced? As recently as 1942, the *Dictionnaire de Droit Canonique* forthrightly stated that Carthusian nuns' ritual was distinct from that of Benedictines and Cistercians and could be called a *consecration virginali-diaconissale*, related to the ritual for women deacons of the early church.[80]

It appears that contemporary discussion on the restoration of the female diaconate, and concurrent (theologically unrelated) discussion about the possibility of women priests, has raised significant disagreement regarding the historical facts as they have traditionally been received. The fact that Carthusian nuns to this day retain a ritual that includes investiture with appurtenances of diaconal status, and do so with the clear approbation of Rome, speaks deeply to a tradition of a ministerial diaconate lived by women before the time of Caesarius of Arles, echoed in the life of Radegund, and brought forward outside the monastery by secular and religious women today.

What that tradition has to say to the future is unclear. It is, however, a tradition that should be remembered because (or perhaps in spite of) the extensive discussion and commentary on the ordination of women in general and the ordination of women to the diaconate in particular. Even though the distinct roles of deacon and priest have been codified,[81]

---

[79] This despite the fact that other local churches seem to have retained women deacons. Macy notes, for example, that "in 1018, Benedict VIII conferred on the Cardinal Bishop of Porto the right to ordain bishops, priests, male or female deacons (*diaconibus vel diaconissis*)," a privilege repeated by John XIX in 1025 and by Leo IX in 1049. Macy cites the following papal documents: Benedict VIII, *Quotiens illa* (August 1, 1018); John XIX, "Quoniam semper" (May 1025); and Leo IX, "Supplicantium desideriis" (April 22, 1049) (*Hidden History*, 35 and 172–73 nn. 78, 79, 80).

[80] D. L. Ray and D. Pierre Mouton, "*Chartreuses (regle des moniales)."*

[81] Following the *Catechism of the Catholic Church*, Pope Benedict XVI issued the *motu proprio, Omnium in mentem* (October 26, 2009) clarifying canon law regarding the distinction: priests are ordained to act in the person of Christ, the head

confusion as to their relationship remains, giving rise to the argument that ordination of a woman as deacon presages ordination of a woman as priest. Such opposition ignores the fact that the diaconate has been restored as a permanent (as opposed to "transitional") order in the church. For the tradition to be fully remembered, it must include women.

---

of the Church; deacons are ordained to serve the people of God in and through the Word, the liturgy and charity.

11

Varieties of Ministries
and Diaconal Renewal

Yves Congar

Review of *New World, New Deacons*[1]

All that could be said has been said.
Many interesting things have been said about the diaconate as a permanent order. Almost everything has already been said. We would feel rather weary about it. We always say it is coming and I cannot help but think of what Clémenceau once said: "We recognize a sentence of Jaurès regarding this: all the verbs are in the future." At other times this reminds me of the first decades of Catholic Action, with meetings where we kept asking ourselves: What is it? Who is in? Who is not in? In short, we are saying today with more insistence what we wrote ten years ago: "Only an experience sufficiently prolonged and varied will allow the blessings and the difficulties, the exact status, and the specific organization of the restored diaconate as a permanent ministry to be revealed" (*Vie Spirituelle* [July 1959]: 90). Yes, truly, we have said all that could be said, we have anticipated all that we could have. Now we must try.

"Variétés des ministères et renouveau diaconal," *Diacres aujourd'hui* 7 (1969): 2–3.

---

[1] The bold-faced heading and subheadings are by the author, who has also emphasized (in bold) certain passages to aid reading of the text. H. Bourgeois and R. Schaller. "Nouveau monde, nouveaux diacres. Demain, dans une Eglise renouvelée quells ministères?" ("Called into question") (Desclée, 1968). Matthieu Knudde, OP, in *La Maison de Dieu* 96, no. 4 (1968): 106–14 presents a very interesting report on the theology of the diaconate: very descriptive of the ecclesiological problems in the question.

Toward the declericalization of the notion of Church

The book by H. Bourgeois and R. Schaller, however, does not repeat the work of others. It has over these the advantage of using a number of actual evidence and assembled documentation, even in the realm of ideas and testimonials, by the diaconal community. And this allows me to comment: to a great extent Bourgeois and Schaller state the criticism or objections that have been articulated against the establishment of a new diaconate, either as it leans toward the priesthood or toward laity. Will not the new married deacons appear like sub-priests? Does not the baptismal priesthood allow all Christians to fulfill the functions, even liturgical, that we want to assign them? And yet, on the other hand, does not the fact of married deacons risk taking from the laity good features and unduly clericalizing them? These are not small difficulties, and Bourgeois and Schaller's book tries to answer some of these. One senses, however, a fairly strong feeling of division between them [these difficulties] and the arguments supporting the diaconate. If the term was not too common and disparaging, we might say that the difficulties leave the impression of being cooked up by clerics and the supporting arguments of rising sentiment to the expression of a spiritual fact.

Of course that depends, first of all, on the literary genre of each text: a witness's statement always bears the personal, existential, mark of the person asked. Yet we would willingly think there is more and that the impression felt is an indication of the ecclesiological significance of the problems presented. In fact, we think increasingly that the problems evoked call for a prophetic development of the ecclesiological vision outlined by Vatican II: **a People of God Church where the main value is not the distinction between laity and clergy** (these latter granted jurisdiction and "powers"): it is rather a life of grace given by Christ and by his Holy Spirit, the source of "charisms" or spiritual gifts. That leads to the idea that the People of God as Church, while still being intrinsically structured through the sacraments, are entirely responsible for the Church's mission and its service to the world. Within the framework of these fundamental values, are *some* **diverse ministries** that certainly do not all have the same status or importance: some are properly "hierarchical" and founded on a sacrament, meaning founded on an intention and act of the Lord. To the extent that one frees oneself from a mainly juridical notion, which has dominated to the point of prevailing and leaves the narrowness of a vision of the Church as a fixed established institution, yet without denying this reality, one sees her as being created unendingly and freely by the Lord, rising from the instruments of his design of grace. Such must apply to **the restoration of a theology of the variety of ministries**. In this direction we should search for a declericalization of the notion of Church, carrying, in my view, more truth and more importance than the "declergification" of the presbyteral priesthood.

We should not prefabricate diaconal behaviors.

More and more, we will think in terms of functions within the priestly people, without disregarding the sacramental and instituted nature of functions of a hierarchical level and importance. (See Bourgeois-Schaller, 102.)

There have been many attempts to precisely define the ministerial diaconate. Very interesting ideas have been proposed, but none seems entirely satisfactory.[2]

In the perspective and in the spirit of what we just said, we approve on the other hand the following lines of Bourgeois-Schaller (p. 131):

Can we now partly specify what the particular "functions" of deacons will be? The project is ordinary but ambiguous. "There is a danger in believing that the deacon will only have defined functions to fill" (a candidate, employed, married, six children). "This would lead to prefabricating diaconal behaviors and, once it is restored, the diaconate would be fixed and structured" (a candidate, insurance agent, married, three children). In addition, we have previously underlined the risk there would be in determining the sphere of responsibilities reserved for deacons. It would be better to wait until the deacons gradually find their place in collaboration with the bishop, the priests, and the laity. As one priest hopes: "One must not say: we create deacons, now what are we going to do with them?"—But we must create these deacons because we have felt the calls of the Spirit and of the Church."

[2] The latest proposal I have seen is that of Tibor Horvath, SJ, "Theology of a New Diaconate" in *Revue de l'Université d'Ottawa* 38 (1968): 248–76 and 495–523. The author begins with a historical review of the relationships between the episcopacy, presbyterate, and diaconate, which allows him to present an answer to the question: why has the permanent diaconate declined and nearly disappeared? He proposes to consider the presbyterate as a service of the Church insofar as it offers to serve the world in its reality and its difficulties. But, neither bishops nor priests will agree to be isolated from such service to the world, which evidently they must exercise according to their aim, within their orders, and through the ways appropriate to what they are. (*N.D.L.R.* cf. in the following pages of this journal.)

We could expect that these calls are in harmony with those who at present guide the life of the Church as a whole. But today one fact imposes itself. It characterizes the postconciliar era more than the work of the Council, during which it was only announced. **The problems, even the internal problems of the Church, are today presented starting from the world and by the world.** It is clear that there might be a danger here insofar as one might not only look for demands and specifications but also for the principle of norms and responses within the world.

"The world's expectations of the Church's manifestation of the diaconate."

It is very informative to follow the question of the diaconate as do Bourgeois and Schaller, by retracing its history, a history they sum up thusly: "The idea of the diaconate has gone from **the perspective of help for priests** to the input of **the needs of the Church,** and then to that of **the expectation of a world** to which the Church must manifest its diaconate (p. 54). Without systematizing as Horvath does, we might accept what could be interesting in his thesis (cf. fn. 2). We would especially welcome as instructive the answer he gives with regard to knowing why the permanent diaconate declined and was replaced by the presbyterate in its role of service to the bishop. It is, he says, that the priesthood adapted itself to the changes in the world at that time, whereas the diaconate did not. Could this be because the Church did not then really have a world **before it** to serve? This question should be studied more profoundly.

The deacon will be "leader in service."

We said there are no theoretical problems to deal with before moving on to the actual practice. However, perhaps there are still some. **Are we perfectly clear on the question of knowing if the diaconate is a degree of the ministerial or hierarchical priesthood, that is to say, is it part of the sacrament of Order?** In my opinion no one can doubt the latter. The patristic tradition may not be unanimous. On the contrary, the liturgical facts place the ordination of deacons on the same level as that of priests and bishops. The Council of Trent is more favorable to our thesis;[3] Vatican II affirms it expressly.[4] That raises a question. Vatican II

---

[3] Session XXIII, c.2 and can. 6 (Denzsch, 1765 and 1776).
[4] Dogmatic Constitution on the Church, *Lumen gentium*, 28, 29.

says that the hierarchical priesthood represents Christ as Head in the priestly community of the faithful.[5] What does this say regarding the deacon? In the Christian community, each person as a disciple is devoted to *diakonia*. The deacon will be a leader in service and in this role will "equip the saints for the work of ministry" (Eph 4:12). And the deacon will be leader of prayer.

Our brother and friend, Father Gy, has in this regard, attracted our attention to an interesting and significant episode in the life of St. Anthony the Hermit: "He wished that all clerics take precedence over him (. . .) . If a deacon came to him for enlightenment, he said what was necessary; but, when it came to prayer Anthony ceded his place, unembarrassed to learn."[6] What a beautiful illustration of the relationship between the charismatic order and the hierarchical order in their respective responsibilities! The superior of monks understood it was the deacon's place to lead or preside at prayer.

Women deacons?

This is a question that, finally, Bourgeois and Schaller do not deal with but which will be asked about sooner or later, that of conferring the diaconate on women. The question will be asked some day, because that of the priesthood has already been asked, sometimes a bit noisily (for example by the Joan of Arc Federation, the Third World Congress of the Apostolate of the Laity in Rome, in October 1967), sometimes with motivations I do not despise. **I have, however, taken a stand against the feminine priesthood**, for reasons that look to me still valid.[7] I would not have the same objections for the diaconate. Of course, if this is the first grade of the sacrament of Order, it confers in the Church a certain position of representing Christ as Head, which indeed I have just recognized. The position a deaconess would hold in the order of charity and prayer would not exceed that which many women already hold, at the head of religious communities or service organizations. In my opinion, the question of preaching carries with it some difficulties, which could become limitations of its practice. The difficulties would also arise within the solemn celebration of the eucharistic liturgy. On the other hand, if it

---

[5] Implicit in *Lumen gentium* (21, 28, 37) this idea is explicated in the decree *Presbyterorum ordinis*, 2, para. 3; 6, para 1.

[6] Saint Athanasius, *Vie de Saint Antoine*, chap. 67, trans. B. Lavaud (Lyon, 1943).

[7] See *le Concile au jour le jour, troisième session* (Paris, 1965), 93–97.

becomes a question of the distribution of Communion, laity, both men and women, already do that. We return to the question found posed several times in the pages of Bourgeois and Schaller: **Why are there deacons where the royal priesthood authorizes laity to exercise ministries that are not strictly hierarchical? So much so that the question of the diaconate partly depends on the laity** on this question, within the framework of an ecclesiology of the People of God and of the varied ministries, the life of the Church has not pronounced its last word.

Translated by Gabrielle Corbally, Carmela Leonforte-Plimack,
and Phyllis Zagano

12

Conclusions Regarding the Female Diaconate

Peter Hünermann

The problem whether or not at this time to introduce the female diaconate into the Church involves a series of separate questions: (1) Dogmatically speaking, is it possible to confer this order on women? The response to this question will take Scripture and tradition as its point of departure. (2) Can the factors which led to the blossoming and demise of the female diaconate be brought into relief? From this there might ensue points which are important for a fruitful revival of this female office in the Church. (3) Assuming its feasibility in light of dogma, should the reasons for such a reanimation be examined? (4) Should—with an eye to the second question—something be said about what should determine the functions of this diaconate and what relationship the holder of this office would have today to other ministers? These two points are vital to the healthy development of such an office.

I

The gospels and other books of the New Testament bear witness to the immense and irreplaceable role women played in the growth of the early Church. In the context of a still relatively fluid structure, one where the distribution of offices and services was not yet fixed, they functioned: as prophetesses,[1] their charisma being as much one of service and just

"Conclusions Regarding the Female Diaconate," Theological Studies 36, no. 2 (1975): 325–33.

[1] Cf. 1 Cor 11:2 (regarding the apparently contradictory text 1 Cor 14:33b-36, cf. H. Conzelmann, *Der erste Brief an die Korinther* [Göttingen, 1969], 289f.); Acts 21:9, Ap 2:20. It was not until the pastoral epistles were written that women were expressly forbidden to teach; cf. 1 Tim 2:11-14. (The gloss 1 Cor 14:33b-36 also

as prominent and vigorous as the apostleship and the office of teachers and evangelists; as proselytes who in the various cities ranked with the "notables" of the young community[2] and thus took part in its direction; and as those who undertook missionary and charitable activities.[3] It may well be said that without this committed female collaboration and its full recognition by the Church, the spread of Christianity would have been unthinkable.

It is in the context of such activity on the part of women in the early Church that Romans 16:1 mentions Phoebe, whose missionary and charitable work is indicated by the title "deaconess of the church at Cenchreae." Because there was still no specific use of the words *diakonein* and *diakonos* in reference to ministry and the office of service in the Church, it would be false to call this a testimony to the existence of the female diaconate as a specific office. The formation of official structures was a whole process still in embryo.

The situation reflected in the pastoral epistles is of considerable interest. Modern exegetes unanimously hold that these writings are post-Pauline in character and have the double purpose of showing that apostolicity was inherent in the structure of the early catholic Church and of making the retention of this structure a matter of obligation. On the one hand, the letters speak of an ingrained institution, the order of widows, with its conditions of admission and formulary of duties, etc. On the other, they give a directive for women at 1 Timothy 3:11, right in the middle of a description of the office of diaconate. Is it a question here of the deacons' wives or of deaconesses? The reasons for supposing the former are judged by present-day exegetes to be of questionable validity. More attractive, they say, is the latter view.[4] The suspicion that the directive is a later interpolation cannot be adequately supported. Ultimately stemming from a certain embarrassment in the face of the text, it is nowadays disregarded by almost all exegetes.

Merely on the basis of the evidence from the New Testament, it is impossible unambiguously to say whether or not dogma leaves room for the office of deaconess. A text from Origen, however, seems to me to

---

belongs in this context.) With the struggle against Montanism and Gnostocism the arrangement became permanent.

[2] Cf. Acts 14:16; 1 Cor 16:19.

[3] Cf. Rom 16:1f.; 16:3-5; 16:11.

[4] Cf. A. Vögtle, *Die Tugend- und Lasterkataloge im NT* (Münster, 1936), 53; and N. Brox, *Die Pastoralbriefe* (Regensburg, 1969), 154; further references in the latter.

be important for an elucidation of all sides of the question. In his commentary on the Epistle to the Romans he writes of 16:1f.:

> This passage shows with apostolic authority that women too were designated for the Church's ministry. Paul is commending and greatly praising Phoebe, who had been installed in this office in the Church at Cenchreae. So this passage shows two things: first, as we have said, that there were female ministers, and secondly, that it was expected that those who had been of so much help and by their good services had gone so far as to merit apostolic praise would be taken into the ministry.[5]

Here "ministry" and "female ministers" translate respectively the Latin text's *ministerium* and *feminas ministras*. Essential to understanding this text is the observation that in Origen's time there were no deaconesses in his ecclesiastical province. Also, Origen seems to understand Romans 16:1 in terms of the by then quite institutionalized diaconate familiar to him. The least that follows, then, is that he was not opposed on principle to admitting women to the diaconate; and quite likely he knew from tradition that women had been deaconesses.

In referring to "one of" the two epistles to Timothy—which one is not clear—Clement of Alexandria had already written:

> The women whom . . . the apostles . . . took around with them were not wives but, as befitted the apostles' dedication to an undistracted preaching ministry, sisters, fellow ministers to the women who kept house. So the Lord's teaching made its way into the women's quarters too, and in a manner above reproach, for we know what the honorable Paul in one of his letters to Timothy prescribed regarding female deacons.[6]

One may well conclude from both texts that for these two eminent and discerning theologians, pertinent passages from the New Testament, viewed in conjunction with its over-all theology of the Church and church offices, clearly granted the possibility of admitting women to the office of deaconess.

The witness of Pliny the Younger, from a letter (111–113) dispatched to Trajan from northwest Asia Minor, is a neat chip in this entire mosaic of evidence. The writer had "judged it . . . necessary to extract the real

---

[5] PG 14:1278.
[6] *Stromata* 3, 6, 53 (PG 8:1158).

truth, with the assistance of torture, from two female slaves, who were styled deaconesses."[7]

As for tradition, the earliest text that gives formal and unequivocal evidence of the existence of the office of deaconess is the *Didascalia*, the Syrian document dating from the first decades of the third century.[8] Pertinent passages show what place the office of deaconess had amid the other ministerial offices and outline its duties in detail. So this ecclesiastical code presupposed an established communal practice, the appointing of deaconesses, which, though perhaps not yet established among all those addressed by the document, the bishops were being exhorted to continue.

Exactly as the deacons, the deaconesses were chosen and ordained by the bishop. Their ministry was of both a liturgical and a nonliturgical nature. In the first area, they were mainly expected to assist at baptisms of women and perform the accompanying anointings. In the other, calling on women, sick ones in particular, for whom they performed nursing duties, and giving religious instructions and guidance to newly baptized women made up their responsibilities.

The rapid expansion of the female diaconate in the Eastern churches brought a number of other responsibilities to the office and gave it further definition. In the area of liturgy, deaconesses in certain churches were granted the right to distribute Communion from the rail to women and children. As to the rest, they occasionally administered the Anointing of the Sick to women, were responsible for the order and cleanliness of the sanctuary, and functioned, in church and outside of it, as portresses, the community's guardians as it were of women and children. They were supposed to take an interest in all women and children, healthy or ill.[9]

The exact meaning of the Council of Nicaea's nonadmission (canon 19) of the ordination of deaconesses through the laying on of hands is disputed. Canon 15 of the Council of Chalcedon, however, does speak

---

[7] Pliny, *Letters 2*, trans. William Melmoth (Cambridge, MA, 1957), 405.

[8] Funk, ed., *Didascalia et constitutiones apostolorum* (Paderborn, 1905).

[9] Along with the *Constitutions apostolorum*, cf. especially Funk, ed., *Didascalia Arabica*; I. E. Rahmani, ed., *Testamentum Domini nostri Jesu Christi* (Moguntiae, 1899); and the documents of the Monophysite Church in J. S. Assemani, *Bibliotheca orientalis*, vols. 2 and 3 (Rome, 1721 and 1778). Selections from these texts may be found in Josephine Mayer, ed., *Monumenta de viduis diaconissis virginibusque tractantia* (Bonn, 1938); and H. Krimm, *Quellen zur Geschichte der Diakonie 1* (Stuttgart, 1960).

of such an ordination through the laying on of hands. The ordination formulas, the ceremonies (the laying on of hands), the handing over of the stole, etc., all of which had been retained, show that here it is a matter of ordination regarded as on a par with the ordination of a deacon, i.e., an ordination in the strictest sense, not something like a blessing.[10] The formally sacramental character of this ordination cannot be questioned.

In fixing an apportionment of clerics into various types, the *Nouvellae Justiniani* give grounds more or less to infer that deaconesses were part of the clergy as such.

> We decree that no more than sixty priests, one hundred male and forty female deacons, ninety subdeacons, one hundred ten lectors, and twenty-five cantors be appointed to the most hallowed high church, so that the total number of its most reverend clerics be four hundred twenty-five, plus one hundred of those called porters.[11]

Although, like the deacons, the deaconesses were ordained and fully integrated into the liturgical and pastoral ministry and the performance of charitable works, two principles always applied in the various Eastern churches: the deaconesses were not allowed to function at the altar, especially during the consecration of the Eucharist;[12] and they were given no assignments ranking them above men. This applied both to the deaconesses' cooperation with other clerics, i.e., to specifically clerical functions, and to their association with the laity.[13]

That the theological justification for the first point was not easy can be seen in an Egyptian ecclesiastical code from the third century. Through an imaginary conversation between Peter, John, Mary, and Martha it is explained that women had not been allowed to take part in Jesus' celebration of the Last Supper with the apostles because Mary had laughed and because "what is weak will be saved by what is strong."[14]

Theologically unsatisfying as such a response may be, the practice of the Eastern Church allows at least this to be derived as a general

---

[10] For ordination formulas cf. Funk (*Constitutiones apostolorum*), Rahmani, and Assemani.

[11] Justinianus, *Novellae*, in *Corpus juris civilis*, ed. Rudolfus Schoell and Guilelmus Kroll, 3 (Berlin, 1954) 21.

[12] Cf. Epiphanius, *Adv. haer.* (PG 42:743f.).

[13] Funk, *Constitutiones apostolorum*, 530.

[14] Erik Tidner, ed., *Canones ecclesiastici sive canones apostolorum* (Berlin, 1963), 112–13.

principle: the one mission of Jesus Christ which is represented struc-
turally in the many church offices is so many-sided that it prohibits the
conclusion that all ministers who take part in this mission of Christ are
ipso facto partakers of the office of priesthood. This, it seems to me, is
important not only for considering the question of the female diaconate
but also for maintaining the element of independence in the definition
of the male diaconate. In matters regarding the female diaconate, the
Western Church did not follow the same line of development as the
Eastern Church. Nevertheless, a number of women were ordained to
the diaconate in Lower Italy and Gaul. Here the strong influence of the
Eastern churches can be clearly seen.[15] In the context of a study such as
this, it is not necessary to enumerate the individual cases. Rather, it seems
more important to point to two decisive reasons why in the West the
formation of the female diaconate as an institution never occurred. First,
the women in the West were more firmly integrated; so the mission to
them, instructing them, etc., did not require the appointment of women
in any official capacity. Cornelius Nepos had remarked:

> What Roman would blush to take his wife to a dinner-party? What
> matron does not frequent the front rooms of her dwelling and show
> herself in public? But it is very different in Greece; for there a woman
> is not admitted to a dinner-party, unless relatives only are present, and
> she keeps to the more retired part of the house called "the women's
> apartment," to which no man has access who is not near of kin.[16]

Second, in the Roman Church the order of widows did not have diaconal
duties the way it did in the Eastern churches; so it could not, as in the
East, simply be lifted from its original setting and then incorporated into
the office of deaconess as the latter initially took shape.

II

The female diaconate in the Eastern churches gained the greatest
ground during those long periods of peace when the Christian communities imparted momentum to an intensive, ever-growing missionary ac-

---

[15]Cf. the detailed presentation in A. Kalsbach, "Die altkirchliche Einrichtung
der Diakonissen his zu ihrem Erlöschen," *Römische Quartalschrift* 22, Suppl.
(1926).

[16]Cornelius Nepos, *The Book on the Great Generals of Foreign Nations*, trans. John C.
Rolfe (Cambridge, MA, 1947), 371.

tion and took in multitudes. It was the time before the official recognition of the Church, the time of a quite energetic expansion. A greater number of adult baptisms was in evidence; catechumens had to be instructed and after their baptism receive a still further and deeper introduction to the faith. The need to meet the various problems led not only to the creation of the lower clergy but also to the simultaneous entrustment of women with an important office in the Church.

The moment the churches proceeded to lose their missionary character, this office began to die out. So the female diaconate continued to flourish in the large mission churches of the Far East, while in Byzantium it was already showing signs of torpidity and deterioration. Functional weakening brought about the weakening of the office itself. Since there were fewer adult baptisms, the deaconesses' commission to teach became more and more restricted; they were increasingly relieved of the duties of the deacon; and so the stagnation and demise of the office in the "established" churches came relatively quick.

If anywhere, then precisely in connection with this process of deterioration it becomes apparent that hand in glove with an office in the Church go a clear-cut professional image and well-defined, sufficiently variegated portrait of the capacities of the office.

III

The discussion of the New Testament evidence and of the data of tradition makes clear that dogma provides no grounds for misgivings about ordaining women to the office of deacon. In the Latin Church the reasons for opposing the ordination of deaconesses were not of any fundamental nature but derived from conventions of the times. From this starting point we now pursue the question whether the reasons justifying a present reanimation of the female diaconate are sufficient. The following enumeration of them, however, will not go beyond the brevity of an outline. They are all part of much greater complexities, each of which has been often enough expounded upon in the recent discussion of the female office in the Church.[17]

The first thing that must be pointed to is the fundamental transformation of the position of woman in modern society, a society which is so closely connected with an economy characterized by the division of labor. Society's doffing of that form and cultural guise where the guild and the

[17] Cf., for example, H. van der Meer, *Priestertum der Frau* (Freiburg, 1969).

peasantry were the dominant features made woman a partner with equal rights in social and economic life; it opened the doors to equal chances of advancement to positions of leadership in public life. In a large measure, working women are involved in two fields intimately associated with the Church's pastoral activity, those of education and welfare, and hold numerous positions of leadership in these areas. In such a situation the complete exclusion of women from offices in the Church can only be taken as adherence to a bygone conventionality and as discrimination.

Second, to a large degree paralleling the development of the women's professions in society, the collaboration of women within the sphere of the Catholic Church has grown into something bountiful and special- ized. The main thrusts of the effort are differentiated along the lines of catechetical, pastoral, social, charitable, and administrative work. A great many of these women are persons who, in the service of the Church, direct their lives wholly and entirely to the service of Jesus Christ, often remain unmarried, and regard their profession as a lifework. The edu- cational background as well as the personal inner dispositions of many of them constitute the prerequisites for espousing an official ministry that makes a claim on one's entire life. Here the Church has obviously been endowed through the providence of God with a mine of potential authentic vocations, one which no one with a church responsibility can blindly bypass.

Third, like the Church in the third century, the Church today finds itself in a missionary situation which demands an all-out effort. In the so-called Christian countries the Church has turned out to be in a minority posi- tion. The Church needs to take new root in society. What Christian faith bespeaks today, what it can and in fact does mean to people of this age, can only be made visible through the maximum expenditure of energy. The requisite impulses for this have come from the Second Vatican Coun- cil. In conformity with the prompting of John XXIII, it was the Council's intention to freshen the face of the Church. And part of such a process, indeed an essential part, is a renewal of that impression of the faith which the Church's ministerial offices give. The Church can no more forgo the official collaboration of women today than it could during its great mis- sionary drive or during the missionary effort of the third century; their assistance was simply indispensable. The third-century redistribution of the numerous ecclesiastical functions entailed the creation of the entire lower clergy, one marked by the inclusion of an office for women. Like- wise today, the reanimation of such an office in the Church is imperative for the reorganization and differentiation of the ministry.

The above reasons do not from beginning to end and unambiguously betoken the office of deaconess. However, considering that in accord with unbroken tradition in the East and West the episcopal and priestly offices are reserved for men, considering that ecumenical advances toward Orthodox Christianity are under way, the only female office thinkable in the present situation of the Church is the office of deaconess. For it, there is clearly a precedent in the Church's history; about it theology has not the least misgivings.

IV

A single fundamental point, one important for an over-all evaluation of the matter of the female diaconate, is all that the following reflections are designed to bring out.

The question regarding the meaning of ordination perhaps arises with greater trenchancy in connection with the female than with the male diaconate. Would it not be better to continue with what has been the practice until now, namely, of entrusting women with the performance of an abundance of services in the Church? Why ordain them? What is it supposed to empower them specially to do? Indeed, this question feeds on something articulated in lay circles, the fear of an augmented clericalism within the Church. But it is also posed by priests, motivated by the fear of losing that self-identity perceived in the exclusive right to administer the sacraments. Both the male and female diaconate make requisite a thorough consideration of the essence of official ministry in the Church. Such ministry cannot be defined primarily in terms of the sacramental powers. It is much better to understand official ministry with a view to the community and the world, as official *repraesentatio* of the mission of Jesus Christ. An office in the Church is a God-given commission, the power to build up communities and equip them for lives sustained by the one, universally binding mission of Christ.

New Testament exegesis has shown us anew the mission of Jesus Christ in all its breadth and comprehensiveness and thus made clear how necessary it is to take the entire scope of this mission into consideration insofar as it is represented by the official ministry, in the community, for the community and for the people of the world. The cultic and sacerdotal aspect should not be depreciated, but to concentrate on it to such an extent that the diaconal element is slighted would be an anachronism running directly counter to our present knowledge of the New Testament. Seeking its way toward the total person and into all dimensions of society, the mission of Jesus Christ has a scope which can only be represented by way of office to the extent that a plurality of relatively independent offices is envisaged. Naturally, such offices have need of the constitutional and functional integration guaranteed by the office of the episcopate. They should, however, be respected for their independence and not simply be regarded as participating in the "priesthood." There are aspects of the mission of Jesus Christ which cannot be brought into historical effectiveness by the function of the community leader, the presbyter, but which have been reserved for this purpose to the diaconate.

This basic viewpoint on the matter of Church office provides an important standard for the entrustment of deacons and deaconesses with liturgical or sacramental tasks and powers. The liturgy, especially the Eucharist, is the most concentrated of the expressions of faith and at the same time a presentation of what the community in the Lord is. The deacon's or deaconess's function there should be defined, then, in terms of their specific tasks in the life of the community. Bringing the sacrificial gifts to the altar and distributing Holy Communion, for example, make visual what day by day, nonsacramentally takes place in the community through the diaconal ministry. Also, the preaching done by deaconesses and deacons during services should be the expression of such tasks.

These few hints are meant to be no more than illustrative. They are enough to show how the desirable introduction of the female diaconate can be combined with the development and enrichment of the community's life in the area of the liturgy and the sacraments.

Selected Annotated Bibliography

Ansorge, Dirk. "Der Diakonat der Frau. Zum gegenwärtigen Forschungs-stand." In *Liturgie and Frauenfrage*, edited by Teresa Berger and Albert Gerhards, 31–65. Pietas Liturgica 7. St. Ottilien: EOS-Verlag, 1990.
The author deduces that in the case of particular Churches within Christianity and in certain historic periods there was a diaconate of ordained women. From the end of the fourth century, a theology developed determining the liturgical act of ordaining as a *cheirotonia* as an act of granting the grace of the Holy Spirit, and literary sources demonstrate that deaconesses received a *cheirotonia*.

————. "Die wesentlichen Argumente liegen auf dem Tisch. Zur neueren Diskussion um den Diakonat der Frau." *HerKorr* 47, no. 11 (1993): 581–86.

Arichea, Daniel C. "Who Was Phoebe? Translating *Diakonos* in Romans 16:1." *Bible Translator* 39 (1988): 401–9.

Aubert, Marie-Joseph. *Des Femmes Diacres: Un nouveau chemin pour l'Église*. Paris: Beauchesne, 1987.
The author argues that the female diaconate of the ancient East should be closely analyzed as a model for a possible restoration of the tradition today, granting women a specific juridical status within the Church.

Barnett, James Monroe. *The Diaconate: A Full and Equal Order*. Norcross, GA: Trinity Press International, 1983.
Barnett argues that up to the fourth century the diaconate was a ministry featuring a horizontal, organic structure. Around the fourth century the diaconate began to be a step on the path to priesthood. Barnett calls for the restoration of the diaconate to its original place, as a full and equal order.

Beyer, Herman W. διακονέω, διακονία, διάκονος. *Theologisches Wörterbuch zum Nuen Testament II*, 81–94.

Böttigheimer, Christoph. "Der Diakonat der Frau." *Münchener Theologische Zeitschrift* 47, no. 3 (1996): 253–66.

Bouyer, Louis. *Mystère et ministère de la femme*. Paris: Aubier Monatigne, 1976.
Bouyer discusses the anthropological argument of the relations between man and woman in the light of Pauline teaching (Eph 15 and 1 Cor 15).

Bradshaw, Paul F. *Ordination Rites of the Ancient Churches of East and West*. Collegeville, MN: Liturgical Press, 1990.
Bradshaw parses the primary sources of the texts used in ordination to the offices of greatest antiquity in the Christian Churches of East and West, exploring the core structure of the rituals and commenting on the prayers and ceremonies that accompanied them.

Brandt, Wilhelm. *Dienst und Dienen im Neuen Testament.* Gütersloh: Bertelsmann, 1931.
Brandt reviews German-language studies on women deacons and maintains that in the ancient Church the ordination of deaconesses was of the same character as that of deacons. Such an ordination must be considered a sacrament, as confirmed by the theology of the sacrament of orders as renewed by Vatican II, by which deacons and presbyters according to distinct modalities partake of the same sacrament.

Canon Law Society of America. *The Canonical Implications of Ordaining Women to the Permanent Diaconate.* Washington, DC: Canon Law Society of America, 1995.
A professional study designated to determine the canonical implications of ordaining women to the permanent diaconate. The analysis reaches the conclusion that such an ordination is possible and within authority of the Church, and that this may even be desirable for the United States in the present cultural circumstances.

Collins, John N. *Diakonia: Re-Interpreting the Ancient Sources.* New York: Oxford University Press, 1990, 2009.
A study of the Greek word *diakonia*. Collins analyzes both Christian and non-Christian sources from the second century BC to the second century AD, determining that in most of these sources the meaning of the word is "messenger" or "emissary" and that this sheds new light on the theological discussion on ministry.

Congar, Yves. "Gutachten zum Diakonat der Frau." *Amtliche Mitteilungen der Gemeinsamen Synode der Bistümer der Bundesrepublik Deutsch-lands* 7 (1973): 37–41.
Congar maintains that in the ancient church *ordo, ordinare* meant to establish a certain order in the church. *Ordinare, ordinatio* signified the fact of being designated and consecrated to take up a certain function in the community and at its service. Hence, the question is not whether this is the sacrament of order, but whether the order of the female diaconate is authentic. The author believes it is and hopes for a revival of the office in the present-day church.

———. "Variétés des ministères et renouveau diaconal." *Diacres aujourd'hui* (1969): 2–3.

Daniélou, Jean. *The Ministry of Women in the Early Church.* Translated by G. Simon. London: Faith Press, 1974 (originally in *Maison Dieu* 61 [1960]).
Daniélou argues that in antiquity widows were not ordained by the laying of the hands but that sources demonstrate that deaconesses received the *cheirothesia* from the bishop and therefore may have constituted a minor order.

Davies, John G. "Deacons, Deaconesses and the Minor Orders in the Patristic Period." *The Journal of Ecclesiastical History* 14, no. 1 (1963): 1–15.

Delhaye, Philippe. "Rétrospective et prospective des ministères féminins dans L'Eglise." *Revue théologique de Louvain* 3 (1972).
Delhaye comments on the possibility of restoring the feminine diaconate, highlighting the theological relevance of the historic continuity of ordaining deaconesses in the ancient Church (third and fourth centuries). He maintains

that the fidelity to such a tradition must be preserved and that the ancient practice itself did not aim at creating something new in the Church but at continuing the tradition of Christ and the Apostles.

Diakonia, Diaconiae, Diaconato. Semantica e Storia nei padri della Chiesa. Studia Ephemeridis Augustinianum, 117. Proceedings of the 38th meeting of Scholars of Ancient Christianity. Roma: Istituto Patristicum Augustinianum, 2010. These proceedings lay a foundation for a theological view on the diaconate by returning to the study of the oldest sources, including contributions from specialists on both Eastern and Western traditions. The diverse views on the office of deacon in the Eastern and Western churches are placed under accurate theological scrutiny, so as to establish how the diaconate functioned in different periods and different contexts.

Ditewig, William T. "The Sacramental Identity of the Deacon." *Deacon Digest* 17, no. 1 (January/February 2000): 27–31.

Ditewig, William T., Gary Macy, and Phyllis Zagano. *Women Deacons: Past, Present, Future.* New York: Paulist Press, 2011.

Eisen, Ute E. "Deacons." Chap. 7 (pp. 158–98) in *Women Officeholders in Early Christianity: Epigraphical and Literary Studies,* translated by Linda M. Maloney. Collegeville, MN: Liturgical Press, 2000. *Amtsträgerinnen im frühen Christentum. Epigraphische und literaische Studien.* Göttengen: Vandenhoeck & Ruprecht, 1996.

Eisen investigates the evidence for women officeholders in the first centuries of Christianity, focusing especially on inscriptions and documents (private letters, contracts, official documents). She analyzes the many titles of women and comments on them in the context of the existing literary sources. Includes an extensive bibliography.

Ferrari, Giuseppe. "Le diaconesse nella tradizione orientale." *Oriente Cristiano* 14, no. 1 (1974): 28–50.

Ferrari argues that there existed deaconesses within the Italian-Greek-Albanian communities of Sicily in the sixteenth century. He maintains that these women were ordained deaconesses because had they not been ordained they would not have been entitled to serve at the altar when a priest was celebrating. Lay people in general, and especially lay women, were indeed forbidden to enter the sanctuary. The author maintains that women cannot enter the priesthood but that there are theological grounds for them to enter the diaconate.

Fitzgerald, Kyriaki K. "The Characteristics and the Nature of the Order of the Deaconess." in *Women and the Priesthood,* edited by T. Hopko, 75–95. Crestwood, NY: St. Vladimir's Seminary Press, 1983.

———. *Women Deacons in the Orthodox Church: Called to Holiness and Ministry.* Brookline, MA: Holy Cross Orthodox Press, 1998.

Fitzgerald makes the case that women were ordained rather than appointed to the diaconate, including evidence that the essential characteristics of the Byzantine ordination rite for women distinguish it as for a major order.

Frohnhofen, Herbert. "Weibliche Diakone in der frühen Kirche." *Stimmen der Zeit* 111 (1986): 269–78.

238   *Women Deacons?*

Galot, Jean. *La donna e i ministeri nella Chiesa.* Assisi: Cittadella, 1973.
An exploration of women's early church ministries focused on historical evidence of the institutionally recognized positions widows, virgins, deaconesses, and later abbesses held within the church.

Gryson, Roger. *The Ministry of Women in the Early Church.* Translated by Jean Laporte and Mary Louise Hall. Collegeville, MN: Liturgical Press, 1976; originally *Le ministère des femmes dans l'Église ancienne.* Éditions J. Duculot. Gembloux, Belgium, 1972.
Gryson maintains that history testifies to the existence of widows and deaconesses as separate and non-overlapping institutions. He demonstrates a connection between ministries and specific functions and defines the position held by women deacons in the ancient Church as analogous to that of deacons, as proved by use of the term *diakonos* for both. From a detailed analysis of the literary sources he deduces that women deacons belonged to the clergy.

———. "Un diaconat féminin pour aujourd'hui?" *La Libre Belgique* (May 11, 1981): 12.

Goltz, Eduard von der. *Der Dienst der Frau in der christlichen Kirkche.* Potsdam: Stiftungsverlag, 1914.

Goodspeed, Edgar J. "Phoebe's Letter of Introduction." *Harvard Theological Review* 44 (1951): 55–57.

Gvosdev, Matushka Ellen. *Female Diaconate: An Historical Perspective.* Minneapolis: Light & Life Publishing Company, 1991.
A study of the female diaconate in the early Byzantine Church using biblical, historical, and canonical sources.

Hauke, Manfred. "Excursus on Deaconesses." In *Women in the Priesthood: A Systematic Analysis in the Light of the Order of Creation and Redemption*, translated by David Kipp, 440–44. San Francisco, Ignatius Press, 1986. Original: *Die Problematik um das Frauenpriestertum vor dem Hintergrund der Schöpfungs- und Erlösungsordnung.* Paderborn: Verlag Bonifatius-Druckerei, 1986.
Hauke maintains the restoration of the ancient female diaconate would be anachronistic, but the inclusion of women in the contemporary diaconate would be viewed as a step toward women in priesthood.

———. "Il diaconato femminile: osservazioni sul recente dibattito." *Notitiae 418*, no. 37 (2001): 195–239.
Hauke maintains that the unicity of orders provides that the possible sacramental ordination of women deacons would contradict the teaching on women priests. He affirms that since the deacon receives the sacramental character, at the foundation of acting *in persona Christi*, should a woman receive the diaconal order there would then not be any valid theological principle to exclude her from the other degrees of the sacrament of order.

Hentschel, Anni. *Diakonia im Neuen Testament.* Tübingen: Mohr Siebeck, 2007.
The Greek terms *diakonia* and its cognates are important in the texts of early Christian communities because they refer to commissioned tasks and imply the notion of a mandate and a personal obligation, often involving a mediating activity. The author examines the way New Testament writers used these

words, providing new insights into the different ways early Christians used the term *diakonia.*

Hiebert, David Edmond, "Behind the Word 'Deacon': A New Testament Study." *Bibliotheca Sacra* 140 (1983): 151–61.

Hilberath, Bernd Jochen. "Das Amt der Diakonin: ein sakramentales Amt?" In *Diakonat. Ein Amt für Frauen in der Kirche—Ein frauengerechtes Amt?*, edited by Peter Hünermann, Albert Biesinger, Marianne Heimbach-Steins, and Anne Jensen, 212–18. Ostfildern: Schwabenverlag, 1997.

Hofrichter, Peter. "Diakonat und Frauen im kirchlichen Amt." *Heiliger Dienst* 50, no. 3 (1996): 140–58.

Hoping, Helmut. "Diakonat der Frau ohne Frauenpriestertum?" *Schweizerische Kirchenzeitung* 18 (June 14, 2000).

Hopko, Thomas, ed. *Women and the Priesthood.* Crestwood, NY: St. Vladimir's Seminary Press, 1983.

Essays by Alexander Schmemann, Nicholas Afanasiev, Georges Barrois, Nonna Verna Harrison, and others discuss the reasons why Orthodoxy has never ordained women to serve as bishops and priests. All agree that the Church has had women deacons and that careful consideration must be given to the office as it existed in the past, and as it may once again exist.

Hünermann, Peter. "Conclusions Regarding the Female Diaconate." *Theological Studies* 36 (1975): 325–33.

Hünermann supports the ordination of women deacons and the revival of the female diaconate in the Church, affirming that aspects of the mission of Jesus Christ cannot be brought into historical effectiveness only by presbyters.

———. "Gutachten zur Bestellung des Diakons (der Diakonin) zum ordentlichen Spender der Krankensalbung." *Diaconia Christi* 9, no. 3 (1974): 25–28.

———. "Lehramtliche Dokumente zur Frauenordination." In *Frauenordination,* edited by Walter Groß, 83–96. München: Erich Wewel Publications, 1996.

———. "Stellungnahme zu den Anmerkungen von Professor Otto Semmelroth SJ betreffend Votum der Synode zum Weihediakonat der Frau." *Diaconia Christi* 10, no. 1 (1975): 33–38.

———. "Theologische Argumente für die Diakonatsweihe van Frauen." In *Diakonat. Ein Amt für Frauen in der Kirche—Ein frauengerechtes Amt?*, edited by Peter Hünermann, Albert Biesinger, Marianne Heimbach-Steins, and Anne Jensen, 98–128. Ostfildern: Schwabenverlag, 1997.

Jensen, Anne. "Das Amt der Diakonin in der kirchlichen Tradition der ersten Jahrtausend." In *Diakonat. Ein Amt für Frauen in der Kirche—Ein frauengerechtes Amt?*, edited by Peter Hünermann, Albert Biesinger, Marianne Heimbach-Steins, and Anne Jensen, 32–52. Ostfildern: Schwabenverlag, 1997.

———. *God's Self-Confident Daughters: Early Christianity and the Liberation of Women.* Translated by O. C. Dean, Jr. Louisville, KY: Westminster John Knox, 1996.

Jewett, Robert. "Paul, Phoebe, and the Spanish Mission." In *The Social World of Formative Christianity and Judaism: Essays in Tribute to Howard Clark Kee,* edited by J. Neusner et al., 144–64. Philadelphia: Fortress Press, 1988.

Jorissen, Hans. "Theologische Bedenken gegen die Diakonatsweihe von Frauen." In *Diakonat. Ein Amt für Frauen in der Kirche—Ein frauengerechtes Amt?*, edited by Peter Hünermann, Albert Biesinger, Marianne Heimbach-Steins, and Anne Jensen, 86–97. Ostfildern: Schwabenverlag, 1997.

Kalsbach, Adolf. "Diakonisse." In *Reallexikon fir Antike und Christentum*, 917–28. Vol. 3. Stuttgart: Hiersemann, 1957.

———. *Die altkirchliche Einrichtung der Diakonissen bis zu ihrem Erlöschen.* Freiburg im Breisgau: Herder, 1926.

Kalsbach connects the feminine diaconate with the institution of widows and maintains that within the ancient Church their roles and status coincided. Further, he posits that their official *ministerium* was distinct from the ministry of male deacons and that they were excluded from major orders, rather receiving a special blessing.

Karras, Valerie. "The Liturgical Function of Consecrated Women in the Byzantine Church." *Theological Studies* 66 (2005): 96–116.

Even though the ordained order of deaconesses effectively died out in the Byzantine Church, some women continued to perform, either formally or informally, various liturgical functions in public church life. Karras explores evidences of three groups of women: noblewomen incense-bearers, matrons, and the possibly ordained order of myrrhbearers in the Church of Jerusalem.

Kasper, Walter. "Der Diakon in ekklesiologischer Sicht angesichts der gegenwärtigen Herausforderungen in Kirche und Gesellschaft." *Diaconia Christi* 32, nos. 3–4 (1997): 13–33.

———. "The Ministry of the Deacon." *Deacon Digest* 15, no. 2 (March/April 1998): 19–27.

Keener, Craig S. *Paul, Women and Wives: Marriage and Women's Ministry in the Letters of Paul.* Peabody, MA: Baker Academic, 1992.

Lague, Micheline. "Le diaconat permanent pour les femmes: une question ouverte dans l'Eglise?" *Pretre et pasteur* 114, no. 7 (2011): 414–27.

The author examines the possibility of offering women more responsibilities and opening up new spaces and roles for them within the Catholic Church. He concludes that the female diaconate would accomplish this purpose and dismisses the iconic argument as an impediment to this accomplishment.

Lochmann, Andreas Christof. *Studien zum Diakonat der Frau.* Univ. diss., Siegen 1996.

The author argues in this dissertation that in antiquity, both in the West and the East, there were equivalent notions to sacramentality. There existed a widely received theology that understood the imposition of the hands as the act that mediated the empowerment and the grace of the Holy Spirit on the ordained. The imposition of hands entailed the substance of sacrament, even if the word is not used. Ordination was understood in terms of what we today would call a sacrament, and sources prove that women deacons were ordained.

Lohfink, Gerhard. "Weibliche Diakone im Neuen Testament." In *Die Frau im Urchristentum*, edited by G. Dautzenberg et al., 320–38. Freiburg: Herder, 1983.

Macy, Gary. *The Hidden History of Women's Ordination: Female Clergy in the Medieval West.* Baltimore: The Johns Hopkins University Press, 2005.

———. "Ordination of Women in the Early Middle Ages: An Historiographic Problem." *Essays in Medieval Studies* 29 (2013): 1–16.

Madigan, Kevin, and Carolyn Osiek. *Ordained Women in the Early Church: A Documentary History.* New York: Oxford University Press, 2007.

Martimort, Aimé Georges. "A propos des ministères feminins dans l'Église." *Bulletin de Littérature Ecclésiastiques* 74 (1973): 103–8.

In this response to Gryson and Delhaye, Martimort surveys some primary sources and maintains that deaconesses belonged to a minor order, performed a limited liturgical ministry, and were substantially different from male deacons.

———. "La question du service des femmes à l'autel." *Notitiae* 16 (1980): 8–16.

———. *Les diaconesses: Essai historique.* Rome: Edizioni Liturgiche, 1982.

Martimort argues that evidence of a feminine diaconate in the Eastern Churches demonstrates that it changed in response to the needs of the church but was never at the same level as the male diaconate. He finds women deacons rare in Western churches and non-existent after the twelfth century. While he argues that a true female diaconal order never existed, he leaves open the question of the theological possibility for such in the present.

Marucci, Corrado. "Il 'diaconato' di Febe (Rom. 16:1-2) secondo l'esegesi moderna." In *Diakonia, Diaconiae, Diaconato. Semantica e Storia nei padri della Chiesa, Studia ephemeridid Augustinianum,* 685–95. Rome: Istituto Patristicum Augustinianum, 2010.

An exploration of the etymology of the term "deacon" as used referring to Phoebe in the New Testament, and a brief survey of its interpretation by ancient authors and modern Scripture translations. Marucci concludes that the term expresses a title, a stable function, and an ecclesial ministry, even though it is not possible to specify whether these were of a sacramental nature.

———. "La donna e i ministeri nella Bibbia e nella tradizione." *Rassegna di teologia* 17 (1976): 273–96.

An exploration of the biblical and historical data concerning the role of women in Scripture and a discussion of the ministries held by women in antiquity and during the Middle Ages.

———. "Storia e valore del diaconato femminile nella Chiesa antica." *Rassegna di Teologia* 38 (1997): 771–95.

Marucci examines women deacons of the first millennium, in particular with regard to their functions and the sacramental nature of the feminine diaconate. He concludes that their ordinations had a sacramental dignity equal to that of ordained male deacons.

Mayer, Josephine. *Monumenta de viduis diaconissis virginibusque tractantia.* Bonn: Peter Hanstein, 1938.

Greek and Latin ancient texts that mention widows, women deacons, and virgins and their rites of institution or ordination and their functions.

McKenna, Mary Lawrence. *Women of the Church: Role and Renewal.* New York: P. J. Kenedy, 1967.
McKenna argues in this study of the ancient orders of women, argues that women held the status of ecclesiastical order in antiquity and definitive functions in the Church's official structure.

McManus, Frederick. "Book Review: *Deaconesses: An Historical Study.*" *The Jurist* 47 (1987): 596–98.

Merklein, Helmut, and Müller Karlheinz, eds. *Die Frau im Urchristentum.* Freiburg: Herder, 1983.

Meyer, Charles R. "Ordained Women in the Early Church." *Chicago Studies* 4 (1965): 301.
Meyer suggests reexamination of the question of the ordination of women in the early Church and contends that to argue too strongly against the sacramentality of the ordination of deaconesses would be to deny the sacramentality of the order of deacons.

Müller, Gerhard L. *Priesthood and Diaconate: The Reception of the Sacrament of Holy Orders from the Perspective of Creation Theology and Christology.* San Francisco: Ignatius Press, 2002.
Müller extends the iconic argument against the priestly ordination of women to the question of women deacons, stating women cannot image Christ and cannot act *in persona Christi.*

Rahner, Karl, and Herbert Vorgrimler, eds. *Diaconia in Christo: Uber die Erneuerung des Diakonates.* Questiones Disputatae 15/16. Freiburg: Herder, 1962.

Rand, Laurence. "Ordination of Women to the Diaconate." *Communio: International Catholic Review* 8, no. 4 (2014): 370–83.

Raming, Ida. "Bestrebungen zum Diakonat der Frau im 20. Jahrhundert." In *Diakonat der Frau—Chance für die Zukunft? Dokumentation zu den Tagungen am 18. Mai 1993 and 19. Mai 1995 in der Katholisch—Sozialen Akademie,* edited by A. Urban. Münster, 1995.

Reininger, Dorothea. *Diakonat der Frau in der einen Kirche.* Ostfildern: Schwabenverlag, 1999.

Richardson, Peter. "From Apostles to Virgins: Romans 16 and the Roles of Women in the Early Church." *Toronto Journal of Theology* 2, no. 2 (1986): 232–61.

Romaniuk, Kazimierz. "Was Phoebe in Romans 16,1 a Deaconess?" *Zeitschrift für die Neutestamentliche Wissenschft* 81 (1990): 132–34.

Scimmi, Moira. *Le antiche diaconesse nella storiografia del XX secolo.* Milano: Edizioni Glossa, 2004.
A detailed critical analysis of the literary and epigraphic sources on deaconesses in the ancient Church.

Semmelroth, Otto. "Anmerkungen zu dem Votum der Synode zum Weihediakonat der Frau." *Diaconia Christi* 10, no. 1 (1975): 29–32.

Sorci, Pietro. "Diaconato e altri ministeri liturgici della donna." In *La Donna nel pensiero cristiano antico,* edited by Umberto Mattioli, 331–64. Genova: Marietti, 1992.

Explores the issue of the female diaconate and of other feminine liturgical ministries through a detailed historical retrospective, spanning from antiquity to the Middle Ages and covering both the Eastern and Western traditions.

Stiefel, Jennifer H. "Women Deacons in 1 Timothy: A Linguistic and Literary Look at 'Women Likewise. . .' (1 Tim 3.11)." *New Testament Studies* 41 (1995): 442–57. By analyzing the structure of both passages and scrutinizing the syntax of 3:11 Stiefel presents new evidence for the identification of the women mentioned in 3:11 as partners in ministry with the men of the passage.

Swidler, Arlene, and Virginia Ratigan. *A New Phoebe: Perspectives on Roman Catholic Women and the Permanent Diaconate.* Kansas City, MO: Sheed & Ward, 1990. Individual personal commentaries from women in Germany and the United States on the possibilities for women in the ordained diaconate. Includes an interview with the first chair of the US bishops' Committee on the Permanent Diaconate.

Synek, Eva M. *Heilige Frauen der frühen Christenheit. Zu den Frauenbildern in hagiograpischen Texten des christlichen Ostens.* Das östliche Christentum, NF 48. Würzburg, 1994.

Taddei Ferretti, Cloe. "In margine agli antichi riti di ordinazione delle diaconesse." *Studium* 95 (1999): 225–72. Starting from a historical overview of the ancient rites of ordination for women deacons, the author discusses the possibility of restoring women to the diaconate today, emphasizing that all humans are in God's image and therefore capable of exercising different roles in different epochs, and that a diaconal order truly expressing the reality of Christ the servant would include women.

Theodorou, Evangelous. "Das Amt der Diakoninnen in der kirchlichen Tradition. Ein orthodoxer Beitrag zum Problem der Frauenordination." *Una Sancta* 33 (1978): 162–72. Theodorou presents the most authoritative research on women deacons in Orthodoxy, noting that their ordination was a *cheirotonia* analogous to the ordination of men deacons and identical to the *cheirotonia* of other major orders. He finds that both deacons and deaconesses belong to the clergy.

———. "The Institution of Deaconesses in the Orthodox Church and the Possibility of Its Restoration." In *The Place of the Woman in the Orthodox Church and the Question of the Ordination of Women*, edited by G. Limouris, 207–380. Katerini: Tertios Publications, 1992.

———. "The Ministry of Women in the Greek Orthodox Church." In *Orthodox Women: Their Role and Participation in the Orthodox Church*, edited by World Council of Churches, 37–43. Geneva, 1977.

———. *The 'Ordination' (χειροτονια) or 'Appointment' (χειροθεσια) of Women Deacons.* Doctoral Dissertation, Athens, 1954.

Thiermeyer, Andreas. "Der Diakonat der Frau." *Theologische Quartalschrift* 173, no. 3 (1993): 226–36. Thiermeyer links the concept of sacrament to the notion of *mysterion*. Women deacons are documented in the history of the undivided Church. He deduces the sacramentality of the ordinations of women as deacons through the application of the term *mysterion* to it. He argues that neither an ecumenical council nor a fundamental text in the tradition of the Church dogmatically rules out including women in the diaconate.

Trabace, Ilaria. "La figura della diaconessa negli scritti dei padri cappadoci." Pages 639–51 in *Diakonia, Diaconiae, Diaconato. Semantica e Storia nei padri della Chiesa*. Roma: Istituto Patristicum Augustinianum, 2010.

Trabace explores the role of female deacons in Cappadocia in antiquity, mentioning the discreet and yet essential role they played within the Church and the trust bishops put in them.

Turner, Cuthbert H. "Ministries of Women in the Primitive Church: Widow, Deaconess and Virgin in the First Four Christian Centuries." *Constructive Quarterly* 7 (1919): 434–59.

Turner explores the three names under which the various ministries of women in the early ages of the Church are grouped—widows, virgins, deaconesses—to determine to what extent these names were those of distinct offices or orders.

Vagaggini, Cipriano. "Le diaconesse nella tradizione bizantina." *Il Regno* 32 (1987): 672–73.

Vagaggini's intervention before the 1987 Synod of Bishops on the Laity explains his research demonstrating the sacramental nature of the ordination of women to the diaconate, which points to the possibility of women being included in the contemporary ordained diaconate.

———. "L'Ordinazione delle diaconesse nella tradizione greca e bizantina." *Orientalia Christiana Periodica* 40 (1974): 145–89.

Vagaggini argues that within the Byzantine tradition the ordination of deaconesses belonged for nature and dignity to the major orders, and, despite differences between their functions, men and women deacons belonged to the same diaconal order. He writes that the sources show that deaconesses were allowed to perform liturgical tasks, having qualified for them by diaconal ordination. They received a *cheirotonia*, which distinguished the major orders from the minor orders, before the altar.

van Beneden, Pierre. "Aux origins d'une terminologie sacramentelle: *ordo, ordinare, ordinatio* dans la littérature chrétienne avant 313." *Spicilegium sacrum Lovaniense. Etudes et documents* 38 (1974).

A linguistic and theological study of the terms *Ordo, Ordinare, Ordinatio* in Latin Christian literature to AD 313 that argues that later theology of *Ordo* should not applied to early terminology.

Vanzan, Piersandro. "Le diaconat permanent feminin. Ombres et lumieres." *La documentation catholique* 2203 (1999): 440–48.

This article examines women deacons from historical and theological-sacramental points of view, offering a retrospective of studies supporting or rejecting the possibility of ordaining women as deacons.

Viteau, Julien. "L'Institution des diacres et des veuves." *Revue d'histoire ecclésiastique* 22 (1926): 513–36.

Viteau explores the passages in the New Testament where the word *diakonia* is mentioned, examining them from an etymological and linguistic perspective.

Vorgrimler, Herbert. "Gutachten über die Diakonatsweihe für Frauen." *Diaconia Christi* 9, no. 3 (1974): 19–24.

Ware, Kallistos. "Man, Woman and the Priesthood of Christ." In *Women and the Priesthood*, edited by T. Hopko, 9–37. Crestwood, NY: St. Vladimir's Seminary Press, 1983.

Wijngaards, John. *Women Deacons in the Early Church: Historical Texts and Contemporary Debates*. New York: Continuum, 2002.
A review of historical evidence, including literary an epigraphical documentation of women deacons in the early Church.

Wild, Ute. "Unsere Schwester Phoebe." *Diakonia* 20 (1989): 101–5.

Winkler, Dietmar W., ed. *Diakonat der Frau*. Vienna: Lit Verlag, 2010.

Ysebaert, Joseph. "The Deaconesses in the Western Church of Late Antiquity and Their Origin." In *Eulogia, Instrumenta Patristica* 24, edited by G. J. M. Bartelink, A. Hillhorst, and C. H. Kneepkens, 421–36. Hague: Nijhoff International (1991).
Ysebaert addresses deaconesses in the West and concludes that Churches in both the East and West ordained women to the diaconate.

Zagano, Phyllis. "Catholic Women's Ordination: The Ecumenical Implications of Women Deacons in the Armenian Apostolic Church, the Orthodox Church of Greece, and Union of Utrecht Old Catholic Churches." *Journal of Ecumenical Studies* 43, no. 1 (Winter 2008): 124–37.
Examination of three Churches in dialogue with the Catholic Church and able to ordain women to the diaconate: the Armenian Apostolic Church, the Orthodox Church of Greece, and certain Union of Utrecht Old Catholic Churches. Since the Catholic Church recognizes the validity of sacraments and orders in these Churches the question arises of whether it also recognizes the validity of these ordinations of women.

———. "Grant Her Your Spirit: The Restoration of the Female Diaconate in the Orthodox Church of Greece." *America* (February 7, 2005): 18–21. Translated as: "Ortodosse all'Altare." *Adista* 16 (26 febbraio 2005), and as "Chiesa Ortodossa Greca: Il ripristino del diaconato femminile." *Dimensione speranza* (April 4, 2005).

———. "The Historical Debate about Women in the Diaconate." *Doctrine and Life* (March 2013): 32–41.
An overview of the history of women ordained and consecrated in the ancient Church in relation to the 2002 International Theological Commission study document on women in the diaconate.

———. *Holy Saturday: An Argument for the Restoration of the Female Diaconate in the Catholic Church*. New York: Crossroad/Herder, 2000.
A seven-point argument supporting the restoration of women to the ordination diaconate based on the Church's need for the ministry of women, which distinguishes the question of women deacons from the question of women priests.

———. "Ministry by Women Religious and the U.S. Apostolic Visitation." *New Blackfriars* 92, no. 1041 (September 2011): 591–606.
An evaluation of the Vatican investigation of women religious in the United States.

———, ed. *Ordination of Women to the Diaconate in the Eastern Churches: Essays by Cipriano Vagaggini*. Collegeville, MN: Liturgical Press, 2014.
Translations of two essays by Vagaggini, one written in response to a request by Pope Paul VI and a second a summary of that response delivered as an intervention before the 1987 Synod of Bishops.

———. "The Question of Governance and Ministry for Women." *Theological Studies* 68 (2007): 348–67.
Formal participation in Church governance and ministry by women hinges on their admission to the clerical state, which is demonstrably possible by their readmission to the diaconate, now supported by extensive historical exegesis.

———. "Remembering Tradition: Women's Monastic Rituals and the Diaconate." *Theological Studies* 72, no. 4 (December 2011): 787–811.
An examination of ceremonies for women that demonstrates the tradition of the women ordained as deacons, distinguishing between and among monastic profession, consecration of virginity, and diaconal ordination.

———. "The Revisionist History of Benedict XVI." *Harvard Divinity Bulletin* 34, no. 2 (Spring 2006): 72–77.

———. *Women and Catholicism: Gender, Communion, and Authority*. New York: Palgrave-Macmillan, 2011.

———. "Women and the Church: Unfinished Business of Vatican II." *Horizons* 34, no. 2 (2007), 205–21.

———. *Women in Ministry: Emerging Questions about the Diaconate*. New York: Paulist Press, 2012.
Essays from *Horizons, Journal of Ecumenical* Studies, and *Theological Studies*.

Zanetti, Ugo. "Y eut-il des diaconesses en Égypte?" *Vetera Christianorum* 27 (1990): 369–73.
An historical and linguistic investigation of deaconesses in the Egyptian and Ethiopian churches in antiquity concluding there were women who performed diaconal ministry.

Index